Contemporary Vulnerabilities

Contemporary Vulnerabilities
Reflections on Social Justice Methodologies

Edited by Claire Carter,
Chelsea Temple Jones,
and Caitlin Janzen

UNIVERSITY *of* **ALBERTA** PRESS

PUBLISHED BY

University of Alberta Press
1-16 Rutherford Library South
11204 89 Avenue NW
Edmonton, Alberta, Canada T6G 2J4
amiskwaciwâskahikan | Treaty 6 | Métis Territory
ualbertapress.ca | uapress@ualberta.ca

Copyright © 2024 University of Alberta Press

Library and Archives Canada Cataloguing in Publication
Title: Contemporary vulnerabilities : reflections on social justice methodologies /
    edited by Claire Carter, Chelsea Temple Jones, and Caitlin Janzen.
Names: Carter, Claire, 1976- editor. | Jones, Chelsea Temple, editor. |
    Janzen, Caitlin, 1982- editor.
Description: Includes bibliographical references.
Identifiers: Canadiana (print) 20230541534 | Canadiana (ebook) 20230541550 | ISBN
    9781772127386 (softcover) | ISBN 9781772127577 (PDF) | ISBN 9781772127560 (EPUB)
Subjects: LCSH: Social change—Research—Methodology.
Classification: LCC H62 .C66 2024 | DDC 303.4072—dc23

First edition, first printing, 2024.
First printed and bound in Canada by Houghton Boston Printers, Saskatoon, Saskatchewan.
Copyediting and proofreading by Jenn Harris.

All rights reserved. No part of this publication may be reproduced, stored in a retrieval system, or transmitted in any form or by any means (electronic, mechanical, photocopying, recording, generative artificial intelligence [AI] training, or otherwise) without prior written consent. Contact University of Alberta Press for further details.

University of Alberta Press supports copyright. Copyright fuels creativity, encourages diverse voices, promotes free speech, and creates a vibrant culture. Thank you for buying an authorized edition of this book and for complying with the copyright laws by not reproducing, scanning, or distributing any part of it in any form without permission. You are supporting writers and allowing University of Alberta Press to continue to publish books for every reader.

This book has been published with the help of a grant from the Federation for the Humanities and Social Sciences, through the Awards to Scholarly Publications Program, using funds provided by the Social Sciences and Humanities Research Council of Canada.

University of Alberta Press gratefully acknowledges the support received for its publishing program from the Government of Canada, the Canada Council for the Arts, and the Government of Alberta through the Alberta Media Fund.

Contents

Preface · *ix*
    Chelsea Temple Jones, Claire Carter, and Caitlin Janzen

Introduction · *xix*
    Claire Carter, Caitlin Janzen, and Chelsea Temple Jones

I · **Vulnerable Moments**

1. NRI/Outsider/Returnee: The Location of Trust in Ethnographic Practice · 3
   Shraddha Chatterjee

2. To Whom Are We Accountable? The Vulnerability of Deep Listening in Feminist Ethnographic Research · 17
   Rebecca Lennox

3. Discard or Save the Leftovers? What To Do with Truths That Cannot Be Told · 33
   Brenda Rossow-Kimball and Kristyn White

II · **Reflections on Challenges and Hard Decisions in Research Processes**

4. Un(rendered) Stories: Ethical Considerations of Translation Work in Research · 51
   Anh Ngo

5. "Crossroad" Moments and the Choice to Respond: Diverging from Textbook Ethics · 67
   Yuriko Cowper-Smith and Preeti Nayak

6. The Messiness of Applying Feminist Research Principles: Reflections on Researching Rape Culture on Campus · 85
   Rebecca Godderis, Debra Langan, and Marcia Oliver

III · Reflections on Contemporary Approaches to Key Methods and Concepts

7. Disrupting Codified Academic Norms through Decolonization · 103
   Emily Grafton, Moses Gordon, Cheyanne Desnomie, Cassandra J. Opikokew Wajuntah, and Bettina Schneider

8. A Familiar Stranger: Hindsight and Foresight Reflexivity, Multiple Interviews, and a Young Academic Interviewing a Young Mother · 123
   Amber-Lee Varadi

9. Queering the Activist/Academic: An Autoethnography of Queering Research with/in Community Spaces · 139
   Amelia Thorpe

10. Even with the Best of Intentions: An Accounting of Failures in a Participatory Research Project · 157
    Lori Ross, Merrick Pilling, Kendra-Ann Pitt, Jijian Voronka

IV · Reflections on Creative Research Collaborations and Relationships

11. Building Collaboration through (Embodied) Conversation: An Indigenist and a Feminist Reflect on Writing and Learning Together · 179
    Melissa Schnarr and Eva Cupchik

12. Working Collectively across Our Minoritized Differences: Vulnerabilities and Possibilities of ReVisioning Fitness · 195
    Aly Bailey, Meredith Bessey, Carla Rice, Evadne Kelly, Tara-Leigh McHugh, Bongi Dube, Paul Tshuma, Skylar Sookpaiboon, Kayla Besse, Salima Punjani, and seeley quest

13. "Sorry, My Child Is Kicking Me under the Desk": Intersectional Challenges to Research during the COVID-19 Pandemic · 215
    Irene Shankar and Corinne L. Mason

14. "It Was the Worst Place I Ever Lived"..."It Was the Best Place I Ever Worked": Exploring the Productive Potential of Narrative Discrepancies and Bias in Qualitative Research · 241
    Madeline Burghardt

V · Reflections on the Methodologically Unresolved

15. Decolonial Co-Resistance as Indigenous Methodology: Deepening Resistance and Decolonizing the "Co-" · 267
    Jess Notwell

16. The Weight of It All: Methodological Implications to Community-Engaged Research on Violent Memory · 287
    Jen Rinaldi, Kate Rossiter, and Siobhán Saravanamuttu

17. Vulnerabilities, Affects, and Solidarities: A Rape Survivor's Tale · 305
    Athanasia Francis

Conclusion: Finding (a) Dwelling in Vulnerabilities · 323
    Caitlin Janzen, Chelsea Temple Jones, and Claire Carter

Contributors · 329

Preface

Chelsea Temple Jones, Claire Carter, and Caitlin Janzen

Dear Readers,
We are writing to you, at the opening of this collection, to share our own vulnerabilities and ground what follows in (research) stories (along with many conversations, reflections, and additional moments) that motivated us to draft the call for papers and begin work on bringing vulnerability to the fore—as it has been for us and so many others who engage in social justice research.

In treating this book as an invitation to linger in vulnerability and to dwell upon the vulnerable, we mean to move with you toward a reciprocal reading process that mobilizes your own relationship to vulnerability in whatever way fits your story. We would, therefore, be remiss to propose an activation of your story without reciprocating by sharing our own moments of vulnerability.

As three white settler, queer scholars, variously positioned within the academy and living and working within different treaty territories, our stories are grounded in a range of experiences—graduate student, the ambiguous place of post-defence contract work, attending conferences as a junior academic—echoing the positions embodied, moments encountered, and spaces occupied by many of the contributors to this collection.

Caitlin

Thirteen years ago, when I was working as a research assistant on a project about street sex work in Canada, I had the opportunity to interview a woman who was a new mother to a little baby boy who laid quietly in her arms the entire time we spoke. Something this woman told me continues to haunt me over a decade later: she said that though she did not enjoy sex work and would like to quit it altogether, she did see a social benefit to her work. In her words, "it was almost a protection thing because if we weren't out there for them to feed off of, you never know what they would do." She continued to share that if she and other street sex workers were not available for men to enact their violent sexual urges upon, those same men "would rape the innocent."

My heart broke right there in the room, which is to say, something in me shattered, fragilized in that moment.

It pained me that she believed that this was her role in society. I gave a "good feminist" response. I said: "You don't think you're the innocent? But you are." Abandoning my politicized repertoire and instead entering her linguistic frame, I said, "You shouldn't have to be the go-between." By which I meant that this was not her burden to bear.

In the moment of the interaction, I was upset at how patriarchal bio-determinist myths had infiltrated her identity, about how discourses surrounding the insatiability and urgency of the male sex had seemingly determined her position in the world. My outrage at this unjust asymmetry in the experience of being a woman reached its pinnacle when she recounted an experience in which a man walked up to her in a grocery store parking lot, exposed himself, and then headbutted her in broad daylight. "And I thought, you know what, not a single person—I know oodles of people saw it—and not a single person did anything." This prompted me to ask a follow-up question about the distribution of vulnerability between women as a social group:

> **Me (researcher):** What about women, like middle class-looking women, who chose to do nothing. This is something, like how women turn their backs on other women."
>
> **Her:** You know what, because I feel that they get it. They know. They've been there and they're scared. Come on, you can't tell

me that they don't know. Yeah, I would have to say they've been there, done that.
Me: Even if it's not prostitution?
Her: Even if it's not prostitution. In some way they've been in that type of lifestyle, in the sex trade or not, they've been there. They've been in survival mode. Because when you're in survival mode, you only look out for yourself.

Returning to this interaction now, I feel these words travelling along their original fault line, but this time the rupture does not leave us isolated on either side of a subjective scansion the way I initially interpreted it. This is still a narrative of what Ellen Gordon-Bouvier has termed "relational vulnerability," a theory of vulnerability that recognizes individuals as "situated within an unequal network of relationships in which they are marginalised, and exposed to harm on an economic, emotional, and spatial level."[1] It is undeniable that she and I were positioned differently due to material conditions such as age and class, conditions that mark the body in particular ways and open onto other structural inequities such as criminalization (especially as this research took place prior to the decriminalization of sex work in Canada) and barriers to accessing healthcare and protection. And yet, when I return to our exchange now, I see both *relational* vulnerability and the *relationality* engendered by an acknowledgement of a shared and distributed vulnerability. In other words, the fluidity of vulnerability, who it resides with in what moments, and the way in which it shades that individual as a social-legal subject is less absolute, less static than I initially thought. Prior to this interview, I was more closely aligned with feminist academic research that considered women who engage in street sex work as agentic but categorically vulnerable; "at risk" of myriad things, from problematic substance use to stigmatization and marginalization, to violence and murder. In this exchange, however, she challenged the notion of a vulnerability that could be ascribed once and for all. For her, there were "the innocent"—girls and women who were even more vulnerable and for whom she felt a sense of protective responsibility. This is relational vulnerability in its most distilled form: She put her body, the same body her little baby depended upon so fully, on the line for other women.

For me, this interview tells a story of how vulnerability brings us into relation with one another.

Claire

In the space between defence, graduation, and moving across the country to take up a term position, I did contract work for a research institute in Toronto, affiliated with a hospital. My role was to interview women living in five different communities in southern Ontario as part of research evaluating a program around housing and women's experiences of intimate partner violence. In the short time I worked on this project, I experienced several critical moments layered with vulnerabilities that gave me significant pause and have offered lessons beyond what any course could teach. I share three of those moments here.

Moment One

I was asked during my interview for the position whether I had experienced any form of intimate partner violence and shared that I had been raped by my boyfriend in high school. I was told that it was important for the research team that people working on the project had some experiential as well as more general knowledge about intimate partner violence. This moment spoke to an effort at relational vulnerability—that the team was trying to foster and work from a space of shared vulnerability between everyone involved. Upon later reflection, after having done some of the interviews, I realized that I had no idea whether any of the women being interviewed knew that I had experienced sexual violence, nor whether the women participating knew that the research team had made this decision and prioritized this in their selection of interviewers. I felt a tension between following the interview guide and engaging in feminist interviewing, which would involve more of an exchange of shared vulnerabilities rather than conventional question (interviewer) and answer (interviewee). I often felt uncomfortable going into women's homes, aware of how differently we were positioned. I had many moments of feeling that my presence as a middle-class, white settler graduate student and my role as the interviewer further reproduced dynamics of power and inequity that likely caused harm. For example, in moments where women would engage in self-blame about their life choices and situation, I would pause the tape recorder and speak about systemic and structural inequality. My whiteness and economic social capital had not been a part of the reflexive research team conversations in my interview, but undoubtedly, they critically informed the interviews (how I was read/how women responded and felt) and analysis (of which I was not a part).

Moment Two

As a junior qualitative researcher, I was getting used to drafting open-ended questions, engaging in conversation, and being open to where the interviewee/co-researcher wanted to take the conversation. In this instance, though, which involved a mixed-methods approach, the research team wanted us to follow the interview guide with each person in exactly the same way; there was a set list of questions, and we were discouraged from deviating from it. This felt inappropriate and counter to the social justice focus of the research and for myself, as a researcher. There were moments that brought to the fore what Oakley references, where women asked me questions and it would have been disingenuous—unethical—to simply move on to the next question.[2] One of these moments involved being questioned by a woman of colour about why she had been placed in social housing in a more rural community, where, as a new immigrant, she faced numerous barriers to employment that were largely tied to racism and minimal employment opportunities. Given that I represented university/research/public service employment, she wanted answers: What should I do? How can I get a job? How can I support myself and my child if they won't hire me? I felt unprepared for these moments and unsure of how to respond given the parameters of the interview protocol. Upon reflection, there was an inherent vulnerability evident in this approach to research, specifically the framing of this research project, in its inability or failure to be relevant to the women they sought to support.

Moment Three

During the third interview in one day, a woman talked about her most recent experience of intimate partner violence and disclosed that her ex knew where she lived, that he was active with a violent organization in the community, and that she often worried he would come by her house. Sitting in the dark listening, I became afraid—afraid for her and afraid for my own safety. As part of the interview protocol, I would get a check-in call from a designated member of the research team after a set time to debrief and make sure everything was okay. This interview went on longer than most, and I did not receive a check-in call. When it finally ended, I sat in my car quite shaken and called to check in. A friend later asked if there was support available for me (and other interviewers on the project) to debrief what was shared with us; there wasn't. It hadn't occurred to me that there might be and I was left wondering how to make space for my vulnerability within the traditional conceptions of power dynamics in research. Later, I tried to follow up with a member of the research team after the interviews were done—I wanted to know if the women were doing okay, better/safer than when we had met. I was told there had been no contact or follow-up, which troubled me deeply. These moments reveal ways we are undone by each other, and as Butler states, "if we're not, we're missing something" (2004, 19). Overlapping layers of vulnerability— failure of research protocols, of follow-up care, and of relationality have stayed with me and reveal the dissonance between research in practice with the ideals or desired goals of research and what vulnerability can shed light on.

Chelsea
It is a sunny June day with a crisp breeze on the University of British Columbia campus, and my friend, Kim, is sitting beside me. She has ushered me out of a large academic conference because I have lost my breath, and the buildings around me are spinning. "I don't know—" I gasp, "I don't know what is happening." Kim is a calm wonder who is not scared off by madness. She assures me that it's okay not to know what is happening. It's okay to take a break from academic networking. Having forged ahead quickly through the publish-or-perish path of academia into a precarious but sought-after post-doctoral position, I don't believe her. But I cannot figure a way to reverse this panic. I haven't slept in days. I might throw up. I sink into a chair and stare off into the sky, my mind scaling thoughts like a fast-forwarded film: What will happen if I don't get the grant I applied for? What if I never get a job, and my community-based research halts, and is rendered ineffective? What if I do get a job, but the reward of employment makes my research seem extractive? I try not to think about the folks with whom I do research—they are the people I have been trying to represent in my conference presentations. Of course, it would be better if they could be here, representing themselves,

but there was no funding for the access features that would be required to bring disabled people across the country: personal support workers, sign language interpreters, accessible hotel rooms.

Kim sat with me for over an hour. Later another friend, Fady, would sit with me, too, holding my shaky hand as I tried to steady myself. At one point, I spot Claire across campus, walking into a building. I want to call out, but I cannot move. Still, I feel lucky to have allies nearby and within view in this moment. A few days later I return home and weep in my doctor's office—I still don't know what is happening and why it won't stop. A day later, heavily medicated, I sleep. I finally slow down, for the first time in weeks.

For me, vulnerability is connected to severe bouts of acute anxiety. Both vulnerability and anxiety are a pain in the ass, really. Both are uncomfortable, draining, dizzying, and often force me to take a longer, more tedious route through life than I had hoped. Both are affective states tightly stitched through the quilt of research I have gradually patched together as I move through academia. Ironically, both are also the antithesis to the fast-paced research machine that values product over process and, too often, progress over people. And oh, how easy, how tempting it would be, to be the kind of researcher who could just produce inquiry and be done with it. But that is not how the bodymind works when embedded in action research.[3] Instead, vulnerability is corporeal. And amid this felt, affective vulnerability, that I have access to these things—education, a doctor, medication—speaks to my immense privilege. I am also white, which is a signifier of difference against the vulnerabilities embodied by Indigenous, Black, and people of colour, for whom anxieties of many types are generational and incessantly pushed upon them by the ongoing violence of racism and colonialism. Indeed, we cannot talk about the body without understanding that the body is in relation to others, and that relationality includes a dependency on infrastructural conditions and legacies of discourse and institutional power that precede its existence. As Butler reminds us, "we cannot understand bodily vulnerability outside this conception of social and material relations."[4] I come to this collection thinking about vulnerability as something embedded in the social and material relations, and it sparks our curiosity about how justice-oriented research happens today. I am here, in these pages, wanting to focus in on the contours of vulnerability, which include but also stretch beyond its use as a pejorative label against minoritized groups who try to participate in research. I am here because I am implicated in vulnerability and its many faces in all that I do. Mine is not a story of overcoming vulnerability, but a story of being steeped in it—though, thankfully, I am not alone.

―――――― / / ――――――

How do we navigate the tensions between different requirements, protocols, academic spaces, and particular institutions, on the one hand, and our sense of shared vulnerabilities and political commitments to social justice and community engaged ethics on the other? How can we learn to disrupt protocols that seek to categorically determine who is vulnerable in research? How do we speak out against traditions that are unethical, may cause more harm, and/or that encourage detachment? How can we ask for and provide necessary support for ourselves, our collaborators, and our students so that we can sit with the tensions, process what is being offered, and endeavour to be present and grounded? And how can we continually engage in critical reflexivity about our positionality and the impact on people with whom we collaborate in research? The aforementioned moments of shared vulnerability have prompted a long consideration of these questions and have ultimately lead to this collection, motivating us to collaborate with other researchers, first to discuss and listen to their moments of vulnerability in research and then to read and learn from their earnest reflections. By sharing their research practices with such humility and openness, the authors in this collection reveal just how generative vulnerability can be.

Notes
1. Ellen Gordon-Bouvier, "Relational Vulnerability: The Legal Status of Cohabiting Carers," *Feminist Legal Studies* 27 (2019), 164.
2. Ann Oakley, "Interviewing Women: A Contradiction in Terms," in *Doing Feminist Research*, ed. Helen Roberts, 30–62 (London, Routledge, 1981).
3. Margaret Price, "The Bodymind Problem and the Possibilities of Pain," *Hypatia* 30, no. 1 (2015): 268–284; Judi Marshall, *First Person Action Research: Living Life as Inquiry* (London: SAGE Publications, 2016).
4. Judith Butler, "Rethinking Vulnerability and Resistance," in *Vulnerability in Resistance*, eds. Judith Butler, Zeynep Gambetti, and Leticia Sabsay (Durham: Duke University Press, 2016), 16.

Bibliography

Butler, Judith. "Rethinking Vulnerability and Resistance." In *Vulnerability in Resistance*, edited by Judith Butler, Zeynep Gambetti, and Leticia Sabsay. Durham: Duke University Press, 2016.

Gordon-Bouvier, Ellen. "Relational Vulnerability: The Legal Status of Cohabiting Carers." *Feminist Legal Studies* 27 (2019).

Marshall, Judi. *First Person Action Research: Living Life as Inquiry*. London: SAGE Publications, 2016.

Oakley, Ann. "Interviewing Women: A Contradiction in Terms." In *Doing Feminist Research*, edited by Helen Roberts, 30–62. London, Routledge, 1981.

Price, Margaret. "The Bodymind Problem and the Possibilities of Pain." *Hypatia* 30, no. 1 (2015): 268–284.

Introduction

Claire Carter, Caitlin Janzen, and Chelsea Temple Jones

An Invitation

This book is an invitation to dwell in vulnerability. We recognize this invitation may sit a little uneasily, as the fundamental role of vulnerability in social science and humanities research remains largely unacknowledged and its relational qualities and productive capacities remain unexplored. When it arises in the curriculum for methodology courses, it does so in the context of research ethics where particular groups are pre-assigned to the category of so-called "vulnerable populations" in a matrix of risk where intersections of structural inequality aggregate until certain people become "high risk" and difficult to access. Paradoxically, the effect of such protection is exclusion. Such exclusion can result in narrative silencing, lack of engagement in evaluating interventions or policies that directly affect people's daily lives, or missed opportunities for co-constructing knowledge on the community's own terms. Such an understanding of vulnerability in research has led van den Hoonaard to call for the end of vulnerability as a framing concept in social science research. In fact, he states, "with very few exceptions, we are better off disowning the term 'vulnerability.'"[1]

Van den Hoonaard makes a compelling case; however, we wonder what might be lost in doing away with the concept of vulnerability altogether.

What sites of inquiry or research relations might be foreclosed upon should we eschew the idea of vulnerability *qua* co-dependency and embodied limitations? It is this second conceptualization of vulnerability that we adopt in this book, using it as an invitation to dwell in vulnerable moments of research. If you are like us, you know that research and vulnerability are inseparable because you have experienced how muddled the work of knowledge production in one form or another can be. Everyone experiences vulnerable moments differently, but often these moments are overshadowed by traditionally positivist ways of knowing that would position researchers as unflappable investigators existing on a separately imagined plane of knowledge from others involved in the research. Orienting toward vulnerability imagines a possible disruption of this researcher/subject binary and instead renews our positioning in a multitude of ways: as learners, collaborators, wonderers, mistake-makers, creators, community members, and embodied creatures still bearing the wounds of knowledge production under institutional violence. It is into this unsteady, ever-changing orientation that we, as researchers and post-secondary educators, have tried to mentor our students who are learner-researchers studying qualitative research and methodologies. Sometimes, within both our research and our classrooms, we are not sure what to do and our own vulnerabilities bubble to the surface in uncomfortable and ultimately revelatory ways that prompt later reflection. We know we are not alone in experiencing these moments, nor in our understanding that they speak to new, different, and more socially just ways of being in relation in our work. Here, with an understanding that vulnerability is inextricable from research, we invite you to join us in facing and reflecting on the contours of research vulnerability together.

Orienting to Vulnerability

Working in the Canadian post-secondary sector, we concurrently engage in community research and teach undergraduate and graduate students about what it means to do qualitative, social justice–driven research in its many forms. Through conversations with each other and with students, we have noticed that our deep commitment to foregrounding vulnerability praxis is met with a scarcity of resources. There are a few pieces focused on the vulnerability of research though feminist reflections that have lit our way forward. Such works include those by Ruth Behar,[2] Kathryn

Church,[3] and Bain and Nash's "Undressing the Researcher."[4] For its awkwardness, openness, and hints of amusement that reside in the pages of their discussion, "Undressing the Researcher" is rife with moments of vulnerability. Doing research at a queer women's bathhouse in Toronto, Bain and Nash make space for tensions that arise around the contrast between textbook advice and the reality of their research space, as well as how the boundaries between researcher and community member, lesbian and queer, impact research relations. Bain and Nash share concerns that their role as researchers engaged in participant observation, but not as active participants in the bathhouse, contributed to a sense of voyeurism, and potentially "dishonest and exploitative" moments. Not participating in public sex led, they felt, to a potential lack of community credibility by bathhouse organizers and, further, marked a boundary between lesbian and queer. Moments like this—moments of vulnerability—challenge the oft simplistic research binary about who is vulnerable within research. But more than just stating that vulnerability was present, Bain and Nash are reflexive about what vulnerability reveals about us as researchers, our community connections, and relations. Researchers who reflect on their own vulnerability invite us to do the same and to inhabit moments of uncertainty that inevitably emerge in justice-driven scholarship.

Though it has been possible to lace our respective course outlines with moments of vulnerability, we know that contemporary conversations to this end are often hidden or covert—the research blips you discuss with only trusted colleagues. After all, even following decades of narrative and affective turns that highlight vulnerability, vulnerability in practice is still often taken up as a problem or understood as a side effect of research. And as feminist scholar Sara Ahmed points out, the person who points out the problem often *becomes* the problem in institutional settings.[5] This was the case for one of the co-editors, Chelsea, who has openly scrutinized her own experiences of regret and resilience amid navigating capacity-to-consent and competence procedures in research alongside intellectually disabled people who are too easily labelled "vulnerable" by institutional ethics protocols.[6] While there has been an awareness of vulnerability within feminist/social justice academic spaces, for an awareness of its presence within research processes, we have had to look to critical disability studies for a "sustained consideration of how vulnerability might sit with methodological choices and commitments" and what it could offer or make possible.[7] Following this tradition of critical thought, we come to this collection with an awareness that vulnerability is a wide-reaching concept that leaves an impression on various bodies—the researcher's, those of others involved in the project, learners', and decision-makers' bodies. Amid this complexity, we have adopted or revised ways of the doing the research in which we had been trained or instructed by reflecting upon past moments of vulnerability in our research—or even on the fly when we were confronted by inadequate, unethical, and/or unknown ways forward.

Motivated by our respective and overlapping critical, intersectional ontologies of queer feminist, psychosocial, and critical disability studies, we felt a desire to figure out where vulnerability emerges in current research methodologies, including methodologies informed by queer, disabled, and Indigenous worldviews. This desire was compounded by the realization that what counts as knowledge or research is expanding and becoming more interdisciplinary, shifting the relations between researcher and communities in social justice-based inquiry. Institutional praxis has changed over the course of our careers. Significantly, this includes the mainstreaming of equity, diversity, and inclusion (EDI) practices and calls to decolonize the academy, or what Ahmed calls diversity agendas, alongside intensification of conditions under neoliberalism that have left some more vulnerable than others.[8] From within higher education institutions, whose pervasive grip on research so profoundly impacts our experiences and analysis of vulnerability, we find ourselves stretched for contemporary, theoretically informed resources about how to navigate the unexpected, vulnerable moments that emerge in research, that are deepened by our own and our students' commitments to social change. We felt compelled to listen to what vulnerability speaks to, what it reveals, even demands and to provide space for sustained dialogue about what emerges and/or shifts when we recognize and incorporate vulnerability in research production. In other words, we wondered: How are research relations transformed in and by vulnerable moments? What instances give us pause, demand thoughtfulness, creativity, and reflexivity? In what ways are we called to make space for the unexpected and unresolved as we reassert our commitment to community-informed ethics and shared learning in social justice research? How do we confront and seek to disrupt systemic and traditional academic barriers that encode our praxis?

These questions, posed in our 2020 call for papers, have guided contributors toward exploring the many vulnerabilities that communities and researchers navigate as they work toward research for social change. Our call received over fifty submissions, suggesting that we were far from alone in feeling troubled, curious, and uncertain about how to navigate vulnerability—individually and collectively as researchers committed to social change. While each chapter addresses the aforementioned questions differently, all authors build their discussion around the impact of vulnerable moments in research. In this way, vulnerability serves as a central concept for the collection, giving a distinct shape and unique perspective to writing focused on qualitative research methods. We offer this collection as one that fills a gap in contemporary research discourse by focusing on first-hand accounts of uncertainties and entangled realities between theory and praxis that demonstrate vulnerable positionings.

Why Vulnerability/What is Vulnerability?

It is useful at the outset to explain the two key ways that we arrive at thinking about vulnerability. First is through the often-assumed vulnerability of people who are researched. In particular, the assumed vulnerability of marginalized folks with whom research is considered "too risky" and who are often thought of as incapable of agency or giving consent.[9] We are aware that traditionally, social justice research has been bound up in ideas and ethics about who is vulnerable, and that these ideas are continually being challenged. Specific groups have historically been subject to violence, and this violence continues to proliferate at the intersections of sexist misogyny, transphobia, heterosexism and queer hatred, racism, colonialism, ableism, ageism, fatphobia, and poverty—each of these intersections are represented in *Contemporary Vulnerabilities*.

Crucially, the conflation between vulnerability and violability leads to a problem to which the most appropriate ethical response becomes that of protection. The assumed heightened risk for identified "vulnerable populations" is described in the *Tri-Council Policy Statement: Ethical Conduct for Research Involving Humans* (TCPS 2), which is concerned with the "limited decision-making capacity" of these groups.[10] The flipside of the "vulnerable populations" coin, however, is that categorizing some people as fundamentally vulnerable (again, the notion of vulnerability as a characteristic) has resulted in the exclusion of marginalized groups from the very research creation that seeks to represent them and may impact their lives.[11] Circumstances in which researchers, often working under guidelines of funding bodies and ethics boards, are in a clear "power-over" relationship with groups (for example, in contexts of incarceration, where participants' income, employment, or housing is dependent on participation, or where the participant does not understand the terms of consent) are indeed rife for exploitation. As Linda Tuhiwai Smith has persuasively argued, Western academic research is the progeny of European imperialism and colonial expansion, and in many cases, it continues that legacy through paternalist epistemic assumptions and appropriative practices that procure both resources and knowledge at the expense of Indigenous Peoples.[12] Indigenous scholars critique universalist and generalized notions of vulnerability in research, stating that these marginalize Indigenous ways of knowing; further, they say that in practice, research ethics boards are not adequately educated on collective processes of consent, decision making, and knowledge sharing and thus privilege Eurocentric individualist models at the expense of the established ethical protocols of specific Indigenous communities.[13] All this said, perhaps the questions of who is vulnerable, independent of the research relationship, and on what basis, are the wrong questions to be asking. Reiterating the argument made by Ron Iphofen,[14] that the question should instead be whether participation in our research makes a subject *more vulnerable* than they would otherwise be in their daily lives, van den Hoonaard[15] declares that "ethics codes should, with very few exceptions, get out of the business of defining what populations are vulnerable."

Second, we consider more broadly what vulnerability means, what it tells us, and how it informs and connects to the ethics of research committed to social justice. In her book *The Ethics of Vulnerability: A Feminist Analysis of Social Life and Practice*, feminist philosopher Erinn Gilson systematically works toward a conceptualization of vulnerability that challenges common conflations of the term with "liability to injury, weakness, dependency, powerlessness, incapacity, deficiency, and passivity."[16] In so doing, Gilson, in conversation with thinkers such as Judith Butler, Hèléne Cixous, Gilles Deleuze, and Maurice Merleau-Ponty, advances her own concept of vulnerability. Rather than a negative quality held by some (the vulnerable) and not others (the invulnerable), Gilson's notion of vulnerability is an experience—rather than a label—common to all beings. This evocative notion of vulnerability echoes early feminist debates about vulnerability that ground this inquiry including Kathryn Church's[17] push to expose the uncertain, entangled moments of research that emerge with the collision of our own positionalities and research expectations. Shortly afterward, on a qualitative inquiry trajectory that found space for vulnerabilities in narrative inquiry, Art Bochner and Katie Ellis[18] solidified the value of the partial, situated story woven with moments of vulnerability.[19] Drawing on a research trajectory that has solidified vulnerability as a valid mode of being in theory and praxis,[20] Gilson posits that "vulnerability is both ambivalent and ambiguous in how it is experienced and...has a diversity of manifestations."[21] Gilson's notion of vulnerability presents an important counter to traditional designations and thus provides a productive launch for our reimagining of vulnerability as a vital part of research praxis. Kovach and Fast articulate that what is vulnerable is honourable within Indigenous research, and that for them, "it is our vulnerabilities that connect us and the teachings of the sacred circle tells us that it is our connections that keep us strong."[22] Telling our stories as researchers can be uncomfortable and messy, but they suggest that "the beauty of this act is that it gives pause as the researcher and invites a shared story to come through."[23]

Vulnerability is something shared among humans (and, indeed, other-than-human life), but, as both Gilson and Judith Butler suggest, to varying degrees across social structures, political systems, circumstances, and lifespans. Butler's[24] conceptualization of vulnerability emerges out of the context of state-sanctioned violence and war and the ethical implications (particularly for those in so-called Western democracies) pursuant to the various conceptualizations of vulnerability. Drawing out the discursive links that bind vulnerability to practices of normativity by way of opposition, Butler challenges an idea of vulnerability as a quality conferred upon a particular individual or group, instead arguing that the very basis of human life is its precarity, its openness to violation. Not only does Butler challenge the distinction between vulnerability and normativity by making the former central to the very experience of embodiment (we are all vulnerable at various points in our lives, though to varying degrees and durations), she also highlights the social, political, and ethical norms that surround our understandings of vulnerability, namely our sense of responsibility for those deemed vulnerable. While Butler strives toward the argument that vulnerability is a shared, albeit specific, experience, her conceptualization remains problematically grounded in the equation of vulnerability as susceptibility to violation and harm. In other words, vulnerability to violence.

It is perhaps feminist legal scholar Martha Fineman who has most concretely linked the universal and inevitable experience of vulnerability to social and state responsibility. Like Butler, Fineman's notion of vulnerability is grounded in the body and the "ever-present possibility of harm, injury, and misfortune from mildly adverse to catastrophically devastating events, whether accidental, intentional, or otherwise."[25] Fineman's theory of vulnerability reminds us that counter to the liberal subject, the embodied subject may at any time become dependent. Thus, she has spent the last decade building upon and reconceptualizing her earlier work on dependency to construct a working theory of vulnerability that might serve as a more complex and promising basis upon which to build more equitable societies. Expounding her "vulnerability thesis," Fineman states the following:

> I want to claim the term "vulnerable" for its potential in describing a universal, inevitable, enduring aspect of the human condition that must be at the heart of our concept of social and state responsibility. Vulnerability thus freed from its limited and negative associations is a powerful conceptual tool with the potential to define an obligation for the state to ensure a richer and more robust guarantee of equality than is currently afforded under the equal protection model.[26]

Determining social, legal, and political responses would then require an analysis of levels of vulnerability a subject is experiencing as well as the resources they have available to mitigate against detriment.

For our purposes, we borrow from the aforementioned theorists in considering the social, economic, and political conditions that contribute to our understanding and response to vulnerability. And if vulnerability is something shared, inherent to all lived experience, how can we reimagine our research relations, processes, and ethical commitments in ways that recognize our shared capacity to be vulnerable, while still recognizing the inequitable distribution of resources to protect against the damages that can accompany vulnerability and dependency? Reconceptualizing vulnerability in such a way would also disrupt models that measure risk based on assumptions that certain groups in society are fundamentally vulnerable. Institutionally based ethics protocols follow this approach and may in fact reinforce normative societal relations that deny agency to equity-deserving groups through protectionist discourses.

With these nuances of vulnerability in mind, our collection resists paternalism and advocates for community and individual engagement with knowledge production on each author's own terms. Vulnerability in these chapters speaks to accounts that have been marginalized or actively silenced, from painful memories of experiences of institutional violence and to a geopolitical context surrounding the struggle to exist. Rather than serving to speak for as a means of "protecting" from further violence, these authors endeavour to make space for and negotiate vulnerability in new ways. These chapters offer moments of pause and reflection and, we hope, facilitate an opening to acknowledge our vulnerability as researchers. In offering their own experiences of vulnerability in research, the contributors provide examples of how we might pause to wonder what it is about vulnerability that breeds discomfort and to question why conventional approaches to teaching research methods may fail to prepare us for experiences of vulnerability when they arise or recognize what vulnerable moments can teach us within our research.

Structure of the Book

Considerations of the social location and identification of the researcher in relation with and to the research and community is of central concern to this collection. The precise point of our inquiry, however, is the site at which these considerations intersect with the critical conceptualization of vulnerability outlined previously and the material realities of research. Posed as a question, we ask:

> If we were to understand vulnerability as a shared human potential that is experienced contextually, relationally, and with embodied specificity, how might research relations shift from an ethical responsibility to protect research participants to a capacity to respond ethically in and through the practice of research?

The importance of this query is heightened when we consider that researchers are not somehow outside of the social relations of research. The authors included in this collection share a reflexive approach to knowledge production. Such an approach recognizes the role of the researcher (both their social locations and corresponding interpretations) and the research relationship on the findings or offerings. Reflexivity in research also attends to the particular research contexts, as well as how we endeavour to negotiate the different needs and bodies—funding bodies, community groups, research partners, among others.

Contemporary Vulnerabilities considers the ways in which researchers and the research itself are implicated in and constituted by experiences of vulnerability. To this end we have structured the book into the following sections—Vulnerable Moments; Reflections on Challenges and Hard Decisions in Research Processes; Reflections on Contemporary Approaches to Key Methods and Concepts; Reflections on Creative Research Collaborations and Relationships; and Reflections on the Methodologically Unresolved—which are reflective of the following areas of consideration:

- Moments of vulnerability: making hard decisions, disappointments, moments when where we're not really sure what to do, discomfort and community building, and ethical tensions. For example, Chapter 6 focuses on the use of the phrase *rape culture* within research. Rebecca Godderis, Debra Langan, and Marcia Oliver share that the original desire to have students focus on the *cultural* elements of rape culture was impossible given the deeply personal experiences of sexual violence. They reflect that using a different term might have engaged a wider group of participants into critical conversations about rape culture but that this would have also had troubling implications for them as feminist researchers.
- Spaces of research: how research changes through reimaginings of reflexivity and disruptions to oppressive systems and spaces. In the chapter "Disrupting Codified Academic Norms through Decolonization," the authors speak of the necessary changes to academic spaces as part of moving toward decolonization. Emily Grafton, Moses Gordon, Cheyanne Desnomie, Cassandra Opikokew Wajuntah, and Bettina Schneider suggest

that shifting power relations are displacing vulnerability and "it might soon be that those institutions unwilling or unable to follow suit with cultural humility and cultural competence are left vulnerable in the wake of decolonial practices."
- Temporal disjunctures and allowances: the time it takes to build relationships, nurture knowledge, and notice/grapple with the unexpected. Chapter 12, set within the COVID-19 pandemic, focuses on the lack of engagement with feminist expertise within the current mainstreaming of EDI (equity, diversity, and inclusion) in academia. Irene Shankar and Corrine L. Mason draw attention to the expectation to keep up with their research amid a global health pandemic, which fundamentally contradicts EDI commitments to address structural inequalities within the workplace.
- Multiple forms of resistance and creative knowledge production: research that critically attends to the appropriation of others' narratives and experiences, including Indigenous methodologies, critical translation work, arts-based research, insider/outsider relations, dialogic collaborations, unconventional writing practices, and naming power dynamics within research relationships. The opening chapter of the collection is a sustained reflection on Shraddha Chatterjee's identity following a comment made by a hoped-for participant that positioned Chatterjee as a non-resident Indian (NRI). This labelling emerged in contrast to how she identifies—as a queer activist-scholar in India doing fieldwork mediated by a Canadian university. This disruptive moment sparked what she calls a "sense of ethnographic crisis" and her chapter reflects on how a brief remark can upset self-identity, contextualized within the global power relations informing research.
- Challenges of research: doing Indigenous/community-engaged/intersectional research within the neoliberal academy and other colonial institutions, including timing, funding, traditional dissemination, accessibility, and/or recognition (issues of power/binaries reproduced). In the chapter "It Was the Worst Place I Ever Lived"... "It Was the Best Place I Ever Worked," Madeline Burghardt juxtaposes two sets of experiences—those of people

who worked and those who lived at an institution for people labelled as having intellectual disabilities. The significant contrasts between their depictions reflect personal and structural inequities. Speaking of the challenges she faced listening to former staff's positive stories, Burghardt found that the bias she had for residents' experiences was productive and critical for social justice research.

How to Read This Book

The politics of academic reading have much to do with how certain voices are represented and included in intellectual conversations. Max Liborion encourages a reciprocal style of reading—not reading for extraction of knowledge, but for ethical exchange that recognizes the relation between research, researcher, and wider communities.[27] In this spirit, we imagine this book as an invitational dialogue that moves from one vulnerable moment to the next, through the voices and stories of 41 different authors and co-authors. These authors detail moments of difficult decision making, creative method making, collaboration, and uncertainty—some of which are left unresolved. This is a book of reflection, not of answers. Though there are moments of fixed problems in these pages, we are aware that to read vulnerability as a problem with a solution would be to flatten its vibrant contribution to knowledge production. We hold vulnerability as complex and unresolvable.

Structurally, we have organized the chapters into themes to amplify discussions taking place between authors while also developing the book's central argument across chapters in a coherent manner. However, we invite you into this book in whatever way suits your process. We anticipate that some of these pieces might sit alongside you during difficult research moments of your own, while others will be part of the larger dialogues you are having in classrooms, communities, and institutions about vulnerability and research. Some of these chapters might be easy to digest, while others may be difficult. While we invite you into the entire collection, we are counting on your non-linear, possibly sporadic, or partial read, mainly because we know that there is no simple beginning, middle, or end to the vulnerable processes imbued in our lives and on these pages.

Tempting as it is to extend bell hooks's "come closer" approach to reading, we anticipate that you will dip in and out of this book.[28] We imagine that you will come to this book carrying your own overlapping personal and political contexts. You might find yourself reflecting on a past moment, still uncertain about a decision. You might even find yourself backing away from the pages, not wishing to tip too close to the pain that vulnerability can evoke. You may or may not find yourself represented here. For this reason, our invitation to dwell in vulnerability is meant to be open-ended: We invite you to join this conversation so that we might hold space for each other and extend connections to each other via moments of vulnerability. But we leave it to you to decide what this looks like.

Notes

1. Will C. van den Hoonaard, "The Vulnerability of Vulnerability: Why Social Science Researchers Should Abandon the Doctrine of Vulnerability," in *SAGE Handbook of Qualitative Research Ethics*, eds. Ron Iphofen and Martin Tolich (Thousand Oaks: SAGE, 2018), 317.
2. Ruth Behar, *The Vulnerable Observer: Anthropology That Breaks Your Heart* (Boston: Beacon Press, 1996).
3. Kathryn Church, *Forbidden Narratives: Critical Ethnography as Social Science* (New York: Routledge, 1995).
4. Alison L. Bain and Catherine J. Nash, "Undressing the Researcher," *Area* 38, no. 1 (2006): 99–106.
5. Sara Ahmed, *Complaint!* (Durham: Duke University Press, 2021).
6. Chelsea Temple Jones, "'Wounds of Regret': Critical Reflections on Competence, 'Professional Intuition,' and Informed Consent in Research with Intellectually Disabled People," *Disability Studies Quarterly* 40, no. 2 (2021).
7. Catherine J. Nash and Kath Browne, *Queer Methods and Methodologies: Intersecting Queer Theories and Social Science Research* (London: Routledge, 2010).
8. Sara Ahmed, *On Being Included: Racism and Diversity in Institutional Life* (Durham: Duke University Press, 2012).
9. Alan Santinele Martino, and Ann Fudge Schormans, "When Good Intentions Backfire: University Research Ethics Review and the Intimate Lives of People Labeled with Intellectual Disabilities," *Forum, Qualitative Social Research* 19, no. 3: (2018), https://doi.org/10.17169/fqs-19.3.3090.
10. Canadian Institutes of Health Research, Natural Sciences and Engineering Research Council Canada, Social Sciences and Humanities Research Council of Canada, and Interagency Secretariat on Research Ethics, *Tri-Council Policy Statement: Ethical Conduct for Research Involving Humans* (TCPS-2) (Ottawa: Interagency Secretariat on Research Ethics, 2018).
11. Jackie L. Scully, "Disability and Vulnerability: On Bodies, Dependence, and Power," in *Vulnerability: New Essays in Ethics and Feminist Philosophy*, eds.

Catriona Mackenzie, Wendy Rogers, and Susan Dodds, 204-221. New York: Oxford University Press, 2014; Øyvind Ibrahim Marøy Snipstad, "Concerns Regarding the Use of The Vulnerability Concept in Research on People with Intellectual Disability," *British Journal of Learning Disabilities* 00, no. 1 (2020): 1-8.
12. Linda Tuhiwai Smith, *Decolonizing Methodologies: Research and Indigenous Peoples* (London and New York: Zed Books, 1999).
13. Juan M. Tauri, "Research Ethics, Information Consent and the Disempowerment of First Nations Peoples," *Research Ethics* 14, no. 3 (2018); Kathleen E. Absolon (Minogiizhigokwe), *Kaandossiwin: How We Come to Know* (Halifax: Fernwood, 2011); Nathalie Piquemal, "Four Principles to Guide Research with Aboriginals," *Policy Options* (December 2000).
14. Ron Iphofen, *Ethical Decision-Making in Social Research: A Practical Guide* (Basingstoke: Palgrave Macmillan, 2009).
15. van den Hoonaard, "The Vulnerability of Vulnerability," 307.
16. Erinn Gilson, *The Ethics of Vulnerability: A Feminist Analysis of Social Life and Practice* (New York: Routledge, 2014), 5.
17. Church, *Forbidden Narratives*.
18. Arthur P. Bochner, and Carolyn Ellis, *Ethnographically Speaking: Autoethnography, Literature, and Aesthetics* (Walnut Creek: AltaMira Press, 2002).
19. Tony E. Adams, Robin M. Boylorn, and Lisa M. Tillman, *Advances in Autoethnography and Narrative Inquiry: Reflections on the Legacy of Carolyn Ellis and Arthur Bochner* (New York: Routledge, 2021).
20. Rosi Braidotti, "A Theoretical Framework for the Critical Post-humanities," *Theory, Culture & Society* 36, no. 6 (2018): 31-61.
21. Gilson, *The Ethics of Vulnerability*, 7-8.
22. Margaret Kovach and Elizabeth Fast, "Community Relationships Within Indigenous Methodologies," in *Applying Indigenous Methodologies*, eds. Sweeney Windchief and Timothy San Pedro, 21-36 (New York: Routledge, 2019), 26.
23. Kovach and Fast, "Community Relationships," 26.
24. Judith Butler, *Frames of War: When is Life Grievable?* (New York: Verso, 2016).
25. Martha Albertson Fineman, "The Vulnerable Subject: Anchoring Equality in the Human Condition," *Yale Journal of Law and Feminism* 20, no. 1 (2008), 9.
26. Fineman, "The Vulnerable Subject," 8-9.
27. Max Liborion, "Exchanging," in *Transmissions: Critical Tactics for Making and Communicating Research*, ed. K. Jungnickel (Massachusetts: MIT Press, 2020), 90-107.
28. bell hooks, *Feminism is for Everybody: Passionate Politics* (London: Pluto Press, 2000).

Bibliography

Absolon, Kathleen E. (Minogiizhigokwe). *Kaandossiwin: How We Come to Know*. Halifax: Fernwood, 2011.

Adams, Tony E., Robin M. Boylorn, and Lisa M. Tillman. *Advances in Autoethnography and Narrative Inquiry: Reflections on the Legacy of Carolyn Ellis and Arthur Bochner*. New York: Routledge, 2021.

Ahmed, Sara. *Complaint!* Durham: Duke University Press, 2021.
Ahmed, Sara. *On Being Included: Racism and Diversity in Institutional Life.* Durham: Duke University Press, 2012.
Bain, Alison L, and Kath Browne, eds. *Queer Methods and Methodologies: Intersecting Queer Theories and Social Science Research.* London: Routledge, 2010.
Bain, Alison L., and Catherine J. Nash. "Undressing the Researcher: Feminism, Embodiment and Sexuality at a Queer Bathhouse Event." *Area* 38, no. 1 (2006): 99-106.
Behar, Ruth. *The Vulnerable Observer: Anthropology That Breaks Your Heart.* Boston: Beacon Press, 1996.
Bochner, Arthur P., and Carolyn Ellis. *Ethnographically Speaking: Autoethnography, Literature, and Aesthetics.* Walnut Creek: AltaMira Press, 2002.
Butler, Judith. *Frames of War: When is Life Grievable?* New York: Verso, 2016.
Butler, Judith. *Precarious Life.* New York: Verso, 2009.
Braidotti, Rosi. "A Theoretical Framework for the Critical Posthumanities." *Theory, Culture & Society* 36, no. 6 (2018): 31-61.
Canadian Institutes of Health Research, Natural Sciences and Engineering Research Council Canada, Social Sciences and Humanities Research Council of Canada, and Interagency Secretariat on Research Ethics (Canada). *Tri-council Policy Statement: Ethical Conduct for Research Involving Humans* (TCPS-2). Ottawa: Interagency Secretariat on Research Ethics, 2018.
Church, Kathryn. *Forbidden Narratives: Critical Autobiography as Social Science.* New York: Routledge, 1995.
Fineman, Martha Albertson. "The Vulnerable Subject: Anchoring Equality in the Human Condition." *Yale Journal of Law and Feminism* 20, no. 1 (2008): 8-40.
Gilson, Erinn. *The Ethics of Vulnerability: A Feminist Analysis of Social Life and Practice.* New York: Routledge, 2014.
hooks, bell. *Feminism is for Everybody: Passionate Politics.* London: Pluto Press, 2000.
Iphofen, Ron. *Ethical Decision-Making in Social Research: A Practical Guide.* Basingstoke: Palgrave Macmillan, 2009.
Jones, Chelsea Temple. "'Wounds of Regret': Critical Reflections on Competence, 'Professional Intuition,' and Informed Consent in Research with Intellectually Disabled People." *Disability Studies Quarterly* 40, no. 2 (2021).
Knight, Michelle, Bentley, Courtney C., Norton, Nadjwa, et al. "(De)constructing (in)Visible Parent/guardian Consent Forms: Negotiating Power, Reflexivity, and The Collective Within Qualitative Research." *Qualitative Inquiry* 10, no. 3 (2004): 684-699.
Kovach, Margaret, and Elizabeth Fast. "Community Relationships Within Indigenous Methodologies." In *Applying Indigenous Methodologies*, edited by Sweeney Windchief and Timothy San Pedro, 21-36. New York: Routledge, 2019.
Liborion, Max. "Exchanging." In *Transmissions: Critical Tactics for Making and Communicating Research*, edited by Kat Jungnickel, 90-107. Massachusetts: MIT Press, 2020.

Martino, Alan Santinele, and Ann Fudge Schormans. "When Good IntentionsBackfire: University Research Ethics Review and the Intimate Lives of People Labeled with Intellectual Disabilities." *Forum, Qualitative Social Research* 19, no. 3 (2018). https://doi.org/10.17169/fqs-19.3.3090.

Piquemal, Nathalie. "Four Principles to Guide Research with Aboriginals." *Policy Options* (December 2000): 49-50.

Scully, Jackie L. "Disability and Vulnerability: On Bodies, Dependence, and Power." In *Vulnerability: New Essays in Ethics and Feminist Philosophy*, edited by Catriona Mackenzie, Wendy Rogers, and Susan Dodds, 204-221. New York: Oxford University Press, 2014.

Smith, Linda Tuhiwai. *Decolonizing Methodologies: Research and Indigenous Peoples*. London and New York: Zed Books, 1999.

Snipstad, Øyvind Ibrahim Marøy. "Concerns Regarding the Use of The Vulnerability Concept in Research on People with Intellectual Disability." *British Journal of Learning Disabilities* 00, no. 1 (2020): 1-8.

Tauri, Juan M. "Research Ethics, Informed Consent and The Disempowerment of First Nation Peoples." *Research Ethics* 14, no. 3 (2018): 1-14.

van den Hoonaard, Will C. "The Vulnerability of Vulnerability: Why Social Science Researchers Should Abandon the Doctrine of Vulnerability." In *The SAGE Handbook of Qualitative Research Ethics*, edited by Ron Iphofen and Martin Tolich, 305-320. Thousand Oaks: Sage.

I

Vulnerable Moments

1

NRI/Outsider/Returnee
The Location of Trust in Ethnographic Practice

Shraddha Chatterjee

One evening, in the early days of my fieldwork in New Delhi, I was texting Imkaan some details about my research and asking if he would give me an interview. Imkaan was a queer activist of some repute, having appeared on a major television show to discuss homosexuality almost a decade ago. I no longer remember whether I had met Imkaan at a Delhi Queer Pride event or protest before moving to Toronto for my PhD or if we had simply begun following each other on social media at some point. Their social media presence was curated to reflect their political stance on various issues, with their queer Muslim identity often at the centre, and they would post about their negotiations with love and loss, their cooking skills, and sometimes their intimate familiarity with the lanes and monuments of old Delhi. Since my research was attempting to map the connection between queer activisms and Hindu majoritarianism in contemporary India, Imkaan was an obvious choice as a participant. When I shared with them a few lines about my research with them, they immediately wrote back, "Absolutely, let's meet and chat. I think I know you...You're that NRI queer who wrote some book right?" I had viscerally flinched at this comment and was quite surprised at how much it continued to bother me for days afterward.

NRI stands for non-resident Indian, and for many middle- and upper-class communities, the NRI remains an aspirational figure, embodying a dream of upward mobility in a postcolonial landscape with dwindling freedoms and worsening quality of life. At the same time, the NRI is a figure fraught with negative charge and affect. As Visvanathan puts it, rather distastefully:

> The NRI does not quite fit the colonial categories of the Anglophile and the Orientalist...He is an aspirational, upwardly-mobile creature who leaves home to seek a more affluent and opportunistic world... There is an economic power to the NRI which is obvious...Our current prime minister, Narendra Modi, dotes on their support... The NRI loved Modi for decisiveness, his passion, his celebration of their success, his masculinity...the NRI loves India, it is Indians he finds obtuse and intolerable...The NRI is a happy composite of the Gujarati in Rutgers, the Silicon Valley technocrat...the NRI academic who has internalized the rituals of the American university, who has mastered its academic table manners if not its intellectual ideals, the Sikh in Canada creating bits of Chandigarh at Montreal and Ottawa. The political emergence of the NRI is twofold. He is an influence on the regime here as he struggles to make his presence felt abroad.[1]

Having grown up in an upper-caste, upper-middle-class family in metropolitan New Delhi, where the NRI was, indeed, an aspirational figure, I had moved into other social communities through student politics and queer activism in my twenties, where the NRI affiliation was seen with disdain or at least suspicion. Therefore, being called an NRI by Imkaan was upsetting to me. What was even worse was learning that, despite my international student status in Canada (a status I experienced as relatively precarious), I could be considered an NRI in any given calendar year based on whether I had spent a certain number of days outside India. The irony was that, based on that arbitrary metric of days spent abroad versus in the "homeland," while I had briefly been an NRI the previous year, returning for fieldwork had disqualified me as one.

Clearly, in this interaction between Imkaan and myself, I had come face to face with a flexible and porous category that, while having roots in taxation laws, had acquired a social life of its own. The increasingly popular presence of the NRI in the mainstream Indian imaginary can be attributed to almost three decades of economic liberalization and corresponding sociocultural discourses that facilitated an invested desire in India's upwardly mobile classes to work toward a life "abroad," most often in countries like the US, Canada, the UK, and Australia.[2] In these last three decades, the NRI has emerged as a predominantly Hindu, family oriented, economically rich figure who embodies the "virtues of consumerism and devotion and of cosmopolitanism and roots."[3] This NRI figure is deeply imbricated in the cultural politics of the Bharatiya Janata Party (BJP), the authoritarian Hindu nationalist government in power in India at this time, and the massive success of events such as the "Howdy Modi" rally in Houston in 2019 provides proof that the Indian diaspora is culturally and materially invested in the kind of Hindu revivalism that is in line with the BJP's vision. Therefore, the NRI is consequently viewed unfavourably by a significant portion of the Indian population, who bear the brunt of the government's repressive policies within the borders of the subcontinent. As such, it was difficult to read being called an NRI by Imkaan as anything but a hostile gesture, primarily because of the overdetermined relationship between the NRI and Hindu nationalist politics, and also because the NRI figure embodied a sense of cultural purity, economic wealth, and stability, all of which I decidedly lacked and most of which I fundamentally despised.

However, this chapter is not a genealogical enquiry into what makes a non-resident Indian, nor is it about enlivening the complexities of who is, or can be, an NRI. Rather, it is an attempt to demystify an affectively charged ethnographic moment where I was referred to as an NRI and about the perceived meanings behind that gesture. Why was I called an NRI and what did that mean, especially in the context of my previous work as a queer activist-scholar in India? How did this labelling brush against the already existing and problematized category of the returnee in anthropology? What are the implications of an ethnographic encounter with so much negative charge? In other words, what produced the specific vulnerability of this ethnographic moment and what can we learn, from staying with this vulnerability and sense of ethnographic crisis, about the field and about the process of fieldwork? In the following sections, I will offer two interrelated explanations through which this encounter can be given meaning within my research context. Through these readings of the cultural semiotics of this exchange, I will highlight what crisis and anxiety can offer the work of ethnography.

The First Possibility: I Had Not "Returned" to What I Had Left Behind

Any ethnographic encounter is framed by the expectations of the ethnographer and how they are upheld, disrupted, or entirely cast aside by the field and by the participants. One way of reading the incident I describe above, between Imkaan and myself, is through the disruption of my expectations as an ethnographer. Even though I was conducting fieldwork mediated by my affiliation with a Canadian university, I had expected to be treated by my participants as an "insider" at best, and a "returnee" at worst. There were many reasons for this expectation: New Delhi was my childhood home, and I had indeed returned there for fieldwork; I wanted to believe that my past experience with queer spaces and politics in the city qualified me as an insider to those life-worlds; and I did not want to feel like an outsider to the landscapes and people among whom I had spent most of my life. In other words, I did not want to believe that my leaving for a PhD had changed anything about my belongingness in the communities and geographies I had grown up in and with. In this way, perhaps the ethnography itself was a way for me to "return home." Even though Imkaan was not, in the conventional sense of the term, a friend, they belonged, for me, within a loosely knit community that I considered my own.

There hasn't been too much ethnographic research conducted with queer communities in India, and Naisargi Davé's research has been foundational to this oeuvre of work, which is now beginning to proliferate. When Davé had conducted fieldwork with lesbian communities in New Delhi in the early 2000s, of their experience they had written:

> Queerness and gender were shown to matter infinitely more than nationality or social race in matters of access and trust. I was out in the field as a queer woman—the semiotics were such that this was never in any doubt. This minimum level of commonality was

critical for the quality of relationships I could forge. While lesbians and gay men sometimes queried the motivations for and necessity of my research, they never doubted my solidarity and sympathy. The importance of identity in the queer landscape seemed to prequalify me for trust and often brought me close to people before I even had the chance to try.[4]

Why, then, did I have a different experience when I set out on this ethnographic project in early 2020? What had made me an outsider, or at best, an untrustworthy returnee, whereas Davé had been welcomed with so much trust?

Staying with this question threw into sharp relief the ways in which queer activisms have changed in India generally, and in New Delhi in particular, since the early 2000s. The proliferation of social media,[5] neoliberal and global cultural influences,[6] and the decriminalization of homosexuality in 2013 and 2018 have all made enormous differences to queer life and activisms in the past two decades. I was no longer returning to the emergent field of queer activisms that Davé[7] had described; in fact, I was not even returning to the landscape I myself had left behind when I moved to Toronto in 2017. It was quite clear that the decriminalization of homosexuality in 2018 has caused a significant shift in how queer activisms are being organized and oriented in the last two years, and there has been a rapid expansion of groups, collectives, and organizations working on various queer issues in this time. Queer mainstreaming in the form of inclusion and diversity initiatives in workplaces has also become popular,[8] even though such measures are strongly critiqued by a section of queer activists and other scholars.[9] Critiques of queer activisms that were previously withheld in public spaces due to an implicit understanding of a shared vision for decriminalization are now being spoken of freely.[10] There has been a definite increase in queer visibility and representation, however problematic, since 2018. As such, the loosely knit community I had left in 2017, the one to which I was so eager to "belong" again, was simply no longer there and had morphed into something else.

Even though I had known these shifts were taking place while I was away, I had been unable to experience the fullness of these changes from another location. My own psychic investments in returning to the "homeland" had also led me to minimize the shifts in queer activisms that I had been aware of, as well as to disregard, at least affectively, the large body of anthropological research that has problematized notions of return, of the "homeland," of static cultures, of "native anthropologists."[11] In this way, my ethnographic sensibilities were overridden by the affective charge of homecoming. Similar negotiations are experienced by ethnographers across different contexts, and remaining attuned to these complex grids and often contradictory moments can produce more robust ethnographies. In fact, Pandian argues that these encounters can be experienced as contradiction, unease, or rupture precisely because anthropology has a disciplinary legacy of "colonial relations of power and knowledge in the formal structures of the discipline"[12] that demand seamless representations of cultures and communities. Relatedly, Boyce, Engbretsen and Posocco argue that these negotiations are central to anthropology's queer sensibilities. They write:

> A key problematic in the sub-field of queer anthropology, institutionalized by now in the US, and a fractured special interest network at dispersed locations elsewhere, is to do with these connections—and inevitable ruptures. These (dis-)connections evoke tensions between empiricism and theory, concept and reality, activist and academic sensibilities. Such tensions are productive and necessary, albeit oftentimes they do create feelings of discomfort negative vibes, or even disdain and anger.[13]

Imkaan's comment had forced me to become an outsider, and once I attempted to situate that gesture within a larger grid of cultural semiotics, it enabled me to better understand the changes that had occurred not only with respect to my position and affiliations, but also with respect to the queer landscape and the research field. The question of the "field" is perhaps as old as anthropology itself, and has evolved in relation to developments in understanding what culture is as well as how ethnography can be constituted as method, praxis, and worldmaking. Moving from the rigid boundaries that defined the field as an enclosed physical or spatial location, multi-sited at best, recent scholarship in anthropology has come to the "realization that the field site is in certain ways constructed rather than discovered."[14] Within "this newer conception, the movement of objects, of individuals, of ideas, of media, and of the fieldworker is attended to, uncovering insights and objects of inquiry that were not visible in studies that assumed culture was spatially fixed."[15] Through Imkaan's comment and the corresponding anxiety it generated in me, an orientation to the field site as a dynamic, mobile, and heterogeneous space—not restricted by location but rather defined by context—had become possible, and I was able to identify the ways in which the landscape of queer activisms had changed over the past few years. Opening myself to the possibility of the field as a dynamic construction, simultaneously a situation and location, I was able to pull away from the simplistic myth of anthropological "return."

The Second Possibility: Those Who Leave and Those Who Stay
Just as ethnographies are determined by the ruptured expectations of the ethnographer, they are also driven by the perceptions of ethnographic subjects. Another possible explanation for my interpellation as an NRI could be that my departure had made me untrustworthy—in moving away from queer communities and choosing academic advancement, I had demonstrated a lack of commitment to those queer communities. As such, rather than being perceived as someone researching queer life from within the queer community, my departure and return had coded me as an outsider—as a researcher no longer invested in queer lives but in their own career goals.

Even though, as I mention above, there hasn't been too much ethnographic research on queer lives and communities in India, there is a burgeoning field of social scientific inquiry that is attempting to understand and explain the multiple contours of queer experience in the subcontinent, and this research is marked by a certain politics of representation. Dutoya[16] demonstrates how a significant portion of queer research in India emerges from within queer activisms and relies on participatory reflections and observations. Therefore, existing "scholarship does not only 'make visible' what already exists, but participates in the emergence of a collective 'we,' grounded on a shared identity."[17] For better or worse, this results in research that tends to remain imbricated within questions of representation, authenticity, authorship, and legitimacy. It is my contention that the popularity of social media in determining certain queer activist discourses in India also contributes heavily to the importance given to these questions. Within this atmosphere, the specific question of who can speak for whom is ossified even further.

Additionally, Dutoya documents that this body of scholarship tends to exclude lower-class, lower-caste queer communities, as well as queer Muslim populations. More research is also needed on lesbian and bisexual women's queer sensibilities and politics, and research on transmasculine persons is virtually nonexistent as well. I argue that this is directly related to the kinds of subjects who are centred in queer activisms in India. In other words, those who are at the margins of queer activisms are also at the margins of queer theory emerging from and about India. Relatedly, those who are seen as the beneficiaries of queer activisms are also, often, only understood as objects of analysis. Within this context, Gee Semmalar and Living Smile Vidya, two lower-caste trans activist-scholars, discuss how they get requests from graduate scholars to give interviews and how those interviews produce knowledges that remain interested in Othering lower-caste trans communities. Vidya states, "I never got anything from any of these research projects. They [researchers] get funding and support, travel from various cities in India, even across the world and use my life experiences, but give me nothing in return. Neither payment, nor even the finished work."[18] This problematic, I would argue, is heightened when it is overdetermined by the imbalance created by the researcher being located in the Global North (even if institutionally and not in terms of nationality or citizenship), like myself.

While it is not unusual that hitherto marginalized communities remain suspicious of researchers and their intentions, this suspicion and untrustworthiness, signalled by Imkaan's comment, became an important gesture through which I came to terms with my "foreign" location and outsider status. Many times in the course of fieldwork, potential participants disappeared after promising interviews or left my requests for interviews unanswered even as we continued to talk on the same email thread, text message chain, or social media chat service about other things. These were uniquely frustrating and interesting moments—they were not disappearing from my life completely, but only refusing, in a rather persistent way, the request I was making as an ethnographer. I interpret these moments to mean that they were refusing to trust me as a researcher, but my previous experience among those activist communities remained grounds for forays into friendship, camaraderie, and solidarity.

Toward Patchwork, Queered, Uneasy Ethnographies

While describing the merits of thick description, Geertz[19] argues that the task of ethnography is to interpret, within a matrix of cultural semiotics, whether the contracting of one eyelid is a twitch or a wink. In doing so, he locates the object of ethnography precisely between the process of making the actor and their gesture visible. He writes that the object of ethnography is to create "a stratified hierarchy of meaningful structures in terms of which twitches, winks, fake-winks, parodies, rehearsals of parodies are produced, perceived, and interpreted, and without which they would not…in fact exist."[20] In this chapter, I have tried to demonstrate how such a gesture—in my case, being called an NRI—can be populated and how the task of ethnography, of interpreting these gestures, is necessarily grounded in vulnerability, crisis, rupture, bad feelings, and fractures of trust. It is precisely when experience is fractured that the resultant slippages in cultural signification, those moments of things being lost in translation, begin to hold worlds of possibility. In our life-worlds, which are characterized by the contradictions of (post)modernity and repeated and overlapping crises, perhaps what would be really suspicious was an experience of ethnography that progressed really smoothly.

Of course, it is possible that Imkaan didn't think too much before calling me an NRI; what was an agonizing moment for me may have simply been them making a flippant, offhanded joke. And yet, as Freud[21] (1960) reminds us, jokes have deeper meanings and can alert us to other textures of cultural experience that require humour in order to be articulated. Given our previous associations within the same queer communities, it might have been difficult for Imkaan to say no to being my research participant directly, and indeed, they did say yes to giving me an interview. However, in the weeks and months that followed, Imkaan ignored all my messages about scheduling a conversation. When we ran into each other at a protest a few weeks after this exchange, they introduced me to their friend as an NRI, again as if in jest. The joke, that I was an NRI, allowed Imkaan to convey that they did not necessarily trust me as a researcher. The repetition of the joke cemented for me that I would not be able to interview Imkaan, even as the modality of the joke ensured that there wouldn't be any souring of our association outside the research setting.

How do we mobilize such ruptures and moments of crisis in productive ways in ethnographic research? Queering anthropological methods seems to offer unique possibilities. Manalansan argues that:

> Queer anthropological research is not about reaching and arriving in "the field," since processes such as globalization and colonialism have put this very concept into question. Indeed, the acceptance of queer anthropology as an analytical frame and methodology should not be about its comfortable emplacement in the study of cultural things. It is, rather, about the messy and uncomfortable enmeshment of both anthropologists and the communities they study in the lived realities of life and death, of suffering and exuberance, and therefore, of quotidian mutabilities and contingencies.[22]

Similarly, Ghaziani and Brim suggest that queer methods are often interdisciplinary, resisting disciplinary boundaries because of a commitment to the messiness of everyday life, and their promise lies in "disrupting ideals of stability, rationality, objectivity, and coherence"[23] and moving beyond binaries into multiplicity, pluralism, assemblages, and other forms of radical networking as worldmaking.

In the same vein, recent provocations by Gunel, Varma, and Watanabe[24] argue that ethnographies must take into account the crises surrounding researched communities and researchers as well. They call for a reorientation that makes space for patchwork ethnographies that consider neoliberal university conditions, global events like the COVID-19 pandemic, and other "financial, environmental, political, and temporal constraints." They write:

> By *patchwork ethnography*, we refer to ethnographic processes and protocols designed around short-term field visits, using fragmentary yet rigorous data, and other innovations that resist the fixity, holism, and certainty demanded in the publication process...Patchwork ethnography offers a new way to acknowledge and accommodate how researchers' lives in their full complexity shape knowledge production. In the process, we argue that

anthropological knowledge itself must be transformed. Patchwork ethnography helps us refigure what counts as knowledge and what does not, what counts as research and what does not, and how we can transform realities that have been described to us as "limitations" and "constraints" into openings for new insights.

In this chapter, I argue for similar orientations toward fieldwork and ethnographic research. In doing so, I take the provocations of Springgay and Truman seriously, where they demand that we imagine research methods as "practices of being inside an event,"[25] as the "speculative middle" of research that can only come into being through the process of research but cannot be determined beforehand. This requires that we unlearn our temporal lessons as researchers, and remain at ease with the unease caused by speculative and fractured methodologies that are made, invented, adopted alongside the research.

Notes

1. Shiv Viswanathan, "The NRI: Consumer of Civilizations and a Threat to Culture," *The Telegraph (India)*, October 22, 2019.
2. Sareeta Amrute, "The 'New' Non-Residents of India: A Short History of the NRI," in *A New India? Critical Reflections in the Long Twentieth Century*, ed. Anthony P. D'Costa (UK: Anthem Press, 2012), 127–150.
3. Ingrid Therwath, "'Shining Indians': Diaspora and Exemplarity in Bollywood," *Samaj: South Asia Multidisciplinary Academic Journal* 4 (2010), 3.
4. Naisargi Davé, *Queer Activism in India: A Story in the Anthropology of Ethics* (Durham: Duke University Press, 2012), 25.
5. Rohit Dasgupta, *Digital Queer Cultures in India: Politics, Intimacies and Belonging* (London: Routledge, 2017).
6. Srila Roy, "New Activist Subjects: The Changing Feminist Field of Kolkata, India," *Feminist Studies* 40, no. 3 (2014): 628–656; Srila Roy and Debanuj Dasgupta, "Aparajita and Nishith Chetana: The City's Contested Fabric," *Contemporary South Asia* 28, no. 4 (2020): 434–445.
7. Dave, "Queer Activism in India."
8. Parmesh Shahani, *Queeristan: LGBTQ Inclusion in the Indian Workplace* (Chennai: Westland Books, 2020).
9. Oishik Sircar, "New Queer Politics: Notes on Failure and Stuckness in a Negative Moment," in *Violent Modernities: Cultural Lives of Law in the New India* (New Delhi: Oxford University Press, 2021).

10. Akhil Kang and Vqueeram Aditya Sahai, "The Story of a Movement: The Law, the Leaders, the Lies," *Akademi Magazine*, September 24, 2020; Charu Pragya, "Understanding Homonationalism and Pinkwashing," *Akademi Magazine*, June 26, 2021.
11. Clifford Geertz, "Thick Description: Toward an Interpretive Theory of Culture" and "The Politics of Meaning," in *The Interpretation of Cultures* (New York: Perseus Books, 2000); Kirin Narayan, "How Native is a 'Native' Anthropologist?" *American Anthropologist* 95, no. 3 (1993): 671-686; Kamala Visweswaran, *Fictions of Feminist Ethnography* (Minnesota: University of Minnesota Press, 1994).
12. Anand Pandian, *A Possible Anthropology: Methods for Uneasy Times* (Durham: Duke University Press, 2019), 1.
13. Paul Boyce, Elisabeth L. Engebretsen, and Silvia Posocco, "Introduction: Anthropology's Queer Sensibilities," *Sexualities* 21, no. 5-6 (2018), 844.
14. Jenna Burrell, "The Field Site as a Network: A Strategy for Locating Ethnographic Research," *Field Methods* 21, no. 2 (2009), 182.
15. Burrell, "The Field Site," 183.
16. Virginie Dutoya, "Defining the 'Queers' in India: The Politics of Academic Representation," *India Review* 15, no. 2 (2016): 241-271.
17. Dutoya, 249.
18. Living Smile Vidya and Gee Imaan Semmalar, "Transphobia is a Kind of Brahmanism: A Conversation between Living Smile Vidya and Gee Imaan Semmalar," in *Gender, Caste and the Imagination of Equality*, ed. Anupama Rao (New Delhi: Women Unlimited Press, 2018), 59.
19. Geertz, "Thick Description."
20. Geertz, "Thick Description," 7.
21. Sigmund Freud, *Jokes and Their Relation to the Unconscious*, trans. J. Stratchey (New York: W.W. Norton & Company, 1960).
22. Martin F. Manalansan IV, "Queer Anthropology: An Introduction," *Cultural Anthropology* 31, no. 4 (2016), 596-597.
23. Amin Ghaziani and Matt Brim, eds., "Queer Methods: Four Provocations for an Emerging Field," in *Imagining Queer Methods* (New York: New York University Press, 2019), 15.
24. Gökçe Gunel, Saiba Varma, and Chika Watanabe, "A Manifesto for Patchwork Ethnography," *Society for Cultural Anthropology*, June 9, 2020.
25. Stephanie Springgay and Sarah E. Truman, "On the Need for Methods Beyond Proceduralism: Speculative Middles, (In)Tensions, and Response-Ability in Research," *Qualitative Inquiry* 4, no. 3 (2018), 204.

Bibliography

Amrute, Sareeta. "The 'New' Non-Residents of India: A Short History of the NRI." In *A New India? Critical Reflections in the Long Twentieth Century*, edited by Anthony P. D'Costa, 127-150. London: Anthem Press, 2012.

Boyce, Paul, Elisabeth L. Engebretsen, and Silvia Posocco. "Introduction: Anthropology's Queer Sensibilities." *Sexualities* 21, no. 5-6 (2018). https://journals.sagepub.com/doi/abs/10.1177/1363460717706667.

Burrell, Jenna. "The Field Site as a Network: A Strategy for Locating Ethnographic Research." *Field Methods* 21, no. 2 (2009). https://journals.sagepub.com/doi/10.1177/1525822X08329699.

Dasgupta, Rohit. *Digital Queer Cultures in India: Politics, Intimacies and Belonging.* London: Routledge, 2017.

Davé, Naisargi. *Queer Activism in India: A Story in the Anthropology of Ethics.* Durham: Duke University Press, 2012.

Dutoya, Virginie. "Defining the 'Queers' in India: The Politics of Academic Representation." *India Review* 15, no. 2(2016): 241-271.

Freud, Sigmund. *Jokes and Their Relation to the Unconscious*, trans. J. Stratchey. New York: W.W. Norton & Company, 1960.

Geertz, Clifford. "Thick Description: Toward an Interpretive Theory of Culture" and "The Politics of Meaning." In *The Interpretation of Cultures*, 3-36 and 333-348. New York: Perseus Books, 2000.

Ghaziani, Amin, and Matt Brim. "Queer Methods: Four Provocations for an Emerging Field." In *Imagining Queer Methods*, edited by A. Ghaziani and M. Brim, 3-26. New York: New York University Press, 2019.

Gunel, Gökçe, Saiba Varma, and Chika Watanabe. "A Manifesto for Patchwork Ethnography." *Society for Cultural Anthropology*, June 9, 2020. https://culanth.org/fieldsights/a-manifesto-for-patchwork-ethnography.

Kang, Akhil, and Vqueeram Aditya Sahai. "The Story of a Movement: the Law, the Leaders, the Lies." *Akademi Magazine*, September 24, 2020.

Manalansan IV, Martin F. "Queer Anthropology: An Introduction." *Cultural Anthropology* 31, no. 4 (2016): 595-597.

Narayan, Kirin. "How Native is a 'Native' Anthropologist?" *American Anthropologist* 95, no. 3 (1993): 671-686.

Pandian, Anand. *A Possible Anthropology: Methods for Uneasy Times.* Durham: Duke University Press, 2019.

Pragya, Charu. "Understanding Homonationalism and Pinkwashing." *Akademi Magazine*, June 26, 2021.

Roy, Srila. "New Activist Subjects: The Changing Feminist Field of Kolkata, India." *Feminist Studies* 40, no. 3 (2014): 628-656.

Roy, Srila, and Debanuj Dasgupta. "Aparajita and Nishith Chetana: The City's Contested Fabric." *Contemporary South Asia* 28, no. 4 (2020): 434-445.

Shahani, Parmesh. *Queeristan: LGBTQ Inclusion in the Indian Workplace.* Chennai: Westland Books, 2020.

Sircar, Oishik. "New Queer Politics: Notes on Failure and Stuckness in a Negative Moment." In *Violent Modernities: Cultural Lives of Law in the New India.* New Delhi: Oxford University Press, 2021.

Springgay, Stephanie, and Sarah E. Truman. "On the Need for Methods Beyond Proceduralism: Speculative Middles, (In)Tensions, and Response-Ability in Research." *Qualitative Inquiry* 4, no. 3 (2018): 203–214.

Therwath, Ingrid. "'Shining Indians': Diaspora and Exemplarity in Bollywood." *Samaj: South Asia Multidisciplinary Academic Journal* 4 (2010): 1–19.

Viswanathan, Shiv. "The NRI: Consumer of Civilizations and a Threat to Culture." *The Telegraph (India)*, October 22, 2019. https://www.telegraphindia.com/opinion/the-nri-consumer-of-civilizations-and-a-threat-to-culture/cid/1713566.

Visweswaran, Kamala. *Fictions of Feminist Ethnography*. Minnesota: University of Minnesota Press, 1994.

Vidya, Living Smile, and Gee Imaan Semmalar. "Transphobia is a Kind of Brahmanism: A Conversation between Living Smile Vidya and Gee Imaan Semmalar." In *Gender, Caste and the Imagination of Equality*, edited by Anupama Rao, 58–75. New Delhi: Women Unlimited Press, 2018.

2

To Whom Are We Accountable?
The Vulnerability of Deep Listening in Feminist Ethnographic Research

Rebecca Lennox

This chapter is dedicated to Judith Taylor, who taught me to listen.

Introduction

According to Michel Foucault, the ancient sport of dressage—which involves extensively training horses to perform stylized movements for carefully judged competitions—is much less about human-animal cooperation than it is about human-animal control.[1] In the sixteenth century, dressage athletes coerced horses into cantering, pirouetting, and vaulting by placing live hedgehogs under horses' tails, forcing their heads under water, or using spurs and bits engineered to cause pain.[2] In contemporary dressage, these draconian methods are eschewed, and riders extract horses' compliance by offering them rewards for obeying commands. While dressage has become more humane, its status as a spectacle of control is unchanged. As the International Federation for Equestrian Sports puts it, a successful dressage performance still requires that the horse "submit...generously to the control of the Athlete...thus *giv[ing] the impression* of doing, of its own accord, what is required" (my emphasis).[3] In this contemporary version of human-animal domination, control is so complete that trainers command not only the acquiescence of their trainees, but also a bizarre façade of partnership.

In summer 2021, as I completed this chapter, I finished a round of one-on-one interviews with Canadian women about their responses to men's violence in urban public places. As I endeavoured to write reflexively about what conducting feminist, participant-centred research means to me, the imagery of dressage routinely and unsettlingly entered my mind. Many of the qualitative methods guides I reviewed as I researched this chapter invited me into what I felt was an extractive model of research in which interviewees were figured as subordinates. These interviewees/subordinates were — not unlike ill-trained dressage horses — cast as in need of probing, prompting, and pulling into a tightly structured performance written and directed by interviewers alone.

This hierarchical model of research, which I term the horse training approach to qualitative research, is predicated on a subject-object split wherein researchers alone are conceived as authoritative knowers.[4] In the horse training approach to research, interviewees are cast as ill-spoken subjects who are easily swayed by the intelligence of the distanced researcher; generally inarticulate and in need of direction; and, not unlike a spooked horse, liable to bolt if given the opportunity. Interviewing guides that exemplify a horse training approach encourage new researchers to "master...the art of controlling an interview." This art is mastered first by recognizing that interviewers "have a better understanding than the respondent...of what will be helpful...to learn." Once researchers internalize the truism that they know better than respondents what is worthy of investigation, researchers should reign in "big talkers" by pulling them back on course when they go "off track."[5] One strategy is to "nudge [interviewees]...into...the right channel,"[6] by redirecting them with targeted "motivational probes,"[7] which are especially necessary when interviewees prove "hard to control."[8] All of these horse training-esque tactics ostensibly make the interview "*feel like* a conversation for the interviewee."[9] Explicit in many guides, however, is the admonition that interviews are *not* conversations.[10] Although skilled interviewers should create this illusion to get good data, the researcher and researched — or more accurately, the trainer and trained — are on epistemologically distinct planes. As such, the researcher leads but never follows the participant, simultaneously extracting, but never revealing, personal information.

Most of us who consider ourselves feminist researchers find it easy to eschew the horse training approach to research at the interviewing stage. When we meet participants whose stories we want to learn, we practise principles like mutuality and egalitarianism instead of distance and hierarchy.[11] We conceptualize interviews not as a strict one-way interrogation, but rather as a reciprocally shaped dialogue where interviewer and interviewee together determine the focus, number, and nature of questions posed.[12] During interviews, the spectre of dressage fades easily into the background as we discover that people love to be listened to and that informants know much better than we do what needs to be documented. Sometimes—as happened when I interviewed middle-aged Canadian women about their responses to gender-based violence—our interviewees tell us what to ask future respondents, how to frame our findings, and what we should have asked them. We write this down, delighted to be embarking upon what appears to be an unproblematic and non-hierarchical exercise in knowledge co-creation.

Yet the egalitarianism that characterizes feminist interviewing approaches is rarely mirrored in the analysis phase of research. Once we leave the field and are on our own with piles of passive transcripts, the positivist stance and epistemological arrogance that informs the hegemonic, horse training-esque approach to research becomes harder to eschew. When we turn to analysis, participants' words have typically been transcribed, and in this process, respondents are transformed from active co-constructors of knowledge into passive pieces of textual data.[13] At the same time, as we move out of the field and into a solitary writing space, questions about the analysis we will produce intrude on our consciousness, and we begin to hold accountability to participants in tension with unsettling images of our future readers and critics.[14] Too often, in the researcher-centric alchemy of transforming participants' stories into the abstract theory that is valued in disciplinary peer-reviewed journals, participants as whole subjects disappear and our imagined readers and reviewers silently take precedence over respondents in our decisions about how to write up participant accounts.

Against this backdrop of honouring ethical commitments to interviewees post-fieldwork, this chapter explores a question that ethnographer

Michelle Fine[15] identifies as an existential concern for researchers: *to whom are we accountable?* I focus my exploration of this question on the analysis phase of qualitative research, a phase in which our face-to-face interactions with respondents have typically ended, and feminist commitments to egalitarianism, mutuality, and knowledge co-creation begin to exist in tension with the felt presence of our "epistemic communities"—the disciplinary circles "wherein our work is located, read, reviewed, and received."[16] Building on the work of feminist ethnographers Andrea Doucet[17] and Marjorie DeVault,[18] I offer the methodological and political practice of *deep listening* as a strategy for maintaining accountability to participants during the analysis phase of research.

Deep listening is, to echo the words of the editors of this volume, a feminist invitation to "dwell in vulnerability" and become comfortable with eschewing the posture of the "unflappable investigator...[who] exist[s]... [on a separate] plane of knowledge from others involved in the research."[19] As a methodological practice, deep listening entails commitments that run counter to hegemonic analytical approaches. Rather than assuming we know better than participants what is important to analyze, deep listening involves ensuring that the interests of informants—rather than those prescribed by pre-existing disciplinary concepts, debates in our subfields, or gaps in the literature—guide how we write up participants' accounts. Deep listening calls upon researchers to dwell in vulnerability by following participants, rather than leading them. While disciplinary norms may assume that researchers alone extend or create theory, deep listening calls for a slow and uncertain research process wherein the analysis and write-up of our work is directed by respondents.

I use listening instead of reading to denote a style of analysis in which the researcher envisions her respondents beside her, silently observing her as she analyzes and writes up their stories.[20] Through listening deeply to rather than simply reading participants' accounts, researchers invite interlocutors into dialogue throughout the analysis phase of research. Depending on the foci and goals of a given project, deep listening might take various forms, such as writing in a creative genre, sending write-up drafts to respondents for their commentary, or playing and replaying audio recordings of participants' words post-fieldwork. In what follows, I outline my approach to deep listening in my research on cis and trans women's experiences of gender-based violence. As the aforementioned examples suggest, deeply listening to interlocutors is an expansive practice that can take many forms. What I offer below is intended to serve as one example of how accountability to participants can continue to be foregrounded after feminist researchers leave the field.

One Researcher's Deep Listening Practice
Standpoint Theory and Deconstructionist Coding

In my ethnographic research on cis and trans women's fears of gender-based violence in urban public places, I examine how women make sense of their ascribed responsibilities to prevent men's violence in public places. In one-on-one and group interviews, I listen to women of varied ages, social class locations, racial/ethnic identities, and sexual orientations enumerate a never-ending list of taboo gendered activities: going out alone after dark, having more than two drinks at the bar, going out without a cell phone, accepting a ride home from a date on the first time out together, ignoring the just-trying-to-be-friendly guy at the bar—and the list goes on. The women I speak to often cast these taboo activities as proxies for much more explicit gendered prescriptions: don't provoke men, don't get raped, don't be a bitch, don't be a whore.

Since 2019, I've talked to over 100 Canadian women about these explicit and implicit gendered prescriptions. In this chapter, I focus on my deep listening strategy for analyzing the first round of interviews I completed. These initial interviews assessed Greater Vancouver women's violence-management practices in public places. I recruited participants for this research at two universities in Greater Vancouver, and I facilitated interviews using open-ended questions about women's use of public places, the kinds of activities they did in public, their feelings of safety in various locales, and the practices they used most frequently in situations where they felt unsafe. Seventeen cis-identified, able-bodied women participated in the initial round of interviews. The majority of participants self-identified as heterosexual, and the sample was racially and ethnically diverse, with most of the women I spoke to self-identifying as visible minorities, including as Chinese, Indian/Indo-Canadian, Korean, and Filipino. All the women who spoke with me were between 19 and 26 years old, and none were married.

I began my research with a general interest in understanding how women navigated what I perceived as highly contradictory discourses about women's safety. When I looked at resources on women's safety produced by the Vancouver police before I began my interviews, I was puzzled by the persistent focus on public stranger crime and the minimization of intimate violence, given decades of research showing that women are most at risk of harm in their own homes. In reviewing gendered safety messaging, I noticed that most of the materials contained lengthy instructions for avoiding danger by using strategies such as carefully watching one's drink in the bar, being vigilant after dark, and fighting back against assailants.[21] Yet in spite of being positioned as responsible for preventing men's violence, women were also implicitly represented as frail, destined to be weaker than their attackers, and generally incompetent in self-protection. I felt patronized by the gendered safety materials I read, betrayed by the lack of attention given to domestic violence, and ambivalent about a set of discourses that assume women are incapable of defending themselves yet nonetheless mandate us to do just that.

I wanted to learn how other women negotiated these gendered safety messages. How did women navigate a masculinist discourse that mandated them to prevent men's violence, yet simultaneously cast them as defenceless? While these general questions guided my research recruitment, I was uncertain about my ultimate research trajectory. I had an admittedly broad research *topic* (women's responses to men's violence), yet even after I had completed several in-depth interviews, my research *question* remained elusive. Would my findings contribute to knowledge about gendered patterns in fear of crime? Women's embodied responses to sexual harassment? Neighbourhood-level differences in women's perceptions of safety? As I puzzled over my research focus, I simultaneously navigated demands for a polished research pitch from ethics boards, funders, conference audiences, and peers. As Sherryl Kleinman and Martha Copp[22] tell us, uncertainty is not an uncommon emotion in ethnographic work, since qualitative research is inherently emergent. While a key strength of qualitative work is its iterative nature, academic norms pressure researchers to present themselves as competent, in-control knowledge producers.[23] These pressures are at odds with an emergent research process guided by deep, careful listening, and it can be tempting to simply map participant accounts onto existing disciplinary frameworks, efficiently tying up projects without the uncertainty and time investment that deep listening demands. Rather than capitulating to these impulses, deep listening calls upon researchers to conscientiously construct themselves in opposition to positivist ideals of researcher-controlled inquiry. In practice, this can mean submitting ethics protocols without research questions clearly articulated, presenting in-progress research without a clearly mapped analysis after several months in the field, or summoning the courage to respond "I don't know" when colleagues ask us what our research question is months and months into a project of inquiry. All of these practices, given the hegemony of the horse training approach to qualitative research, may make us feel uncomfortable and foolish. Deep listening thus invites researchers to sit with uncomfortable emotions and embrace the vulnerability this entails.

In my analysis of women's accounts of avoiding men's violence, I sought to prioritize participants' vantage points and knowledges, and I was wary of the ways in which my own preconceived understandings of violence, which were shaped by my immersion in sociology and criminology, informed my thinking. I thus avoided a descriptive coding approach in my research. While descriptive coding is often defined as a technical, atheoretical process of data sorting,[24] descriptive coding methods are researcher-centric and, at worst, provoke a descent into meaninglessness in which the researcher's epistemic community silently takes precedence in determining how participants' words will be categorized, sorted, and written up. When we rely on our preconceived disciplinary understandings to guide coding, curiosity falls by the wayside, and "the voice [of the research participant] is recovered *only to be silenced.*"[25]

The discipline (sociology) and subfields (feminist criminology and gender studies) I conduct my research within are ripe with concepts explaining the patterns I observe in my interviews. Drawing on existing disciplinary frameworks, I could, for example, categorize the anxieties women routinely report feeling in urban public places as "fear of crime,"[26] and I could label women themselves either as "survivors" or "victims."[27] While these frameworks offer valuable theoretical tools for making sense of women's narratives about men's violence, categorizing interview data within existing theoretical frameworks can create a redundant research loop in which participants' narratives are covered over, distorted, or misrepresented.

As feminist standpoint theorists including Patricia Hill Collins[28] and Dorothy Smith[29] have argued, the topics and frameworks that shape established academic disciplines originated in small, elite circles of men. These frameworks traditionally advanced androcentric, Eurocentric, cisnormative, and heteronormative value systems—often while claiming value neutrality.[30] For qualitative feminist researchers working in academic disciplines, the process of research thus entails ensuring that participants' lived experiences, as articulated in interviews, are not arbitrarily placed within disciplinary frameworks that may distort them. If we interview women but fit their narratives within hegemonic concepts such as work/leisure, public/private, and victim/survivor, we effectively replace *the actual* (women's narrated experiences from their subjugated positions in the gender order) with *the conceptual* (disciplinary themes, concepts, and topics), resubjugating women's experiences beneath male conceptualizations of the world.[31]

In this context, standpoint epistemology is central to my own practice of deep listening. I understand standpoint theory as a disruption of traditional interviewing approaches that cast interlocutors as epistemologically passive. In contrast to these framings, standpoint epistemology positions interlocutors who occupy marginalized social positions as knowledge-creators.[32] The notion of epistemic privilege, which is central to standpoint theory, suggests that subordinated social groups have superior vantage points from which to understand social reality. Not only do subordinated groups view the social through their own eyes, as subordinates, but their continuous participation in social relations determined by the dominant class means that they can also access dominant-class perspectives.[33] For standpoint researchers, beginning research in the subjugated perspectives of women and other marginalized groups means that research objectivity can be maximized, and partial understandings of social phenomena produced from dominant class perspectives can be corrected.[34]

I operationalized standpoint epistemology in my interview analysis using a deconstructionist coding approach. In contrast to descriptive coding approaches that use disciplinary concepts or researcher interests to sort the manifest content of interview transcripts thematically, deconstructionist coding involves close analytical attention to what is not or cannot be said by participants; places in the transcript where participant narratives are ambiguous, contradictory, or do not continue; and the existence of regularities, such as repeated words or phrases, both within and between participant accounts.[35] By focusing on areas of women's accounts that were truncated, hesitant, or discontinuous, deconstructionist analysis proved generative as a feminist method for recovering experiences that, as feminist researcher Marjorie DeVault[36] conceptualizes them, exist at the periphery of what can be thought, said, and conveyed within a masculinist gender order and discipline.

I began my analysis of women's accounts with a mind full of the criminological literature on violence against women that I had consumed in my research preparations. A deconstructionist coding approach was thus an anchor toward curiosity, discouraging an unreflexive mapping of women's words into descriptive codes influenced by my epistemic community. The critical questions deconstructionist analysis poses—that is, "what cannot be said?" and "what are the contradictions, tensions, and ambiguities here?"—encouraged me to practise a vigilant closeness to participants' words. I summarize key outcomes of this deep listening below.

Listening to Women and Hearing their Words: Beyond Safety Work

In the subfield of scholarship that examines how women strategize every day to stay safe from gender-based violence on the street, "safety work" is a hegemonic concept for describing women's efforts. Originally coined by Liz Kelly,[37] "safety work" refers to the embodied strategies women use in public spaces to prevent, avoid, and manage male violence. Such strategies include, for example, avoiding appearing in public alone, wearing plain clothing, displaying an unfriendly facial expression, and wearing sunglasses.[38] Scholars who invoke Kelly's concept argue that women practise safety work either because it tangibly mitigates gendered risks in public[39] or because women *perceive* that it mitigates risk and therefore feel less fearful as a result.[40] Both of these explanations implicitly presume that women do safety work because it is effective.

Given this context, I began my research analysis expecting to easily document how safety work made women feel safer. Using a deconstructionist coding approach, I was surprised to identify a disconnect between women's narratives of genuinely *feeling* safe and performing the labour of *being* safe. As I listened to women's words, I noted that most women linked the safety work strategies they used to a general goal to minimize risk and reported being hypervigilant in public or carrying would-be weapons in public places. At the same time, and in an unsettling echo of the paternalistic attributions of hegemonic research approaches that construct some groups as inherently vulnerable, many participants insisted that they were inherently vulnerable as women and could never successfully fight back against a violent man. Thus, a decided tension existed between women's ostensible readiness to physically fight attackers and their simultaneous acknowledgment that they would never undertake such a fight.

For example, Analyn (Filipino, heterosexual, dating) described herself as constantly ready to fight off attackers in public places. She stated: "I might have...something that I could punch with. Um, I guess something kind of sharp if I have it. Um, I'll have my keys in my pocket." Shilpi (Indo-Canadian, heterosexual, dating) similarly emphasized her readiness to fight crime and reported regretting the fact that "it's...illegal to carry pepper spray." Parisa (Iranian, heterosexual, dating) shared that she "use[d] to carry dog spray" whenever she left her own home after dark. As these examples suggest, the women I interviewed exerted considerable efforts to be perpetually physically ready to deter gender-based violence with force.

However, as I listened to women's words in the interview transcripts, I became aware that women's accounts were highly contradictory. Although they spoke spiritedly of their physical readiness to fend off violent crime, most of the women I spoke to also cast themselves as inherently weak, incapable of self-defence, and generally reliant on men for protection if "something ever happened" (Alicia; European-Middle Eastern, heterosexual, single). For example, although Alicia reported that she carried an umbrella to "use as a weapon," "being attacked" was her "number one fear." She told me:

> I would not be able to fight back. It's like I don't have any strength... So *whatever happens would just happen*. (My emphasis)

Despite her apparent readiness to deter crime, Alicia's words—like those of the other women I interviewed—suggested that she understood herself as incapable of self-defence.

Joana's (Caucasian, heterosexual, single) account contained a similar contradiction illuminating the fact that women's physical readiness to deter assault had little to do with ensuring physical safety. As Joana stated in our one-on-one conversation, "[I walk with] my hand[s] like fists...I know nothing's going to *really* happen, but [I do it] *just to make me feel better*" (my emphasis). When I considered Joana's statement in the context of responsibilizing gendered safety messaging, it became apparent that her desire to "feel better"—even though she knew that "nothing's going to *really* happen"—signalled a desire to be read as vigilant and risk-averse.

Identifying this incongruity allowed me to challenge the usefulness of the widely used term "safety work"[41] for describing women's vigilance. Much less than creating an enhanced sense of physical safety, participants' narratives showed that being constantly vigilant to the possibility of men's violence often *exacerbated* their fear. In addition, the disjuncture between women's apparent physical readiness to fight and their simultaneous understanding of themselves as unable to fight cued me to the fundamentally performative nature of women's safety behaviours. Thus, rather than seeing women's vigilance and clenched fists as strategies for preventing physical harm, I recognized women as engaged in pre-emptive, carefully staged performances of risk aversion for the mostly male audiences in courtrooms, police stations, and newsrooms that would ultimately adjudicate their deservingness as survivors, should they encounter men's violence. Focusing analytically on textual inconsistencies thus pointed me toward an emotionally taxing, deeply exhausting, yet widely unrecognized form of gendered labour in public places: the sexual and embodied labour of performing innocent victimhood.

By listening deeply to women's narratives, I identified women's vigilance as oriented *not only* to safety, but to visible, performative compliance with the gendered prescriptions identified at the beginning of this section: don't provoke men, don't get raped, don't be a bitch, don't be a whore. In offering this analysis, I joined other feminist scholars in speaking back to patronizing explanations for women's vigilance that, for example, benevolently indulge the supposed irrationality of women who carry rape alarms in public, despite the rarity of stranger rape.[42]

Conclusion

Deep listening, as I discussed at the outset of this chapter, may take many forms. The labour and ethics of resisting a horse training approach to research might involve analyzing transcripts with a team of respondents or co-writing manuscripts with them, creative writing, or subjecting taken-for-granted explanations for women's behaviour—such as safety work—to rigorous empirical analysis. Whatever method feminist researchers choose, deep listening refuses the intrusion of epistemic communities on qualitative analyses in order to remain perceptive to participants' insights, and it pushes us to transcend mundane disciplinary imperatives to find answers to questions that extend our subfields' literature and to be more vulnerable and open to being challenged by our encounters with interlocutors.

By being curious about what participants have to tell us, and being open to being surprised by them, we refuse to bury participants' accounts beneath hegemonic disciplinary logics, theories, and frameworks. When we invite women to speak with us but fail to do the difficult and time-consuming work of listening deeply, we are complicit in a kind of academic extraction that uses participants only as convenient props for churning out commodified forms of knowledge that are used to advance through graduate school, seek promotion, or extend a career. While research conducted under the banner of feminism is often far from non-extractive, deep listening provides one roadmap for methodologically and politically committing to following where interlocutors lead—even, and especially, after we leave the field.

Notes
1. Michel Foucault, *Discipline and Punish* (New York: Random House, 1995).
2. Stephen Smith, "Human-Horse Partnerships," in *Sport, Animals, and Society*, eds. James Gillett and Michelle Gilbert (New York: Routledge, 2013), 35-51.
3. Fédération Equestre Internationale, "Object and General Principles of Dressage and Para Dressage," 2023.
4. Sharlene Nagy Hesse-Biber and Michelle Yaiser, *Feminist Perspectives on Social Research* (New York: Oxford University Press, 2004).
5. Annette Lareau, *Listening to People* (Chicago: University of Chicago Press, 2021), 99.
6. Irving Seidman, *Interviewing as Qualitative Research* (New York: Teachers College Press, 2006), 80.
7. Monique Hennink, Inge Hutter, and Ajay Bailey, *Qualitative Research Methods* (London: Sage Publications, 2011), 120.
8. Lareau, *Listening to People*, 99.
9. Hennink et al., *Qualitative Research Methods*, 109, emphasis added.
10. See, for example, John Creswell and Cheryl Poth, *Qualitative Inquiry and Research Design* (Los Angeles: Sage Publications, 2018).

11. Adrianna Kezar, "Transformational Elite Interviews: Principles and Problems," *Qualitative Inquiry* 9, no. 3 (2003): 395–415.
12. Britta Wigginton and Michelle Lafrance, "Learning Critical Feminist Research: A Brief Introduction to Feminist Epistemologies and Methodologies," *Feminism & Psychology* 0, no. 0 (2019): 1–17.
13. Andrea Doucet, "'From Her Side of the Gossamer Wall(s)': Reflexivity and Relational Knowing," *Qualitative Sociology* 31, no. 1 (2008): 73–87.
14. Doucet, "From Her Side"; Sherryl Kleinman and Martha Copp, *Emotions and Fieldwork* (London: Sage, 1993).
15. Michelle Fine, "Just Methods in Revolting Times," *Qualitative Research in Psychology* 13, no. 4 (2016): 347–365.
16. Doucet, "From Her Side," 73.
17. Doucet, "From Her Side," 73.
18. Marjorie DeVault, "Talking and Listening from Women's Standpoint: Feminist Strategies for Interviewing and Analysis," *Social Problems* 37, no. 1 (1990): 96–116.
19. Claire Carter, Chelsea Temple Jones, and Caitlin Janzen, "Introduction," this volume, xx.
20. Doucet, "From Her Side," 77; DeVault, "Talking and Listening," 101.
21. Vancouver Police Department, "Personal Safety," https://vpd.ca/crime-prevention-safety/personal-safety/.
22. Kleinman and Copp, *Emotions and Fieldwork*.
23. John Warren, "How Much Do You Have to Publish to Get a Job in a Top Sociology Department? Or to Get Tenure? Trends over a Generation," *Sociological Science* 6, no. 1 (2019): 172–96.
24. Creswell and Poth, *Qualitative Inquiry and Research Design*.
25. Martin Packer, *The Science of Qualitative Research* (Cambridge: Cambridge University Press, 2011), 69.
26. Stephanie Riger, Margaret T. Gordon, and Robert LeBailly, "Women's Fear of Crime," *Victimology* 3, no. 314 (1979), 274.
27. Jennifer L. Dunn, "'Victims' and 'Survivors': Emerging Vocabularies of Motive for 'Battered Women Who Stay,'" *Sociological Inquiry*, 75, no 1 (2005), 1.
28. Patricia Hill Collins, *Black Feminist Thought: Knowledge, Consciousness, and the Politics of Empowerment* (New York: Routledge, 2009).
29. Dorothy Smith, *The Everyday World as Problematic: A Feminist Sociology* (Boston: Northeastern University Press, 1987).
30. Hesse-Biber and Yaiser, *Feminist Perspectives on Social Research*.
31. Smith, *The Everyday World as Problematic*.
32. Collins, *Black Feminist Thought*.
33. Collins, *Black Feminist Thought*.
34. Hesse-Biber and Yaiser, *Feminist Perspectives on Social Research*.
35. Barbara Stern, "Textual Analysis in Advertising Research: Construction and Deconstruction of Meanings," *Journal of Advertising* 25, no. 3 (1996): 61–73.
36. DeVault, "Talking and Listening," 104.

37. Liz Kelly, *Surviving Sexual Violence* (Oxford: Polity Press, 1998).
38. See, for example, Fiona Vera-Gray, *The Right Amount of Panic* (Bristol: Policy Press, 2018).
39. Fiona Vera-Gray and Liz Kelly, "Contested Gendered Space: Public Sexual Harassment and Women's Safety Work," *International Journal of Comparative and Applied Criminal Justice* 44, no. 4 (2020): 265-275.
40. See, for example, Bianca Fileborn, "Doing Gender, Doing Safety? Young Adults' Production of Safety on a Night Out," *Gender Place & Culture* 23, no. 8 (2016): 1107-1120.
41. Vera-Gray and Kelly, "Contested Gendered Space," 266.
42. Elizabeth Stanko, "Warnings to Women: Police Advice and Women's Safety in Britain," *Violence Against Women* 2, no. 1 (1996), 20.

Bibliography

Collins, Patricia Hill. *Black Feminist Thought: Knowledge, Consciousness, and the Politics of Empowerment*. New York: Routledge, 2009.

Creswell, John, and Cheryl Poth. *Qualitative Inquiry and Research Design: Choosing Among Five Approaches*. Los Angeles: Sage, 2018.

DeVault, Marjorie L. "Talking and Listening from Women's Standpoint: Feminist Strategies for Interviewing and Analysis." *Social Problems* 37, no. 1 (1990): 96-116.

Doucet, Andrea. "'From Her Side of the Gossamer Wall(s)': Reflexivity and Relational Knowing." *Qualitative Sociology* 31, no. 1 (2008): 73-87.

Dunn, Jennifer L. "'Victims' and 'Survivors': Emerging Vocabularies of Motive for 'Battered Women Who Stay.'" *Sociological Inquiry* 75, no. 1 (2005): 1-30.

Fédération Equestre Internationale. 2023. "Object and General Principles of Dressage and Para Dressage." April 9, 2023. https://inside.fei.org/system/files/Object%20and%20General%20Principles%20of%20Dressage%20and%20Para%20Dressage.pdf.

Fileborn, Bianca. "Doing Gender, Doing Safety? Young Adults' Production of Safety on a Night Out." *Gender, Place, & Culture* 23, no. 8 (2016): 1107-1120.

Foucault, Michel, *Discipline and Punish: The Birth of the Prison*. New York: Random House, 1995.

Hennink, Monique, Inge Hutter, and Ajay Bailey, *Qualitative Research Methods*. London: Sage Publications, 2011.

Hesse-Biber, Sharlene Nagy, and Michelle Yaiser, *Feminist Perspectives on Social Research*. New York: Oxford University Press, 2004. Kelly, Liz. *Surviving Sexual Violence*. Oxford: Polity Press, 1998.

Kelly, Liz. *Surviving Sexual Violence*. Oxford: Polity Press, 1998.

Kezar, Adrianna. "Transformational Elite Interviews: Principles and Problems," *Qualitative Inquiry* 9, no. 3 (2003): 395-415.

Kleinman, Sherryl, and Martha Copp, *Emotions and Fieldwork*. London: Sage, 1993.

Lareau, Annette. *Listening to People*. Chicago: University of Chicago Press, 2021.

Packer, Martin. *The Science of Qualitative Research*. Cambridge: Cambridge University Press, 2011.

Riger, Stephanie, Margaret T. Gordon, and Robert LeBailly. "Women's Fear of Crime: From Blaming to Restricting the Victim." *Victimology* 3, no. 3-4 (1978): 274-284.

Seidman, Irving. *Interviewing as Qualitative Research*. New York: Teachers College Press, 2006.

Smith, Dorothy. *The Everyday World as Problematic: A Feminist Sociology*. Boston: Northeastern University Press, 1987.

Smith, Stephen. "Human-Horse Partnerships." In *Sport, Animals, and Society*, edited by James Gillett and Michelle Gilbert, 35-51. New York: Routledge, 2013.

Stanko, Elizabeth. "Warnings to Women: Police Advice and Women's Safety in Britain." *Violence Against Women* 2, no. 1 (1996): 5-24.

Stern, Barbara B. "Textual Analysis in Advertising Research: Construction and Deconstruction of Meanings." *Journal of Advertising* 25, no. 3 (1996): 61-73.

Vancouver Police Department. "Personal Safety." August 8, 2021. https://vpd.ca/crime-prevention-safety/personal-safety/.

Vera-Gray, Fiona. *The Right Amount of Panic*. Bristol: Policy Press, 2018.

Vera-Gray, Fiona, and Liz Kelly. "Contested Gendered Space: Public Sexual Harassment and Women's Safety Work." *International Journal of Comparative and Applied Criminal Justice* 44, no. 4 (2020): 265-275.

Warren, John. "How Much Do You Have to Publish to Get a Job in a Top Sociology Department? Or to Get Tenure? Trends over a Generation." *Sociological Science* 6 (2019): 172-196.

Wigginton, Britta, and Michelle N. Lafrance. "Learning Critical Feminist Research: A Brief Introduction to Feminist Epistemologies and Methodologies." *Feminism & Psychology*, 0, no. 0 (2019): 1-17.

3

Discard or Save the Leftovers?
What To Do with Truths That Cannot Be Told

Brenda Rossow-Kimball and Kristyn Rebecca White

Introduction

As a young woman in my twenties, I worked in the field of disability services. Most of my work was focused on facilitating inclusive community experiences for adults labelled with intellectual disabilities. I worked as a summer recreation programmer, whereby I sought out and arranged accessible and inclusive activities in the community. We visited parks and museums, we had picnics and parties, we cooled off at splash parks and pools. If funding allowed, we took a day trip outside the city to a tourist farm or to one of many lakes to enjoy the summer and sun-soaked beaches.

My work eventually progressed into more responsibilities as I took on the role of house mother—now known as a group home operator—supporting middle-aged adults living with intellectual disabilities in a government-funded, residential setting. During my time working in homes, I was surprised at the lack of self-determined behaviours demonstrated by those living there. Houses operated around staff preferences, scheduled maintenance, and chores. Activities involved everyone in the home and were scheduled down to the minute, leaving little room for personal expressions of choice. I was intrigued by the lack of leadership, self-directed participation, and personal influence of the residents in their own home. I made the choice to create space for decision making and choice making. I chose to study these self-determined moments in group homes for my master's thesis.

To work toward trustworthiness in my work, I spent time in two group homes. One home I was very familiar with, as I had worked in it for a number of years and was a key player in facilitating self-determined experiences for those living there. The second home I chose to study was operated by a different community-based organization. I was somewhat familiar with the executive director, and I sent her a letter asking her to consider allowing that home to participate in my research. She agreed, and I acted as a volunteer in the home while I observed activities. Because I had only worked in environments that encouraged self-determination, I assumed all environments offered similar experiences. I quickly came to learn that this was not the case.

One home created a self-determined environment whenever possible. Preferences were listened to and responded to in nearly every aspect of home life: meals, activities, TV shows, clothing, visitors, and personalized bedroom spaces. The other home operated under strict management and honed schedules. For example, menus were made two weeks in advance to accommodate the grocery budget. If cereal was slated for Tuesday breakfast but someone wanted toast, one was relegated to cereal to stay on schedule. Activities were imposed upon residents to address at-home idle time, and weekly community outings were enforced to meet community inclusion policies of the agency. And there was a lot of behaviour management: staff telling residents to "stop." Stop talking. Stop rocking in the chair. Stop eating your food that way. Stop dragging your feet. Stop looking at others. Stop asking when you can see your family. Stop asking when we can go. Stop asking when we can leave. It was emotionally taxing for me when staff would exercise their power in the home, which, in my perspective, manifested a lack of freedom and autonomy for others. It felt like the story being told about the residents in the home was: *You are not smart enough. You are not strong enough. You are not well enough. You are not good enough. You are not experienced enough. You have not proven yourself enough. You are not trusted.* They were not enough for a lot of things. Historically, this is not an uncommon practice; this culture can still be found in some institutional spaces.

Nearly every time I left the home, I cried. I turned to my supervisor for support. I shared what I had seen and heard. She cried alongside me. She agreed that it was problematic, ethically problematic, and neither of us had expected this would happen. Finally, I said, "I don't think I can continue like this. What should I do?" We considered the possibility—and potential consequences—of taking up a meeting with social services. But what might that conversation unleash? Would staff lose their jobs? Would people lose their homes? Would families become overwhelmed with the caregiving responsibilities they fought so hard to establish in community? Institutional ethics did not prepare me for questions of morality, dignity, and discernment. Simply asking, "What is the *right* thing to do?" was not enough. After all, my study and presence as a researcher wasn't harming anyone; the research activities were ethically carried out. So was I expected to be necessarily bothered by what I witnessed in the home? And what if my presence actually *offered* safety and dignity to the people with whom I was engaging? What if I could be an example for dignifying care? But in doing this, would I influence the study? There were too many considerations and too many queries to resolve.

We decided that I had earned the trust of the group home, and if the unsettling stories inside were revealed, it might jeopardize any future engagement between university-housed researchers and disability service programs. My supervisor and I talked about the role of a researcher and how sometimes we see and hear things we do not expect. We talked about how I could share my observations in a way that would dignify everyone and not place blame. We agreed that a component of dissemination would be a presentation to the leadership in the homes, as well as to the government ministry funding the homes, highlighting the positive aspects of each environment and gently offering suggestions to engage all residents in the project of their lives. Essentially, we agreed that I could write what could be stomached, and the rest would end up in a folder on my computer named "Other Stories," not to be revisited.

Fast forward 20 years. I'm sitting in a restaurant waiting for my graduate student. She is bright, enthusiastic, and talented. She has spent the last 10 years working in group homes supporting people living with developmental disabilities, further labelled with complex needs. She is genuinely concerned for the well-being and rights of those she supports. Through her relational living alongside, she has come to learn that some people who are supported in the community are often denied the opportunity and/or are unprepared to express their sexuality. Individuals living with disabilities experience systemic, attitudinal, and personal barriers to fully experiencing their sexual potential,[1] most often due to heteronormative perceptions of sex and who should be doing it,[2] and ableist notions of the corporeal standard.[3] There is little research about sex positivity in the lives of people living with developmental disabilities; a great deal of the research focuses on abuse,[4] training,[5] and behaviours.[6] And while the student can situate her lived experiences within the literature, she can confirm that there is so much more going on that is not being talked/written about. Part of her work allows her to have intimate conversations with people with disabilities, other support workers, advocates for sex positivity, sexual health educators, parents, teachers, and more. She has listened to others' stories of secretly supporting individuals to safely acquire pornography. She talks with individuals about how to protect themselves from pregnancy and infection. She works with other organizations to advocate for personal privacy, sex positivity, and dignifying sexual experiences in the lives of those defined as vulnerable. Yet in doing this work, she exists in a "tension-filled midst,"[7] as she considers the needs and desires of those she cares for/about while being challenged by heteronormative and ableist notions of sexuality imposed by important others in people's lives. She feels strongly about the value of sharing her lived stories with others but is also aware of the potential consequences of doing so. How much can she share? How will her career be affected? What if someone figures out who the stories are about? What is ethical?

Methodological Approach

And so today we are meeting, once again, to contemplate the ethics of sharing stories. We humbly arrive at this work within the framework of narrative inquiry, a research methodology and phenomenon conceptualized by Jean Clandinin and Michael Connelly.[8] Our work encourages us to become awakened to who we are in people's lives and who they have/ might become in ours. We see our role in research as one to "describe lives, collect and tell stories of them, and write narratives of experience,"[9] because "people by nature lead storied lives and tell stories of those lives."[10] We discuss tensions that we have experienced, specifically bumping points between the professional knowledge landscape and practical knowledge, concepts developed by Clandinin and Connelly through their observations of teacher's lives.[11] We situated our tensions, our stories, as talking moments; we developed a co-constructed dialogue to make sense of them in a relational way,[12] considered how we might live with the tensions in an educative way, and how others might learn, too. We discuss past, current, and anticipated future tensions in research [and practice] that have resulted from our living alongside individuals identified as vulnerable: people labelled with intellectual disabilities.

We agreed to record our conversation in preparation for this chapter, and we present it here as a co-constructed narrative developed from that dialogue, which also includes recollected moments from rich conversations we have shared over the last three years of her graduate work. In-text citations have been added to credit scholarly work. The narrative reveals threads of coherence and shared tensions.

Conversation and Context
Why Stories Matter

Supervisor: So, I know some of the stories you're thinking about sharing in your research are stories, that, well, the story itself doesn't cause tension for you but it's the idea of sharing it. Like, wondering what can you write, or what are you allowed to write. So, first, why don't you tell me about why the stories are important to share.

Student: I just feel like a lot of people in the field are not aware of what's going on, or they witness something that [startles] them and they just pretend it doesn't exist. They don't talk about it because it's so incredibly uncomfortable. And so I think the stories are really important because it brings light to the struggles people in our community are having. It's the fact that caregivers have zero support when it comes to a lot of different areas. I mean, specifically about supporting people's sexuality, some people themselves living in [group] homes are basically getting denied what they want. But also the fact that no one knows what to do or say because there's no training and there's no education. It becomes a cycle. People are struggling, they bring something up [to] the caregiver, [the caregiver] is uncomfortable, they dismiss it, and then it repeats itself.

Supervisor: But why you? And why now? Why do you feel a need to share your stories or share the stories that you've lived alongside others?

Student: I think it's just listening to others' stories. I know people are struggling and sometimes I struggle too when I support others in their sexuality. I'm just like, "Whoa, this is just so much." I thought, either I talk about this and get support, or I can't go on anymore. But no one knows what to do and no one really knows what to say and nothing's getting better and nothing's changing.

Supervisor: What isn't getting better?

Student: I've had the privilege and the opportunity to learn about some areas that aren't commonly talked about in [group homes]. Like [in terms of sexuality] I learned this past year that, like, [sexual] pleasure is a human right. Well, so is privacy. But I've heard stories from other support workers or people with disabilities that bedroom doors are taken off in some group homes because the person behaved badly or [was] caught doing something wrong, or the staff want to know what everyone is doing at all times. Some homes don't have bedrooms that lock because it's perceived to be too dangerous. And sometimes people are not allowed to masturbate or have their partner over. Is that ethical? Is anyone asking about the ethics of that? And I didn't know that until I started listening to others. So now that I know that, I feel like I'm just very hyperaware of times that personal rights might be jeopardized.

Bumping Up against Dominant Narratives of Practice

Supervisor: In coursework, we talk about how things have changed. Institutions are closing, employment is more inclusive, accessibility legislation is on the way. Paradigms have shifted and we're progressive, and I think person-centred is the language that is used now.

Student: But within these, like, little institutions, [these] group homes, even though [supports] are like, "We're personal-centred, this is what's best for them."

Supervisor: That's the landscape of professional knowledge that Clandinin and Connelly[13] refer to. The space where professionals "know what is best." Government policy and experts are the key informants who determine what is best and ultimately compose others' lives. Clandinin and Connelly call those dominant narratives of practice *sacred stories*. Sacred stories tell us about how things *should* be.

Student: But what's actually happening is what makes the caregiver feel more comfortable instead of what's actually best for the person that they're supporting. So, some support staff are trained to do something a certain way and it's not working for the people they support. So I wonder if sometimes support staff in group homes learn about how to support people to live a life they want, but do they realize that maybe sometimes they come close to denying people their rights? And what if caregivers support in ways that are not allowed? Like supporting sexuality?

Supervisor: You're situating yourself on the practical knowledge landscape[14] now. In a way, you're practising outside the professional knowledge landscape because you have to, because you're living stories behind the scenes that haven't yet emerged onto the professional knowledge landscape. You're practising support without the watchful eye of experts; Clandinin and Connelly[15] refer to these as secret stories.

Student: Secret stories. That sounds about right. Sometimes, when I talk to others, they say, "I've never told anyone this before, but...." And it's nothing. They'll say something like, "Oh, I took So-and-So, a 40-year-old man, to buy pornography. But I might get in trouble from his parents or my supervisor, so I haven't told anyone. It's a secret between me [support worker] and So-and-So. Everyone just acts like everything is okay, but they live with secrets. Secrets that really aren't that bad!

Supervisor: So you're telling or acting a cover story.[16] You're telling a story that would be acceptable on the professional knowledge landscape, but it's not exactly the truth. It's not wrong or bad, but it's just how some people have to practise.

Student: Oh, there's lots of those! And no, it's not like anyone is doing anything wrong, but it's not necessary to get everyone [families, staff, leadership] worked up over what support workers are doing or how they're doing things to support people to express their sexuality.

The Ethics of Sharing Stories

Supervisor: Here's the big question: Would the Other in your story be okay that you are writing about a shared lived experience?

Student: The fact is that the stories are really personal and private and deal with taboo topics. And they're topics [that] me, you, none of us would want written about or shared. You know I wouldn't want someone writing about my sexual life. I wouldn't want someone writing about times that I did something sexually promiscuous or wrong or did something I regretted or was embarrassed about. I don't know anyone who would feel comfortable with some of their, you know, most embarrassing or shameful and private moments being retold.

Supervisor: Is it ethical?

Student: That's exactly it. Is it ethical to share a story that I lived alongside someone, even if I change their name, change the details, change the location and share it as a form of, I guess, education? Is that wrong, or is that helpful? We know that this person, the people whom these stories are about will never read the papers. They'll never know that I'm writing this, they'll never see it. Their names and details will be changed. So they won't know it's about them, but [I'll] know. And so, the question is: is that okay? Is that allowed? Does that make me a bad caregiver? Or a good researcher? Both or neither?

Supervisor: I remember asking myself those questions. And I was thinking about these two group homes, and I was wondering how I could represent each, as they were so vividly different from one and other. When I started writing the draft of my thesis results, it was like, "Here's Group Home A and it was all lovely and flowery and happy. And then here's Group Home B, it feels like it has a lot of tension to me. It feels depressing and sad and shitty." But I knew I couldn't do that. You have to be as gentle as possible. You have to write the story, so that the person reading it, the group home, could stomach it. But it can feel like you aren't accurately representing lives in your research.

Student: I remember being told once that sadness is a passive emotion and anger is sort of an active emotion, and that if you read something or watch something and you feel anger, you're more likely to make a change and you're more likely to want to act and do differently. But if you watch something or hear something and feel sad, you just feel sad about it and you don't necessarily have the drive to do something. So, I sometimes think about that. I think, "Oh I could write stuff and it would, you know, make people feel emotional or sad." But I want to write something that says, "Something has to change. This is really bad."

Supervisor: I'm reliving my story as you tell yours. I wanted to make change. I wanted to tell the truth about what I saw and how it hurt people, and how I was hurt, too. I felt angry and helpless. And the worst was I felt responsible. But I couldn't interfere. I'd drive home from data collection days, just crying from the tensions I lived through and saw. And I was always wondering about what was happening when I wasn't there. I wanted to blow the lid off the whole place. But I had the trust of the leadership in the group home.

Student: But sometimes it's just like, isn't it worth pissing off one person to help 100 people?

Supervisor: Interesting. So, you're thinking the risk is small for the greater benefit of everyone?

Student: Exactly. But you still wonder if it's worth it.

Supervisor: Well, is it?

Student: Maybe it's worth it. Isn't it better that I share the story, knowing that the person who had the experience that I lived alongside probably won't find out, and potentially open a bunch of other people's eyes to the fact that people need support and others' rights are at risk of being jeopardized?

Supervisor: I always wondered about that. About the ethics of writing about someone who won't read the paper, simply because they can't, they can't read. So, we study the Other because they are different[17] and then remove them from their own lived experience as we interpret it for our own benefit. Sometimes I wondered why I was doing the work. Why am I doing this graduate work? Who is really benefiting from this? Anyone other than me?

Student: It's like exploiting people....

Supervisor: Or even the loyalty. You're committed to the people and to the policy and the organization and your colleagues and now it's like, no, here's someone from the inside telling the truth.

Student: That's the thing, like, it almost feels like some undercover journalist. And if I think of where I work, relationships are so emphasized and they're so important. And so you go into it and you, you actually do end up building relationships with people [you support] that are bigger than just a paycheque.

Relational Ethics: Beyond the Research

Supervisor: You want to honour that relationship. Because you're practising—and living—in a relational way.

Student: I suppose....

Supervisor: You are. Living in a relational way, in research anyways, means that you're caring beyond institutional ethics.[18] You and your well-being, and the well-being of those you research alongside, are at the forefront of your work. You are mindful about relational ethics, about caring for the story and the people in the story, regardless of their participation in the research. I always tell students to write as if the person you are writing about will read it. You can write the truth, but be sure you dignify their experiences and who they are as a person. Consider how and why—and by whom—others' lived stories are composed, why they might be bumping up against sacred, secret, or cover stories. It helps us to understand why tensions exist.

Student: And then another part of me is like, am I only writing these stories because "these" people have disabilities? Would I write these stories about anyone else in my life? Am I okay with it because we are so comfortable with documenting everything that people with disabilities do?

Supervisor: More exploitation....

Student: In some homes, caregivers constantly document what [people with disabilities] are doing during their day, constantly filling out a chart on someone's mood. Writing reports when someone gets mad and throws something. Writing reports when people are sad and they express something and share something personal. So, it's like the industry [of disability services] is so used to doing all this. I don't necessarily think any of that is right, but then I wonder, is what I'm doing [in my research] any different? That's another layer of the dilemma. Because if you're someone who recognizes that documenting people's lives isn't normal, and it's only been made normal by an institutional paradigm…So, if I don't think that it's okay that I write a report every time someone yells at me, then I ask myself: is it okay that I write a whole paper on people's experiences that I just happened to witness or I just happened to be there for?

Supervisor: I understand everything you're saying. I understand your tensions and your desire to do what is right, and to do what will make the biggest difference in people's lives. We want others to benefit from our research. And it is so lovely that you are thinking beyond institutional ethics. Like I said, you're thinking in a relational way, about who the people are in your life, and who you are in theirs, and there is reciprocity in how our lives are composed by one and other. We want to be sure we represent people with dignity.

Student: I didn't know that I'd be writing about my own experiences, because you know when you're living them you don't realize that they're important. You more so just view them as like, "Whoa that happened to me, that happened to someone else, that was interesting." Or you know, you almost just view events as another day in the life of someone. But as I started thinking about things narratively, and that my experiences might be similar to anyone who's worked as a caregiver, and how my own practice composes other's lives, then I realized that my stories are important.

Supervisor: And that's why it matters. You might create space for others to share their stories, too, or at the very least, create space for them to think about their own lived experiences. And maybe even encourage them to consider their own practical knowledge and how it composes the lives of others.

Preparing for Ethical Conundrums

Supervisor: Is there a way that you could be better prepared for this? So, you take ethical coursework or you talk about ethics in graduate classes to prepare you for all this. But you're not sounding like you feel prepared.

Student: Well, I think about a couple things. I feel like in a lot of grad classes, especially qualitative classes, the focus is methodology, which is obviously important. But learning from others and learning about and from others' lived [research] experiences is so important, too.

Supervisor: And so creating space for those stories, for those stories to be shared in a safe space would be helpful? In my own experience with graduate students, so many have come from a place of lived experience. They're in the midst of living their lives and living alongside others. But they come to graduate work because they are troubled, there are tensions about how professional knowledge bumps up against practical knowledge. In narrative inquiry, Clandinin and colleagues write that tensions are understood in a relational way, as "tensions live between people, events, or things, and are a way of creating a between space, a space which can exist in educative ways."[19]

In my own narrative work, I found that I couldn't necessarily fix the tensions, but I learned from them.

Student: In the human services industry, whether you're a nurse, a caregiver, a social worker, or you work in aging care or a group home, and you have 10 years of storied experience, you may not need to interview the caregiver because you *are* the caregiver. So, what about that? That's not really talked about, you know. And it needs to be. And it needs to be thought about through a relational ethical lens. But how do you do that? In my own stories, I have spent every day with some of these people for years, and I care about them. So, it's an ethical dilemma in terms of research, but then it's also your own personal relational dilemma of wanting to be a good human, and to be a good friend. So I feel like maybe more conversations, more conversations about why we research other's lives without unpacking our own tensions first. Maybe that would help.

Conclusion

This shared narrative between a supervisor and a graduate student reveals our tensions with stories as we live with them in a relational way. Student and supervisor have similar histories, both inspired into graduate work by their living alongside individuals with intellectual disabilities. Laying our experiences side by side helped us to realize that ethical conundrums have always existed, and will always exist, in both research and practice, as we work alongside those labelled with a disability.

Lopez said:

> The stories people tell have a way of taking care of them. If stories come to you, care for them. And learn to give them away where they are needed. Sometimes a person needs a story more than food to stay alive. That is why we put these stories in each other's memory. This is how people care for themselves.[20]

It is stories that tell us about people; who they are, who they are becoming, and who they want to be. Stories reflect what others think of us, too, perhaps showing that we are trusted/not trusted, cared for/not cared for, and seen as equal/not equal, by others. Regardless, we are all in relation to one and other, and we compose our lives accordingly.

Despite the passage of time, stories tend to stay the same. As both supervisor and student consider the shift in paradigms of supports and services for people living with disabilities, we have come to realize that people labelled with disabilities continue to have their lives composed according to the expert(s) who make up the professional knowledge landscape. Rarely do we consider that it is the practical knowledge creators/keepers that witness the living, breathing, meaning-making stories of day-to-day life. And so, this is why it is important for this student, and other students who are currently composing their practical knowledge, to share and unpack their lived stories. It is practical knowledge that has the potential to shift the professional knowledge landscape.

Perhaps the ethical question is not necessarily about how to share others' vulnerable stories, but rather we need to consider whose stories are shared first. We and other practising students have been inspired by Trudy Cardinal's research[21] in which she questioned her responsibilities as an Indigenous graduate student choosing to undertake research with Indigenous peoples in ethically responsible ways. Cardinal was the one and only inquirer throughout the work. She argued that she experienced intense moments of unease and she needed to understand these tensions if she was to move forward as a researcher. Essentially, she had to make sense of her own lived stories, first. And so, we encourage researchers who are composing their practical knowledge, or who are inspired by practical knowledge, to engage in autobiographical work as a stepping stone to furthering their understanding of the importance of lived stories. Perhaps by engaging in reflexive writing and turning the pen toward ourselves, we might better appreciate how marginalized groups have, historically, been represented via the professional knowledge landscape, as it rarely considers who we are in other's lives and who we might be in theirs.

Notes
1. Gina Di Giulio, "Sexuality and People Living with Physical or Developmental Disabilities: A Review of Key Issues," *Canadian Journal of Human Sexuality* 12, no. 1 (2003), 53.
2. Shaniff Esmail, Kim Darry, Ashlea Walter, and Heidi Knupp, "Attitudes and Perceptions Towards Disability and Sexuality," *Disability and Rehabilitation* 32, no. 14 (2010), 1148–1149.

3. Michael A. Rembis, "Beyond the Binary: Rethinking the Social Model of Disabled Sexuality," *Sexuality and Disability* 28, no. 1 (2010), 52.
4. Carmel Digman, "Lost Voices Part 1: A Narrative Case Study of Two Young Men with Learning Disabilities Disclosing Experiences of Sexual, Emotional and Physical Abuse," *British Journal of Learning Disabilities* 49, no. 2 (2021): 195-204.
5. Kirsty Bastable et al., "Availability of Training Programmes on Sexuality for Adolescents with Severe Disabilities: A Review," in *Sexual and Reproductive Health of Adolescents with Disabilities*, eds. Tafadzwa Rugoho and France Maphosa (Singapore: Palgrave Macmillan, 2021), 11-44.
6. Henrique Pereira, "Sexual Behaviors and Sexual Perceptions of Portuguese Adults with Physical Disabilities," *Sexuality and Disability* 39, no. 2 (2021): 275-290.
7. D. Jean Clandinin, M. Shaun Murphy, Janice Huber, and Anne Murray Orr, "Negotiating Narrative Inquiries: Living in a Tension-Filled Midst," *Journal of Educational Research* 103, no. 2 (2009), 82.
8. D. Jean Clandinin and F. Michael Connelly, *Narrative Inquiry: Experience and Story in Qualitative Research* (Hoboken: John Wiley & Sons, 2004).
9. Clandinin and Connelly, *Narrative Inquiry*, 2.
10. Clandinin and Connelly, *Narrative Inquiry*, 2.
11. D. Jean Clandinin and F. Michael Connelly, "Teachers' Professional Knowledge Landscapes: Teacher Stories—Stories of Teachers—School Stories—Stories of Schools," *Educational Researcher* 25, no. 3 (1996), 24-30.
12. Clandinin, Murphy, Huber, Murray Orr, "Negotiating Narrative Inquiries," 81.
13. Clandinin and Connelly, "Teachers' Professional Knowledge Landscapes," 24-25.
14. Clandinin and Connelly, "Teachers' Professional Knowledge Landscapes," 25-26.
15. Clandinin and Connelly, "Teachers' Professional Knowledge Landscapes," 25.
16. Clandinin and Connelly, "Teachers' Professional Knowledge Landscapes," 25.
17. Dan Goodley, "Dis/entangling Critical Disability Studies," *Disability & Society* 28, no. 5 (2013), 637-638.
18. D. Jean Clandinin, *Engaging in Narrative Inquiry* (Walnut Creek: Left Coast Press, 2013), 30.
19. Clandinin, Murphy, Huber, Murray Orr, "Negotiating Narrative Inquiries," 82.
20. Barry Lopez, *Crow and Weasel* (Albany: North Point Press, 1990), 60.
21. Trudy Cardinal, "Stepping-Stone or Saving Story?" *LEARNing Landscapes* 4, no. 2 (2011): 79-91.

Bibliography

Bastable, Kirsty, Shakila Dada, Refilwe Elizabeth Morwane, and Parimala Raghavendra. "Availability of Training Programmes on Sexuality for Adolescents with Severe Disabilities: A Review." *Sexual and Reproductive Health of Adolescents with Disabilities* (2021): 11-44. doi: 10.1007/978-981-15-7914-1_2.

Cardinal, Trudy. "Stepping-Stone or Saving Story?" *LEARNing Landscapes* 4, no. 2 (2011): 79-91.

Clandinin, D. Jean. *Engaging in Narrative Inquiry*. Walnut Creek: Left Coast Press, 2013.

Clandinin, D. Jean, and F. Michael Connelly. *Narrative Inquiry: Experience and Story in Qualitative Research*. Hoboken: John Wiley & Sons, 2004.

Clandinin, D. Jean, and F. Michael Connelly. "Teachers' Professional Knowledge Landscapes: Teacher Stories—Stories of Teachers—School Stories—Stories of Schools." *Educational Researcher* 25, no. 3 (1996): 24-30. doi:10.3102/0013189X025003024.

Clandinin, D. Jean, M. Shaun Murphy, Janice Huber, and Anne Murray Orr. "Negotiating Narrative Inquiries: Living in a Tension-Filled Midst." *Journal of Educational Research* 103, no. 2 (2009): 81-90. doi: 10.1080/00220670903323404.

Di Giulio, Gina. "Sexuality and People Living with Physical or Developmental Disabilities: A Review of Key Issues." *Canadian Journal of Human Sexuality* 12, no. 1 (2003).

Digman, Carmel. "Lost voices Part 1: A Narrative Case Study of Two Young Men with Learning Disabilities Disclosing Experiences of Sexual, Emotional and Physical Abuse." *British Journal of Learning Disabilities* 49, no. 2 (2021): 195-204. doi: 10.1111/bld.12364.

Esmail, Shaniff, Kim Darry, Ashlea Walter, and Heidi Knupp. "Attitudes and Perceptions Towards Disability and Sexuality." *Disability and Rehabilitation* 32, no. 14 (2010): 1148-1155. doi: 10.3109/09638280903419277.

Goodley, Dan. "Dis/entangling Critical Disability Studies." *Disability & Society* 28, no. 5 (2013): 631-644. doi: 10.1080/09687599.2012.717884.

Lopez, Barry. *Crow and Weasel*. Albany: North Point Press, 1990.

Pereira, Henrique. "Sexual Behaviors and Sexual Perceptions of Portuguese Adults with Physical Disabilities." *Sexuality and Disability* 39, no. 2 (2021): 275-290. doi: 10.1007/s11195-020-09657-w.

Rembis, Michael A. "Beyond the Binary: Rethinking the Social Model of Disabled Sexuality." *Sexuality and Disability* 28, no. 1 (2010): 51-60. doi: 10.1007/s11195-009-9133-0.

II

Reflections on Challenges and Hard Decisions in Research Processes

Un(rendered) Stories
Ethical Considerations of Translation Work in Research

Anh Ngo

Introduction

Research conducted in a language other than the one in which the research is reported requires that key decisions be made in the many translation steps that shape the final analysis and report. While the work of translation is an issue of methodological significance fraught with many considerations, the process of translation and the ethical implications for the research product continue to be overlooked and inadequately discussed in the literature. In this chapter, I will reflect on a recent study with the Vietnamese community in Toronto to illustrate the complexities of language translation within research and the many difficult decisions made. Beyond the technical steps of translation, I will present three fundamental ethical tensions I experienced in my work to press the urgency of addressing translation work as a core consideration in social justice research methodology. These tensions are (1) social positionings and the unavoidable operation of power, (2) the subjectivity-forming function of language, and (3) the real possibility of the untranslatable. In addition to guiding those seeking research with a community in which they do not share the same language, centring translation as a core aspect of research methods assists English-language speakers and readers in critically evaluating any given study. This discussion will highlight the decisions made as a researcher when working across multiple languages in efforts to process the multilingual participants' sharing ethically and responsibly. Even more importantly, this discussion will highlight the vulnerability of what is shared in and of itself as something that risks being unrenderable in the translation process.

Including research participants who are not proficient in the dominant Western languages (often English) is a move toward research justice and equity. However, careful translation is required to ensure that research is conducted and reported in an ethical manner that attempts to represent the original speech as closely as possible. Wong and Poon assert that strong translation work in research is possible, and when translation work is transparent, and translators are integrated as vital members of the research team, it allows researchers to access "the richness embedded in research data through multiple layers of interpretation and meaning construction within and across culture."[1] By the very nature of translation—replacing knowledge uttered in one language for another—the knowledge itself is at the mercy of the translator. As such, it is particularly important for knowledge producers and knowledge consumers to demand that the process of translation be considered and discussed explicitly in social justice-oriented research rather than a taken-for-granted process of replacing one word for another.

Background

There are typically two methods of translation work: the researcher partners with a community member who is bilingual in the research community's language and the researcher's language to operate as an interpreter during data collection—so they are present at the interviews and provide interpretation on the spot. The other common method is that the researcher partners with a translator to transform the captured data into the researcher's language, either after transcribing the data in the community's language first or even at times directly translating and transcribing it into the researcher's language. Another common but rightfully critiqued practice is community research, which relies on community participant support for translation in exchange for research training—this, however, takes advantage of unpaid labour from a member of the community being researched.[2] These methods are common and can be effective, if the complexities within this work are reported reflectively and transparently.

Translation is commonly assumed to be an objective and neutral process, with translators as technicians providing an added-on service to the study. In this way, the import of translation to the ethical and scientific integrity of research continues to be overlooked.[3] Temple and Edwards state that translators are often not incorporated as core members of the research team but rather are seen as professional service providers; translators are thus not given insight into the research purpose and objectives and, in return, researchers do not have insight into the translation process when interpreting their findings.[4] When this happens, translation is reduced to word-swapping rather than meaning-based understandings. Wong and Poon argue that the translator holds a vitally important position that allows the research to gain access to the ideas and experiences of the participants, and it is through the translator that the research participants' voices are heard: "translators mediate between the spoken words in interviews and the written texts; they also mediate between the cultural worlds of the researcher and the participants."[5] Sutrisno, Nguyen, and Tangen imagine "translation as a dialogue between the original texts in the source language and the translation in the target language, mediated by the translator, which results in a co-dependence between the two texts."[6] Im, Page, Lin, Tsai, and Cheng state that the language translation process may be the most important part of cross-cultural qualitative studies.[7]

Yet rarely do studies that use translation write sufficiently, if at all, on the power relations that exist between the researchers and translator/interpreter, as well as between the translator/interpreter to the sources and persons from which the original data is sourced. This neglect is particularly troubling, as research participants who are not proficient in dominant Western languages are often positioned as vulnerable and hard-to-access populations. Translation work allows this access, yet the extractive ability of this work is rarely scrutinized. Choi, Kushner, Mill, and Lai found an absolute lack of publications on the researcher-translator relationship, and Esposito points out that in a space-limited journal article, details on the process of translation are not required as part of the methodological write-up.[8] As a mediator, I wrestle with the flattening of identities, as translation itself operates as a sieve, where you are provided with a multitude of narratives and metaphors; contained within them are multiple meanings.[9] The chosen translated outcome then captures a single narrative, and methodological write-ups often omit the "intense personal struggles and philosophical tensions leading up to the research."[10] However, in light of these common challenges, the danger of avoiding research in multiple languages is to exclude non-English participants due to limited funding and resources for translation. This risks further reinforcement of exclusionary research that does not reflect the lived experiences and needs of equity- deserving groups. What is needed in scholarship is a recognition and normalization of the vital and complex role of translation in qualitative research beyond the simple swapping of words. Given the importance of translation in ethical research with linguistically specific peoples, the methodological reporting of data analysis needs to incorporate translation work as a key step. Below, I detail my process of conducting research in Vietnamese to be disseminated in English.

Case Study
It is vital to include translation work during the research planning and interviewing stages to ensure the formulated questions have culturally significant meaning and can capture the experiences and insights the study is seeking. This heightened awareness of another language in the research design requires us to expand our worldviews in attempting to allow space for the worldviews of the people we seek to research. Kamler and Threadgold remind us that the outcomes of translation are also influenced significantly by the social positions of all those involved—researchers, translators, and participants—as "preconceptions and cultural positionings interfere with and obfuscate the process of communication or miscommunication that is actually occurring."[11] This deep embeddedness of the researcher's social location cannot be neutralized by simple statements on positionality and social location but must be continuously interrogated and challenged at every decision made in the

research process to capture the messiness and complexities of critical reflexivity—not as an antidote to the hegemony of research itself, but as a cautionary tale.[12] As researchers across languages, we represent the participants through the research design and analysis as well as through language translation.

As an insider/outsider to the community I studied, I identify as a bilingual heritage speaker, in that I consider both Vietnamese and English as very close to my first languages. My use of Vietnamese was limited to interactions with my parents, elder relatives, and, later, members of the Vietnamese community. People in my situation are now referred to as heritage speakers, where individuals are primarily exposed to the syntax, vernacular, and vocabulary commonly found in familial settings.[13] I am also considered a younger generation and a South Vietnamese from the refugee cohort of the war in Vietnam. These significant details of my identity conditioned my interactions with the study participants in what I was able to ask and to hear. My detailed review of these steps highlights the role of language in researcher-participant relations, and the subjectivity-forming influence language has as both my participant/subject and I move between the two languages. In what follows, I detail the technical steps I took in conducting research across two languages.

In 2015, I conducted a study on the complex negotiations of subjectivity between individuals within communities and between communities within a nation using interview data that were originally presented in Vietnamese and translated into English.[14] My interview questions were formulated first in English and then edited back into Vietnamese, with significant adjustments made to the original English questions in the process. The interviews presented at public events were audio recorded and later translated into English. I rarely conducted translation on my own due to the limitations I shared previously, but also due to the importance of multiple perspectives required in analysis. Working with a team supported my own second-language abilities in Vietnamese but also allowed me to reconsider my worldviews, meaning making, biases, and assumptions in the research process. Translation here was of utmost importance, and the vulnerability of language was duly considered in the study. I embedded translation in key steps of my research process, including in written consent and recruitment documents, formulating interview questions, transcribing in the original language, translating the transcripts into English, and coding between the two languages as the findings were interpreted and re-represented. The studies I discuss employed data collected in Vietnamese, where the interviewer and participant both shared the same language.

With a native Vietnamese speaker as a paid member of the research team, the audio-recorded data was first transcribed into written Vietnamese and then translated into English by the same person. The Vietnamese transcript was then coded in Vietnamese to capture the nuances and deep contextual meaning of the participant narratives and analyzed with the English version on the side to augment translation when needed.[15] The analysis of the data in the language it is presented in allowed me to capture the structure, syntax, and semantics of the language. Hsiung and Wong demonstrated in their study of Chinese women activists the vast gap in meaning of used terms when translated from Chinese to English, as the words' "implied cultural, political, and/or historical meanings are often lost in translation."[16] They argue it is these linguistic operatives that structure and shape our worldviews and the meaning making of our experiences.[17] By keeping both language versions of the transcriptions side by side during analysis and even in the write-up of the study, I ensured the meaning-making process was as reflective of the original language as possible. Any material I personally translated was checked by Vietnamese team members for its coherence from one language to the other, but also for switching from academic jargon to everyday language. With this practice, I kept the audio recordings close during analysis and often read the English translated transcript while relistening to the audio to ensure accuracy in meaning. On a technical note, at the time of my research, I did not find the available transcription and translation software to be reliably accurate. Regardless of the practice used, the key to this work is to collect collateral data, such as observations and journal notes of the interviews, to ensure the transcribed written data does not become decontextualized.[18] As you can see, significant time and costs are associated with multi-language research work. Increasingly, funding bodies (such as Canada's Social Sciences and Humanities Research Council) recognize this expense as essential to conducting rigorous research with diverse language communities and support it as an eligible expense within the overall budget. However, additional resources to studies that work across languages should be provided. Below, I will discuss power dynamics and ethics in translation, attending to the subjectivity enabled and constrained within people's language use as we attempt to make meaning of their narratives, and finally the frequent aversion that we as researchers might feel in leaving some things unspeakable and perhaps unknowable.

Discussion
On Power
Indigenous, racialized, and critical researchers have long called for an expansion, bracketing, and elimination of the Eurocentric methods and worldviews in anthropological studies that were the early predecessors of social research methods.[19] Wong calls for a methodology that accounts for the "sociohistorical contexts of local experiences and the processes by which local cultural meanings are produced or transformed, without assuming culture as static and pure."[20] Doing so spurs us to toward ethical and accurate representation of peoples' knowledge systems and their ways of knowing and being.[21] Qualitative methods continue the colonial legacy of classifying, flattening, and categorizing peoples to be dominated when done without critically interrogating how individual narratives are represented for the consumption of dominant-language readers.

Translation, then, is implicated within the colonializing knowledge production practices that have enabled researchers to abuse and exploit marginalized peoples.[22] It is a constructive process that is fraught with considerations of power that impacts its validity and reliability. Given the importance of knowledge production and language, I situate my work within a Foucauldian analysis of power and its intimate relation to language in knowledge production.[23] Through the poststructural lens, "language is not simply a tool we use to communicate ideas within our sociocultural world; it is implicated in discursive practices that actively construct our sociocultural world through systems of representations and assigned meanings."[24] Translation as a practice is mediated by social relations of power, as participants and researchers negotiate meaning from one language to the other as the translator literally speaks for the Other.[25] With the understanding of translation as an exercise of power, Wong and Poon argue that "the outcomes of translation are influenced significantly by the social positions of the researchers, the translators, and the participants, that is, the extent in which one group assumes absolute authority of knowing over another."[26] When translation work is approached with a deeply ethical stance, researchers are prompted to look for the cultural meanings contained in participants' vocabulary.

With the understanding of translation as an exercise of power, we must be mindful and ethical in our incorporation of our participants' worldviews. As Wong and Poon point out, "The understanding of culture—as a system of dynamic, ambiguous, and conflicting meanings, intertwined with language and discourse, mediated by power, to create and recreate the sociocultural world—is critical to the discussion and debates about translation in cross-cultural research."[27] Gonzales, in reflecting on their work with Indigenous peoples in Latin America, takes this further to assert that the Eurocentric positivistic focus on pure translations omits essential elements of participants' social experiences, such as "the connections between language and embodiment, the influence of language on researcher and participant positionality, and the connections between language, power, land, and materiality."[28]

The colonial muting of voices persists in research today by the very processes that structure knowledge production and dissemination. Gastaldo and Holmes point out that in knowledge production, most of the literature is in English and sources in other languages do not appear in major indexes.[29] Grant applications are urged to allow for translation as a budget item in a research proposal and journal articles can allow for additional space to report findings that must be presented in both languages. As language forms and is informed by our worldviews, the translation process of one language into English inevitably favours the Eurocentric worldview as we attempt to make the original language intelligible and legible to publishing editors, reviewers, and ultimately to predominantly English readers. By meticulously attempting to translate and capture the meaning as closely as possible to the original language, we are attempting to represent the multiple worldviews that are shaped by that language.

On Subjectivity Formation

Language is a living body of history, and it is marked with the wounds of colonization and war. Language conditions the subject positions made (im)possible, used as it is to signify hierarchies in age, kinship, class, and regional origin, as well as—significantly for the Vietnamese Canadian community—wartime allegiances. Language shifts mark major points in Vietnam's and Vietnamese history, as certain terms and phrases were created and ceased after particular events. While popular translation sites such as Google Translate err toward the current Vietnam's Vietnamese, these often did not entirely suit my participants' use of Vietnamese. Political and historical markers in the Vietnamese language were very important in my community research given Vietnam's history of differential regional colonization and a prolonged civil war.

Vietnam has had three major shifts in its modern history that contributed to language changes. In 1956, France's colonial rule was overthrown, but it also divided the country into the North, under communism, and the South, under capitalist democracy.[30] The year 1975 marked the end of the war with American interference, which saw the country forcibly reunited and this is when a great number of Vietnamese people left as refugees.[31] The 1980s and 1990s saw a major shift in economic reform, creating a capitalist socialism within Vietnam. Today it is common to hear different regional dialects of Vietnamese spoken (North, Central, South), and it is just as common to hear Vietnamese people identify themselves along the regions followed by the year as a qualifier. This year as qualifier is important for the Vietnamese to understand if they were recent enemies or not. *Bắc 56* signifies those who were North Vietnamese during 1956 but migrated to the South in protest of the North's communist rule. *Bắc 75* were those who were North Vietnamese during 1975 and fought against the South Vietnamese in the war. For example, the Vietnamese diaspora in Canada have differing views on a historical date in Vietnam: April 30, 1975. For many, this is *Ngày Giải Phóng* or liberation day at the end of a civil war with intensive American and Western intervention. For others, this date is called *Ngày Quốc Hận* or the national mourning day, in what they see as the loss of the country as they knew it. Knowing the political context of these terms enabled me to understand the participants' positioning in relation to this major historical event, which then prompted the growth of the diaspora in Canada. Despite these historical and political signifiers of difference, perhaps even more influential in forming Vietnamese language subjectivity is the use of self-referents.

Self-referents position speakers in a hierarchical social relation to one another, yet this is not a shared aspect of the English language.[32] In Vietnamese, the use of *tôi* [I] is considered rude as it is cold, impersonal, and puts one at equal standing in power to one's conversant. In a linguistic culture where one's ability to navigate social relations is often a matter of survival, this *tôi* is rarely used in community contexts. In place of *tôi*, speakers refer to one another and themselves in kinship terms respective of their age. These self-referents also connote a place in the community kinship structure that not only reflects age, but also status and class.

As a self-identified and presenting female of the second generation who often worked with the elder generation, it was often confusing and difficult to navigate these referents. When I call myself child [*con*], younger sister [*em*], or niece [*cháu*] in relation to my participants, who are referred to as uncles, aunts, elders [*ông, bà, bác, cô, chú*], on the one hand I honour the relational bonds that were historically and politically displaced and severed during the war in Vietnam and the refugee period, but on the other, I am downgraded in my status, my expertise, and my life experience. There is a relational vulnerability here. Outing myself as a younger generation Vietnamese in the language I use, I am forced to let go of my academic expertise, my researcher title and conduct negotiations and discussions with participants as a member of their community and within social hierarchies. I simultaneously resisted and negotiated this subjectivity in relation to the community. When conducting my interviews, I strategically took on the role of student. This honours my research stance as the learner and participants as experts on their lived experiences, but it also aligns with my own upbringing of respect for elders. I do this consciously in my use of language, from speaking Vietnamese with elders, which puts me as the younger kin and learner, to my use of English when I wish to utilize my voice as the scholar and researcher with peers. While not within the text itself, there is a vulnerability in using these self-referents as it requires the researcher to make apparent the multiple social positionings they occupy. Some of these social positionings invoke familial and community hierarchies, which can be experienced as unsettling for a researcher trained to be the knower and expert in dominant Western research paradigms. However, if the researcher can reflexively attune to their negotiations of social relations with the participants, the use of self-positionings can be an ethical reminder of the importance of respectful relationality between researchers and participants as people first. These reflections are important, as they are key to understanding how participants make meaning of their identities and their experiences.

(Un)rendered Stories

Dominant Western research training demands that we uncover and reveal the true meaning of all social phenomena. However, there are terms that do not translate well, and there are utterances that are not made due to the political, social, and personal losses of many in a community. Terms that are value laden and have social-historical linkages require the retention of the original language so that the reader is presented and tasked with considering the worldview of the participants. Wong and Poon shared their challenges in translating Chinese text and struggled with a particular expression equivalent to a good wife. They state: "As there is no language or conceptual equivalence in English for this expression, all the translators (including the authors) were forced into the position of creating a text based on their understanding of the expression."[33]

Given these limitations on translation, Farquhar and Fitzsimons urge us to embrace this unknowability, to be lost, which for them is "to be engaged but uncertain about any final interpretation."[34] They go on to encourage the embrace of uncertainty and reframe the centring of unknowability in translation as a commitment to "restore and re-appropriate meaning, to reveal new modes of being and understandings of each other."[35] Rather than a true translation, the idea of conceptual equivalence is encouraged, which means that efforts must be made in providing comparable concepts or ideas across language.[36] This can be done by providing additional contextual information to help the reader understand the comparison and by sharing the original-language text.

To account for the untranslatable in my work, I presented participant responses in English with key phrases left in Vietnamese and italicized. This asks the reader to take on the viewpoint of the Vietnamese speaker. In doing so, the reader must consciously attempt to see the world through the participants' eyes and to resist their own viewpoints and analytic lens in reading and understanding. The reader must open themselves to the vulnerability of the unknown and to the different worldview Vietnamese people may have, which counters the dominance of the English language in knowledge production. One key idea that was repeatedly articulated by my study participants was the use of tradition and heritage in relation to political stances.[37] In a recent study of the Vietnamese Canadian community, participants repeatedly used several key words in Vietnamese, *truyền thống* [tradition] and *di sản* [heritage], which meant for them a political identity as refugees of communists and the historical community norms associated with honouring the legacy of this seismic, life-shaping, catastrophic event. When translated directly, *tradition* and *heritage* do not adequately capture this sentiment or may even mislead the reader. For many who have not directly embodied a life-shifting event as a war survivor and refugee, we can only work toward conceptual equivalence rather than a true understanding through direct translation.

Conclusion

As an encounter to be embraced, translation within research promises a rich opportunity to understand and grasp the worldviews and meaning making of others.[38] Rather than attempting to fit another's experience within predefined modes of thinking limited by the English language in a quest for the unattainable perfect translation, we should seek beyond what we already can know and capture via language.[39] In this way, translation is not only an encounter but a vulnerability to be embraced. There is vulnerability in the stepping outside the English language, which reinforces the dominance of Eurocentric worldviews and frames of relationality (researcher to participant). There is vulnerability in the untranslatable and the inability to absolutely fix what people share into our available language structures. In reflecting on my experience in research with the Vietnamese-speaking community, I recall the keen curiosity I felt when I encountered the use of a term, metaphor, or vernacular expression I was not familiar with, along with the conversations my inquiries on these terms evoked, not just with research participants but with the team members themselves. In this chapter, I reflected on the power I had as the researcher in making decisions on translations, the political and sociopolitical contexts in which people know themselves and represent themselves through language choices, and the drive for a conceptual equivalence that rejects attempts to directly replace one language text for another in favour of leaving the door open to new understandings. Beyond a vulnerability to be embraced, I press upon the reader that translation is an ethical question to be demanded. I stress the importance of translation work for researchers in approaching their projects with multiple-language speakers. Their study write-ups must consist of more than a few lines on how they arrived at their findings in representing people of another culture, worldview, and language. Attention to translation is also important for the reader in evaluating the methodological rigour of studies as we work collectively as a research community toward social justice.

Notes
1. Josephine Wong and Maurice Poon, "Bringing Translation Out of the Shadows," *Journal of Transcultural Nursing* 21, no. 2 (2010), 157.
2. Laura Gonzales, "(Re)framing Multilingual Technical Communication with Indigenous Language Interpreters and Translators," *Technical Communication Quarterly* (2021), 3.
3. Wong and Poon, "Bringing Translation."
4. Bogusia Temple and Rosalind Edwards, "Interpreters/Translators and Cross-Language Research," *International Journal of Qualitative Methods* 1, no. 2 (2002).
5. Wong and Poon, "Bringing Translation," 153.
6. Agustian Sutrisno, Nga Thanh Nguyen, and Donna Tangen, "Incorporating Translation in Qualitative Studies," *International Journal of Qualitative Studies in Education* 27, no. 10 (2014), 1340.
7. Eun-Ok Im, Robin Page, Li-Chen Lin, Hsiu-Min Tsai, and Ching-Yu Cheng, "Rigor in Cross-Cultural Nursing Research," *International Journal of Nursing Studies* 41, no. 8 (2004).
8. Jaeyoung Choi, Kaysi Eastlick Kushner, Judy Mill, and Daniel W.L. Lai, "Understanding the Language, the Culture, and the Experience," *International Journal of Qualitative Methods* 11, no. 5 (2012); Noreen Esposito, "From Meaning to Meaning," *Qualitative Health Research* 11, no. 4 (2001).
9. Martha Kuwee Kumsa, "Weaving Academic Home: Metaphor, Insurgent Culture, and Transnational Indigeneity," *Qualitative Inquiry* 28, no. 6 (2022).
10. Martha Kuwee Kumsa, "Thinking About Research," *Qualitative Social Work* 15, no. 5-6 (2016), 608.
11. Barbara Kamler and Terry Threadgold, "Translating Difference: Questions of Representation," *Journal of Intercultural Studies* 24, no. 2 (2003), 144.
12. Martha Kuwee Kumsa, Adrienne Chambon, Miu Chung Yan, and Sarah Maiter, "Catching the Shimmers of the Social," *Qualitative Research* 15, no. 4 (2015).
13. Anh Khoi Nguyen, "Space and Time in Vietnamese Heritage Language Maintenance," *Journal of Multilingual and Multicultural Development* 45, no. 5 (2022).
14. Anh Ngo, "The Entanglements of Canada's National Identity Building and Vietnamese Canadian Community Conflicts: Racial Capitalist Democracy and the Cold War Neoliberal Multicultural Subject" (PhD diss., York University, 2019), http://hdl.handle.net/10315/36708.
15. Roselind Wan, "Data Coding for Indigenous Language Research," in *SHS Web of Conferences* 53, 01002. EDP Sciences, 2018.

16. Ping-Chun Hsiung and Yuk-Lin Renita Wong, "*Jie Gui*—Connecting the Tracks: Chinese Women's Activism," *Gender & History* 10, no. 3 (1998), 474.
17. Hsiung and Wong, "*Jie Gui*."
18. Robert M. Emerson, Rachel I. Fretz, and Linda L. Shaw, *Writing Ethnographic Fieldnotes* (Chicago: University of Chicago Press, 2011).
19. Kathleen E. Absolon (Minogiizhigokwe), *Kaandossiwin: How We Come to Know* (Halifax: Fernwood Publishing, 2011); Leslie Brown and Susan Strega, *Research as Resistance: Revisiting Critical, Indigenous, and Anti-Oppressive Approaches*, 2nd ed. (Toronto: Canadian Scholars' Press, 2015).
20. Yuk-Lin Renita Wong, "Reclaiming Chinese Women's Subjectivities," *Women's Studies International Forum* 25, no. 1 (2002), 71.
21. Candace Kaleimamoowahinekapu Galla and Alanaise Goodwill, "Talking Story with Vital Voices: Making Knowledge with Indigenous Language," *Journal of Indigenous Wellbeing* 2, no. 3 (2017).
22. Linda Tuhiwai Smith, *Decolonizing Methodologies: Research and Indigenous Peoples* (London: Zed Books, 2021).
23. Derek Hook, *Foucault, Psychology and the Analytics of Power* (London: Palgrave Macmillan, 2007).
24. Wong and Poon, "Bringing Translation," 152.
25. Mona Baker, *In Other Words: A Coursebook on Translation* (New York: Routledge, 2018); Allison Squires, "Methodological Challenges in Cross-Language Qualitative Research," *International Journal of Nursing Studies* 46, no. 2 (2009); Wong and Poon, "Bringing Translation."
26. Wong and Poon, "Bringing Translation," 153.
27. Wong and Poon, "Bringing Translation," 152.
28. Gonzales, "(Re)framing multilingual," 3.
29. Denise Gastaldo and Dave Holmes, "Foucault and Nursing: A History of the Present," *Nursing Inquiry* 6, no. 4 (1999).
30. Long S. Le, "'Colonial' and 'Postcolonial' Views of Vietnam's Pre-History," *SOJOURN: Journal of Social Issues in Southeast Asia* 26, no. 1 (2011).
31. Albert Lau, *Southeast Asia and the Cold War* (New York: Routledge, 2012).
32. Rebecca Walton and Sarah Beth Hopton, "'All Vietnamese Men are Brothers': Rhetorical Strategies," *Technical Communication* 65, no. 3 (2018).
33. Wong and Poon, "Bringing Translation," 154.
34. Sandy Farquhar and Peter Fitzsimons, "Lost in Translation: The Power of Language," *Educational Philosophy and Theory* 43, no. 6 (2011), 656.
35. Farquhar and Fitzsimons, "Lost in Translation," 660.
36. W. Lawrence Neuman, *Social Research Methods: Qualitative and Quantitative Approaches*, 7th ed. (Boston: Allyn & Bacon, 2011).
37. Anh Ngo, "The Flag of Refugees: Critical Ethnography of a Vietnamese Canadian Community Conflict," *ESC: English Studies in Canada* 45, no. 3 (2019): 73–89.
38. Farquhar and Fitzsimons, "Lost in Translation," 659.
39. Farquhar and Fitzsimons, "Lost in Translation," 659.

Bibliography

Absolon, Kathleen E. (Minogiizhigokwe). *Kaandossiwin: How We Come to Know*. Halifax: Fernwood Publishing, 2011.

Baker, Mona. *In Other Words: A Coursebook on Translation*. New York: Routledge, 2018.

Brown, Leslie, and Susan Strega. *Research as Resistance: Revisiting Critical, Indigenous, and Anti-Oppressive Approaches*, 2nd edition. Toronto: Canadian Scholars' Press, 2015.

Choi, Jaeyoung, Kaysi Eastlick Kushner, Judy Mill, and Daniel WL Lai. "Understanding the Language, the Culture, and the Experience: Translation in Cross-Cultural Research." *International Journal of Qualitative Methods* 11, no. 5 (2012): 652-665.

Emerson, Robert M., Rachel I. Fretz, and Linda L. Shaw. *Writing Ethnographic Fieldnotes*. Chicago: University of Chicago Press, 2011.

Esposito, Noreen. "From Meaning to Meaning: The Influence of Translation Techniques on Non-English Focus Group Research." *Qualitative Health Research* 11, no. 4 (2001): 568-579.

Farquhar, Sandy, and Peter Fitzsimons. "Lost in Translation: The Power of Language." *Educational Philosophy and Theory* 43, no. 6 (2011): 652-662.

Galla, Candace Kaleimamoowahinekapu, and Alanaise Goodwill. "Talking Story with Vital Voices: Making Knowledge with Indigenous Language." *Journal of Indigenous Wellbeing* 2, no. 3 (2017): 67-75.

Gastaldo, Denise, and Dave Holmes. "Foucault and Nursing: A History of the Present." *Nursing Inquiry* 6, no. 4 (1999): 231-240.

Gonzales, Laura. "(Re)framing Multilingual Technical Communication with Indigenous Language Interpreters and Translators." *Technical Communication Quarterly* (2021): 1-16.

Hook, Derek. *Foucault, Psychology and the Analytics of Power*. London: Palgrave Macmillan, 2007.

Hsiung, Ping-Chun, and Yuk-Lin Renita Wong. "*Jie Gui*—Connecting the Tracks: Chinese Women's Activism Surrounding the 1995 World Conference on Women in Beijing." *Gender and History* 10, no. 3 (1998): 470-497.

Im, Eun-Ok, Robin Page, Li-Chen Lin, Hsiu-Min Tsai, and Ching-Yu Cheng. "Rigor in Cross-Cultural Nursing Research." *International Journal of Nursing Studies* 41, no. 8 (2004): 891-899.

Kamler, Barbara, and Terry Threadgold. "Translating Difference: Questions of Representation in Cross-Cultural Research Encounters." *Journal of Intercultural Studies* 24, no. 2 (2003): 137-51.

Kumsa, Martha Kuwee. "Thinking About Research." *Qualitative Social Work* 15, no. 5-6 (2016): 602-609.

Kumsa, Martha Kuwee. "Weaving Academic Home: Metaphor, Insurgent Culture, and Transnational Indigeneity." *Qualitative Inquiry* 28, no. 6 (2022).

Kumsa, Martha Kuwee, Adrienne Chambon, Miu Chung Yan, and Sarah Maiter. "Catching the Shimmers of the Social: From the Limits of Reflexivity to Methodological Creativity." *Qualitative Research* 15, no. 4 (2015): 419-436.

Lau, Albert. *Southeast Asia and the Cold War*. New York: Routledge, 2012.

Le, Long S. "'Colonial' and 'Postcolonial' Views of Vietnam's Pre-History." *SOJOURN: Journal of Social Issues in Southeast Asia* 26, no. 1 (2011): 128–148.

Neuman, W. Lawrence. *Social Research Methods: Qualitative and Quantitative Approaches* 7th edition. Boston: Allyn and Bacon, 2011

Ngo, Anh. "The Entanglements of Canada's National Identity Building and Vietnamese Canadian Community Conflicts: Racial Capitalist Democracy and the Cold War Neoliberal Multicultural Subject." PhD dissertation, York University, 2019. http://hdl.handle.net/10315/36708.

Ngo, Anh. "The Flag of Refugees: Critical Ethnography of a Vietnamese Canadian Community Conflict." *ESC: English Studies in Canada* 45, no. 3 (2019): 73–89.

Nguyen, Anh Khoi. "Space and Time in Vietnamese Heritage Language Maintenance." *Journal of Multilingual and Multicultural Development* 43, no. 5 (2022): 424–437.

Smith, Linda Tuhiwai. *Decolonizing Methodologies: Research and Indigenous Peoples*. London: Zed Books, 2021.

Squires, Allison. "Methodological Challenges in Cross-Language Qualitative Research: A Research Review." *International Journal of Nursing Studies* 46, no. 2 (2009): 277–287.

Sutrisno, Agustian, Nga Thanh Nguyen, and Donna Tangen. "Incorporating Translation in Qualitative Studies: Two Case Studies in Education." *International Journal of Qualitative Studies in Education* 27, no. 10 (2014): 1337–1353.

Temple, Bogusia, and Rosalind Edwards. "Interpreters/Translators and Cross-Language Research: Reflexivity and Border Crossings." *International Journal of Qualitative Methods* 1, no. 2 (2002): 1–12.

Walton, Rebecca, and Sarah Beth Hopton. "'All Vietnamese Men are Brothers': Rhetorical Strategies and Community Engagement Practices Used to Support Victims of Agent Orange." *Technical Communication* 65, no. 3 (2018): 309–325.

Wan, Roselind. "Data Coding for Indigenous Language Research: Attaching Local Meanings in Generating Categories and Themes." In *SHS Web of Conferences* 53, 01002. EDP Sciences, 2018.

Wong, Josephine, and Maurice Poon. "Bringing Translation Out of the Shadows: Translation as an Issue of Methodological Significance in Cross-Cultural Qualitative Research." *Journal of Transcultural Nursing* 21, no. 2 (2010): 151–158.

Wong, Yuk-Lin Renita. "Reclaiming Chinese Women's Subjectivities: Indigenizing 'Social Work With Women' in China through Postcolonial Ethnography." *Women's Studies International Forum* 25, no. 1 (2002): 67–77.

5

"Crossroad" Moments and the Choice to Respond
Diverging from Textbook Ethics

Yuriko Cowper-Smith and Preeti Nayak

Introduction: Women of Colour in the Academy
Women of colour (WoC) are underrepresented in higher education and face a plethora of barriers to full participation in academic life. Some of these barriers include being more likely than white colleagues to be challenged for their expertise, being overly burdened with service responsibilities, and being subjected to racism and sexism in the workplace, which in turn implicitly and explicitly impact their opportunities to thrive and succeed.[1] At the same time, research underscores how WoC scholars are changing the academy by expanding the parameters of whose knowledge counts and why. As expressed by Gloria Anzaldúa,

> Because we are not allowed to enter discourse, because we are often disqualified and excluded from it, because what passes for theory these days is forbidden territory for us, it is vital that we occupy theorizing space, that we not allow white men and women solely

to occupy it. By bringing in our own approaches and methodologies, we transform that theorizing space.[2]

Following Anzaldúa's call to occupy such space, our research goal here is to build on the scholarship that advocates for social justice research methods to be dynamic and flexible and to meet emancipatory research aims.[3] We want to do so because, through our experiences as WoC scholars, we recognized a dearth of writing on research ethics and vulnerability, particularly when we realized that we were not equipped to deal with "crossroad moments." Crossroad moments are instances where we felt we must respond to or engage with the political stakes implied in participants' data, especially when those stakes affected us personally or shifted our subjectivities. The decision to respond diverges from textbook understandings of research ethics—those stating that we should *not* respond, as doing so may undermine trust or the integrity of the data and compromise the ethic of "do no harm." At the same time, standard conceptualizations of vulnerability in research ethics often do not consider the subject position of the researcher. So, we challenge this default position of depicting vulnerability as a feature or sole experience of the participant and instead suggest that researchers' decisions, and most importantly, how we approach vulnerability, are complicated by our positionalities, subject positions, political commitments, and research goals. The aim, then, is to think about methodologies and ethics in ways where we can better support WoC researchers in navigating vulnerability when doing research with dominant groups or with participants who are often assumed to be "vulnerable" on paper.

To this end, in this chapter we explore the question of *how can we better understand how to navigate crossroad moments?* Our response is twofold. First, we interrogate how emerging WoC scholars are initiated into thinking about researcher-participant vulnerability in the context of qualitative, social science research with social justice aims. In doing so, we argue that the conceptualization of vulnerability in research ethics needs to be expanded to be more relational and bidirectional. Second, regarding this nuanced understanding of vulnerability, blanket assumptions of participant vulnerability must be further complicated in social justice research methods and ethics. We read our participants, and we are in turn read by our participants, according to our subject positions.

Thus, vulnerability should be assessed based on the ways we see the data circulating "in the real world" and how it may impact real people and real vulnerable Others, including ourselves. Recognizing that feelings of vulnerability may be contextual and relational, the choice to respond and to talk about vulnerability in more complex ways is especially necessary and critical for WoC, who have experienced oppression and marginalization themselves.

In what follows, we first summarize the methodological approach we took in writing this chapter. Then we turn to our respective reflections on the vulnerability we have experienced during research through introducing two of our own crossroad moments, and we suggest two considerations that would make conversations around vulnerability more nuanced. First, more discussions of researcher vulnerability are needed in research ethics courses and with supervisors for young scholars, especially WoC scholars, to better equip them during data gathering. Second, much like how "writing in" positionality has become normalized across disciplines, multidimensional vulnerability needs to be documented and talked about more explicitly in scholarship. A deeper reflection on different types of vulnerabilities, and how vulnerability changes by who occupies space in the researcher-participant relationship, enriches the concept and makes research more equitable for all.

Methodology

As two young emerging WoC scholars, we have often informally (and passionately) discussed our experiences in the academy, particularly in the realm of research ethics, methods, and beyond. Thus, this chapter began as a therapeutic and cathartic—and intellectually curious—conversation where we shared our personal experiences navigating data gathering while being minority researchers who are situated in the Western academic complex, with its dark history (and present) of oppression in the pursuit of imperialism and hegemonic knowledge. Through these discussions we were able to articulate what we now describe as "crossroad" moments. We knew that because of these delicate experiences, we had respectively started to develop a research orientation that fit within our politics and personal ethics. To set up this chapter, we documented our crossroad moments on paper and then continued to dialogue across our reflections. The commonalities of our experiences form the basis of the chapter discussion.

Learning about Vulnerability

We recalled that throughout our recent respective graduate education experiences, ethics were generally only introduced to us in the process of gaining regulatory approval to conduct our respective projects or when developing data collection instruments. This mirrors broader research findings of how the concept of ethics has increasingly become confounded with the process of gaining regulatory approval required to conduct research.[4] In these processes, discourse on participant vulnerability dominated the discussion. In practice, this looks like receiving guidance from supervisors on how to reword questions to reduce the vulnerability of participants, how to fill out the "participant risks" section on ethics-approval forms, and how to minimize risk. This meant considering, for example, what to wear, where to meet participants, and whether/how to compensate participants. In this view, considerations of vulnerability generally revolve around questions like "who is deemed to be susceptible to greater harm and liable to being taken advantage of?" In asking such questions, vulnerability often relates to ideas such as the ability to give free, uncoerced, informed consent; participants' decision-making ability; diminishment of risks; and if the value of the research is greater than the risks to the participant.[5] This introduction to vulnerability made sense to us; we have always intended to treat participants with care, and we should do our absolute best to make sure they feel safe and protected when participating in research.

Yet because participant vulnerability was depicted as something we would encounter or possibly be responsible to mitigate against, we were less prepared to experience vulnerability ourselves or to understand vulnerability relationally. It was only in the instance of the interview itself that we experienced vulnerability relationally, and this emerged precisely because of gender, race, class, education, socioeconomic status, or other markers of our subject positions—markers that can quickly and substantially shift researcher-participant relationships depending on the context. This kind of researcher initiation for WoC scholars is perhaps overlooked because of the colonial history of the Western university itself.[6] In textbooks and in university discourse about procedural ethics, one is conditioned and socialized to believe that when working with marginalized communities, the researcher wields all the power and must do everything in her power to broach the power relations to make the research experience more equitable. This lesson is important because researchers who are situated in Western universities are trained in institutions that have historically abused and exploited marginalized communities for the purposes of advancing Eurocentric and hegemonic knowledge production. We recognize that much of today's regulatory process and discussion around ethics is a response to this legacy. We are supportive of institutional move(s) that intend to mitigate past and future harms. We recognize that researchers hold tremendous power within the research process. After all, in traditional qualitative research, it is us who decide which questions are asked, which participants are recruited, which methods to employ, and how findings are presented.[7] These "checkpoints" of power demand pause, especially when it comes to notions of vulnerability. As researchers doing social justice–oriented work, it is important to reflect on how and why questions may render participants vulnerable, which methods may be comfortable or intrusive, and what kinds of portrayals we wish to project in our findings. Considering oneself as being in a position of power is a key element in responding to potential participant vulnerability.[8]

However, in nurturing young scholars who have traditionally been excluded and who today still do not quite "fit" into the university, blanket assumptions of participant vulnerability can sometimes lack nuance or at least lead to ambiguous expectations on what the research process should look or feel like. What remains murky to us is the question of how to address researcher vulnerability when doing work with dominant groups and/or those who are often assumed to be "vulnerable" on paper when, in reality, such notions of vulnerability may shift in the microdynamics of data collection. WoC researchers may find themselves in research contexts where the power dynamic is flipped or ambiguous and, as a result, may feel less equipped to navigate ambiguous power dynamics in the process of data collection. Through unexpected conversations or emergent emotions, an interview may generate conditions where vulnerability is continuously shifting between researcher and participant.

Scenario One (Preeti)

In 2019, I was a graduate assistant on a project exploring teachers' approaches to anti-racism in their teaching practices. Part of my role was to conduct a series of final interviews with participants at the end of a 10-month study. The objective of the final interview was to follow up on participants' reflections and gain a better understanding of what they may have learned from the study. I identified as a young, South Asian, middle-class, female graduate student at the time of this research. The majority of participants were white, middle-class, middle-age, female teachers. In one of these interviews, I experienced several crossroad moments with Peggy, a white teacher in her sixties.

In the first crossroad moment, I listened to Peggy trying to describe what it was like to grow up in an Italian family in the 1960s and how she equivocated forms of racial discrimination faced by racial minorities today to the forms of discrimination Italians faced previously. She suggested that she would like to believe that "things will get better" for racial minorities, just like they did for Italians.

In the second crossroad moment, Peggy described the rise and prevalence of what she termed "reverse prejudice"—where white people were subject to race-based discrimination. She described how her white husband feels like he cannot walk down the street by himself without being perceived as an outsider.

In these crossroad moments, I felt a heightened awareness of my own race and age while documenting Peggy's perspectives. I experienced discomfort in hearing her claims of reverse racism or how "things are getting better"; instinctively, I wanted to present her with data or engage in a constructive dialogue on structural racism. But was it appropriate to raise counterclaims to Peggy's perspectives? Why did I feel uncomfortable in doing so?

Part of feeling unsure of how to proceed in these crossroad moments emerged because I thought probing into Peggy's whiteness would push her to become defensive or vulnerable—and making the participant feel vulnerable during data collection was to be avoided at all costs, I thought. I was also fearful that I would lose trust and credibility as the young, racialized researcher asking questions about her whiteness. I felt vulnerable in this interview—how did Peggy perceive me, as a racialized researcher studying race? Was I expected to be sympathetic toward her claims? I did not know how to sit with the data or meaningfully engage with the participant in these moments, precisely because of my own subject position.

In considering Peggy as potentially vulnerable in this work (because she was a research participant) I was overly cautious to not ask questions in a way that would shut Peggy down or censor her responses when talking to me, a WoC. This blanket approach to participant vulnerability was not entirely productive in this interview, as the dynamics indicated that my race, and at times my age, enabled Peggy to perhaps "read" me differently—in ways where I felt undermined or uncomfortable because of assumptions she projected onto me (i.e., that I would not understand her perspective). In the end, I wondered if this interview should have been conducted by a white researcher who could perhaps sit with Peggy's vulnerability more closely than I could.

Choosing to respond to or not engage with oppressive claims that constitute "data" is a difficult choice to make as an emerging WoC scholar. This difficulty speaks to how researchers of colour carry embodied costs in doing social justice research.[9] Bailey reminds us that "Researchers are of course not simply efficient instruments of methodology but embodied actors in a network of intra-acting relations, materialities, contexts, and responsibilities that constitute methodological practice."[10] In this interview, it was difficult to dismiss or ignore the embodied costs to me. The many researchers who study topics that are personally relevant to their lives and livelihoods are faced with difficult microdecisions in data collection. The choice to probe further or not respond to oppressive claims can come from a real desire for self-preservation and credibility in an interview—or not become "too emotional" by what is at stake when doing social justice research. At times, it feels like there is a conflict of interest between promoting learning and research goals versus acting on desires to educate or fight for social justice. There is a tension between collecting data and considering the weight of what is being said by participants from dominant groups—and how statements, if acted upon, can do harm to others. In my exchange with Peggy, I kept wondering how or if her ideas were affecting her students of colour in harmful ways and if it was my responsibility to engage Peggy with counterclaims or other data to consider, as she was articulating her views on race. Ultimately, the researcher cannot control what the participant does with what they share with us. But the grey area we are describing in this chapter is the question of when or if to respond to participants' ideas that we see as possibly harmful to vulnerable others (such as students of colour, in Peggy's case): What is the responsibility of the researcher here, in terms of advancing social justice-oriented learning and action on the part of the participant?

My point in this example is not to fault Peggy, but instead to question how assumptions of participant vulnerability cannot be outrightly assumed. In this light, we stress that positionality is not about signalling intentions as much as it is about considering and weighing what responsibilities you hold, as a researcher with various salient identities.[11] In the immediacy of an interview where we work with participants doing work "in the real world," do academics have responsibilities to intervene or respond to injustice when participants allude to their own complicity? Are we responsible for challenging harmful views, or does our sole responsibility lay in analyzing and theorizing why and how such claims emerge?

Scenario 2 (Yuriko)
During my PhD, I worked with the Rohingya diaspora movement in Canada. Over the past five years, the movement has accomplished incredible feats of intellectual labour and hands-on activism. In its praxis, it is learning how to counter the genocide their community is facing in Myanmar and how to resolve the refugee crisis in Cox's Bazar, Bangladesh, from the diaspora. In April 2017, I initiated the process of getting to know the Rohingya diaspora community when I attended a play, *I Am Rohingya*, in Kitchener-Waterloo. This play was the first time I had the chance to witness Rohingya youths' passionate advocacy for international justice and it galvanized my interest in the work that they were doing. In the fall of that year, the Rohingya diaspora movement started gathering momentum in Canada after approximately 742,000 people[12] crossed from Myanmar to Bangladesh during a period of acute genocidal violence. This turning point made their work even more urgent and critical, and it quickly picked up speed.

I began formal data gathering at the end of 2017. In beginning my data gathering, I had been rightly conditioned and aware that I was working with a community made extremely vulnerable largely by the Burmese state. The Rohingya community has experienced persecution on the largest scale possible—genocide, the wholesale deliberate destruction of a nation of people. I was aware that in working with people who have personally faced genocide, there would be deep power imbalances. In parallel, my ethics training made me recognize that I was part of a colonial legacy, as a PhD student in the academy, and that that legacy could impact the researcher-participant relationship. Thus, I learned a lot about how different types of power relations operate and what I could do to observe, recognize, and counter vulnerability during data gathering. With roots in critical feminist literature, intersectionality dictates an understanding of the processes through which one's social locations contribute to privilege or marginalization and how such elements change in relation to each other and various contexts.[13] Such social locations include gender, ethnicity, class, age, and ability, and these are maintained, reproduced, and naturalized in daily life.[14] As described by Dhamoon, these categories are created through "processes of differentiation" and "systems of domination" (e.g., racism, colonialism, and gendering) that are sustained over time.[15] In order to understand how my positionality might impact the research process, I analyzed how power relations take root and play out across identity markers. My positionality as a young feminist who was a straight, cisgender, second-generation, middle-class Canadian WoC, and an emerging activist-scholar in a Western institution, variously impacted how I learned about and approached research as well as how I am viewed as a researcher. I might not look like someone who could "do harm"—how would the community interpret my presence and the body I am in? How would I know what vulnerability was if the participants in my research look more like me than my academic peers and colleagues?

With these types of questions in mind, in approaching data gathering, one tactic to actively resist imperialist practices and acknowledge power imbalances that I knew might help guide me was to get to know people on a plane that made sense to them. For me, this meant following the social movement organically: going at the pace of the movement, saying "yes" to opportunities that were presented to me, and to meet with people informally and in their comfort zones and spaces. This approach also meant going much beyond what I was taught in ethics training, and it presented me with my first crossroad moment. Constantly being immersed in the movement meant less detachment, less of an ability to remain aloof or ignorant to everything except "the data"; it meant getting to know people as the complicated, conscientious, thinking and breathing, entire-ties that they represent. When encountering bold activist leaders, I thought, *how are these participants vulnerable when they seem anything but?*

Ultimately, it was through this hands-on approach, one that obfuscated a hurried extraction of data, that I recognized that the people who have experienced genocide, statelessness, and forced migration also shoulder the answers to their plight. They are the ones who are developing the tools for their liberation against seemingly impenetrable structural obstacles. They are agentic; they are not vulnerable as people, but the socioeconomic-political power structures have rendered them exposed to vulnerabilities on a scale others can barely imagine. Yes, they are put into conditions and situations that allow for extreme vulnerabilities. However, within structural oppression, there is always agentic power. This recognition meant that participants I encountered were not one-dimensionally vulnerable, as I was socialized to believe throughout academic training and through portrayals in the media. This recognition is not to dismiss or diminish structural oppression, but it is to recognize the complex humanity of the people who face disenfranchisement. It is possible to recognize the agency they inhabit and the labour they are committing to their cause while remaining highly attuned to power differentials. As Tuck underlines, research is harmful when the dominant or only narrative of the participants is focused on their damage and their brokenness.[16]

At the same time, the recognition of agency meant also allowing for vulnerability to be bidirectional. In recognizing that vulnerability is not one-dimensional, I opened myself up to also being vulnerable. For me, this second crossroad moment was not one particular instance, but rather a thought process built over the course of being a young WoC researcher immersed in a social movement during data gathering. Being a young WoC was both an opening to conversations and a source of confidence, but also a potential vulnerability. In particular, discomfort or ambiguity arose throughout data gathering when I was not adequately prepared to be told things, and to hold them, that were deeply personal and/or political in ways that differed from my own politics or that were triggering and meant to elicit a reaction or emotion out of me. This point also goes back to the ethical quandaries that can arise once one is deeply embedded in a social movement. For example, there was a constant, delicate internal negotiation when information was shared with me. Was I told this personal story because I am viewed as a researcher, or is it because I look like someone who can hold space or be an outlet for emotional narratives?

Realizing agency also means realizing that within the confines of a research setting, power flows both ways. This is not to say that I would have changed any way I practised ethical research methods during data gathering and the tools I used to minimize risk. However, had I been trained to understand vulnerability in a more relational manner, I would have perhaps been more aware of the ways in which what participants told me could have also impacted me due to the subject position that I occupy as a young, emerging WoC scholar. This is perhaps a counterfactual that cannot be proven, but it is plausible that the situation would not have been the same for an older white male scholar to enter the research setting in which I was embedded. The power dynamics would have shaped how he was responded to, how he was read, and most importantly, how he ultimately understood, approached, and wrote about the vulnerability of the participants.

Discussion

We do not have clear answers to these tough crossroad moments that we faced or those we will inevitably face in the future. But in this discussion, we present two considerations that we believe will help emerging WoC scholars navigate vulnerability in research.

Potential Researcher Vulnerability in Ethics, Relationships, and Courses
First, we stress that making these tensions explicit in discussions of ethics and vulnerability in graduate courses and supervisory relationships will be insightful for emerging WoC scholars. As discussed, too often procedural ethics work does not initiate WoC researchers into complex considerations of vulnerability. As we stress, vulnerability is bidirectional and participant vulnerability should not be assumed in all research projects. Researchers can also experience vulnerability, and the agency of participants should always be recognized, regardless of how vulnerable they may seem on paper. We encourage all in the academy to consider how the positionalities, politics, research subject matter,

and subject positions of WoC scholars may generate complicated power dynamics between researchers and participants from dominant groups and those deemed vulnerable from the outset.

Raising explicit conversations about potential researcher vulnerability with emerging WoC scholars may help demystify how and what "doing research" can feel like, which may in turn work toward creating a more inclusive ethos of higher education. Complicating discussions of vulnerability works toward making social justice research more rigorous, equitable, and inclusive for WoC scholars—as well as the people we work with. In this light, we encourage all researchers who are doing social justice-oriented research to ask critical questions before, during, and after the data collection process, such as:

- Who is this research for?
- Who does it serve and how will it serve them?
- In what ways may information gathering make the researcher vulnerable and how do we support emerging WoC scholars in navigating these dynamics?
- How can one navigate racism and sexism in an interview? Should one respond or how does one decide when to do so?
- What makes the participant agentic generally and agentic in relation to the researcher?
- What tools can be used, or what plans implemented, to make the research partnership equitable for all?

We believe that making space for these conversations in ethics or methods courses and/or supervisory relationships would help WoC scholars normalize their potential vulnerability in the research process and become better prepared for it, especially if and when interviewing or collaborating with participants from dominant groups or those who have been deemed vulnerable from the outset. It also allows for understanding participant vulnerability in more nuanced ways.

"Writing In" Vulnerability in Scholarship

Second, we encourage "writing in" researcher vulnerability in scholarship when appropriate and when it serves the research aims. We suggest that making explicit the embodied costs of doing social justice research can help nuance common sense approaches to positionality as a "stance." As Bailey argues:

> Despite the productivity of reflexivity as a stance, there is nothing inherently justice-oriented about reflecting on one's subject position in relation to a given project. It depends on a variety of issues, including one's view of oneself, one's view of the subject, one's focus in research, one's political allegiances, and the work such reflexivity enables.[17]

Similarly, such reflexivity is warranted when considering questions around vulnerability in any project. Researcher-participant vulnerability can depend on or be influenced by a variety of issues and positions, as our two examples demonstrate. Therefore, when writing about positionality, there is perhaps an opportunity to also discuss what vulnerability means between researchers and participants.

To be clear, we are not prescribing more focus on the researcher in academic writing, nor that the WoC researcher is writ large vulnerable. Nor are we saying to write in a way where the findings or key ideas are overshadowed by notions of researcher vulnerability. What we are suggesting, based on our experiences, is to make space in academic writing and discussion, when appropriate, to discuss positionality in relation to participants in ways where these sensory and affective experiences of research labour are relevant to the project and its findings. Fraser and Puwar remind us that research as production always holds or contains "sensory, emotional and affective relations [that] are central to the ways in which researchers engage with, produce, understand and translate what becomes 'research' even if they are not vocalized or written as such."[18]

As such, we suggest that writing research this way—engaging with the affective relations of data collection—changes traditional ideas of what we imagine research to be. It is rare to come across published articles where *researcher* vulnerability, relational, and bidirectional vulnerability are exposed or discussed at all. But vocalizing and "writing in" this messiness or exposing these affective experiences during research or data analysis can support emerging WoC scholars to better understand complex researcher-participant dynamics that they may face in the future. Further, it can nuance how WoC scholars produce research or engage with knowledge claims, because emotional and affective relations are actively explored rather than ignored or sidelined; instead of simply focusing on what the data says, we consider how it is said and who it is said to—both of which we argue are important in how knowledge is constructed. This exposure is especially needed for WoC scholars hoping to work in research areas where potential participants occupy positions of power—or conversely, who are labelled as vulnerable from the outset of research design.

As we discussed, growing this type of scholarship can be beneficial in scaffolding graduate learning experiences. To talk about potential researcher vulnerability in courses or supervisory relationships, faculty and educators need scholarship to draw from, to theorize how and why such guidance may benefit their minoritized students. Furthermore, as Page writes, vulnerability as method is "about what unsettles, about relations to the unfamiliar and strange, and about the erasure of the complexities of subjectivity when individuals and bodies and their actions do not fit or adhere to coherent themes of knowledge."[19] Refusing blanket assumptions of participant vulnerability resists the erasure of complex subjectivities found in the researcher-participant relationship that emerge because of race, class, gender, and so forth. This refusal is also generative because it allows for social justice research methods to be dynamic. As Bailey writes:

> A variety of forces shape what "justice" or "equity" might look like in a given context. As forms of power constantly shift, emancipatory practices must remain dynamic and supple. This stance includes keeping open the vision of practices aligned with such inquiries, from considering the context of production, the research imaginary, the micropractices and decisions researchers make during the inquiry, to the analytic processes and final re-presentation.[20]

In the case of Preeti's interview with Peggy, the micropractices and decisions of what to say or what not to ask were shaped by race and age. In retrospect, a clearer understanding of the emancipatory aims of that research project would have probably grounded these decision-making processes for her as she navigated the interview that rendered her vulnerable. In that project, the team never had an explicit discussion of who this research was for, or whom it was serving and why. They also never devised strategies or conversations to unpack what it meant to be a young research assistant of colour interviewing white, middle-aged men and women.

In Yuriko's case, the initial assumption of participant vulnerability on the part of the researcher made the process of recognizing agency, and how it might affect her, much more laborious than it might have been. The interactions that ensued, the learning and unlearning that happened over the course of the information gathering, and the conclusions that were ultimately made could have perhaps been at least more quickly had ethics training around vulnerability been more multidimensional and relational.

Again, having these discussions explicitly in the context of *potential* researcher vulnerability may help in navigating data-gathering processes and producing more rigorous research, as the messiness of such dynamics shaped and continues to shape how we think about knowledge claims made by participants. These discussions also build our confidence and skill sets in data collection, along with what we need to consider prior to building relationships with participants.

Conclusion

In this chapter, we discussed how crossroad moments experienced as WoC scholars compelled us to unpack the concept of vulnerability in researcher-participant relationships. By paying attention to the concept of vulnerability, we each recognized that rather than being unidirectional, vulnerability is contextual and relational, a lesson learned from being a WoC scholar in social justice–oriented research. Moreover, vulnerability should not be assumed. In walking the reader through two scenarios, we assert that (1) more discussions of researcher vulnerability are needed for young scholars, especially WoC scholars, to be better equipped during information gathering; and (2) these instances of vulnerability need to be documented and discussed more explicitly in scholarship, much like how writing in positionality has become normalized across disciplines. By recognizing different types of vulnerabilities, and how vulnerability changes by who occupies space in the researcher-participant relationship and who has voice, we are continuously enriching the concept and making research more equitable for all.

Notes

1. Ryan Rideau, "'We're Just Not Acknowledged': An Examination of the Identity Taxation of Full-Time Non-Tenure-Track Women of Color Faculty Members," *Journal of Diversity in Higher Education* 14, no. 2 (2019): 161-173.
2. Gloria Anzaldúa, *Making Face, Making Soul = Haciendo Caras: Creative and Critical Perspectives by Women of Color* (San Francisco: Aunt Lute Foundation Books, 1990), xxv.
3. Laura Parson, "Considering Positionality: The Ethics of Conducting Research with Marginalized Groups," in *Research Methods for Social Justice and Equity in Education*, eds. K.K. Strunk and L.A. Locke (Cham: Springer, 2019), 15-32.
4. Ariel M. Cascio and Eric Racine, "Person-Oriented Research Ethics: Integrating Relational and Everyday Ethics in Research," *Accountability in Research* 25, no. 3 (2018): 170-197.
5. Dearbhail Bracken-Roche, Emily Bell, Mary Ellen Macdonald, and Eric Racine, "The Concept of 'Vulnerability' in Research Ethics: An In-Depth Analysis of Policies and Guidelines," *Health Research Policy and Systems* 15, no. 1 (2017); Ariel M. Cascio and Eric Racine, "Person-Oriented Research Ethics," 170-197; Florencia Luna, "Identifying and Evaluating Layers of Vulnerability—A Way Forward," *Developing World Bioethics* 19, no. 2 (2019): 86-95; Florencia Luna and Sheryl Vanderpoel, "Not the Usual Suspects: Addressing Layers of Vulnerability," *Bioethics* 27, no. 6 (2013): 325-332; Elizabeth Peter and Judith Friedland, "Recognizing Risk and Vulnerability in Research Ethics: Imagining the 'What Ifs?'" *Journal of Empirical Research on Human Research Ethics* 12, no. 2 (2017): 107-116.
6. Levi Gahman and Gabrielle Legault, "Disrupting the Settler Colonial University: Decolonial Praxis and Place-Based Education in the Okanagan Valley (British Columbia)," *Capitalism, Nature, Socialism* 30, no. 1 (2019): 50-69.
7. Parson, "Considering Positionality," 15.
8. Parson, "Considering Positionality," 15.
9. Lucy E. Bailey, "Thinking Critically About 'Social Justice Methods': Methods as 'Contingent Foundations,'" in *Research Methods for Social Justice and Equity in Education* (Cham: Springer International Publishing, 2019), 92; G. Cannella, "Foreword," in *Disrupting Qualitative Inquiry: Possibilities and Tensions in Educational Research*, eds. Ruth Nicole Brown, Rozana Carducci, and Candace R. Kuby (New York: Peter Lang, 2014), xv-xvi.
10. Bailey, "Thinking Critically," 95.
11. Parson, "Considering Positionality," 15.
12. UNHCR—UN Refugee Agency, "UNHCR—Rohingya Emergency," March 3, 2023, https://www.unhcr.org/rohingya-emergency.html.
13. Kimberlé Crenshaw, "Mapping the Margins: Intersectionality, Identity Politics, and Violence Against Women of Color," *Stanford Law Review* 43, no. 6 (1991): 1241-1299; Patricia Hill Collins, "Learning from the Outsider Within: The Sociological Significance of Black Feminist Thought," *Social Problems* 33, no. 6 (1986): S14-S32.

14. Rita Kaur Dhamoon, "Considerations on Mainstreaming Intersectionality," *Political Research Quarterly* 64, no. 1 (2011): 230-243, 230; Hill Collins, "Learning from the Outsider Within," 132; Robert P. Mullaly, *Challenging Oppression: a Critical Social Work Approach* (Don Mills: Oxford University Press, 2002); Sylvia Walby, Jo Armstrong, and Sofia Strid, "Intersectionality: Multiple Inequalities in Social Theory," *Sociology* 46, no. 2 (2012): 224-240;
15. Dhamoon, "Considerations on Mainstreaming Intersectionality," 233.
16. Eve Tuck, "Suspending Damage: A Letter to Communities." *Harvard Educational Review* 79, no. 3 (2009): 409-427.
17. Bailey, "Thinking Critically," 98.
18. Mariam Fraser and Nirmal Puwar, "Introduction: Intimacy in Research," *History of the Human Sciences* 21, no. 4 (2008): 1-16, 2.
19. Tiffany Page, "Vulnerable Writing as a Feminist Methodological Practice," *Feminist Review* 115, no. 1 (2017): 13-29, 15.
20. Bailey, "Thinking Critically," 92.

Bibliography

Anzaldúa, Gloria. *Making Face, Making Soul = Haciendo Caras: Creative and Critical Perspectives by Women of Color*. San Francisco: Aunt Lute Foundation Books, 1990.

Bailey, Lucy E. "Thinking Critically About 'Social Justice Methods': Methods as 'Contingent Foundations.'" In *Research Methods for Social Justice and Equity in Education*, 91-107. Cham: Springer International Publishing, 2019.

Bracken-Roche, Dearbhail, Emily Bell, Mary Ellen Macdonald, and Eric Racine. "The Concept of 'Vulnerability' in Research Ethics: An in-Depth Analysis of Policies and Guidelines." *Health Research Policy and Systems* 15, no. 1 (2017). https://doi.org/10.1186/s12961-016-0164-6.

Cannella, G. "Foreword." In *Disrupting Qualitative Inquiry: Possibilities and Tensions in Educational Research*, edited by Ruth Nicole Brown, Rozana Carducci, and Candace R. Kuby, xv-xvi. New York: Peter Lang, 2014.

Cascio, M. Ariel, and Eric Racine. "Person-Oriented Research Ethics: Integrating Relational and Everyday Ethics in Research." *Accountability in Research* 25, no. 3 (2018): 170-197. https://doi.org/10.1080/08989621.2018.1442218.

Collins, Patricia Hill. "Learning from the Outsider Within: The Sociological Significance of Black Feminist Thought." *Social Problems* 33, no. 6 (1986): S14-S32. https://doi.org/10.1525/sp.1986.33.6.03a00020.

Crenshaw, Kimberlé. "Mapping the Margins: Intersectionality, Identity Politics, and Violence Against Women of Color." *Stanford Law Review* 43, no. 6 (1991): 1241-1299. https://doi.org/10.2307/1229039.

Dhamoon, Rita Kaur. "Considerations on Mainstreaming Intersectionality." *Political Research Quarterly* 64, no. 1 (2011): 230-243. https://doi.org/10.1177/1065912910379227.

Fraser, Mariam, and Nirmal Puwar. "Introduction: Intimacy in Research." *History of the Human Sciences* 21, no. 4 (2008): 1-16. https://doi.org/10.1177/0952695108095508.

Gahman, Levi, and Gabrielle Legault. "Disrupting the Settler Colonial University: Decolonial Praxis and Place-Based Education in the Okanagan Valley (British Columbia)." *Capitalism, Nature, Socialism* 30, no. 1 (2019): 50-69. https://doi.org/10.1080/10455752.2017.1368680.

Luna, Florencia. "Identifying and Evaluating Layers of Vulnerability—A Way Forward." *Developing World Bioethics* 19, no. 2 (2019): 86-95. https://doi.org/10.1111/dewb.12206.

Luna, Florencia, and Sheryl Vanderpoel. "Not the Usual Suspects: Addressing Layers of Vulnerability." *Bioethics* 27, no. 6 (2013): 325-332. https://doi.org/10.1111/bioe.12035.

Mullaly, Robert P. *Challenging Oppression: A Critical Social Work Approach*. Don Mills: Oxford University Press, 2002.

Page, Tiffany. "Vulnerable Writing as a Feminist Methodological Practice." *Feminist Review* 115, no. 1 (2017): 13-29. https://doi.org/10.1057/s41305-017-0028-0.

Parson, Laura. "Considering Positionality: The Ethics of Conducting Research with Marginalized Groups." In *Research Methods for Social Justice and Equity in Education*, edited by K.K. Strunk and L.A. Locke, 15-32. Cham: Springer, 2019.

Peter, Elizabeth, and Judith Friedland. "Recognizing Risk and Vulnerability in Research Ethics: Imagining the 'What Ifs?'" *Journal of Empirical Research on Human Research Ethics* 12, no. 2 (2017): 107-116. https://doi.org/10.1177/1556264617696920.

Rideau, Ryan. "'We're Just Not Acknowledged': An Examination of the Identity Taxation of Full-Time Non-Tenure-Track Women of Color Faculty Members." *Journal of Diversity in Higher Education* 14, no. 2 (2019): 161-173. https://doi.org/10.1037/dhe0000139.

Tuck, Eve. "Suspending Damage: A Letter to Communities." *Harvard Educational Review* 79, no. 3 (2009): 409-427. https://doi.org/10.17763/haer.79.3.n0016675661t3n15.

UNHCR—UN Refugee Agency. "Rohingya Emergency." March 3, 2023. https://www.unhcr.org/rohingya-emergency.html.

Walby, Sylvia, Jo Armstrong, and Sofia Strid. "Intersectionality: Multiple Inequalities in Social Theory." *Sociology* 46, no. 2 (2012): 224-240. https://doi.org/10.1177/0038038511416164.

6

The Messiness of Applying Feminist Research Principles
Reflections on Researching Rape Culture on Campus

Rebecca Godderis, Debra Langan, and Marcia Oliver

Student activists have been raising their voices for decades about rape culture on campus and the prevalence of sexual violence at universities. We became interested in understanding how students at our own campus understood rape culture following several high-profile incidents at Canadian universities. In September 2013, students at Saint Mary's University and the University of British Columbia were filmed repeating chants that condoned sexually assaulting underage girls during orientation and frosh week activities.[1] Early in 2014, the University of Ottawa made headlines when a student leader from the university was targeted with violent sexual comments in a private Facebook conversation with colleagues[2] and then again when sexual assault allegations were made against the University of Ottawa hockey team.[3] These incidents were widely documented by various media outlets and problematized as a sign of rape culture on university campuses, pushing university administrators at these institutions to take action.[4]

The research we reflect on in this chapter was developed in the months following these incidents and carried out from July 2014 to July 2015.[5] In the years since our research was completed, there has been a shift in relation to addressing the issue of sexual violence at Canadian universities, including several provincial governments passing legislation requiring post-secondary institutions to have stand-alone sexual assault policies and to direct funds toward resources related to education and support.[6] However, at the time our research was conducted, there were few explicit conversations about rape culture and sexual violence on campuses, and there was no separate sexual violence office at our university that provided education, training, or support for survivors. We were keen to understand how our students were responding to the headlines about these incidents and to better understand their views on rape culture.

It was important to us that our approach to studying rape culture was explicitly feminist. Rape culture is evidence of the persistence of patriarchal structures and practices, and feminist research creates opportunities to disrupt these systems and actions. However, as Eleanor Whittingdale writes, "the interface between theory and practice—between thinking as a feminist and doing as a feminist methodologist—is a liminal space where ambivalences, contradictions and anxieties are far from absent."[7] Similarly, we found that applying feminist research principles was a messy endeavour that pushed us to question key methodological choices we had made, leading to a sense of vulnerability. What if we didn't make the right decisions as researchers? What if we made mistakes? This chapter explores these experiences of vulnerability using specific examples from our study about students' perceptions and experiences of rape culture. In addition, we engage with the concept of *situated ethics*, as articulated by Bella Vivat, to consider how we may modify our approach to feminist research principles in the future depending on the specific research context.[8]

A key methodological goal of our research was to explicitly and intentionally apply the following interrelated feminist research principles: (1) reflexivity and recognizing the positionality of the researchers in relation to the research process,[9] (2) reducing the hierarchies of power within the research process itself,[10] and (3) understanding research as an intervention directly connected to feminist goals of changing structures of oppression.[11] To apply these three principles, we decided to form a research team that integrated student research assistants (RAs) from our campus so that we could meaningfully involve the RAs in *all aspects* of the research project, including as focus group facilitators.

The goal of this approach was to address the central power dynamic within the research, which was related to our positionality as full-time permanent faculty. Our campus is relatively small, and it was highly likely that we would know student participants in the focus groups or that we could have them as students in future classes—thereby being in a position of grading their academic work. Even if we did not know the students, we thought the inherent power differentials between faculty and students may make it more difficult for students to talk openly about experiences related to rape culture. Additionally, most students on our campus enter directly from high school, so it is common for there to be a significant age difference between faculty and students, which can also contribute to a hierarchical power dynamic.

Prior to advertising to recruit the student RAs, the faculty researchers felt that organizing focus groups where individuals who identified as women met separately from those who identified as men would create a more comfortable space to speak openly about rape culture. As a result, we decided to hire two RAs who identified as women and two RAs who identified as men. We recognize now that we upheld binary conceptions of gender, which we should have challenged more thoroughly in all aspects of our research. With respect to trans, non-binary, and gender-diverse RAs and participants, we did emphasize that RAs and participants could self-identify their gender; however, we would now employ a much more inclusive concept of gender from the very beginning of project conceptualization through to methodological and analytical decisions. We would also note that challenging the gender binary is particularly important for researchers studying rape culture because, as critics have noted, the concept itself tends to overlook the disproportionate levels of gender-based violence that trans and non-binary communities experience[12] while also "orient[ing] the target of intervention on heteronormative depictions of male-on-female violence—obfuscating and sometimes erasing the intersectional complexities of violence involving same-sex relationships, trans, and gender non-binary people."[13]

In September 2014, the research team was assembled, and we began team development and training. True to the feminist principles of reflexivity and locating oneself in relation to the research, the team meetings involved everyone sharing their own experiences and understandings of "rape culture." Over several sessions, the team worked to build a consensus about the definition of rape culture:

> Rape culture is a complex set of beliefs, values, and practices that normalize and perpetuate sexual violence. In other words, it refers to how we all think [about] and do things in our lives that make sexual violence seem normal. Rape culture affects everyone, but it is also a gendered phenomenon; it is experienced differently by men and women. Additionally, we believe that we are all, at some level, participants in rape culture, but that we can also continue to engage ourselves and others to work towards not perpetuating rape culture.

This definition is important because it represents a collective understanding of rape culture as developed by the team; however, we do want to again acknowledge that the definition upholds the gender binary. If we were to repeat the study this would be brought to the forefront in conversations with the research team.

A unique part of this definition is the recognition that we are all participants in rape culture. This aspect of the definition came from extensive discussions about the nature of rape culture and how deeply embedded rape culture is in our social worlds. For example, we discussed that sexual violence is often normalized in the music we listen to, the movies and TV shows we watch, and the books we read, and thus these ideas seep into our language and our worldviews. As a team we wanted to acknowledge this complicity in rape culture, even if it was unintentional, and to appreciate how hard we all must work to unlearn rape culture. This recognition disrupts the idea that somehow, as researchers, we could exist outside of our own culture and thus be unaffected by it. The process of developing a collective definition was time-consuming, but it was also highly beneficial in terms of developing relationships among members of the research team while also upholding the understanding that the research process itself is a feminist political intervention.

Using this definition as the core concept around which to centre discussions, the RAs completed 11 focus groups (3 groups with men and 8 with women) during a three-month period with 36 participants in total (9 men and 27 women). The research team—faculty and RAs—met weekly throughout the data collection period to debrief what occurred during each focus group. The verbatim transcripts of the focus groups, fieldnotes made during the debriefing sessions, and conversations among faculty researchers about the focus groups following the completion of the research project inform the reflections in this chapter about the messiness of applying feminist research principles in practice. The remainder of this chapter will focus on two significant methodological tensions related to the complexity of peer-to-peer discussions of rape culture that left us feeling the most vulnerable: the significant number of disclosures of sexual violence and the challenges of RAs facilitating discussion groups on this topic with their peers. Integrated into the discussion of these tensions are reflections about our own emotive responses as researchers and what we would consider doing differently in the future.

Disclosures of Sexual Violence during the Women's Focus Groups

As feminist researchers going into this project, we anticipated that if we talked with students—especially students who identify as women—about their experiences of rape culture, there would be disclosures of sexual violence. For decades, studies have consistently demonstrated that approximately 20 per cent of women-identified students in Canada and the United States will experience sexual assault while completing their post-secondary education, and many more individuals experience other forms of sexual harassment and dating violence.[14] We also thought it likely that those who experienced violence would be drawn to the research. Because of these expectations, we specifically focused on preparing the RAs with disclosure training by experts from our local sexual assault centre. However, since the focus of the project was on the broader concept of rape culture, we thought that the conversations would centre more on cultural issues such as norms and myths rather than on individual, personal disclosures of violence. We were, quite simply, wrong.

What we came to understand through the focus groups is that rape culture *is* sexual violence. That is, participants did not distinguish between the more abstract concept of "rape culture" and their experiences of interpersonal violence. Therefore, our original definition, which aimed to separate the "cultural" aspects of rape culture from personal experiences of violence, was a false dichotomy. This was an empirical finding from the research that surprised us; we had considered rape culture in academic and theoretical terms—as a concept that was distinct from other academic concepts—and we had set out to study this single, specific idea. What we did not account for, and what our participants demanded that we see, is that the concept of rape culture cannot exist as disconnected from the impacts of that culture. Women-identified participants spoke about how rape culture and the resulting experiences of a wide range of sexual and gender-based violence, from street harassment to sexual assault, could be an everyday occurrence for them. For example, when asked where she had heard about the idea of rape culture, one participant said, "it's just kind of like being a woman experiencing life on a day-to-day basis," demonstrating how she knows rape culture through her direct experiences of violence.

A wide range of personal experiences of violence were shared during the focus groups, including being followed home from the grocery store, catcalled on the streets around the university, and groped at bars by strangers. Disclosures also included sexual abuse experienced as a child, sexual assault within the context of an ongoing relationship, and rape that occurred after a night out with friends. In some of the women-identified focus groups, *every single participant* in the room disclosed an experience of violence, with some women describing multiple experiences. We found that through disclosing their experiences, the focus groups became sites for collective support and solidarity building among participants. For us as feminist researchers, this was the most valuable aspect of the research, and it spoke to the power of research as feminist intervention. We had an opportunity to see solidarity being fostered among survivors, and many participants were provided with new resources that we hoped could help them heal from the violence they had experienced.[15]

However, the emotional impact of the focus groups on the research team was significant and led to many moments of vulnerability. As faculty members, we became increasingly concerned about what was being asked of the graduate and undergraduate RAs who were running these groups. A significant amount of emotional labour was required for the RAs to navigate the focus groups. Information about the local sexual assault centre was provided to every participant in the focus groups, and warm introductions to the centre's staff were provided when individuals indicated they were interested. However, we continue to wonder if the provision of these resources was enough. More specifically, although our desire was to employ feminist principles to reduce power differentials within the research context, we began wondering whether it was appropriate to ask RAs to lead these groups on their own.

While we had strong relationships with the RAs and debriefed every focus group as a research team and one-on-one if needed, as the project progressed, the nagging feeling grew that it may all be too much. The RAs expressed that they enjoyed leading the groups, but they also spoke of how exhausting it was to constantly be receiving disclosures, hearing stories of violence, navigating the group's responses in those moments, and on top of it all, regulating and processing their own emotional and embodied reactions. As faculty we also felt tired. We carried the concern for our RAs and research participants constantly in our minds and our bodies. We still do. We wonder whether we did enough to help everyone navigate the weight of sharing personal experiences of violence. At the same time, we also worry about whether this interpretation of the project is too paternalistic and makes assumptions that RAs and student participants cannot handle conversations about sexual violence and rape culture. After all, there was a lot of positive feedback about the study in terms of the opportunities it provided to talk about topics that are usually silenced.

These tensions left us feeling vulnerable about whether we had made the best feminist research decisions. In reflecting on the project, we have asked ourselves the following questions: Did we think of power too literally in terms of only considering more traditional, academically defined hierarchical relationships of power between faculty and students? Perhaps we should have thought in more complex ways about the power dynamics involved in navigating conversations about violence. More specifically, the power of our positionality means we have safeguards that could help us better navigate the challenges of leading focus groups about rape culture. For example, as faculty researchers and university instructors, we already had significant experience with disclosures and facilitating conversations about violence. We also have access to supports like a robust health insurance plan that covers services like psychotherapy, medication, and other benefits, all of which contribute to our overall well-being and can be easily accessed during times when we are feeling particularly overwhelmed. Additionally, it is our professional role and responsibility to undertake research, and because of this expectation our research endeavours are supported institutionally in a variety of ways, including having access to supportive colleagues who can debrief difficult research scenarios.

These experiences reminded us of the importance of Bella Vivat's concept of *situated ethics*, which underscores the need for researchers to consider the variety of contexts they encounter in their work and modify research principles to suit the specific situation at hand.[16] In this case, while we were attempting to practise feminist research principles that would reduce hierarchies of power in research, the methodological messiness we encountered pushed us to realize that we did not consider the full complexity of what "power" meant in this context. We focused only on the potential power that was present in the relationship between participant and focus group facilitator. What we did not consider fully were the vulnerabilities of the lower-paid, more precariously positioned RAs who were the members on the research team that were most directly hearing stories of violence and responding to disclosures.

Based on our experiences with this project, we recommend that researchers interested in pursuing rape culture research understand that for many participants rape culture *is* sexual violence. As such, researchers must be prepared for a truly significant numbers of disclosures related to a wide variety of experiences of sexual violence and harassment. We want to emphasize again that we did anticipate there would be some disclosures during the focus group sessions and, as a result, had organized a disclosure training with our local sexual assault centre with the full research team, and we had several other conversations about the topic during team meetings. However, what we did not anticipate was the sheer number of disclosures and the sharing of life-altering experiences of violence such as childhood sexual abuse. Given these experiences, now we recognize that "being prepared" as a research team should involve a more careful consideration who is best positioned to facilitate focus group conversations about violence and what supports are available to those facilitators. As one possible strategy, we recommend allocating funds for a counsellor with specific expertise in sexual violence to lead/co-lead the focus groups or to be present in the session (or immediately after the session) to support the focus group leaders and group participants. A second preparation strategy would be research teams to consider the pace of data collection. We recommend allowing for one to two weeks between focus groups to debrief and process the stories that are heard during the sessions.

Peer-to-Peer Discussions and Unintended Harm

We also did not anticipate how challenging peer-to-peer discussions about rape culture could be and what difficult circumstances could arise for the RAs. When debriefing with the RAs after the focus groups and reading over the transcripts, we became increasingly concerned about the potential for unintended harm, including moments that could be experienced as microaggressions and/or forms of violence against individuals in the room—both RAs and participants. These moments included the reinforcement of damaging myths and stereotypes about rape, rape culture, and gender norms. Below we provide one poignant example of what we have called *demanding interactions* from a focus group with individuals who identified as men to illustrate these concerns. Demanding interactions require the facilitator of the group to find a way to intervene in conversations that uphold oppressive ideas (such as sexist or racist comments) that may lead to an experience of harm toward those in attendance. Whereas positivist approaches to research uphold the idea that the focus group facilitator should remain objective and neutral in these moments, the explicit feminist research principles we were enacting disrupt these assumptions by not only seeing the focus groups as an opportunity to generate data but also as a chance to increase understandings of what rape culture is and how it manifests. Interventions such as these can also contribute to creating spaces where participants feel safe enough to engage in conversation.

The conversation we highlight next took place when the RAs and participants in the focus group were discussing norms relating to masculinity. One of the participants engaged in—what we as faculty interpret as—homophobic comments directed at one of the RAs. This part of the conversation happened after one of the RAs had revealed how he was labelled gay in high school because he did not conform to the "football jock" ideal. The following exchange ensued:

Participant: And, and I can see, uhm, and I mean, I don't mean to be offensive in any way, but I can tell exactly why they would have labelled you gay. You know what I'm saying?
RA: Sure. [Laughing]
Participant: Yeah. [Laughing]
RA: [Laughing] I'm not offended. I've got [inaudible] of my sexuality.

Participant: [Laughing]
RA: Uh, yeah. No, no that's fine. Uh, what are your thoughts, [name of other participant]?

As faculty we read this interaction as a replication of the homophobic harm the RA had previously experienced during high school. As per our research protocols, we had one faculty member on call during each focus group session that could be contacted if the RA needed assistance either during or after the focus group ended. We also debriefed the focus group with the full research team within the week that the group was held. The RAs did not contact us following the focus group and we discovered this interaction during the research team debrief. We talked about it as a group and offered extra debriefing and one-on-one support to the RAs involved in the focus group (including from professionals who were not part of the research team). Both RAs present during this focus group stated they were okay and did not need further support, but we remained uneasy about this interaction, and it weighed heavy on us as faculty members. Again, we were left with many questions: Was our RA harmed in this moment? How were participants impacted? Were we putting too much emphasis on the moment and thus being paternalistic? Is it possible that the RA did not experience this as violence or harm? Or perhaps they experienced it as a negative interaction but not one that had a significant impact?

While we did expect that challenging topics could come up during the group conversations and provided training regarding navigating difficult conversations, upon reviewing the transcripts, we began to wonder whether the peer-to-peer relationship made the negotiation of these moments more difficult than if there had been a greater power differential between researcher and participant. While this is just one example, our experience was that even within the relatively short duration of the data collection period of four months, there were numerous demanding interactions that RAs had to negotiate on their own, including forms of "slut-shaming" that occurred in the women-identified focus groups. It became clear to us that conversations about rape culture opened a complicated social terrain of norms relating to gender and sexuality. We began to question our decision to reduce the power between focus group facilitator and participant because doing so seemed to increase the risk of discussions unfolding in ways that could be harmful to all involved. As discussed in work by Preissle and Han on feminist research ethics, "reducing the ethical tensions of unequal status may only open the way to ethical dilemmas of living among peers,"[17] we wonder whether this was a risk that could have been mitigated by involving facilitators who had more expertise and/or authority.

Thus, similar to the recommendations provided in the previous section, we encourage researchers interested in studying rape culture to carefully consider the use of peer-led focus groups. Our experience with this project points to the importance of understanding how differences in age, experience, and authority may change the nature of demanding interactions and thus increase or reduce the potential for harm. In addition, reflecting on this project has also reminded us that focus groups are a highly complex form of data collection. Researchers may also want to consider other methodologies, such as interviews or surveys, if the research team is unable to secure focus group facilitators who are best suited to lead conversations about rape culture.

Conclusion

Feminist methodology remains a vital component of undertaking research on the topic of rape culture, yet we argue that it is also valuable for researchers to recognize the messiness of applying feminist methodological principles in practice. At the start of our research, we identified three key interrelated feminist methodological principles we wanted to apply in practice: reflexivity and recognizing the positionality of the researchers, reducing hierarchies of power, and understanding research as a feminist intervention. In this chapter, we outlined two significant tensions we experienced when applying these principles to our study of students' experiences of rape culture on campus: the significant number of disclosures of sexual violence and the challenges of RAs facilitating discussion group about rape culture with their peers. These challenges led us to feel a sense of vulnerability and to question some of our methodological choices. As a result, our primary recommendation is that other researchers think carefully about who is best suited to lead focus group discussions about rape culture. These reflections contribute to collective knowledge about how to grapple with maintaining a commitment to feminist principles while acknowledging the vulnerabilities that can arise as we engage in research.

Notes

1. Elizabeth Quinlan, "Introduction: Sexual Violence in the Ivory Tower," in *Sexual Violence at Canadian Universities: Activism, Institutional Responses, and Strategies for Change*, eds. Elizabeth Quinlan, Andrea Quinlan, Curtis Fogel, Gail Taylor (Wilfrid Laurier University Press, 2017), 1–23.
2. Canadian Press, "Anne-Marie Roy, uOttawa Student Leader, Subject of Explicit Online Chat," *CBC News*, March 2, 2014, https://www.cbc.ca/news/canada/ottawa/anne-marie-roy-uottawa-student-leader-subject-of-explicit-online-chat-1.2556948.
3. James Bradshaw, "University of Ottawa Men's Hockey Team Suspended Over Alleged Sex Assault," *Globe and Mail*, March 3, 2014, https://www.theglobeandmail.com/news/national/university-of-ottawa-suspends-hockey-team-over-serious-misconduct/article17201525/.
4. Quinlan, "Introduction: Sexual Violence in the Ivory Tower."
5. This project was made possible with funding from Wilfrid Laurier University. The authors extend their thanks to the Women's Campus Safety Committee, Diversity and Equity Office; Dean, Faculty of Liberal Arts; Dean, Faculty of Human and Social Sciences; and the Office of the Dean of Students at Laurier Brantford.
6. Diane Crocker, Joanne Minaker, and Amanda Nelund, "Introduction to Sexual Violence on Canadian University Campuses: New Challenges, Novel Solutions," in *Violence Interrupted: Confronting Sexual Violence on University Campuses*, eds. Diane Crocker, Joanne Minaker, and Amanda Nelund (Montreal: McGill-Queen's University Press, 2020), 3–17.
7. Eleanor Whittingdale, "Becoming a Feminist Methodologist while Researching Sexual Violence Support Services," *Journal of Law & Society* 48, Suppl. 1 (2021), S10–S27.
8. Bella Vivat, "Situated Ethics and Feminist Ethnography in a West of Scotland Hospice," in *Subjectivities, Knowledges, and Feminist Geographies: The Subjects and Ethics of Social Research*, eds. Liz Bondi, Hannah Avis, Ruth Bankey, Victoria Ingrid Einagel, Amanda Bingley, and Joyce D. Davidson (Lanham: Rowman & Littlefield, 2002), 249, 240–244, 250–51.
9. Sharlene Nagy Hesse-Biber and Deborah Piatelli, "The Feminist Practice of Holistic Reflexivity," in *The Handbook of Feminist Research: Theory and Praxis*, ed. Sharlene Nagy Hesse-Biber (London: Sage, 2012): 557–582.
10. Ann Oakley, "Interviewing Women: A Contradiction in Terms?" in *Doing Feminist Research*, ed. Helen Roberts (London: Routledge, 1981); Ann Oakley, "Interviewing Women Again: Power, Time and the Gift," *Sociology* 50 (2016).
11. Susan Strega and Leslie Brown, "Transgressive Possibilities," in *Research as Resistance: Critical, Indigenous, and Anti-oppressive Approaches*, eds. Leslie Brown and Susan Strega (Toronto: Canadian Scholars' Press, 2005), 1–17.
12. Andrea L. Wirtz, Tonia C. Poteat, Mannat Malik, and Nancy Glass, "Gender-based Violence against Transgender People in the United States: A Call for Research and Programming," *Trauma, Violence, & Abuse* 21, no. 2 (2018): 227–41.

13. Marcus Sibley, "A Genealogy of 'Rape Culture': Knowing and Governing Sexual Violence" (PhD diss., Carleton University, 2021), 12.
14. Walter DeKeseredy and Katharine Kelly, "The Incidence and Prevalence of Woman Abuse in Canadian University and College Dating Relationships," *Canadian Journal of Sociology* 18 (1993): 137-159; Kate Carey et al., "Incapacitated and Forcible Rape of College Women: Prevalence across the First Year," *Journal of Adolescent Health* 56, no. 6 (2015): 678-680; Government of Ontario, "Student Voices on Sexual Violence," March 2019, https://www.ontario.ca/page/student-voices-sexual.
15. For further discussion of these aspects of the research, see Marcia Oliver, Rebecca Godderis, and Debra Langan, "Alternative Practices and Politics of Care: Women Students' Experiences of Rape Culture and Sexualized Violence on Campus," in *Violence Interrupted: Confronting Sexual Violence on University Campuses*, eds. Diane Crocker, Joanne Minaker and Amanda Nelund (Montreal: McGill-Queen's University Press, 2020).
16. Vivat, "Situated Ethics."
17. Judith Preissle and Yuri Han, "Feminist Research Ethics," in *The Handbook of Feminist Research: Theory and Praxis*, ed. Sharlene Nagy Hesse-Biber (Thousand Oaks: Sage, 2012), 593.

Bibliography

Bradshaw, James. "University of Ottawa Men's Hockey Team Suspended Over Alleged Sex Assault." *Globe and Mail*, March 3, 2014. https://www.theglobeandmail.com/news/national/university-of-ottawa-suspends-hockey-team-over-serious-misconduct/article17201525/.

Canadian Press. "Anne-Marie Roy, uOttawa Student Leader, Subject of Explicit Online Chat." *CBC News*, March 2, 2014. https://www.cbc.ca/news/canada/ottawa/anne-marie-roy-uottawa-student-leader-subject-of-explicit-online-chat-1.2556948.

Carey, Kate B., Sarah E. Durney, Robyn L. Shepardson, and Michael P. Carey. "Incapacitated and Forcible Rape of College Women: Prevalence across the First Year." *Journal of Adolescent Health* 56, no. 6 (2015): 678-680.

Crocker, Diane, Joanne Minaker, and Amanda Nelund. "Introduction to Sexual Violence on Canadian University Campuses: New Challenges, Novel Solutions." In *Violence Interrupted: Confronting Sexual Violence on University Campuses*, edited by Diane Crocker, Joanne Minaker, and Amanda Nelund, 3-17. Montreal: McGill-Queen's University Press, 2020.

DeKeseredy, Walter, and Katharine Kelly. "The Incidence and Prevalence of Woman Abuse in Canadian University and College Dating Relationships." *Canadian Journal of Sociology* 18 (1993): 137-159.

Government of Ontario. "Student Voices on Sexual Violence." March 2019. Accessed July 7, 2021. https://www.ontario.ca/page/student-voices-sexual.

Hesse-Biber, Sharlene Nagy, and Deborah Piatelli, "The Feminist Practice of Holistic Reflexivity." In *The Handbook of Feminist Research: Theory and Praxis*, edited by Sharlene Nagy Hesse-Biber, 557-582. Thousand Oaks: Sage, 2012.

Oakley, Ann. "Interviewing Women: A Contradiction in Terms?" In *Doing Feminist Research*, edited by Helen Roberts, 194-97. London: Routledge, 2018.

Oakley, Ann. "Interviewing Women Again: Power, Time and the Gift." *Sociology* 50 (2016): 195-213.

Oliver, Marcia, Rebecca Godderis, and Debra Langan. "Alternative Practices and Politics of Care: Women Students' Experiences of Rape Culture and Sexualized Violence on Campus." In *Violence Interrupted: Confronting Sexual Violence on University Campuses*, edited by Diane Crocker, Joanne Minaker, and Amanda Nelund, 69-86. Montreal: McGill-Queen's University Press, 2020.

Preissle, Judith, and Yuri Han. "Feminist Research Ethics." In *The Handbook of Feminist Research: Theory and Praxis*, edited by Sharlene Nagy Hesse-Biber, 583-605. Thousand Oaks: Sage, 2012.

Quinlan, Elizabeth. "Introduction: Sexual Violence in the Ivory Tower." In *Sexual Violence at Canadian Universities: Activism, Institutional Responses, and Strategies for Change*, edited by Elizabeth Quinlan, Andrea Quinlan, Curtis Fogel, and Gail Taylor, 1-23. Waterloo: Wilfrid Laurier University Press, 2017.

Sibley, Marcus A. "Genealogy of 'Rape Culture': Knowing and Governing Sexual Violence." PhD dissertation, Carleton University, 2021.

Strega, Susan, and Leslie Brown. "Transgressive Possibilities." In *Research as Resistance: Critical, Indigenous, and Anti-oppressive Approaches*, edited by Leslie Brown and Susan Strega, 1-17. Toronto: Canadian Scholars' Press, 2005.

Vivat, Bella. "Situated Ethics and Feminist Ethnography in a West of Scotland Hospice." In *Subjectivities, Knowledges, and Feminist Geographies: The Subjects and Ethics of Social Research*, edited by Liz Bondi, Hannah Avis, Ruth Bankey, Victoria Ingrid Einagel, Amanda Bingley, and Joyce D. Davidson, 236-252. Lanham: Rowman & Littlefield, 2002.

Whittingdale, Eleanor. "Becoming a Feminist Methodologist while Researching Sexual Violence Support Services." *Journal of Law & Society* 48, Suppl. 1 (2021): S10-S27.

Wirtz, Andrea, Tonia C. Poteat, Mannat Malik, and Nancy Glass. "Gender-based Violence Against Transgender People in the United States: A Call for Research and Programming." *Trauma, Violence, & Abuse* 21, no. 2 (2018): 227-241.

III

Reflections on Contemporary Approaches to Key Methods and Concepts

Disrupting Codified Academic Norms through Decolonization

Emily Grafton, Moses Gordon, Cheyanne Desnomie, Cassandra Opikokew Wajuntah, and Bettina Schneider

This chapter is a critical reflection of the research norms that accentuate vulnerabilities and become codified within the Canadian academic system. We confront and disrupt these systemic and Western academic practices that often predetermine what research is, the types of research projects that receive funding, how research is disseminated, and whom it is meant to serve. We examine the challenges of doing Indigenous and decolonial research within the neoliberal academy as a colonial institution and focus on the institutional barriers that have been created through academic norms, research funding models, and mainstream dissemination expectations.

Grounded within an Indigenous research methodology known as *keeoukaywin*, the Visiting Way,[1] we gathered regularly as a group, casting a critical decolonial lens to these challenges. Throughout this chapter, we balance academic scholarship with our discussions or *keeoukaywin*. We ask: how might decolonial approaches to academic norms transform institutional barriers into opportunities? In what ways have we experienced the co-optation of decolonial measures in Western academia? In what ways have we seen an authentic lifting of colonial barriers?

This chapter offers a synopsis of contemporary scholarship concerning Indigenous and decolonial research practices that reflects how Western academia systemically predetermines research procedures and thereby limits the transformation of research in a good way. By this, we mean research that is authentically informed by specific Indigenous worldviews grounded through respectful relationships among beings (human and non-human, those who came before, and those yet to come), lands, skies, waterways, and Indigenous ways of knowing and being. The chapter explores our lived experiences with Indigenous-centred and decolonizing research to transform Western academia and disrupt its codified academic norms that foster vulnerabilities.

Disruptive Methodologies

Indigenous and decolonial research methodologies are relatively new academic disciplines. These require an engaged researcher to respect Indigenous values and ways of knowing, being, and doing. For too long, research involving Indigenous peoples and communities has been based on Western colonial methods of gathering and analyzing data that reduce peoples to repositories of data to be extracted and exploited.[2] Many Indigenous communities believe that Indigenous peoples are among the most studied on Earth,[3] and historically this has often occurred through questionable methods and murky ethics. Fortunately, due to pressures from Indigenous communities and researchers, these practices are being replaced.

Throughout this chapter, we examine the vulnerabilities that result from academic norms, arguing that these vulnerabilities can hold negative outcomes for research, but with a nuanced understanding they hold the potential for positive outcomes. The negative outcomes include those systemic vulnerabilities created by colonially enforced power relations and are reproduced through research that makes Indigenous peoples and communities vulnerable through deficit-setting parameters, racist intent, and colonial constructs. These systemic vulnerabilities created by codified academic norms, while traditionally intended to marginalize Indigenous knowledge systems to benefit colonial orders, have undergone a dialectical reversal and can result in negative outcomes for Western academia. The process of decolonization often entails the creation of new institutional structures or the revision of existing institutional processes that may shift power dynamics away from academic executives toward community stakeholders; this shift involves a relinquishing of power that may be unacceptable for decision makers within university institutions. We argue that colonial institutions become more vulnerable, in a negative way, when they cannot adapt to decolonial research practices. While decolonial research methodologies are increasingly included in research proposals and applications and given lip service by many academics, we are seeing Western institutions failing to adapt to decolonial research practices and instead co-opting decolonial methodologies, engaging in research with suspicious ethical codes, creating reputational damage that impacts their institutions, and producing depleted and stagnant scholarly work that lacks both research innovation and resounding benefit to Indigenous communities.

While codified academic norms result, as noted, in negative systemic vulnerabilities, we also see that relational vulnerability, as defined by Brown, can create positive outcomes.[4] Relational vulnerability creates both discomfort and inner conflict in individuals that, when addressed through worthwhile self-work, can lead to transformation, innovation, and creativity. A key argument of this chapter is that decolonizing methodologies require researchers to do self-work by questioning what they have been taught, what they think and feel, and what they have normalized. When people confront the emotions of discomfort and inner conflict that come from being vulnerable and "having the courage to show up when you can't control the outcome," they often end up experiencing positive outcomes such as resilience, transformation, and innovation.[5] The persistence of Indigenous communities, scholars, and allies in shifting, decolonizing, and taking back research demonstrates resilience and the transformation of systemic vulnerabilities into positive research outcomes.

We see relational vulnerability as a strength in our research programs. For example, while we can point to codified research norms intended to suppress Indigenous resilience, we—the authors—do not see ourselves as vulnerable in this research paradigm. We follow in the wake of renegade Indigenous scholars such as Smith, Kovach, and Wilson,[6] who created space for various Indigenous worldviews beyond Western colonial confines. One example of such an Indigenous worldview is humility. There are many additional values that are Indigenous-oriented.[7] We argue that humility is required in Indigenous and decolonizing research practices.

Being humble takes strength, determination, and resilience. For many Indigenous peoples, the idea of being humble and expressing humility is an understanding that humans are but a small part of a larger picture and just one piece of a whole. To those who do not subscribe to such a worldview, this understanding of humility can often be mistaken for vulnerability, but this is surely not the case in our research experiences.

While the academy remains a colonial and Western space, the harmful manner in which research has been conducted on Indigenous peoples is changing. This colonial space, however, has shaped our lived experiences with codified research norms. For context, imperial colonialism can be described as a global system of political economy that once encouraged European nation-states to invade, conquer, and assimilate peoples and lands around the world. These forces remain entrenched and are often understood as the ongoing projects of settler colonialism. For example, in what has become Canada, Indigenous peoples' lives continue to be regulated by oppressive state structures that are designed to ensure their marginalization.[8] This occurs through, for example, substandard education and healthcare, elevated child apprehension rates, and disproportionate levels of incarceration.[9] Within academia, this colonial presence is demonstrated in the underrepresentation of Indigenous students and faculty, marginalized Indigenous knowledge systems and pedagogies, and the continuation of the harmful research practices discussed above—all of which lead to a range of vulnerabilities for Indigenous peoples in academe.

These practices of colonialism are ongoing in the face of decolonizing efforts in post-secondary institutions. Decolonization in academia relies on the wide-ranging processes and actions intended to dismantle ongoing colonial oppression by addressing inequities.[10] At universities, decolonial efforts typically target research practices, institutionalized power imbalances, and curriculum and pedagogical practices that re-enforce assimilation.[11] These efforts create space for those Indigenous worldviews, which are often viewed incorrectly as vulnerabilities.

This colonial orientation to the academy is further compounded under neoliberalism, which introduces heightened competition in academic practices based on status, merit, and narrowed conceptualizations of innovation.[12] In these ways, neoliberalism fosters an environment of intense rivalry among faculty members and graduate students that results in the insatiable pursuit of ever more and larger research funds and higher-profile publications. Yet we argue that this intensification results in growing institutional vulnerabilities for both Indigenous scholars and colonial institutions. As scholars with no training in disruptive methodologies scramble to engage in innovative decolonial research, surface engagement results in significant deficits in research applications, procedures, and outcomes.

As post-secondary institutions and faculty compete over research funds related to Indigenous peoples and the number of Indigenous students and faculty they can attract, the process of Indigenization, or the recentring Indigenous worldviews in Western-dominated spaces, has become commodified and is inauthentically applied to further colonial institutional pursuit of program dollars, reputation, or publications. These outcomes are dramatically different from their intended purpose, which contributes to the vulnerabilities falsely associated with Indigenous worldviews. As Bettina explained, many Western academic researchers partner with Indigenous scholars and institutions without meaningfully including them in the research. The partnerships are often "more for the institutional name and connections with First Nations communities" and to enhance their own credibility with grant funding agencies than for the academic contributions that these scholars and institutional partners can make. Emily added to this notion of superficiality: "My expertise is not always recognized and instead tokenized, because the complexity of Indigenous worldviews is often unrecognized. Part of this tokenizing process is that we get pulled out of where we are the expert and this process depletes scholarship." Cassandra summarized these lived experiences: "The work is tangential to what you're doing. The tokenization on both a personal level and an institutional level demonstrates so much privilege of those situated to benefit from the colonial institution."

It is in the face of these colonial and neoliberal hostilities that Indigenous communities and Indigenous (and allied) researchers continue to transform research practices to challenge power relations and the resulting negative vulnerabilities. This transformation is evident in the growing number of frameworks and ethics surrounding Indigenous research. Concerns surrounding data governance and data sovereignty are being addressed via the principles of ownership, control, access, and possession (OCAP®) as established through the First Nations Information Governance Centre, the data sovereignty policies developed by the

Inuit Tapiriit Kanatami, or data stewardship with the Métis Nation. Collective concerns around Indigenous populations are also addressed through various commissions and studies, such as the Report of the Royal Commission on Aboriginal People; the Final Report of the Truth and Reconciliation Commission and its Calls to Action; the Final Report of the National Inquiry into Missing and Murdered Indigenous Women and Girls and its accompanying Calls for Justice; Chapter 9 of the Tri-Council Policy Statement; and the United Nations Declaration on the Rights of Indigenous Peoples.

Decolonial and Indigenous research methodologies use these frameworks and ethical alignments but go beyond the regulatory mandates: these are guided by Indigenous epistemologies and worldviews. Smith[13] explains that Indigenous research methodologies tend to recognize that cultural protocols, values, and behaviours are an integral part of methodologies. Kovach echoes this and has stated that the focus of Indigenous research methodologies "ought to be a deep concentration of worldview or paradigm."[14] To engage in these methodologies is to move beyond the confines of traditional academia that is bound in textbooks, archives, and neoliberal competition—it is to be gifted knowledge through relational methodologies that are grounded in specific worldviews of Indigenous nations.

There are distinctions between Indigenous and decolonial research methodologies, but these are not always clear with shifting boundaries determined by the research at hand. We have found that both Indigenous and decolonial research intentionally disrupts, dismantles, and challenges colonial inequities, vulnerabilities, and oppression. Where the two diverge is around Indigenous knowledge systems. Decolonial research sometimes applies Indigenous worldviews to Western practices. Indigenous research, on the other hand, is inherently and unequivocally built from an Indigenous worldview to transcend Western research applications.

While there are distinctions, these research practices are clearly compatible and complementary. In our discussions, Bettina stated that "you can't actually do decolonial research until you decolonize yourself. It's critical to understand what the word *decolonize* means and how that really impacts research." In order to decolonize, non-Indigenous researchers must be open to new ways of knowing introduced by Indigenous worldviews; they must choose cultural humility and cultural competence. Turvalon and Murray-Garcia define *cultural humility* as "a lifelong commitment to self-evaluation and critique, to redressing power imbalances...and to developing mutually beneficial and non-paternalistic partnerships with communities on behalf of individuals and defined populations."[15] Cultural humility requires honesty and humility in interactions with Indigenous peoples and communities as one component to shifting those power relations that, through colonial practices, embed vulnerabilities. Greene-Moton and Minkler explain that *cultural competence* helps researchers to "interact effectively with people of different cultures" while acknowledging that no one can truly be competent in another's culture.[16] In addition to cultural humility and competence, decolonization also requires relational vulnerability, as noted earlier. Brown sees relational vulnerability as a strength and driver of creativity, transformation, and more authentic relationships: "we need to be vulnerable in order to build trust."[17]

Decolonization must not only deconstruct disciplinary ways of valuing and thinking and derived from colonial systems through cultural humility and competence, but it also "must offer a language of possibility, a way out of colonialism."[18] One example is Indigenization, which is often considered an approach that requires one to not only decolonize, but also to provide a way forward that prioritizes Indigenous ways of knowing and methodologies and offers that language of possibility beyond colonial systems and ways of thinking. Both research approaches—Indigenous and decolonial—require researchers to undergo a process of decolonization, and they work complementarily to decentre the intellectual imperialism of Western knowledge and research methods. Both ought to be practised with Indigenous communities, be grounded in ceremony, use culturally appropriate methods of data collection and dissemination that are specific to the community involved, follow appropriate cultural protocols, and privilege that community's lived experiences and worldviews, making time for travel, storytelling, and relational learning.

Neither Indigenous or decolonial research methodologies are meant to dismiss Western approaches completely, but rather to encourage researchers to theorize based on culturally appropriate notions and worldviews to create meaningful and useful research for Indigenous peoples.[19] Due to the diversity of Indigenous groups across the globe, there is also no one definitive way or methodological practice used by researchers to decolonize or Indigenize research methodologies.[20] The first step is to understand that Western post-secondary institutions and academia are steeped in colonial processes of generating knowledge. The best way to understand Indigenous knowledge is to be open to accepting different realities,[21] because to do disruptive research without decolonizing one's methods is to continue to perpetuate colonial norms.

keeoukaywin: The Visiting Way

We are a small group of both Indigenous and non-Indigenous scholars based out of the University of Regina and First Nations University of Canada. We came together to visit and discuss our experiences of engaging in Indigenous and decolonial research and the barriers that we have faced. In order to do so, *keeoukaywin*, or the Visiting Way, was invoked to share stories and experiences and interrogate academic norms.

keeoukaywin as a research methodology demonstrates and reinforces the significance of Indigenous ways of relating that are expressed through visiting and disseminated in research.[22] It builds on Wilson's reflections on storytelling: "When you look at the relationship that develops between the person telling the story and the person listening to the story, it becomes a strong relationship,"[23] which is fundamental to Indigenous research. By coming together as a group on Treaty 4 (the lands of the nêhiyawak [Cree], Nakawēk/Anihšināpēk, Dakota, Lakota, and Nakoda nations and the homeland of the Métis and Michif nations), we were able to participate in what Archibald et al. explain as a shared dialogue:[24] speaking in ways that resonate with each other, we identified common barriers and discussed power relations that reinforce vulnerabilities and create opportunities for disruption. Emily is a member of the Métis Nation and is a guest to this region from Treaty 1. Cheyanne is nēhiýaw-iskwêw from Peepeekisis Cree Nation in Treaty 4 territory. Moses is Saulteaux, Plains Cree, and Métis from the George Gordon First Nation in the Touchwood Hills of Treaty 4 territory. Cassandra is nēhiýaw-iskwêw from Canoe Lake Cree First Nation in Treaty 10 territory in northern Saskatchewan and now lives on Treaty 4 territory with her husband and four children, who are all members of Standing Buffalo Dakota Nation. Bettina is non-Indigenous, originally from the United States, and has been a guest on Treaty 4 since 2006.

Gaudet explains that *keeoukaywin* can equip researchers to recognize the gifts inherent within self, kinship, place, and land. In our discussions, we frequently acknowledged this emphasis on relationships, with gratitude for *keeoukaywin*: Bettina shared, "This has been fun getting to know each other and learning and understanding each other's perspectives and thoughts. And that's so critical because so many research groups come together, and don't know each other." We were also reminded by Gaudet that as researchers who are engaged in decolonial and Indigenous research, we have to ask ourselves how we can give back, uphold respect, receptivity, and reciprocity while being mindful of what our research may unsettle.[25]

Disrupting Codified Research Norms

This section discusses the "research norms" that we, the authors, have experienced as codified within Canadian academic practices. Considering the expansion of Indigenous and decolonial research, we specifically want to flag those barriers that remain within academia that limit the application and effectiveness of this growing field and its ability to disrupt codified Western-based research practices. We specifically consider the institutional barriers that have been created through research funding models and mainstream dissemination expectations. In this section, we balance academic scholarship with our discussions, or *keeoukaywin*, using it as both our research methodology and to disrupt Western standards of scholarship, such as relying on citing the published work of those with whom we are not in relationship or those who might uphold colonial power relations.[26]

Research Funding Models

Codified research norms are expressed in various ways, and research funding models are a critical aspect of setting and maintaining these norms. These models increasingly support research grant applications that include a large number of partners, co-applicants and collaborators; often, the more partners/collaborators, the more successful the grant applications. As noted by Changfoot et al., "In Canada, the national research granting bodies increasingly fund 'partnership'-based research (whether with private, public, or non-profit sector partners)" and expect that those who will benefit from the research are involved in the production and dissemination of the knowledge generated by the research.[27] It is the neoliberal academic model that has led to this increased demand for larger funding grants.[28]

While partnership-based research offers a collaborative model that has many benefits, it can lead to grant applications and proposals submitted by researchers and institutions or communities that have very little association with or understanding of one another prior to the application. Because Indigenous research paradigms are founded on relationality,[29] this lack of relationship and connection—especially given the ideas with which they are expected to engage—can lead to challenges, conflict, and misunderstandings that can derail the research, or worse, mask a lack of meaningful and rich partner involvement.

In order to gain access to research grant funding, many Indigenous communities and early career academics will partner with more established scholars, who typically then serve as principal investigators (PIs) on grant applications. While the applications indicate that research projects will be team/partnership collaborations, in practice the accountability and decision-making frameworks are largely defined by the PIs.[30] Unless an Indigenous community has robust research capacity and/or Indigenous-led research collaborations that prioritize Indigenous concerns and needs, those more senior scholars or PIs will control the research paradigm and accountability frameworks used. Furthermore, PIs, particularly those who serve in a nominated fashion (an NPI), reap additional benefits as their affiliated institutions are sometimes solely awarded indirect research costs.[31] This can lead to conflict for Indigenous scholars and communities when those leading the work are not well-informed about the values and standards of Indigenous-framed or decolonial research—consider the aforementioned brief summary of regulatory bodies—and can disadvantage emerging Indigenous academics who are not PIs or NPIs on grants. Thus, as Last explains, "many international (and local) research projects are driven by agendas or practices that stand in complete opposition to decolonial ideas."[32]

These neoliberal processes of competition further push out Indigenous scholars who have different or non-Western expectations for research, including prioritizing community transformation, well-being, or betterment instead of data collection, publications, professional advancements, or other common Western research-related tenets. Alternatively, Cassandra described "Robin Hooding it": "I don't think that's an actual research term, but that's what we call it." Emily put this in context of commitments to Indigenous communities: "That's the point, isn't it? It's about allocating money in community to address inequity or amplify voices of strength or resilience so that other communities might hear them." Cassandra clarified the importance, as an Indigenous researcher, of reinforcing community priorities over neoliberal academic agendas: "The activism part is the only reason I'm still in academia. I'm much more interested in the advocacy and the activism of it than the tenure track." The allocation of research dollars to "address inequity or amplify voices" is a direct challenge to colonial research norms that have not prioritized cultural humility or competence with Indigenous communities.

As noted by numerous scholars, Indigenous-centred, decolonizing research requires intentions for transformation, but this work ought to also include Indigenous worldviews as central to and guiding the research process.[33] Some argue that Indigenous-framed research starts with and is primarily about relationship[34] and reciprocity,[35] much like we have attempted to model through our practice of *keeoukaywin*. Western methods and theories may dominate when individual researchers and/or research teams attempt to conduct Indigenous research without proper training in and understanding of Indigenous research methodologies. As Datta notes, "Researcher epistemology frames the way we see the world, the way we organize ourselves in it, the questions we ask, and the solutions we seek."[36] Even if some of the co-applicants have this training and understanding, it is often the PI and/or senior scholars on the team who will direct the research methods and the narratives of its findings.

All co-researchers ought to be trained in decolonial and Indigenous-centred epistemological and methodological frameworks. If they are not, research teams may experience significant conflict and even dissolve. Research partners and collaborators can have differing epistemological frameworks, but without training and clarity around appropriate methodologies, many teams will falter. Funding agencies ought to require all those engaging in Indigenous research to train in Indigenous research paradigms and methodologies before they are granted both ethics and funding support to conduct studies with Indigenous research participants. As Bettina states, "Research teams must foster meaningful relationships early on to ensure there is a good methodological and epistemological fit amongst the research team before embarking on a research application together." Relationships lacking this foster, in the face of decolonial research, several vulnerabilities. Colonial institutions might co-opt decolonial methodologies or approach research programs inauthentically. This may jeopardize authentic relationships with Indigenous communities or ignore the community's protocols and dismiss the intended outcomes of decolonization, community benefit, and capacity building.

As we discussed what constitutes researching in a good way with Indigenous communities, our visiting shifted to defining Indigenous-centred research versus Indigenous-framed decolonial research and we exchanged ideas on developing more distinctions between these practices. Emily explained the premise: "I've started to make a clearer distinction between Indigenous and decolonial research. Through studying Cree or sitting in ceremony—these experiences fundamentally changed my understanding of myself and Indigenous worldviews from superficial to deeper. I realized that, because I lack the lens of language, I do decolonial not Indigenous research." Cheyanne responded: "I think that's a really important distinction to recognize that these two research methodologies are different. The impact of colonialism on Indigenous peoples is common globally, and decolonizing research recognizes those commonalities, which is different from Indigenous methodologies that have a specific worldview." Cassandra agreed and suggested more flexibility in defining Indigeneity in Indigenous research: "Just because you're Indigenous, what you do isn't an Indigenous methodology by its nature. Nor does it need to be. We need to expand our definition of who is Indigenous enough to do Indigenous research methodology, because I hear a lot of young Indigenous scholars who say 'Well, I grew up in an urban area. I don't speak the language.' This doesn't make your research any less valid: You have other lenses you can put on it that have value." Our *keeoukaywin* thus demonstrates that for those who remain entrenched in Western norms, colonial research fosters vulnerabilities. However, this landscape is changing and much emerging Indigenous scholarship is ripe with opportunity.

Mainstream Dissemination Expectations

The reach of codified research norms that enforce vulnerabilities extends to mainstream dissemination expectations as well. This can present various challenges to those taking up research with Indigenous communities who might not prioritize the publication of their data and research outcomes within broader academic journals or conferences. All researchers working with Indigenous communities should be aware of the First Nations principles of OCAP®, which "assert that First Nations have control over data collection processes, and that they own and control how this information can be used."[37] The OCAP® principles support First Nations data sovereignty, which emphasizes the laws and governance structures of First Nations that guide how data is to be "collected, protected, used and shared."[38] In the past, many researchers might not have considered the resulting data of a research project to be owned by the communities. This has led to all sorts of misused and abused statistics and understandings of Indigenous peoples that policymakers or program developers might use to reinforce colonial inequities among Indigenous communities.

Expectations of knowledge mobilization, as a codified research norm, insert pressure to publish that can often lead to rushed processes, lower-quality submissions, tenuous research partnerships that have not been properly cultivated, and increased conflict with research partners because of poor communication and misaligned expectations. How research dissemination is codified in academia and the publish-or-perish atmosphere led our *keeyoukaywin* to a discussion of quality versus quantity. Often, it seems that quantity of publications is valued in tenure packages and performance reviews, instead of ensuring quality work that makes contributions to closing a knowledge gap or benefiting the community one is working with. As Emily explained, for Indigenous scholars, there are alternative forms of evaluation at play with publications: "When I think about a potential publication, I think about who I am: I'm not a traditional person, but I do still have responsibilities to Indigenous knowledge systems and the communities who share these with me. I am selective, and say no to projects I deem disingenuous. Publish or perish does not consider contributions to intergenerational knowledge or relational responsibilities."

The publish-or-perish mentality can likewise lead to exploitative research, which occurs when researchers are more committed to their own research agendas and any advantages or benefit the research will afford them rather than the needs and priorities of their research participants or the communities with which they are engaged.[39] That said, we argue that decolonial work can shift these power relations and, through a dialectical arrangement, create new vulnerabilities for those colonial institutions or Western-oriented scholars who do not adapt to authentic decolonial practices: They are made vulnerable by perpetuating ineffective and outdated academic norms and practices, thus producing stagnant and irrelevant research. For example, when Western scholars are not knowledgeable about decolonial and Indigenous research methodologies and protocols, they do not embrace cultural humility and cultural competence. This leads to exploitative power dynamics, distrust, and fractured relationships, placing them (and their research) in vulnerable spaces. According to Wilson, relationality and holding oneself accountable to the relationships one develops through research are fundamental pillars of an Indigenous research paradigm.[40] As Cassandra commented, "Really good community-based research with an Indigenous research methodology is an intimate encounter with an energy exchange. I don't know how anyone could start the research without thinking of reciprocity." This concept of relationality is rooted in traditional teachings about spirituality, reciprocity, and interconnectedness,[41] and it must exist for authentic work to occur that does not enhance vulnerabilities for those unseasoned in disruptive methodologies.

Indigenous research is often community based and can easily be overlooked when pooled with other grant proposals that are deemed to have a broader reach or large-scale impact through knowledge dissemination practices. Western models often stand in contrast to local, community-centred goals. As Bettina explained of this epistemological conflict, "One of the key criteria used to assess research proposals and grant applications is whether research projects can access additional grant funds. Because Indigenous research projects are often community focused and local in their focus, they are not necessarily looking to have national reach." Cassandra responded: "They want to stay local and contextual. That's their strength. They're not looking to scale up because that's not usually the nature of Indigenous work. You don't want to generalize." Bettina: "That's exactly it. This requirement of many larger research grants sets up some Indigenous research proposals for failure when that's one of the key criteria used to assess research proposals. These research projects are focused on community; they are community driven and very locally focused." The notion of generalizability—removing theory from its derived context to be applied in policymaking or program development elsewhere—has historically led to harmful mainstream dissemination practices for Indigenous communities.[42] These processes of generalization conflict with our traditional teachings: take what you want and leave the rest. This is a common reference among knowledge guardians inferring that Indigenous knowledges are inherently based in specific place, time, and relational modes and ought not be removed from these contexts.

We see the normative practices of Western neoliberal post-secondary contexts, which focus on increases in granting dollars and publications, as conflicts for the growing field of Indigenous and decolonial research practices. The Western model of research often views knowledge as an acquirable commodity of the researcher rather than wisdom developed through an equal exchange that is meant to benefit the community as a whole.[43] Such regimented institutional barriers—established through colonial knowledge pursuits and continued through neoliberal competitiveness—limit the application and effectiveness of this growing field and its ability to disrupt codified research norms and do research in a good way, placing colonial institutions and scholars new to the field in increasingly vulnerable positions.

Conclusion

Our work on this chapter has been grounded within an Indigenous research methodology known as *keeoukaywin*, the Visiting Way. We met regularly as a group throughout the development of this work, using the methodological approach as a platform from which to confront the exploitative institutional forces that are pervasive within Western neoliberal academia. Our conversations were candid and took place through a critical and decolonial lens, privileging Indigenous lived experiences within the colonial institutions that make up the academy. We discussed at length the systemic barriers that we face as a community of scholars in conducting Indigenous research within the academy, including conversations revolving around research funding models and mainstream expectations of dissemination and project outcomes. We noted that while these forces directly contradict many basic tenets of Indigenous and decolonial research, we also found that this environment is—at the same time—slowly awakening to the realities of its colonial relationship with Indigenous communities at large. In fact, while exploitative research has historically made Indigenous communities and researchers vulnerable in academia, this is changing: The increase in regulatory safeguards and growing methodological approaches are shifting power relations and it might soon be those institutions unwilling or unable to follow suit with cultural humility and cultural competence that are left vulnerable in the wake of decolonial practices. It is our hope the Indigenous and decolonial research practices continue to gradually and authentically lift systemic colonial barriers and provide meaningful opportunities that can influence positive changes for the Indigenous peoples of this land.

Notes

1. Janice Gaudet, "Keeyoukaywin: The Visiting Way—Fostering an Indigenous Research Methodology," *Aboriginal Policy Studies* 7, no. 2 (2019).
2. Linda Tuhiwai Smith, *Decolonizing Methodologies* (London: Zed Publishing, 2012).
3. Shawn Wilson, *Research is Ceremony: Indigenous Research Methods* (Halifax: Fernwood Press, 2008).
4. Brené Brown, *Dare to Lead* (New York: Random House, 2018).
5. Vanessa Ciccone, "'Vulnerable' Resilience: The Politics of Vulnerability as a Self-improvement Discourse," *Feminist Media Studies* 20, no. 8 (2020), 1316.
6. Smith, *Decolonizing*; Margaret Kovach, "Conversational Method in Indigenous Research," *First Peoples Child & Family Review* 5, no. 1 (2010): 40-48; Wilson, *Research*.
7. For more, see Marie Battiste and James Youngblood Henderson, *Protecting Indigenous Knowledge and Heritage* (Saskatoon: Purich Publishing Ltd., 2000).
8. Joyce Green, "Towards a Détente with History: Confronting Canada's Colonial Legacy," *International Journal of Canadian Studies* 12, no. 1 (1995): 89.
9. James S. Frideres and René R. Gadacz, *Aboriginal Peoples in Canada*, 9th ed. (Don Mills: Pearson Canada, 2012), 4-10.
10. Marie Battiste, *Decolonizing Education: Nourishing the Learning Spirit* (Saskatoon: Purich Publishing Ltd., 2013).
11. Rauna Kuokkanen, *Reshaping the University: Responsibilities, Indigenous Epistemes and the Logic of the Gift* (Vancouver: University of British Columbia Press, 2007).
12. Angela Last, "Internationalisation and Interdisciplinarity: Sharing Across Boundaries?," in *Decolonising the University*, eds. Gurminder K. Bhambra, Dalia Gebrial, and Kerem Nişancıoğlu (London: Pluto Press, 2018), 208-230.
13. Smith, *Decolonizing*.
14. Kovach, "Conversational Method," 40.
15. Melanie Tervalon and Jann Murray-Garcia, "Cultural Humility Versus Cultural Competence: A Critical Distinction in Defining Physician Training Outcomes in Multicultural Education," *Journal of Health Care for the Poor and Underserved* 9, no. 2 (1998), 123.
16. Ella Greene-Moton and Meredith Minkler, "Cultural Competence or Cultural Humility? Moving Beyond the Debate," *Health Promotion Practice* 21, no. 1 (2020), 143.
17. Brown, *Dare*, 30.
18. Smith, *Decolonizing*, 204.

19. Kovach, "Conversational Method"; Wilson, *Research*; Jo-ann Archibald, Jenny Bol Jun Lee-Morgan, and Jason De Santolo, "Introduction: Decolonizing Research: Indigenous Storywork as Methodology," In *Decolonizing Research: Indigenous Storywork as Methodology*, eds. Jo-ann Archibald, Jenny Bol Jun Lee-Morgan, and Jason De Santolo (London: Zed Books, 2019).
20. Archibald, Lee-Morgan, and De Santolo, "Introduction."
21. Battiste and Henderson, *Protecting*.
22. Gaudet, "Keeyoukaywin."
23. Shawn Wilson, "What is an Indigenous Research Methodology?" *Canadian Journal of Native Education* 25, no. 2 (2001), 178.
24. Archibald, Lee-Morgan, and De Santolo, "Introduction."
25. Gaudet, "Keeyoukaywin," 53.
26. Sara Ahmed, *Living a Feminist Life* (London: Duke University Press, 2017).
27. Nadine Changfoot, Peter Andrée, Charles Z. Levkoe, Michelle Nilson, and Magdalene Goemans, "Engaged Scholarship in Tenure and Promotion: Autoethnographic Insights from the Fault Lines of a Shifting Landscape," *Michigan Journal of Community Service Learning* 26, no. 1 (2020): 256.
28. Last, "Internationalisation."
29. Robert A. Innis, "Elder Brother as Theoretical Framework," in *Sources and Methods in Indigenous Studies*, eds. Chris Anderson and Jean M. O'Brien (New York: Routledge, 2017), 135-142.
30. Bob Kayseas, personal communication to Bettina Schneider, June 11, 2021.
31. Research Support Fund, "Grant Calculations," 2023, https://www.rsf-fsr.gc.ca/apply-demande/calculations-eng.aspx?pedisable=true.
32. Last, "Internationalisation," 216.
33. Bettina Schneider and Bob Kayseas, "Indigenous Qualitative Research," in *The SAGE Handbook of Qualitative Business and Management Research Methods*, eds. Catherine Cassel, Ann Cunliffe, and Gina Grandy (Thousand Oaks: Sage, 2017), 154-72; Smith, *Decolonizing*.
34. Innis, "Elder."
35. Wilson, *Research*.
36. Ranjan Datta, "Decolonizing Both Researcher and Research and its Effectiveness in Indigenous Research," *Research Ethics* 14, no. 2 (2018): 9.
37. First Nations Information Governance Centre, "The First Nations Principles of OCAP," 2021, https://fnigc.ca/ocap-training/.
38. First Nations Information Governance Centre, "First."
39. Smith, *Decolonizing*; Datta, "Decolonizing."
40. Wilson, *Research*.
41. Bagele Chilisa, *Indigenous Research Methodologies* (London: Sage, 2012); Schneider and Kayseas, "Indigenous."
42. Smith, *Decolonizing*.
43. Schneider and Kayseas, "Indigenous," 159.

Bibliography

Ahmed, Sara. *Living a Feminist Life*. London: Duke University Press, 2017.

Archibald, Jo-ann, Jenny Bol Jun Lee-Morgan, and Jason De Santolo. "Introduction: Decolonizing Research: Indigenous Storywork as Methodology." In *Decolonizing Research: Indigenous Storywork as Methodology*, edited by Jo-ann Archibald, Jenny Bol Jun Lee-Morgan, and Jason De Santolo. London: Zed Books, 2019.

Battiste, Marie. *Decolonizing Education: Nourishing the Learning Spirit*. Saskatoon: Purich Publishing Ltd., 2013.

Battiste, Marie, and James Youngblood Henderson. *Protecting Indigenous Knowledge and Heritage*. Saskatoon: Purich Publishing Ltd., 2000.

Brown, Brené. *Dare to Lead*. New York: Random House, 2018.

Changfoot, Nadine, Peter Andrée, Charles Z. Levkoe, Michelle Nilson, and Magdalene Goemans. "Engaged Scholarship in Tenure and Promotion: Autoethnographic Insights from the Fault Lines of a Shifting Landscape." *Michigan Journal of Community Service Learning* 26, no. 1 (2020): 239–263.

Chilisa, Bagele. *Indigenous Research Methodologies*. London: Sage, 2012.

Ciccone, Vanessa. "'Vulnerable' Resilience: The Politics of Vulnerability as a Self-improvement Discourse." *Feminist Media Studies* 20, no. 8 (2020): 1315–1318.

Datta, Ranjan. "Decolonizing Both Researcher and Research and its Effectiveness in Indigenous Research." *Research Ethics* 14, no. 2 (2018): 1–24.

First Nations Information Governance Centre. "The First Nations Principles of OCAP." 2021. https://fnigc.ca/ocap-training/.

Frideres, James S., and René R. Gadacz. *Aboriginal Peoples in Canada*, 9th edition. Don Mills: Pearson Canada, 2012.

Gaudet, Janice. "Keeyoukaywin: The Visiting Way—Fostering an Indigenous Research Methodology." *Aboriginal Policy Studies* 7, no. 2 (2019): 47–64.

Green, Joyce. "Towards a Détente with History: Confronting Canada's Colonial Legacy." *International Journal of Canadian Studies* 12, no. 1 (1995): 85–105.

Greene-Moton, Ella, and Meredith Minkler. "Cultural Competence or Cultural Humility? Moving Beyond the Debate." *Health Promotion Practice* 21, no. 1 (2020): 142–145.

Innis, Robert A. "Elder Brother as Theoretical Framework." In *Sources and Methods in Indigenous Studies*, edited by Chris Anderson and Jean M. O'Brien, 135–142. New York: Routledge, 2017.

Kovach, Margaret. "Conversational Method in Indigenous Research." *First Peoples Child & Family Review* 5, no. 1 (2010): 40–48.

Kuokkanen, Rauna. *Reshaping the University: Responsibilities, Indigenous Epistemes and the Logic of the Gift*. Vancouver: University of British Columbia Press, 2007.

Last, Angela. "Internationalisation and Interdisciplinarity: Sharing across Boundaries?" In *Decolonising the University*, edited by Gurminder K. Bhambra, Dalia Gebrial, and Kerem Nişancıoğlu, 208–30. London: Pluto Press, 2018.

Schneider, Bettina, and Bob Kayseas. "Indigenous Qualitative Research." In *The SAGE Handbook of Qualitative Business and Management Research Methods*, edited by Catherine Cassel, Ann Cunliffe, and Gina Grandy, 154-172. Thousand Oaks: Sage, 2017.

Smith, Linda Tuhiwai. *Decolonizing Methodologies*, 2nd edition. London: Zed Publishing, 2012.

Tervalon, Melanie, and Jann Murray-Garcia. "Cultural Humility Versus Cultural Competence: A Critical Distinction in Defining Physician Training Outcomes in Multicultural Education." *Journal of Health Care for the Poor and Underserved* 9, no. 2 (1998): 117-125.

University of Regina. "Research Cost Recovery." 2015. https://www.uregina.ca/policy/browse-policy/policy-RCH-030-005.html.

Wilson, Shawn. *Research is Ceremony: Indigenous Research Methods*. Halifax: Fernwood Press, 2008.

Wilson, Shawn. "What is an Indigenous Research Methodology?" *Canadian Journal of Native Education* 25, no. 2 (2001): 175-179.

8

A Familiar Stranger
Hindsight and Foresight Reflexivity, Multiple Interviews, and a Young Academic Interviewing a Young Mother

Amber-Lee Varadi

Stress: Excerpt from Second Interview

Amber: [turns on recorder] Okay. So, I guess—we were just talking so it's kind of weird to try and act like we weren't. [laughs]

April: It's okay. [laughs]

Amber: So, how have things been since we last interviewed you? It sounds like it's, ah—

April: Um, they've been good, but generally just, like, super busy and super stressful because...I'm graduating so I'm not coming back here...we were figuring out what I'm gonna do for college and...it's just been chaos for the last little bit...[My daughter] might be getting sick and there's, like, two weeks left of her school. About a week left of mine.

I really need her to be in school this week! Ugh! [sighs] Let's just pray. Just pray. [pauses] Stress. Busy. [groans]

Amber: Phew!

April: Yes![laughs]...I don't have energy to do anything at all. [forced laugh]

In her influential chapter on qualitative interviews, Oakley states that textbook paradigms often position interviewing as a "one-off affair,"[1] which has particular consequences for how one's data is to be collected. As a one-off affair, the interviewer must be clear and direct with her questions and make space for her interviewee to respond, typically through thoughtful prompts and maintaining one's role as a neutral, emotionally detached "silent listener."[2] With much methodological literature bolstered by this understanding of the objective one-off interview and dispassionate interviewer, there has been a lack of research discussing the longitudinal interviewer-interviewee relationship and the vulnerable and affective elements of interviewing. This traditional understanding of interviews has been challenged by a growing feminist literature that works to undermine the idea that the interviewer must be "tight and impenetrable."[3] Instead, feminist methodologies encourage interviewers to be engaged and interactive, suggesting that "[i]dentification with respondents enhances researchers' interpretive abilities, rather than jeopardizes validity...[and] can be a powerful source of insight."[4]

Attempting to use these traditional and feminist knowledges together in practice, however, can quickly create a tension in how the researcher feels she should approach her interviews, and this tension is precisely what I encountered across my first set of research interviews as an inexperienced interviewer. Indeed, it was one week before my twenty-third birthday and several months into my master's program when I conducted formal interviews as a graduate research assistant. With an intimate research team made up of two child and youth studies faculty members and me, we set out to learn about the impact of a summer mentorship program developed to support student parents. This was done with a sample of 11 young mothers attending the Young Parents Support Program (YPSP), a local alternative high school and childcare program for young parents, whom we planned to interview up to three times each across a seven-month period, where the same researcher would speak with the same interviewee in February, June, and September. Notably, some of the participants, such as the interviewee discussed in this chapter, only participated in two interviews due to their graduation from the program in July.

Accordingly, this chapter discusses the two interviews I had with a young mother (pseudo)named April, whose humorous, frank, and honest personality fostered an openness between us that undermined my textbook how-to knowledge of interviews. As my first formal interview in a paid research position, I held certain expectations with how I ought to behave in our first interview together, which aligned with my understanding of the researcher as "a certain type-of-person"[5]: rational and calculated yet warm and friendly. This balancing act of playing the good researcher, as suggested by much feminist research, produces irreconcilable contradictions within and beyond the interview, especially for researchers holding multiple interviews.[6] The analysis provided herein is threefold: (1) to discuss some tensions between traditional textbook knowledges and feminist knowledges on interview practices, (2) to introduce the concepts of hindsight reflexivity and foresight reflexivity, and (3) to consider the emotionality and vulnerability that become apparent in the interviewer-interviewee relationship through hindsight and foresight reflexivity.

Traditional Interviews versus Feminist Interviews: Knowledges in Tension

Key to the success of an interview, as suggested by traditional methodological knowledges, is the interviewer's professional competence and character: pleasant yet stoic, reserved yet interested.[7] As a novice researcher, I felt anxious that I would be perceived as too young, where my age would raise questions about my credibility as an effective researcher who could reliably learn about our participants' experiences. In an effort to minimize my anticipated problematic youthfulness, I visited YPSP in the guise of a capable and sophisticated professional, donning my only pair of dress pants and my then-girlfriend's work blazer while carrying around my university-branded clipboard and heaviest pen. In this sense, I simultaneously worked to differentiate myself from my similarly youthful participants while maintaining the power divide in our interviewer-interviewee relationship. This guise made me feel slightly more qualified—if not emotionally, then physically—and suggested, "Let there be no mistake…I am the researcher here to get information from you the respondent! We are not having any relationship but that of researcher and respondent."[8] As an aspiring feminist researcher, however, I soon realized how this guise could not only help me be read as more accomplished but also as more privileged, "bougie," and, consequently, judgmental and incapable of understanding or relating to this group of mostly working-class young mothers. Through my attempt to act and dress up as the "good" and legitimate researcher, I unintentionally played into the "paradigmatic representation of 'proper' interviews in the methodological textbooks…[that adopt] a masculine social and sociological vantage point than to a feminine one,"[9] where the researcher's detached objectivity maintains a hierarchy that grants them "The Power" to extract particular information from the interviewee,[10] and appeals to colonial and exploitative logics fuelling traditional knowledges about interviewing and Western research more generally.[11]

Fortunately, appearances can only go so far and April, my first interviewee for my research team's first set of interviews, was immediately warm, open, and seemingly comfortable with me when we started our interview, telling me about her semi-chaotic morning of running late to class and, in that process, stepping into a puddle of melted snow and getting her socks wet. Over an hour later, we finished our interview and I was feeling optimistic. *With an interview that long, how could it not be great? Think of all the useful data that will inform our research!* More than that, April and I seemed to get along well, where we shared laughter rather than any (dreaded) moments of silence.

After later reviewing this interview's transcript, however, I noticed areas of discussion surrounding April's mental health challenges that were missed. Compared to discussions about her dog and fiancé's side of the family, among other things, our conversations about mental health, feelings of loneliness, and stress seemed to be truncated and stopped short. This realization was initially shocking, as I was certain that no question went without an in-depth response (and subsequent banter). Through applying what I conceptualize as hindsight reflexivity, I was able to recognize where April's honesty and openness were met with dismissive humour and laughter, which I will discuss further below. I will also introduce foresight reflexivity to discuss how this form of reflexivity attends to a future, which can shape how one engages with both their transcript and next steps with interviewing.

Hindsight Reflexivity and Foresight Reflexivity

As I revisited April's transcript, I recognized a familiar stranger across the text. While I could recall many moments of vulnerability and honesty, I struggled to remember how I did not notice when some topics—especially poignant subjects concerning her well-being—were skimmed over. To address this gap in my memory and fieldnotes, I used what I call hindsight reflexivity to acknowledge where my expectations and beliefs about April's interview unravelled.

I define hindsight reflexivity as recognizing and making legible particular possibilities or limitations within the interview after it has occurred. Hindsight reflexivity is rooted in feminist methodological values to deepen our understanding of women's lives and experiences to reveal manifestations of inequality and oppression and produce transformative social change. This is done through a critical retrospection that is made possible through this practice's time-based positioning. As a form of reflexivity that is located and to be practised at any—and, better yet, several—moments *after* the interview, hindsight reflexivity recognizes how time is both cohesive and disintegrating, where our memories and affect(ion)s toward an interview, interviewee, or self as an interviewer may hold and mould across the days, spaces, events, and experiences we find ourselves in. With this, memories of our research practices are vulnerable—*exposed* to changes in time, place, and attitude; *at risk* of losing credibility to partiality; *at the mercy of* each individual researcher—and vulnerabilities in themselves.

Examples of this reflexivity can be revealed as one reflects on or relistens to an interview, and include feelings such as the loss or frustration of not probing after an interviewee's answer or the slight embarrassment of noticing how often you would chime in with a certain word in response to an interviewee's comments (as I had with the word *awesome* in my first interview with April), or noticing the ways that you related to (or only now presently relate to) an interviewee's circumstances due to similar social roles or events happening in your own life and how that sense of solidarity translated in your responses (e.g., "I totally understand") or subsequent analysis.

Using this hindsight reflexivity, I noticed various scenarios where April's laughter prompted me to move on from topics demanding her vulnerability. Grønnerød suggests that laughter is a diverse interactional resource used to relate with others that "has no universal meaning, so it must be interpreted in its context."[12] Accordingly, the reasons I moved on from some topics following laughter were not immediately clear to me, but hindsight considerations allowed me to notice how I unconsciously read April's laughter as an "established defenc[e] working to protect her from her own painful experiences"[13] and vulnerabilities. An example of this is when I asked April about her acts of self-care, and she admitted that she does not do any (see "Self-care" excerpt). Had I not been subconsciously prompted to move on from questions like this, it would have been clearer to me that the stressors in her life were having a much more detrimental effect on her than she made it seem. In other instances, shared moments of laughter simply distracted me from probing further about particular challenges, especially surrounding April's mental health struggles (see "Petty" excerpt).

Self-care: Excerpt from First Interview
Amber: So, do you take part in any self-care activities? So, like, right here [motioning to interview guide on the table we are sitting at] we have: take a bath, a nap, calling friends, going for a walk—
April: No.
Amber: No?
April: No. Like, I walk my dog every night, pretty much, after the kids go to bed, if it's not too cold. I've been slacking on that because it's been wet and cold and shitty.
Amber: Yeah.
April: I just cop out. I'm just like [to the dog], "go in the backyard." [laughs] Yup.
Amber: So—
April: I don't really—yeah.
Amber: No?
April: No.
Amber: Okay.
April: [laughs]

Petty: Excerpt from First Interview
April: You should've seen me yesterday. *I had a mental breakdown on my man* [fiancé] *for many, many reasons, but yesterday was a bad day.* I was very childish. [laughs] I'm petty when I get angry. Very petty. [italics added for emphasis]

Amber: Oh, a lot of people are. [laughs]
April: [laughs]

Indeed, while laughter in many ways fostered a sense of connection and understanding—an idea I will discuss further below—it also served as an affective tool for self-protection.

Beyond a self-scrutiny that prompts researchers to vulnerably acknowledge flaws and blind spots in their interviewing, hindsight reflexivity can also reveal how the interviewer's reactions can have consequences that highlight her inevitable bias, which may then shape an interviewee's response in both its content and form. This prompts one to consider how an interviewee's answer is hardly one that is stable, transparent, and "truth" beyond a particular point in time. Hindsight reflexivity, then, also works to destabilize the belief that it is possible to collect accurate and unbiased data by asking the "right" questions. Here, the benefit of multiple interviews becomes apparent, as they allow the interviewer to notice how responses and feelings change as an interviewee's circumstances shift across time and space, just as the interviewer's might have. Following hindsight reflexivity, I propose the importance of foresight reflexivity when using multiple interviews.

Foresight reflexivity involves the practice of anticipating what will be needed in the future based on affective insights and realizations from the previous interview. This is done by carefully reading the previous interview's transcript with an attentive intuition and emotional framing. Without this framing, the transcript will appear as nothing more than text, thereby eliding one's analysis of the valuable influence of affect and embodied performance in the interview context.[14] Foresight reflexivity consequently stands at tension with hegemonic understandings of the interviewer as in control and urges the interviewer to embody vulnerability as she makes space for the unresolved. This reflexivity works to normalize uncertainty and prompts interviewers to follow their hunches in order to seriously consider what they will do in their next interview.

After recognizing areas in April's transcript that were missed due to my being distracted or implicitly uncomfortable, foresight reflexivity encouraged me to consider how I could use these vulnerable moments to better prepare myself for our next interview, held four months later. With its emotional framing, my application of foresight reflexivity allowed me to develop some reflective questions for our second interview: How can I remain committed to April's narrative without moving on from a topic that is met with friction by April or myself? How can I engage with these unexpected moments of emotionality in a way that is not harmful, if at all?

These questions pushed me to thoughtfully consider how I could approach the sensitive topics that were often skimmed in April's first interview without being demanding, confrontational, or insensitive. These considerations were necessary, as this emotional navigation allowed me to better approach a part of April's life that perhaps many other young women and young mothers share. Without this foresight reflexivity, it is possible that I would have simply moved on from the same topics that were previously resisted with laughter. When I asked April about her wellbeing in our second interview, I was met with her familiar brief yet honest comments suggesting her "super unhealthy" coping mechanisms, followed by her laughter. Rather than mumble out the neutral "mhm" or repeat my clumsily stammered responses from our first interview (see "Self-care" excerpt), I made space for April to elaborate before asking a follow-up question to learn about her available supports and capacities for self-care (see "Coping" excerpt).

> **Coping: Excerpt from Second Interview**
> **Amber:** Is there anything you're doing right now that you feel is bad for you?
> **April:** ...My coping mechanisms are super unhealthy but I, like, need to focus on other things right now. So, for now, we're just gonna keep bottling things up. [laughs] For the next couple weeks.
> **Amber:** I think you said that a few months ago, too, though.
> **April:** And I've had quite a few mental breakdowns in between, and then I got new stuff [stressors], so we're gonna do that again. [laughs]
> **Amber:** Is there anything you feel that you could do to kind of tackle that now?

While April's laughter had both distracted and implicitly signalled me to move on from a particular topic to avoid potential discomfort for her or myself in our first interview, I was better prepared to address her humour, which often worked as a half-hearted follow-up in lieu of a personal response. Not included in the previous excerpt is April's in-depth response discussing how she was attempting to manage current stressors while new challenges continued to appear. These conversations prompted intimate moments of vulnerability—vulnerabilities that no textbook chapter prepared me for in the infamous one-on-one interview—that I felt better ready to handle through the questions and considerations that were developed using foresight reflexivity.

After reviewing April's transcripts, a "flaw" that I noticed in my interview technique included my quick comments following some responses in an attempt to be more lighthearted in comparison to the textbook classic: "mhm" (see "Stress," "Petty," and "Crying" excerpts). Applying hindsight reflexivity allowed me to consider the consequences of these quips, however, and while they may have indeed shaped April's responses, I believe that they fostered a solidarity between us, not just as young women, but as people with emotions and vulnerabilities who ought to make space to share those intimacies in whatever way we comfortably can with another person (see "Stress" and "Crying" excerpts). It is these vulnerable moments of togetherness where a researcher can step outside her role as the "good" interviewer who is an "attentive listener" in order to make the interview mutually nourishing for both her and her interviewee.[15]

Crying: Excerpt from Second Interview
Amber: Do, um—do you want to keep talking about this? We can, like, skip to positive things now.
April: [crying] No, it's okay. It doesn't matter. I'm fine. It doesn't matter, yeah.
Amber: Okay, okay.
April: I just haven't cried in a really long time, that's why I'm crying…It's just gonna come out cuz it's been a while.
Amber: It sounds like you're putting up—yeah. You're putting up a really tough front. Yeah.
April: [wiping away tears]
Amber: I always cry, so—
April: I cry all the time. It's so ridiculous! Ugh. But it does help.

Amber: It does.

April: I haven't cried in a long time, actually. It's been weeks, which is pretty good cuz I went through a crying-all-the-time phase. [wiping away tears]

With this, it is important for each interviewer to recognize the particular dynamics active in their interviewer-interviewee relationship. In the two interviews discussed, I spoke with an extroverted, honest, and headstrong young mother who was two years younger than myself. It is possible that our rapport was as jovial, open, and vulnerable as it was due to our similarities in age, gender, race, and challenges maintaining mental health and work-school-life balance.

The interview, moreover, is a "specialized location," where roles are "revealed, negotiated, and reframed."[16] With the more I got to know April, the more she reminded me of my sister, as they are about the same age and have similar fiery, straightforward, and good-humoured personalities. It is perhaps this negotiated role of familiarity that allowed us to "develop a relationship more akin to or resembling friendship or sisterhood than the conventional middle ground between stranger and friend,"[17] which helped me gently approach moments of discomfort when sharing emotional responses. As familiar strangers, our rapport was fostered through our similarities and solidarities and, perhaps most importantly, our shared awareness of the fleeting nature of our interviews. At one point in our second interview, April shared her feelings about the interview process: "It's actually nice cuz I don't know you. It's like I can go all verbal diarrhea." Thus, while our communication felt genuine, we nonetheless remained strangers.

The limitations and tensions following my textbook knowledges of interviews manifested in a sort-of-awkward, sort-of-funny way once April and I completed our final interview. Once I turned off the recorder, we shared some final remarks as we headed to the door of the interview room. Before reaching the door, however, April turned to me and asked if we could hug. I did not have the chance to respond before she hugged me and remember feeling slightly tense, wondering if we had crossed some ethical boundary that I should have made clearer across our two interviews. Thus, while emotionally entangled interviews may not be a part of everyone's research experience, I argue that it is valuable for qualitative research textbooks to highlight the emotionality, vulnerability, and solidarity that can arise across and beyond the interview process. To do this, however, these same textbooks must be committed to acknowledging the messiness of research, discuss the lack of control, objectivity, and neutrality the interviewer really holds, and therefore dismantle positivist assumptions that still have an insidious influence over qualitative research.

Embodied, Intuitive Interviewing and the Vulnerable Interviewer-Interviewee Relationship

While reviewing our transcripts, I noticed that I did not share much about myself, as encouraged across feminist research, to make our interview more of a fair exchange. At the same time, I hardly maintained the dispassionate and neutral disposition that I believed was expected from the interviewer, which may have worked as a subtle form of self-disclosure. Indeed, while I did not often stray from my research team's carefully composed interview guide, my genuine reactions reveal how interviewers are not neutrally positioned in the interview but, rather, play an active role. Moreover, my reactions of surprise (e.g., "oh my god!," "wow," "phew!") inherently bias or "contaminate" the data. While an interviewer's reaction does not explicitly suggest an opinion that immediately "colours" an interviewee's response, these reactions are produced through experiential knowledge, personality, and "attitudinal stances"[18] that open or close various ways that an interviewee may choose to respond across the rest of the interview. The emotional labour of balancing one's warm openness versus closed, business-like character, while often unstated, is expected from interviewers in traditional methodological textbooks outlining the "how-tos" of interviewing, where "[t]he motif of successful interviewing is 'be friendly but not too friendly.'"[19] All of this is possible, apparently—"[i]t is just a matter of following the rules."[20]

Reviewing the transcript for April's first interview, I often wondered if I maintained the acceptable friendly/too friendly balance. Through hindsight reflexivity, I determined that I may indeed have been "too friendly," as far as textbook expectations go. However, I also determined that this openness and playful rapport made it possible to discuss some deeper and more difficult topics later in our interviews (see "Stress," "Petty," and "Bleeding" excerpts).

Bleeding: Excerpt from First Interview

Amber: So, who or where do you commonly turn to when you need help?

April: ...I talk to my fiancé's dad a lot. I talk to him a lot cuz...I feel like he doesn't really listen but, like, at the same time, I can just, like, verbal diarrhea everything that's wrong and he's just like, "yeah, I totally get it." And I'm like, "you're not even listening but whatever. I got it all out at least."

Amber: "I hate having my period." He's like, "yup, me too."

April: Yeah! I'm like, "god, I'm bleeding! It's like *The Shining* elevators!" And he's like, "oh, girl, I get it."

Amber: ...[laughs] That's funny.

April: He's like, "you made me really uncomfortable." And I'm like, "yeah, well, I make a lot of people uncomfortable. Doesn't really make me uncomfortable."

This inability to determine the difference between appropriate friendliness and too much friendliness reveals how one's ability to be a "successful" interviewer is not simply a matter of following "the rules" but, rather, one's ability to follow their intuition. Foresight reflexivity, then, can be practised before or during an active interview, as it urges interviewers to not only consider what they will do in their next interview—if there is a next interview at all—but what they will do *next*, whether that is in their reaction or response or how they will ask the following questions. Moreover, applying foresight reflexivity during an interview further underscores how interviewing is not simply a matter of taking on a specific role (e.g., the feminist interviewer, the detached interviewer), but a process that is embodied, intuitive, and, at times, a communion between both interview participants.[21]

I believe that an interviewer's open disposition and ability to react, laugh, and share emotions may be a way to navigate the ethical tensions that some feminist researchers have considered with the practice of sharing calculated parts of themselves in order to cultivate rapport with their interviewees. Bloom and Grønnerød similarly suggest that laughter can work to strengthen the connection shared in the interviewer-interviewee relationship[22] by fostering mutuality and a feeling of togetherness that "reduce[s] the barriers of status, gender and other differences,"[23] which can help feminist researchers mitigate the power imbalance often imbued within this relationship. Indeed, much reflexive research by feminists questions their capacity to make these relationships less hierarchical when interviewers "are more free to leave the relationship than are the participants...[and] walk away with the interview data they wanted."[24] I often think about my interviews with April, which took place six years ago, and wonder if the fond and emotionally vivid memories I have of these "pseudo-conversations"[25] are a sign that I have not fully "walked away" from them. Perhaps an interviewer's ability to share her honest emotions through her reactions and interactions across the interview, whether that is in front of the interviewee or through practices of hindsight and foresight reflexivity, may foster a form of intimacy and connection that is genuine and transcends the interview setting.

Conclusion

Analyzing the strengths of multiple interviews revealed how each interview is a collaborative creation that results in data that is fundamentally shaped by the interviewer-interviewee relationship and the responses and reactions of both interview participants. While I had initially believed that I succeeded as a neutral researcher through my efforts to follow the interview guide and avoid self-disclosure, so as not to take priority from or bias my interviewee's "authentic" responses, my use of hindsight and foresight reflexivity across my interviews with April allowed me to notice the many ways I shaped the interview, for better or worse. This analysis reinforced the reality that "the complex emotional and intellectual forces that influence the conduct of our inquiry...are at once the source of our insight and our folly."[26]

The concepts of foresight and hindsight reflexivity have practical implications for feminist qualitative researchers. These contemporary approaches to the concept of reflexivity not only allow researchers to differently approach their (multiple) interviews, but also foster a careful reimagining of the possibilities of the interviewer-interviewee relationship and the key role of rapport and emotion in these relationships. An affective, personal rapport should not only be given to the interviewee across from us, but to the transcript afterwards as well. This rapport offers a responsibility to the transcript that is attentive to the moment of the interview as well as what we will do with this data next.

Interviewers are urged not to "lose themselves" to their own humanity in the interview. While they are expected to produce a conversational interview with a sense of ease, "good" interviewers must not become overly sociable, effusive, or personally invested.[27] My analysis, however, suggests that emotions and vulnerability, personal investment, and the acknowledgement and negotiation of our multiple social roles are not only necessary for foresight and hindsight reflexivity, but also beneficial for (multiple) interviews and one's understanding of themselves as an interviewer. With these considerations, it is valuable to reflect on the often-repeated question: *what makes a "good" interviewer?* It is possible that these vulnerable and personal reflections can bring us towards social change within our research relationships.

Notes

1. Ann Oakley, "Interviewing Women: A Contradiction in Terms," in *Doing Feminist Research*, ed. Helen Roberts (London: Routledge and Kegan Paul, 1981), 41.
2. Leslie R. Bloom, *Under the Sign of Hope: Feminist Methodology and Narrative Interpretation* (Albany: SUNY Press, 1998), 50.
3. Bloom, *Sign of Hope*, 22.
4. Bloom, *Sign of Hope*, 18.
5. Timothy J. Rapley, "The Art(fulness) of Open-Ended Interviewing: Some Considerations of Analysing Interviews," *Qualitative Research* 1, no. 3 (2001), 308.
6. Oakley, "Interviewing Women," 41.
7. Oakley, "Interviewing Women," 33–34.
8. Bloom, *Sign of Hope*, 48.
9. Oakley, "Interviewing Women," 38.
10. Oakley, "Interviewing Women," 34.
11. Linda Tuhiwai Smith, *Decolonizing Methodologies: Research and Indigenous Peoples*, 2nd ed. (London: Zed Books), 62.
12. Jarna Soilevuo Grønnerød, "On the Meanings and Uses of Laughter in Research Interviews: Relationships between Interviewed Men and a Woman Interviewer," *Young* 12, no. 1 (2004), 33.
13. Wendy Hollway and Tony Jefferson, *Doing Qualitative Research Differently: A Psychosocial Approach*, 2nd ed. (Thousand Oaks: Sage, 2013), 30.
14. Douglas Ezzy, "Qualitative Interviewing as an Embodied Emotional Performance," *Qualitative Inquiry* 16, no. 3 (2010): 163.
15. Bloom, *Sign of Hope*, 23.
16. Bloom, *Sign of Hope*, 27.
17. Bloom, *Sign of Hope*, 27.

18. Oakley, "Interviewing Women," 36.
19. Oakley, "Interviewing Women," 33.
20. Oakley, "Interviewing Women," 33.
21. Ezzy, "Qualitative Interviewing," 164.
22. Bloom, *Sign of Hope*, 20.
23. Grønnerød, "On the Meanings," 41.
24. Bloom, *Sign of Hope*, 35.
25. Oakley, "Interviewing Women," 32.
26. David N. Berg and Kenwyn K. Smith, *The Self in Social Inquiry: Researching Methods* (Thousand Oaks: Sage, 1988), 11, quoted in Wendy Hollway and Tony Jefferson, *Doing Qualitative Research Differently*, 30.
27. Oakley, "Interviewing Women," 34.

Bibliography

Berg, David N., and Kenwyn K. Smith. *The Self in Social Inquiry: Researching Methods*, 2nd edition. Thousand Oaks: Sage, 1988.

Bloom, Leslie R. *Under the Sign of Hope: Feminist Methodology and Narrative Interpretation*. Albany: SUNY Press, 1998.

Ezzy, Douglas. "Qualitative Interviewing as an Embodied Emotional Performance." *Qualitative Inquiry* 16, no. 3 (2010): 163-170. https://doi.org/10.1177/1077800409351970.

Grønnerød, Jarna Soilevuo. "On the Meanings and Uses of Laughter in Research Interviews: Relationships between Interviewed Men and a Woman Interviewer." *Young* 12, no. 1 (2004): 31-49. https://doi.org/10.1177/1103308804039635.

Hollway, Wendy, and Tony Jefferson. *Doing Qualitative Research Differently: A Psychosocial Approach*, 2nd edition. Thousand Oaks: Sage, 2013.

Oakley, Ann. "Interviewing Women: A Contradiction in Terms." In *Doing Feminist Research*, edited by Helen Roberts, 30-61. London: Routledge and Kegan Paul, 1981.

Rapley, Timothy J. "The Art(fulness) of Open-Ended Interviewing: Some Considerations on Analysing Interviews." *Qualitative Research* 1, no. 3 (2001): 303-323. https://doi.org/10.1177/146879410100100303.

Smith, Linda Tuhiwai. *Decolonizing Methodologies: Research and Indigenous Peoples*, 2nd edition. London: Zed Books, 2012.

9

Queering the Activist/Academic
An Autoethnography of Queering Research with/in Community Spaces

Amelia Thorpe

Introduction

This chapter is an experimental work of queer autoethnography[1] in which I consider the challenges and contradictions presented through my research with/in queer communities on unceded Wolastoqiyik territory in the region known as New Brunswick. What began as a dissertation project exploring the educational value of Pride[2] soon evolved to include an effort to queer spaces of 2SLGBTQ+ organizing. This work examines the tensions that arose during my doctoral research and data collection as both an insider and outsider: a queer activist and novice academic. I draw on my experiences of queering Pride while embedded in the volunteer non-profit organization Fierté Fredericton Pride and conducting a series of in-depth interviews with 2SLGBTQ+ activists engaged in my local community.

I engage in autoethnography, a form of recalling, reflecting, and self-writing, to find meaning in my experiences within specific social, political, and cultural contexts.[3] I am drawn to autoethnography as a means of bringing lived experience into research, and I present my memories, as an individual deeply entrenched in 2SLGBTQ+ activism, as a lens through which to gain "understanding of a societal culture."[4] Autoethnography, not unlike ethnographic research, creates space to recognize and reflect on the fluid nature of the researcher's status, disrupting the fixed positions of insider and outsider and instead acknowledging how status and identity are continually renegotiated within embedded research.[5] Autoethnographic data can be collected in myriad ways, including analyzing the self, engaging in reflection, and recalling, a "free-spirited way of bringing out memories about critical events, people, place, behaviors, talks, thoughts, perspectives, opinions, and emotions pertaining to the research topic."[6] This piece recalls four memories that are critical to my experiences engaging in this project as an activist and academic.

Jones and Adams propose that both autoethnography and queer theory "take up selves, beings, or 'I's, even as both work against a stable sense of self-subjects or experience."[7] I look to queer theory[8] as an invitation to identify and disrupt discourses that contribute to the oppression of individuals, bodies, and identities deemed non-normative and relegated to the margins, and queer autoethnography as form of critical, political, and reflexive self-writing that makes visible the discourses of power and oppression that inform my context and positionality.[9] By weaving fragments of the personal with the theoretical, I seek to capture and convey not only my experiences embedded in Pride, but the emotions I felt in this space. I present my memories and subsequent reflections as autoethnographic data to investigate the tensions between the dichotomous and interconnected positions of activist and academic (insider and outsider).

My research began as an investigation of Pride as an educational space. However, despite the organization's radical roots and potential as a site for social change, I quickly came to realize that this goal necessitated that I extend my work of queering Pride as an activist to queering Pride within my research. My roles as both activist and academic are entwined yet discordant. In what follows, I present a series of autoethnographic excerpts to bring you into the world of advocacy in which I have been embedded for the past 15 years. These memories share my experiences as an activist and provide a glimpse into histories of organizing to preface my exploration of the challenges that arose during my research process. They contextualize a handful of the (largely unresolved) moments of vulnerability I have experienced in this liminal space as both an activist and an academic in the subsequent sections: Queering the Activist and Disrupting the Academic. I take up these constructed and conflicting subject positions to structure this reflective work and to delve into the tensions present in my queer organizing and doctoral research, my entangled efforts to queer Pride.

Memories

The contents of my first "Pride Purse" included a hammer, nails, and duct tape as well as sunscreen and bandages. I was proud of my preparedness. It was the height of summer, 2008, and I felt I was carving a space within the local 2SLGBTQ+ community of Kjipuktuk[10] by being useful. As I helped paint wooden cacti for our queered western-themed Pride float in the basement of my workplace, the Youth Project, I felt at home in a way I had not previously experienced. I had just graduated high school and couldn't conceive of a better summer gig before heading off to university in the fall of 2008. Finally, I was beginning to find my place in the 2SLGBTQ+ community after years of advocacy work.

I grew up in a small village in the Maritimes some 40 minutes from the "big city." The type of village where a good portion of the population might tell you, "We don't have any of those [people] here." Where resources like the Youth Project, a non-profit community centre for 2SLGBTQ+ youth, did not exist. Growing up in a small rural community was isolating, yet over time, too familiar. Despite not existing in this place, it was too small to keep secrets and too small to blend in. Discussions of 2SLGBTQ+ identities and histories were absent from my school experience. I began seeking out community and advocacy organizations, desperate to find and build community and address the erasure I experienced in my schooling. Enamoured with the raw potential of grassroots organizing and alternative spaces of education, I never expected to end up theorizing queer activism in pursuit of a PhD.

I've been in colonially named Fredericton for longer than I had intended. Following my time working with organizations like the 519 Church Street Community Centre in Toronto, the move back to the Maritimes to pursue another degree was especially jarring. Seeking community here was reminiscent of my early experiences in small-town

Nova Scotia. It took years to carve inroads in local activist circles and after much persistence, I received a message inviting me to join the board of directors for the 2018 Pride festival. In my time as a quasi-board member, it was soon evident that the longstanding board executive were very much set in their ways and arguably hesitant to engage in any programming that might be considered too political or radical for fear of endangering the sense of progress they had cultivated over the past decade. Following a tense season of planning and the execution of the 2018 festival, the executive announced their retirement and myself and a continuing board member decided to run for the position of co-chairs in 2019. This marked the beginning of my interminable journey to queer Pride as an activist.[11]

Year One: June 2019
I've been staring at the screen long enough to finish two iced espressos, writing and erasing words that feel hollow and unmoored. Organizing Pride this summer is taking a toll on my productivity, but the delay in completing my dissertation proposal can't be blamed on this alone. My heart isn't in it. I saw one of my advisors at the café just last week, and I've accomplished little since. She mentioned writing about Pride, again. I still can't envision it—nor can I articulate the ties between advocacy and education. It doesn't seem like a legitimate academic option, rather it seems like I'm playing pretend to even consider it. Still, I keep coming back to the notion. I had added a small notebook to my Pride Purse at the beginning of the season, encouraged to take fieldnotes "just in case." The act of writing them has sparked something indescribable, a dizzying array of possibilities that I can't yet grasp but I can sense.

Year Two: August 2020
This year, my partner joins me as I reprise my role as co-chair. Having pivoted my dissertation proposal late last year, the realization that the COVID-19 pandemic had decimated our Pride plans is doubly concerning. Following my third interview explaining our decision to pivot to a provincewide collaborative festival Pride NB with mere months to go, I vowed to purge the buzzword from my vocabulary. While we may well have pivoted, the term fails to capture the reality of stressed, scrambling, unpaid volunteers spiralling ever deeper into burnout trying to spin

the pandemic's restrictions as an unprecedented opportunity. We avoid talking about it, but I find myself writing it into my dissertation, perhaps hopeful I'll leave my disenchantment between the watery blue lines, quickly filled with aggressive exclamation points and underlines that dig at the fibres of these crisp pages.

Year Three: August 2021
Last night I found one of my Pride shirts from the 2019 festival. That feeling of pride, of doing something valuable for my communities, of belonging, has waned. The board has been referring to Pride as being "back" this summer, following our entirely virtual slate of programming in 2020 for Pride NB, a tumultuous collaborative project we now refer to in hushed tones. This year I'm directing the festival, despite having stepped off the board. My Pride Purse is smaller, a crossbody bag that holds my phone, walkie talkie, mask, sanitizer bottle, and Pride bank card, thanks to my partner's "Pride Car" brimming with the excess. I recall our excitement at the prospect of a hybrid festival with in-person and virtual offerings. It's a faint memory now, the palpable energy of knowing Pride was "back," buried under utter exhaustion. We tell ourselves we're going to step back, but I'm not sure how truthful this is.

Year Three: November 2021
A reviewer referenced Pride as a "dumpster fire" that can't be salvaged after engaging with a piece that discusses my research. I appreciate their honest feedback—and my visceral reaction reaffirms that my heart is in this project. However, I haven't been able to shake the descriptor since. Pride is a constant in my life. Moreover, it has crept into the cracks in my psyche, fissures eroded by worry that I've spent much of my life organizing my Pride Purse yet I am still unprepared. Have I stoked the dumpster fire? I'm apprehensive that I've engaged in advocacy without creating any change, that my research is inconsequential and may damage the insider status necessary to continue engaging in said advocacy, that I'm an outsider and imposter in academia studying community building and informal education while others cure disease and curb emissions. As I reach the final stages of my dissertation, I feel more uncertain than ever before, the tensions between activist and academic complicated even further.

Queering the Activist

I began work on this project years ago. I've been immersing myself in the spaces I wish to study long before I ever believed they had a place in academic pursuits. While my doctoral work explores my experiences embedded in Pride, I had been deeply involved as an activist before I assumed the uncomfortable title of academic. In this way, I consider myself an intermittent insider in both advocacy and academia more frequently than an outsider.

I started writing about Pride in our first year as a new and quixotic board back in 2019. I had plans. Plans emboldened by my recent discovery of José Esteban Muñoz's work on queer futurity.[12] Plans to disrupt the ways in which this organization contributed to the growing discourse of homonormativity[13] complicit in fracturing 2SLGBTQ+ communities on this territory. The new board wanted to reimagine an organization that had long failed its local 2SLGBTQ+ communities, particularly racialized, disabled, gender-diverse, young, and aged individuals. We wanted to queer this exclusionary legacy, creating a radically inclusive festival aware of its historical roots, true to its history as a response to police brutality led by queer and trans women of colour. We wanted to strengthen our fragmented communities in a city that saw its mayor refuse to read the Pride Proclamation less than two decades prior. It took several years, but my arguably "insider" status as an out and active queer individual and activist in this small city slowly developed. Despite this, my doctoral research, including my in-depth qualitative interviews and foray into autoethnography, provoked discomfort as my personal and professional worlds became increasingly entwined.

Organizing with Pride could be viewed a perpetual exercise in vulnerability, balancing a commitment to queer the organization's politics with its undeniable precarity. Unlike many larger organizations across Turtle Island, our organization was run entirely by volunteers and had no operational funding. We were constrained by our modest budget and our commitment to introducing more accessible, community-centred events that did not revolve around party culture and the consumption of alcohol. Our early actions, including limiting police participation and developing a sponsorship policy that largely excluded corporations, reflected our commitment to radical change while simultaneously opening the door to debate that exposed the fractured nature of our communities and the exclusionary, homonormative attitudes that we sought to disrupt. One year prior to assuming a leadership position on the board, I would have been quick to engage in such discussions; however, speaking on behalf of this non-profit organization brought new tensions to the surface.

In a space where I had long sought to establish my identity as an activist, the tensions of this new role unsettled the distinction between insider and outsider. Organizing became a balancing act to maintain a relationship with the municipal government while queering their rules and expectations, to afford executing engaging events without using free space inside bars and clubs, to reject corporate sponsorship and pinkwashing while paying speakers and performers, and to create change while refereeing the discord it provoked. Being responsible for an organization I believed could create space for inclusive, unapologetic queer existence, community building, and education in this place was undoubtedly harder than I had anticipated.

While our new board's vision of what Pride could be was intended to disrupt the exclusion and barriers of preceding years and recreate the annual festival to actively prioritize accessibility, inclusion, and community care, we were struck by the pushback. For example, our choice to limit the presence of law enforcement, including a ban on uniformed participation in the parade, was met with a barrage of vitriolic messages and calls for an outright boycott. Our decision to limit corporate and political participation in the annual parade to local companies and political groups that could provide evidence of their actions or policies in support of 2SLGBTQ+ individuals and communities sparked aggressive messages and social media posts denouncing our organization for engaging in discrimination and exclusion.

From the early days of organizing for the 2019 festival, our commitment to unsettle the structures we inherited left us with unsteady footing. As the individual who handled festival planning and communications for Pride, I felt particularly exposed, vulnerable to the anger of those who opposed our desire for change, to the entitlement of the businesses I tried to pacify, and to losing favour with the city officials we needed onside to continue the festival. Most of all, I felt the tension between the potential of creating change and the potential for harm that the process entailed.

While trying to remain transparent about our methods and intentions, our posts on social media created unsafe online spaces, where the comments were laced with harmful rhetoric that denied the ongoing exclusion of racialized, disabled, older, and otherwise Othered 2SLGBTQ+ individuals.

I had already committed to queering Pride as an activist and working to identify and disrupt the oppressive systems embedded in the organization; however, my growing discomfort as an academic exploring this space spoke to a need to expand this work. Further, as both activist and academic, the unforeseen vulnerability I felt when discussing Pride with my participants and in my writing, along with the gnawing fear that I might be in some way associated with the Pride of years prior, prompted me to interrogate this relationship further. Reflecting on my critique of the organization's history, a legacy I so desperately wished to position in opposition to my project of queering, I recognized that the project of queering must extend past the institutions that shape my position, to me. I am in no way immune to the discourses that had shaped the homonormative, whitewashed festivals that came before our collective takeover. In recognizing this, I endeavour to acknowledge and unpack the ways I am shaped by innumerable relations, structures, and histories of power and reinscribe them through my engagement in Pride. My very involvement in an organization that held the potential to either destabilize or reinforce the oppressive structures required me to take pause.

As a queer, female-identified, mad, and chronically ill individual entering academia, it wasn't long before I learned the extent to which minoritized populations have long been subject to unethical, intrusive, and often pathologizing research conducted by outside researchers.[14] My research is deeply entwined with my insider status with regard to sexual diversity, a position broadly understood to be advantageous to qualitative research, such as interviewing.[15] While "being part of the community" may have distinct advantages for my research with local 2SLGBTQ+ activists, it remains vital for me to continually engage in critical reflexivity and actively identify and disrupt the innate imbalance of power present in my interactions.[16] It is necessary to call attention to my positionality as I approach this work and to acknowledge that my privilege as a white cisgender woman allows me to engage in advocacy, to take on a position of leadership within this organization, and to explore these experiences within the context of academia.

Disrupting the Academic

While my work seeks to engage with Pride as a space for disruption and radical rethinkings of queer futures, this reality is punctuated not only by the awareness that my participation within these spaces itself may reify discourses of oppression, but that I simultaneously hold the privileged title of academic. As a graduate student, I exist within an institution that reinscribes exclusory norms and discourses that privilege whiteness, heterosexuality, binary understandings and performances of gender, and ability.[17]

When I decided to begin writing about Pride, I neglected to draw on my experiences of activism in their entirety, in part conflicted by the discomfort of bringing my position as insider/activist into the institution of academia. I saw the potential of bringing the positive experiences, the possibilities Pride could offer to academia, but none of the messiness or contradictions. In my excitement, I failed to engage my critical, queer feminist lens. I was taken by the idea of an idealistic space of inclusion, education, and community building. However briefly, I painted Pride as an imagined queer utopia, a symbol of queer futurity that drives me to engage in continual disruption.

The reality of this research shattered my rainbow rose-coloured glasses almost instantly. I knew the organization's history upon embarking on this journey. In the board's collective experience, Pride in this city had been known to cater to a very narrow demographic, predominantly white, middle class, cisgender, and Anglophone, with a focus on events at bars and nightclubs. In grappling with the discomfort of hearing some of my participants share their experiences of racism, sexism, transphobia, ableism, and more within spaces purported to be by and for the 2SLGBTQ+ community and feelings of exclusion from spaces associated with the growing homonormativity of Pride, I realized that queering Pride as an activist was insufficient. How could I work toward the radical reimagining of a community space with one hand and paint the organization as an answer to the ongoing erasure of gender and sexual alterity within educational institutions with the other? I needed to disrupt Pride in my academic work as well. In some ways, I expected this to be easier than navigating the project of queering Pride from within an organization. However, I soon realized that the entwined nature of my activist and academic positions was no less fraught.

Due to the size of the city and the circles in which I engage, I was known to each of my participants and they to me. While in some ways an insider, who had at times worked alongside each individual as an activist, it was difficult to shake the anxiety attached to my secondary position as an academic outsider. During the interview process, I became concerned that my insider history and outsider context might negatively impact the engagement. I had stepped down from the board of directors before beginning data collection. While not the sole impetus, I hoped this manufactured distance would allow my participants to feel more at ease sharing honest opinions about their experiences in queer organizing locally. Maintaining this distance proved to be one of the greater challenges.

I anticipated some discomfort throughout the interview process as I represented not one but two institutions that had long failed minoritized populations: academia and the local Pride organization I sought to queer. Further, as an individual with one foot on the normative map of the institution and one foot venturing into the queer unknown, I thought I was equipped for complex negotiations relating to the politicized nature of my work in both worlds. I hoped my insider position, experience working with/in community, commitment to radical politics of queering, and intentional subversion of research norms and methods would help belay this friction. However, I was unprepared for the complexity of the frictions at the intersection of activism and academia and the ways in which this discord challenged my politics and my position.

When I decided to write myself in to my dissertation, melding queer theory, autoethnography, and narrative inquiry with a nod to postqualitative methodology, I made the decision to embrace the necessary vulnerability of writing my politics in as well.[18] I believe Pride is inherently political, despite the growing depoliticization fuelled by homonormativity, neoliberalism, and capitalism, and to undertake queering this space, as both activist and academic, requires engaging and writing politically.[19] My misstep here can be traced to the ways in which I theorized these politics, reducing the commitment to queering that I grasped so tightly to an oppositional binary of homonormative and radical politics.

Likely stoked by personal insecurities associated with engaging in work that would be useful and generative for 2SLGBTQ+ communities and the internalized terror of failing to be queer and critical enough, particularly after my brief and misguided foray into utopian longing,[20] I had constructed a standard of radical queerness. This became clear upon broaching my standard set of questions about the involvement of police in Pride. In contrast to other participants, Sebastián, a gay, racialized immigrant and community planner, spoke of his frustration with the restrictions placed on police involvement and vehement support of the inclusion of law enforcement in events such as the parade. I was caught off guard. I had not considered addressing diverging political stances of this magnitude, an assumption that not only projected my constructed standard on my participants but an unconscious judgment not unlike that which I feared.

As an academic, I considered my role to be clear: control my reaction, continue the interview, engage my participant further on this topic without bias. As an activist, I was conflicted. The political queer inside wanted to put the interview on hold, to ask questions personally as a friend and comrade, to articulate the homonormative dangers of narratives that position law enforcement as protectorates instead of disrupting the institution that represents ongoing racism, colonialism, and systemic oppression.[21] Instead, I continued my line of questioning, frozen in a vulnerable, liminal state between action and inaction, activist and academic, considering the ways in which my silence might betray my commitment to queering. Several minutes had passed, during which Sebastián had raised the militarization of Pride. Aware of my recent role as co-chair of the local Pride organization, he then queried whether a sign that read "All Cops are Bastards (ACAB)" would be permitted in the annual parade. I didn't have a good answer.

A group of Prides across Turtle Island have released statements in recent years limiting the involvement of the institution of policing, while others have welcomed cops with arms outstretched.[22] In our efforts to queer and reimagine Fierté Fredericton Pride, one of our first actions was to implement a policy limiting police and military involvement, a priority raised by racialized and gender-diverse community members, swiftly followed by restrictions on corporations and political parties. While a political party, for instance, would be prohibited from using the ACAB slogan, unaffiliated persons would not be. I stumbled over my words, trying to remain as diplomatic as possible while rapid-fire questions raced through my head. Who is carrying the sign? Should that matter? Is it the sentiment or the verbiage that would be problematic?

I consider this question the most salient moment of vulnerability in my data collection. Despite being committed to queering as both an activist and academic, this question complicated my position as I grappled with a response—disrupting my constructed standard of radical queerness and the assumptions it held and making visible the discourses of power that allow me, a white woman, to wear an ACAB patch on my jacket or wield a sign that calls for defunding the police and the military industrial complex. Blurring the already murky lines between activist and academic, insider and outsider, I considered not only how to respond in the moment, to affirm my participant's lived experience as a gay man of colour nearly two decades my senior and engage in this necessary discussion in meaningful ways, but how I would write about this unexpected tension without pathologizing my participant? Did my decision to craft a discreet answer based solely in policy negate this commitment? I remain unsure.

Conclusion: Embracing a Queer and Liminal State

The uncertainty that accompanied the question just discussed mirrors my discomfort around the ambiguous and oppositional titles used cautiously throughout this chapter: activist and academic, insider and outsider. I consider these labels to represent a constructed distinction that serves to obscure differences of power, experience, and privilege. As articulated by scholar Nancy Naples, "insiderness and outsiderness are not fixed or static positions, rather, they are ever-shifting and permeable social locations that are differentially experienced and expressed by community members."[23] Going into this research, I'd attached the uncomfortable title of insider to my activist work, in many ways due to feeling like an outsider within academia. However, my attempts to segment my thoughts and experiences along these largely arbitrary and oft-entwined lines has been unsuccessful.

My experiences negotiating the politics of Pride and my efforts to queer the organization as both activist and academic throughout my doctoral work have broken down the binary between insider and outsider, requiring attention to the contradictions and conflicts therein. Unable to place my feet firmly in these constructed binaries, I adopt a queer, liminal position that defies categorization and embraces assemblage.[24] This shifting positionality seeks not to reconcile the power and privilege of participation in academia with my experiences as a queer activist; rather, it serves to make visible these contradictions, complicities, and challenges in acknowledging, interrogating, and resisting the systems of power that shape me and the institutions with which I engage.

To embrace the messiness of deconstructing the insider/outsider dichotomy and the uncertainty of a queer and liminal state requires the sort of vulnerable precarity Butler cites as a precursor of resistance to be mobilized as "a deliberate and active form of political resistance."[25] While perhaps tenuous, I consider my attempts to pin down my position(s), to separate the activist and academic, insider and outsider, as symptomatic of my unrelenting desire to feel a sense of belonging and kinship. From my first Pride Purse to my Pandemic Pride Purse iteration this past summer, I have sought to arm myself with the tools that allowed me to be prepared, to respond to the unknown, to be useful to my communities. Perhaps subconsciously, I have long conflated being useful with belonging in the spaces I inhabit. Ahmed argues that the real or imagined requirement to be useful, "while often presented as general or even universal, tends to falls upon some more than others."[26] Upon looking inward to identify the internalized discourses that instilled this desire to be viewed as useful, to be a part of the fleeting utopian construct I'd imagined, I'd confronted a discomfort not unlike the moments of vulnerability discussed in this chapter.

Far from my imagined project, the challenges that arose during my doctoral research have left me with more questions and more uncertainty. However, it is these questions and moments of vulnerability that have shaped the trajectory of my work and strengthened my commitment to critical and reflexive queering, that have led me to embrace this queer and liminal space between activist and academic, that have invited political resistance. I close this chapter without concrete answers or revelatory findings, but with a new selection of tools in my Pride Purse: a deeper awareness of my positionality and the inextricable nature of my insider and outsider identities, questions that propel my research forward and blur the lines between activism and academia, an uneasy acceptance of the vulnerability of engaging in this work, and a renewed commitment to disruption in the unending pursuit of radical, political queer futures of possibility and belonging.

Notes

1. Carolyn Ellis, "Lingering in the Closet," *Journal of Autoethnography* 1, no. 1 (2020): 69-80; Stacy L.H. Jones and Anne M. Harris, eds., *Queering Autoethnography* (New York: Routledge, 2019).
2. I capitalize Pride throughout this work to gesture to established 2SLGBTQ+ organizations and events involved in the annual observation of what is now known as "Pride," a political, social, and/or celebratory gathering of 2SLGBTQ+ individuals that prioritizes community visibility and resilience and that emerged from the Stonewall Riots of 1969.
3. Heewon Chang, *Autoethnography as Method* (New York: Routledge, 2008); Stacy L.H. Jones and Tony E. Adams, "Autoethnography is a Queer Method," in *Queer Methods and Methodologies: Intersecting Queer Theories and Social Science Research*, eds. Kath Browne and Catherine J. Nash (New York: Routledge, 2016), 195-214.
4. Chang, *Autoethnography as Method*, 49.
5. Jill A. McCorkel and Kristen Myers, "What Difference Does Difference Make? Position and Privilege in the Field," *Qualitative Sociology* 26 (2003): 199-231.
6. Heewon Chang, "Individual and Collaborative Autoethnography as Method: A Social Scientist's Perspective," in *Handbook of Autoethnography*, eds. Tony E. Adams, Stacy Holman Jones, and Carolyn Ellis (Walnut Creek: Left Coast Press, 2016), 113.
7. Jones and Adams, "Autoethnography is a Queer Method," 197.
8. José Esteban Muñoz, *Cruising Utopia: The Then and There of Queer Futurity* (New York: New York University Press, 2009); Roderick A. Ferguson, *One-Dimensional Queer* (Cambridge: Polity Press, 2019); David M. Halperin, "The Normalization of Queer Theory," *Journal of Homosexuality* 45, no. 2-4 (2003): 339-343.
9. Elizabeth Ettorre, *Autoethnography as Feminist Method: Sensitising the Feminist "I,"* (London: Routledge, 2017).
10. This is the Mi'kmaq name for the city colonially known as Halifax in the province of Nova Scotia.
11. For me, to queer Pride meant to disrupt its recent history of exclusion, to dismantle the structures (or lack thereof) that upheld this divide, to bring more eyes, hands, and voices together to reimagine and rebuild an organization that truly reflected and served all community members, an organization that would continually reflect and reconstruct itself toward a goal of radical, queer inclusion and futurity.
12. Muñoz, *Cruising Utopia*.
13. *Homonormativity* refers to the ways in which heteronormative ideals and constructs are reproduced within segments of 2SLGBTQ+ communities (predominantly politically conservative, white gay men) in a move away from radical activism and queer politics and toward assimilation to white, middle-class, cisgender norms, ideals of respectability and progress, and participation in systems that uphold the oppression of gender and sexual alterity.

14. Nado Aveling, "Don't Talk about What You Don't Know: On (Not) Conducting Research with/in Indigenous Contexts," *Critical Studies in Education* 54, no. 2 (2013), 203-214; Travis S. Kong, Dan Mahoney, and Ken Plummer, "Queering the Interview," in *Inside Interviewing: New Lenses, New Concerns*, eds. James A. Holstein and Jaber F. Gubrium (London: Sage, 2002), 91-110.
15. Kathy Absolon and Cam Willett, "Putting Ourselves Forward: Location in Aboriginal Research," in *Research as Resistance: Critical, Indigenous and Anti-Oppressive Approaches*, eds. Leslie Brown and Susan Strega (Toronto: Canadian Scholars Press, 2005), 97-126; Suzanne Day, "A Reflexive Lens: Exploring Dilemmas of Qualitative Methodology Through the Concept of Reflexivity," *Qualitative Sociology Review* 8, no. 1 (2012): 60-85.
16. Wanda Pillow, "Confession, Catharsis, or Cure? Rethinking the Uses of Reflexivity as Methodological Power in Qualitative Research," *International Journal of Qualitative Studies in Education* 16, no. 2 (2003), 182.
17. Amelia Thorpe, "Pride And (Learned) Prejudice: Education, Activism, Identity," PhD thesis, University of New Brunswick, forthcoming.
18. Elizabeth Adams St. Pierre, "Why Post Qualitative Inquiry?" *Qualitative Inquiry* 27, no. 2 (2021): 163-166; Stacy L.H. Jones, "Writing a Hard and Passing Rain: Autotheory, Autoethnography, and Queer Futures," in *Gender Futurity, Intersectional Autoethnography: Embodied Theorizing from the Margins*, eds. A.L. Johnson and B. LeMaster (New York: Routledge, 2020).
19. Amelia Thorpe, "Queering Pride Facilitation: An Autoethnography of Community Organizing," in *Facilitating Community Research for Social Change: Case Studies in Qualitative, Arts-Based and Visual Research*, eds. Casey Burkholder, Funké Aladejebi, and Joshua Schwab Cartas (New York: Routledge, 2022), 178-192.
20. Muñoz, *Cruising Utopia*.
21. Thorpe, "Queering Pride Facilitation: An Autoethnography of Community Organizing."
22. Emma K. Russell, "A 'Fair Cop': Queer Histories, Affect and Police Image Work in Pride March," *Crime, Media, Culture* 13, no. 3 (2017): 277-293; Alexa DeGagne, "Pinkwashing Pride Parades: The Politics of Police in 2SLGBTQ+Q2S Spaces in Canada," in *Turbulent Times, Transformational Possibilities? Gender and Politics Today and Tomorrow*, eds. Fiona MacDonald and Alexandra Dobrowolsky (North York: University of Toronto Press, 2020), 258-280.
23. Nancy Naples, "The Outsider Phenomenon," in *Feminist Perspectives on Social Research*, eds. Sharlene Nagy Hesse-Biber and Michelle L. Yaiser (New York: Oxford University Press, 2004), 373.
24. Jasbir K. Puar, "'I Would Rather Be a Cyborg than a Goddess': Becoming-Intersectional in Assemblage Theory," *PhiloSOPHIA* 2, no. 1 (2012): 49-66.
25. Judith Butler, *Notes toward a Performative Theory of Assembly* (Cambridge: Harvard University Press, 2015), 184.
26. Sara Ahmed, *What's the Use?: On the Uses of Use* (Durham: Duke University Press, 2019), 10.

Bibliography

Absolon, Kathy, and Cam Willett. "Putting Ourselves Forward: Location in Aboriginal Research." In *Research as Resistance: Critical, Indigenous, and Anti-Oppressive Approaches*, edited by Leslie Brown and Susan Strega, 97-126. Toronto: Canadian Scholars Press, 2005.

Ahmed, Sara. *What's the Use?: On the Uses of Use*. Durham: Duke University Press, 2019.

Aveling, Nado. "Don't Talk about What You Don't Know: On (Not) Conducting Research with/in Indigenous Contexts." *Critical Studies in Education* 54, no. 2 (2013): 203-214.

Butler, Judith. *Notes toward a Performative Theory of Assembly*. Cambridge: Harvard University Press, 2015.

Chang, Heewon. *Autoethnography as Method*. New York: Routledge, 2008.

Chang, Heewon. "Individual and Collaborative Autoethnography as Method: A Social Scientist's Perspective." In *Handbook of Autoethnography*, edited by Tony E. Adams, Stacy Holman Jones, and Carolyn Ellis, 107-122. Walnut Creek: Left Coast Press, 2016.

Day, Suzanne. "A Reflexive Lens: Exploring Dilemmas of Qualitative Methodology Through the Concept of Reflexivity." *Qualitative Sociology Review* 8, no. 1 (2012): 60-85.

DeGagne, Alexa. "Pinkwashing Pride Parades: The Politics of Police in 2SLGBTQ+Q2S Spaces in Canada." In *Turbulent Times, Transformational Possibilities? Gender and Politics Today and Tomorrow*, edited by Fiona MacDonald and Alexandra Dobrowolsky, 258-280. North York: University of Toronto Press, 2020.

Ellis, Carolyn. "Lingering in the Closet." *Journal of Autoethnography* 1, no. 1 (2020): 69-80.

Ettorre, Elizabeth. *Autoethnography as Feminist Method: Sensitising the Feminist "I."* London: Routledge, 2017.

Ferguson, Roderick A. *One-Dimensional Queer*. Cambridge: Polity Press, 2019.

Halperin, David M. "The Normalization of Queer Theory." *Journal of Homosexuality* 45, no. 2-4 (2003): 339-343.

Jones, Stacy L.H. "Writing a Hard and Passing Rain: Autotheory, Autoethnography, and Queer Futures." In *Gender Futurity, Intersectional Autoethnography: Embodied Theorizing from the Margins*, edited by A.L. Johnson and B. LeMaster. New York: Routledge, 2020.

Jones, Stacy L.H., and Tony E. Adams. "Autoethnography is a Queer Method." In *Queer Methods and Methodologies: Intersecting Queer Theories and Social Science Research*, edited by Kath Browne and Catherine J. Nash, 195-214. New York: Routledge, 2016.

Jones, Stacy L.H., and Anne M. Harris, eds. *Queering Autoethnography*. New York: Routledge, 2019.

Kong, Travis S., Dan Mahoney, and Ken Plummer. "Queering the Interview." In *Inside Interviewing: New Lenses, New Concerns*, edited by James A. Holstein and Jaber F. Gubrium, 91-110. London: Sage, 2002.

McCorkel, Jill A., and Kristen Myers. "What Difference Does Difference Make? Position and Privilege in the Field." *Qualitative Sociology* 26 (2003): 199-231.

Muñoz, José Esteban. *Cruising Utopia: The Then and There of Queer Futurity*. New York: New York University Press, 2009.

Naples, Nancy. "The Outsider Phenomenon." In *Feminist Perspectives on Social Research*, edited by Sharlene Nagy Hesse-Biber and Michelle L. Yaiser, 373-381. New York: Oxford University Press, 2004.

Pillow, Wanda. "Confession, Catharsis, or Cure? Rethinking the Uses of Reflexivity as Methodological Power in Qualitative Research." *International Journal of Qualitative Studies in Education* 16, no. 2 (2003): 175-196.

Puar, Jasbir K. "'I Would Rather Be a Cyborg than a Goddess': Becoming-Intersectional in Assemblage Theory." *PhiloSOPHIA* 2, no. 1 (2012): 49-66.

Russell, Emma K. "A 'Fair Cop': Queer Histories, Affect and Police Image Work in Pride March." *Crime, Media, Culture* 13, no. 3 (2017): 277-93.

St. Pierre, Elizabeth Adams. "Why Post Qualitative Inquiry?" *Qualitative Inquiry* 27, no. 2 (2021): 163-166.

Thorpe, Amelia. "Pride And (Learned) Prejudice: Education, Activism, Identity." PhD thesis, University of New Brunswick, forthcoming.

Thorpe, Amelia. "Queering Pride Facilitation: An Autoethnography of Community Organizing." In *Facilitating Community Research for Social Change: Case Studies in Qualitative, Arts-Based and Visual Research*, edited by Casey Burkholder, Funké Aladejebi, and Joshua Schwab Cartas, 178-192. New York: Routledge.

Even with the Best of Intentions
An Accounting of Failures in a Participatory Research Project

Lori Ross, Merrick Pilling, Kendra Ann Pitt, and Jijian Voronka

Introduction

Participatory research is a valuable and widely used social justice research methodology.[1] It fundamentally challenges more traditional research methodologies through its principle of power sharing, which arguably situates greater control over research processes within the communities that are the subjects of study.[2] However, critiques of participatory methodologies highlight the possibility for this power sharing to be incomplete and ultimately tokenistic,[3] and in turn, to potentially cause harm within the communities intended to benefit.[4] Failures of participatory research, however, are seldom shared publicly, inhibiting a more fulsome understanding of these approaches and their potential limitations.

In this chapter, we take up the editors' call to "dwell in the vulnerable moments of research" through an examination of what we see as the failures of one of our own participatory research projects. The Peers Examining Experiences in Research Study (PEERS) was a participatory investigation of the practice of hiring peer researchers (i.e., individuals with lived experience) as research staff—a common strategy to mitigate power imbalances in participatory research.[5] Here, in our capacities as academically situated study investigators and project coordinators on the PEERS study, we offer an analysis of our collaborative reflections on our experiences working on this project. In particular, we document what we see to be the failures of our participatory research project as they relate to the social justice goal of equitable power sharing. We do this through an analysis of the macro-, meso-, and micro-level contributors to these failures, with particular attention to our roles as *proximal actors* on behalf of more distal forces. In doing so, we examine how a research approach intended to mitigate vulnerabilities associated with power imbalances can in fact reproduce them, and does so by using us—the researchers—as tools in this process. Rather than offering suggestions or recommendations, we close with our collective questions about the possibilities for participatory methodologies to achieve their social justice aims when operating within the constraints of the neoliberal academy, and the implications and potential harms for the communities intended to benefit from the work.

Background

Participatory research approaches challenge traditional distinctions between "researcher" and "researched" by actively engaging with members of the community under study to use research for social change.[6] These approaches are taken up across a range of disciplines, including psychology, sociology, social work, geography, and health studies.[7] Participatory research is celebrated for its potential to maximize the impact of research on affected communities,[8] to address issues of mistrust among communities who have been harmed by research in the past,[9] and to address the power imbalance between academic researchers and (often marginalized) communities to more equitably include those affected by the research[10] in the knowledge production process.

However, some writers have critiqued the extent to which these emancipatory intentions are achieved and have described the limited benefits of participatory research as a tool for empowerment.[11] Much of this writing has examined the role of power in participatory research, including the effects of power as it is enacted both within teams (i.e., in relationships between differentially situated team members) and upon teams (i.e., in the impact of structural and institutional forms of power on the research process).[12] For example, speaking to research with mental health service users in particular, Happell et al.[13] highlight the impact of hierarchies structured on the basis of both research roles (e.g., academic investigator, community-based researcher) and academic disciplines (i.e., with medicine dominating all others), and note how these two forms of hierarchies together produce paternalism toward those who are not academics and/or have lived experience of the mental health system.

Other writers have focused their critique more specifically on limitations of participatory research in a neoliberal context, where resources in the community sector are scarce, thus constraining possibilities to sustain the temporary gains in capacity that research can bring.[14] Current policy contexts that mandate community engagement (e.g., in Canada, the *Tri-Council Policy Statement: Ethical Conduct for Research Involving Humans*[15]) are noted to contribute to this, by requiring researchers to engage with communities without providing the support necessary to enable communities to engage in ways that will maintain community control over the research process.[16] Among other unintended harms, this leads to what Brunger and Wall[17] have termed "engagement creep": the burden borne by communities in supporting the research enterprise, much of it in the form of un- or underpaid work. Cook and Kothari[18] have called this the "tyranny of participation": the phenomenon wherein participatory approaches promise empowerment but in actuality reproduce or reinforce colonial (and other oppressive) relations of power.[19]

This literature exposing the potential limitations and pitfalls of participatory research offers an important complement to more widely cited scholarship celebrating its potential benefits,[20] as well as to policy recommendations and directives promoting community engagement in research.[21] A clearer understanding of the limitations and even failures of participatory research can better equip researchers to anticipate, honestly discuss, and perhaps mitigate the challenges documented by others. To this end, our objective in this chapter is to analyze reflections recorded over the course of a two-year participatory research project to document what we see as the failures of our project. We particularly reflect upon the project's lack of success in achieving the participatory principle of equitable power sharing, and the implications and harms associated with this failure, in order to offer questions about the possibilities for participatory methods to achieve their social justice aims when carried out in the context of the neoliberal academy.

Methodology

The PEERS study was a two-year, federally funded participatory study of the practice of hiring peers (i.e., people with lived experience) as research staff.[22] The study specifically focused on four communities of identity/experience that face structural oppression in the Canadian context, and we hired one research assistant with experience working as a peer researcher from each of the four communities (hereafter referred to as "research assistants"—see Authors' Note at end of chapter). Given the nature of structural oppression, these four communities of focus were inherently intersectional and overlapping, and in turn there was intersectional overlap in our staff's self-identities. The research assistants were involved in developing data collection tools, co-interviewing, analyzing the data, and disseminating the findings. The "meta" nature of this study—as a peer research project examining the experiences of peer researchers—provided a rich opportunity to treat our (investigators' and project staff's) own experiences as data in addressing our research questions about the potential benefits and harms of the practice of hiring peer researchers.

The investigator team for this study collectively had many years of experience leading participatory research with all four communities of focus, and it also included investigators who themselves had experience working as peer researchers. We intentionally followed many of the practices that have been recommended in participatory research,[23] including developing a research agreement, involving peers, incorporating paid training opportunities for project staff (e.g., in qualitative interviewing), and paying staff on par with what non-peer research assistants would be paid for the same work.

The study incorporated an autoethnographic component, in which the research staff and the principal investigator and project coordinators each recorded reflections on our experiences working on this project over its duration. The project had two coordinators: one who held the position for less than a year and then moved into a co-investigator role, and a second who then took over the role for the remainder of the project. This chapter is based on the reflections, recorded during meetings, of the principal investigator and current (at the time) project coordinator. The meetings were held approximately every two months, specifically for the purpose of collaboratively recording our reflections. The data were entered into a Google document, which we then took turns typing simultaneous with our conversation. On one occasion, we invited Jijian Voronka, a project co-investigator, and both the current and former project coordinators to join in our reflections; thus, the text analyzed for this review is based primarily on conversations between two people and one conversation between four people.

Analysis for this chapter involved all authors independently reviewing the reflections document, noting key themes and ideas potentially of interest for closer analysis. Through conversation, we then decided to focus our analysis on macro-, meso-, and micro-level factors that influenced the success/failure of the project, as further described below. Lori Ross then coded the document with attention to these three levels, and in so doing, identified the overarching theme of focus in our findings (*proximal actors*). She then undertook a second round of coding to identify all sections of the document that spoke to this theme. After preparing summaries of her analyses, the findings were reviewed, verified, and expanded upon by Merrick Pilling, Kendra Ann Pitt, and Jijian Voronka, resulting in the final version of our analysis, which follows in the next section.

Findings

In analyzing our reflections, we aimed to better understand the failures of our participatory research project to achieve the methodology's intended social justice aims by identifying macro-, meso-, and micro-level contributors and, by extension, to illuminate the implications and potential harms of these failures to communities and researchers. At the macro level, we were attuned to the impact of intersecting forms of systemic oppression and privilege (most prominently racism, classism, sanism, and ableism), alongside neoliberalism in shaping the politics of knowledge production— that is, in determining whose knowledge and expertise was valued in the academic space and whether or how lived experience was accounted for in this. At the meso level, we attended to the impacts of institutions, most notably our federal funder and the principal investigator's university, in shaping the research processes in ways that at times came into direct conflict with the values of participatory research. Finally, at the micro level, we examined how power circulated in relationships within the research team, across differences in project roles as well as across our varying social positions. We attended to how these relationships shaped team dynamics, communication, and engagement.

Our reflections call into question how much difference participatory methods can make in the face of persistent, intersecting systemic oppressions and structural forces that shape all of the actors' encounters with one another and with the involved institutions. While our intentions were to mitigate power imbalances through the tenets of participatory research, we became acutely aware of the limits to what participatory methods could accomplish. As we noted in our reflections:

> Even with all good intentions/attempts—creating the spaces doesn't end systemic discrimination...peoples' lives exist outside of these seven hours a week, structural systems in place are being recreated even within this project that is thinking critically about the way peers are being engaged...[There is an inevitable] disconnect between the hope of what you would like to create and the reality produced by the systems.

Our analysis highlights that factors at the micro level (e.g., tensions in relationships within the team) and meso level (e.g., funding constraints) are both profoundly shaped by forces at the macro level. That is, structures outside of the participatory project authorize people to take up space (or not), determine how peoples' contributions and qualifications are valued, and ultimately shape their experience of meaningful power sharing (or a lack of it) within the research project. These same forces also constrain the policies and practices of the institutions; for example, in limitations on who can be named as an investigator on a grant, what kinds of expenses are considered appropriate (and so whether a participatory project is adequately budgeted), and human resources and other institutional policies and practices that do not take adequately into account economic precarity. However, in the moment of a particular "failure" in the project, it can be difficult to see the macro-level forces at play, thus obscuring their primacy. In our analysis, we sought to make explicit these forces as they shaped the meso- and micro-level factors that were more obviously apparent in our everyday experience of carrying out this project. Here, we explore one particular manifestation of the obscured impact of macro-level forces: the notion of *proximal actors*. In this context, we define proximal actors as those actors who appear to be responsible for a particular action and its consequences but who are in fact acting on behalf of (or within the constraints defined by) a more distal actor. Below, we draw from our reflections to illustrate.

"Proximal Actors"

Our reflections illustrate that each of the actors in this project inevitably came to carry out the functions of the more macro actors or forces at play. In this way, the institutions (our federal funder, the university that held the grant and hosted the research) became the most proximal actors of neoliberalism, and we (the investigators and research coordinators) became the proximal actors of the institutions. In our reflections, this reality led to difficult questions about responsibility: when one actor is obligated to carry out the work of another, who is ultimately responsible for the harms that are done? In what follows, we explore this notion of proximal actors through examples from our project.

We begin with the very origin of our participatory research project. In order to be successful in the competitive pool of federal research grants we applied to, we submitted a fully fleshed out research proposal, with identified research questions, theoretical framing, and methodology. In our team's experience, this was necessary in order to secure funding in the amount required to carry out a multi-year participatory project, since the more developmental "planning" or "engagement" grant mechanisms offer typically in the range of $10,000 to $25,000, which would not be sufficient to adequately engage and compensate peer researchers. However, securing funds through the larger funding envelope meant contravening one of the key tenets of participatory research: that communities should be involved in all stages, including the development of the research questions. Although we had co-investigators with past experience as peer researchers, their present academic roles (as tenure-track faculty or graduate students) positioned them quite differently than most peer research assistants with respect to their current access to formal education and economic precarity, for example. Thus, at the point that we hired our research assistants (as well as our project coordinators), the capacity for their engagement was constrained by the research plan we had to develop for the funder. In this way, the competitiveness of federal grant funding, as a manifestation of neoliberal constraints on government funding, played a profound role in setting out the boundaries of possibility for meaningful community engagement in our study. It also established from the beginning of the project a hierarchy that participatory research is meant to trouble, with the principal investigator and then academically situated co-investigators holding the most power (given they were the ones involved from the outset of the study in developing the questions and research plan). In fact, this project was probably more "top heavy" than most: given our desire to include expertise with/from all four communities of study, the project had six co-investigators in addition to the principal investigator (seven, once the initial project coordinator moved into a co-investigator role). This hierarchal team structure, which we established in an attempt to maximize our competitiveness within a limited funding pool, inevitably influenced the power relationships within our research team as the project unfolded.

The constraints of our funding also led to a tension that was apparent for the life of the project: conflict between the budget and timeline required by our funder, and our commitment to meaningful engagement with our research assistants (and their communities more broadly). This tension was ever-present and continuously manifested a clash between the values of the neoliberal institution (federal funding body) and the values of participatory research. In our case, the funder reduced our requested budget by one-third. Given our intention to prioritize meaningful community engagement, we chose not to apply this cut to the salary line for our research assistants but instead to reduce the salary support for the project coordinator position and to condense the project activities from three years into two. In retrospect, our funder, as a proximal actor of neoliberalism, thus tied us to an unrealistic budget and timeline, and as proximal actors of the funder, we (the PI and coordinators) were seen by our staff to insufficiently accommodate the ways and extent to which they wanted to engage with the project, given that we found ourselves needing to curtail engagement on certain products and processes in order to keep the project moving along.

The cut to our proposed budget also led us to reproduce the precarious working conditions so often critiqued in relation to peer research—including by participants in our own study[24]—given that it meant that all staff, including both project coordinators and research assistants, were on part-time contracts (one day per week for research assistants, and 2.5 days per week for the coordinators). As a result, most staff were working more than one job (creating challenges in scheduling and availability), there was staff turnover/staff were rarely available to work together at the same time (which impacted team relationships and dynamics), and there was stress created by the part-time availability of the staff in light of the full-time, ongoing work of the project (resulting in people either working at times when they were not scheduled to work or project tasks going undone). It also meant that only certain members of the team were regularly available to attend research team meetings (typically the principal investigator, project coordinator, and some of the co-investigators), which further contributed to the hierarchical team structure, given that most team decision making happened at these meetings.

These tensions between our commitments to the funder and our commitments to the values of participatory research became particularly complicated for us when they bumped up against our desire and intention to accommodate of our staff's various needs in relation to their disability accommodation, employment precarity, and other issues that affected their availability for work—especially given that these issues were often very directly related to the lived experience we hoped for them to draw upon in their work on our project:

> What's happening on our project is that a deadline is given, the deadline is missed, the project has to move forward, and then people feel like they weren't given the opportunity to contribute.

For example, at times, staff were unable or unavailable to complete work tasks for disability-related or other legitimate reasons (e.g., responsibilities to another, less precarious position), for weeks or even months after tasks were assigned. While in principle we were very supportive of this, in practice, the work of the project had to continue regardless (given the funder's requirements, but also our broader accountability to our research participants and their communities). We struggled with what to do about this. Given the nature of their casual positions at the university, research assistants were paid on the basis of biweekly timesheets that were submitted indicating their hours worked, so that if they did not work, they did not get paid—but also that it was hypothetically possible for them to work their hours later, at a more convenient time. As a result, our ideal solution would have been to have the project coordinator pick up the very time-sensitive portions of our work, leaving the bulk of it for our staff when they were next able to work, but this was not possible given the budget cuts we had had to make to the coordinator's salary budget line. While we typically ended up reassigning work to other staff, this meant fewer hours and fewer opportunities to contribute for the staff originally hired in the role. These challenges with individual staff also had broader implications in terms of representation within our team of the specific communities the staff were connected to; we found that we were in a position to have to choose between accommodating the needs of our staff (i.e., holding their hours for when they were able to work them) or significantly reducing, for the periods of time that they were unavailable, the engagement we had intended (in project decision making, etc.) with these communities. These limitations in regard to providing accommodations also highlight how structural inequities, by definition, come to bear differently on different individuals, as mediated by their social positioning. That is, staff who were members of one, or sometimes more than one, of the socially marginalized communities our study aimed to work with were differently impacted by the budget cut and attending implications for accommodation than would be individuals who were located in more privileged positions (and thus less in need of accommodation).

In retrospect, we feel that the funder's cut to our budget set this project up to fail, from the perspective of the power-sharing principles of participatory research. Much has been written about the additional time required to meaningfully engage communities in participatory research;[25] the budget and timeline we originally submitted to the funder reflected our understanding of this reality. As a proximal actor of neoliberalism, the funder enforced cuts that ultimately reproduced dominant power structures in relation to knowledge production; as proximal actors of the funder, we (the PI and coordinators) were required to substantially curtail intended community engagement in order to complete project deliverables on time. In this process, existing power relations, wherein academics maintain control of knowledge production about communities, were reproduced—despite our plans and intentions otherwise.

The second example highlights the (presumably unintended) impacts on our research staff of university policies, particularly those related to hiring and compensation. The complexities of payment when hiring peer researchers have been discussed elsewhere;[26] in our study, the only available option was to hire our research assistants as staff of the university, given that their total payment per calendar year would exceed the amount allowed to be paid by honorarium. While this offered some benefits to staff (e.g., in terms of a formal employment relationship to list on their resumes, and the opportunity to pay into, and thus later access, government benefits such as the Canada Pension Plan), it also presented challenges. As one example, the university's policies required that our research assistants be designated as casual staff due to the small number of hours per week they were working. This designation limited us to offering contracts of maximum six months in length to the research assistants. Thus, even though we knew we had the budget for two years of work, we were unable to formalize this commitment to our staff, leading to precarity, presumably stress and reduced engagement with the project, and for some, the need to look for other work in case the contracts were not renewed. In this way, the policy was associated with harms to both research staff (with respect to the impacts of precarious work) and to the research project (with respect to the limitations in community engagement produced by having staff so precariously attached to the project).

As another example, university policies and practices related to compensation were organized around the assumption that all university staff would have bank accounts—an assumption that was incorrect in the case of our project. Payment was only possible by direct deposit to a bank account, and exceptions to this were made only on a very temporary basis while staff did the work required to set up a bank account. The possibility that someone might be unable to open a bank account, for example, as a result of not having the necessary identification, seemed never to have been encountered or considered. In our project, during the period that staff were attempting to navigate all the necessary systems to enable pay by direct deposit, there was ongoing pressure (on research staff directly as well as the projector coordinator and PI) from the institution via our departmental administrative staff, who were themselves under pressure from central administration to alleviate the burden on their part of processing manual cheques. This pressure presented challenges to the relationships between all involved parties and produced extra work for the project coordinator (who, as noted, was already trying to do the work of the project with insufficient hours) in trying to advocate for staff, identify workarounds, and determine what role (if any) the project should play in supporting our staff to set up bank accounts. The policy also produced (presumably unintended) harms for our staff in terms of uncertainty when they would receive their pay, along with the added labour (emotional and otherwise) required to negotiate their way through these administrative hurdles.

Although the institutional policies described in this section likely create problems for investigators and their staff in other (non-participatory) research projects as well, in our reflections, we noted that framing our work as a participatory project

> places different responsibilities on the academic members of the team, who have more access to resources and power (institutional and otherwise) than do the peer researchers, and [participatory research] calls us to be attentive to and actively attempt to mitigate these power imbalances. At the same time, there are real, concrete limits to our power within the institution to address or work around oppression or unsupportive policies.

Our attention to, and attempts to mitigate, the power imbalances that are centred in participatory research led us to be particularly attuned to the implications and harms of being so severely constrained in our capacity to mitigate them. Further, this analysis of our autoethnographic reflections enabled us to recognize how these constraints directly serve the interests of the neoliberal institutions involved—in reproducing power relations with respect to who is authorized to produce knowledge in the academic space.

Conclusions

In this analysis, we have drawn on our collaborative reflections to illustrate how, despite intentions of contributing to the emancipatory goals of participatory research, our project was unable to overcome macro-level constraining forces, and as a result, reproduced vulnerabilities that participatory research is intended to address. We have traced back failures that could be perceived to be happening on the micro level (e.g., staff turnover) to make visible the profound role of macro-level forces in creating research contexts that made them inevitable (or at least predictable). We have shown how we, as researchers, contribute to the reproduction of macro-level forces when we are required to become the proximal actors of our institutions, and ultimately, of the structural oppressions and neoliberal forces that underpin those institutions. On the basis of these experiences, we have shown how structural violence is diffused through research projects that attempt to be community based but are administrated through the constraints of university and funding cultures. In so doing, we have raised questions about who is responsible for the harms done by way of this diffusion of structural power. These harms are manifold, including tangible harms affecting individual research assistants (e.g., the harms associated with precarious work) and practical harms affecting the quality and quantity of the research outputs (i.e., due to underfunding and the amount of staff time that ends up being redirected to address meso- and micro-level failures). Together, this context produces epistemic harms to communities, whereby power relationships that leave control of knowledge production in the hands of those with academic privilege are reproduced at the same time as claims are made to be disrupting them, silencing the knowledge of communities as they continue to be denied meaningful access to the academic space.

Our findings align with the critiques of others who have highlighted the gaps between the goals and actualities of participatory methods[27] and, for us, raise questions about the possibilities and ethics of participatory research in the context of the neoliberal academic institution. Others have written about the harm that happens when peer researchers are tokenized, not appropriately accommodated, and further stigmatized in peer research positions.[28] We fear that despite our best intentions, in this project, these harms occurred—and not because we were unaware of the issues or unwilling to address them; rather, because the academic research enterprise severely constrained us in our capacity to do so.

Our analysis has some important limitations. Most significantly, it is based on the reflections of academic members of our research team, and while some of these individuals also have experience as peers on prior research projects, their roles on the current project limited our reflections to the experiences (and harms) that were visible to us in this capacity. The research assistants have recorded their own reflections,[29] and it will be necessary to consider those reflections alongside our own for a more complete understanding of the failures of this project. A second important limitation of this work is that we are constrained in the specific failures we can discuss, and the level of detail that we can provide to support our arguments, by the need to maintain the privacy of the individual members of the research team. For example, certain failures of the project fall within the scope of human resources issues and thus must remain confidential. However, our collective experiences across multiple projects signal for us that these sorts of failures happen commonly, in the context of many different participatory projects, suggesting that they, too, can likely be traced back to some of the macro-level forces discussed in this chapter. As a result, we are necessarily limited in our capacity to achieve our aim of sharing our failures for the purpose of enabling others to anticipate and/or mitigate them in future participatory projects.

While we remain committed to the principles of participatory research and continue to believe that meaningful engagement with the communities who will be affected is a precondition for ethical research, our experiences (in this specific project, and collectively across the various participatory projects we have been involved with) have left us skeptical about the extent to which it is possible to realize the proposed power-mitigating objectives of participatory research in an academic environment. Based on each of our positionalities in relation to participatory work, we are collectively left with a range of questions about whether and how we engage with these methodologies in the future. Until we are able to change institutional policies and practices that serve to further marginalize peers, is it ethical to ask them to come work in this space? And what are the implications of engaging in research that purports to actively deconstruct power relationships from within an institution that is founded upon (and continues to profit from) colonialist, racist, and ableist (among other) underpinnings? What promises can we ethically make to our community partners in this context? We do not have answers for these questions, and indeed, between us would answer them in different ways, ranging from more reformist positions to decisions to eschew peer research altogether. However, we hope that by sharing our failures and offering the questions they have raised for us, we can contribute to the growing scholarship that calls for participatory researchers to take a more critical and cautious approach in this work.

Authors' Note

There was a lack of consensus within our team regarding the most appropriate language to describe the role of our research staff. While some of the investigators feel that, given the project's orientation to centring lived experience, it is important and necessary to distinguish the peer aspect of the role, some of our staff felt that the term *peer research assistant* devalued or delegitimized their contributions. We note that this sentiment may itself be a manifestation of macro-level forces and the valorization of academic/empirical knowledge over lived experience. Thus, in order to err on the side of minimizing the harm done by the project, we adhere to these staff's stated preference and use the term *research assistant* while explicitly valuing the essential contributions to the project brought by their lived experiences.

Notes

1. Gina Higginbottom and Pranee Liamputtong, *Participatory Qualitative Research Methodologies in Health* (London: Sage, 2015); Nina Wallerstein et al., *Community-based Participatory Research for Health: Advancing Social and Health Equity* (Hoboken: John Wiley & Sons, 2017).
2. Barbara A. Israel et al., "Review of Community-based Research: Assessing Partnership Approaches to Improve Public Health," *Annual Review of Public Health* 19, no. 1 (1998): 173–202.
3. Randy Stoecker, "Are We Talking the Walk of Community-Based Research?" *Action Research* 7, no. 4 (2009): 385–404; Saara Greene et al., "Between Skepticism and Empowerment: The Experiences of Peer Research Assistants in HIV/AIDS, Housing and Homelessness Community-based Research," *International Journal of Social Research Methodology* 12, no. 4 (2009): 361–373.
4. Fern Brunger and Darlene Wall, "'What Do They Really Mean by Partnerships?' Questioning the Unquestionable Good in Ethics Guidelines Promoting Community Engagement in Indigenous Health Research," *Qualitative Health Research* 26, no. 13 (2016): 1862–1877.
5. Brenda Roche, Sarah Flicker, and Adrian Guta, *Peer Research in Action: Models of Practice* (Toronto: Wellesley Institute, 2010), http://www.wellesleyinstitute.com/wp-content/uploads/2011/02/Models_of_Practice_WEB.pdf.
6. John Gaventa et al., "Participatory Research in North America; A Perspective on Participatory Research in Latin America; Participatory Research in Southern

Europe," *Convergence: An International Journal of Adult Education* 21, no. 2-3 (1998): 19-48.
7. Mary Brydon-Miller, "Education, Research and Action: Theory and Methods of Participatory Action Research," in *From Subjects to Subjectives: A Handbook of Interpretive and Participatory Methods*, eds. Deborah Tolman and Mary Brydon-Miller (New York: New York University Press, 2001), 76-89; Davydd J. Greenwood and Morten Levin, *Introduction to Action Research: Social Research for Social Change*, 2nd ed. (Thousand Oaks: Sage, 2007); Budd L. Hall, "From Margins to Center? The Development and Purpose of Participatory Research," *American Sociologist* 23, no. 4 (1992): 15-28; Israel et al., "Review of Community-based Research," 173-202; Geoff P. Whitman, Rachel Pain, and David G. Milledge, "Going with the Flow? Using Participatory Action Research in Physical Geography," *Progress in Physical Geography* 39, no. 5 (2015): 622-639.
8. Justin Jagosh et al., "A Realist Evaluation of Community-based Participatory Research: Partnership Synergy, Trust Building and Related Ripple Effects," *BMC Public Health* 15 (2015): 725.
9. Suzanne Christopher et al., "Building and Maintaining Trust in a Community-Based Participatory Research Partnership," *American Journal of Public Health* 98, no. 8 (2008): 1398-1406.
10. Sandy Lazarus et al., "Community-Based Participatory Research as a Critical Enactment of Community Psychology," *Journal of Community Psychology* 43, no. 1 (2015): 87-98; Joanna Ochocka, Rich Janzen, and Geoffrey Nelson, "Sharing Power and Knowledge: Professional and Mental Health Consumer/Survivor Researchers Working Together in a Participatory Action Project," *Psychiatric Rehabilitation Journal* 25, no. 4 (2002): 379-387.
11. Amy Salmon, Annette J. Browne, and Ann Pederson, "'Now We Call It Research': Participatory Health Research Involving Marginalized Women Who Use Drugs," *Nursing Inquiry* 17, no. 4 (2010): 336-345.
12. Matias I. Golob and Audrey R. Giles, "Challenging and Transforming Power Relations within Community-based Participatory Research: The Promise of a Foucauldian Analysis," *Qualitative Research in Sport, Exercise and Health* 5, no. 3 (2013): 356-372.
13. Brenda Happel et al., "'Chipping Away': Non-consumer Researcher Perspectives on Barriers to Collaborating with Consumers in Mental Health Research," *Journal of Mental Health* 28, no. 1 (2018): 49-55.
14. Brunger and Wall, "What Do They Really Mean by Partnerships?," 1862-1877.
15. Canadian Institutes of Health Research, Natural Sciences and Engineering Research Council of Canada, and Social Sciences and Humanities Research Council, *Tri-Council Policy Statement: Ethical Conduct for Research Involving Humans* (Ottawa: Government of Canada, 2018), https://ethics.gc.ca/eng/documents/tcps2-2018-en-interactive-final.pdf.
16. Brunger and Wall, "What Do They Really Mean by Partnerships?," 1862-1877; Robb Travers et al., "'Community Control' in CBPR: Challenges Experienced

and Questions Raised from the Trans PULSE Project," *Action Research* 11, no. 4 (2013): 403-422.
17. Brunger and Wall, "What Do They Really Mean by Partnerships?," 1862-1877.
18. Bill Cooke and Uma Kothari, *Participation: The New Tyranny?* (New York: Zed Books, 2001).
19. Brunger and Wall, "What Do They Really Mean by Partnerships?," 1862-1877.
20. Wallerstein et al., *Community-based Participatory Research for Health*.
21. For example, see Canadian Institutes of Health Research et al., *Tri-Council Policy Statement*.
22. Kinnon R. MacKinnon, Adrian Guta, Jijian Voronka, Merrick Pilling, Charmaine C. Williams, Carol Strike, and Lori E. Ross, "The Political Economy of Peer Research: Mapping the Possibilities and Precarities of Paying People for Lived Experience," *British Journal of Social Work* 51 (2021): 888-906.
23. Israel et al., "Review of Community-based Research," 173-202.
24. Jijian Voronka and Carole King, "Reflections on Peer Research: Powers, Pleasures, Pains," *British Journal of Social Work* 53, no. 3 (2023): 1692-1699.
25. See, for example, Wallerstein et al., *Community-based Participatory Research for Health*.
26. Alissa Greer and Jane Buxton, *A Guide for Paying Peer Research Assistants: Challenges and Opportunities* (Vancouver: BC Centre for Disease Control, 2017), https://towardtheheart.com/assets/uploads/1502392095pS7Cr8pMMC3xed4576edy2mH-GOyNxJnLFCmcbzU.pdf.
27. Brunger and Wall, "What Do They Really Mean by Partnerships?," 1862-1877; Travers et al., "Community Control," 403-422.
28. Stoecker, "Are We Talking the Walk of Community-Based Research?," 385-404; Greene et al., "Between Skepticism and Empowerment," 361-373.
29. Voronka and King, "Reflections on Peer Research: Powers, Pleasures, Pains," 1692-1699.

Bibliography

Brunger, Fern, and Darlene Wall. "'What Do They Really Mean by Partnerships?' Questioning the Unquestionable Good in Ethics Guidelines Promoting Community Engagement in Indigenous Health Research." *Qualitative Health Research* 26, no. 13 (2016): 1862-1877. https://doi.org/10.1177/1049732316649158.

Brydon-Miller, Mary. "Education, Research and Action: Theory and Methods of Participatory Action Research." In *From Subjects to Subjectives: A Handbook of Interpretive and Participatory Methods*, edited by Deborah Tolman and Mary Brydon-Miller, 76-89. New York: New York University Press, 2001.

Canadian Institutes of Health Research, Natural Sciences and Engineering Research Council of Canada, and Social Sciences and Humanities Research Council. *Tri-Council Policy Statement: Ethical Conduct for Research Involving Humans*. Ottawa: Government of Canada, 2018. https://ethics.gc.ca/eng/documents/tcps2-2018-en-interactive-final.pdf.

Christopher, Suzanne, Vanessa Watts, Alma Knows His Gun McCormick, and Sara Young. "Building and Maintaining Trust in a Community-based Participatory Research Partnership." *American Journal of Public Health* 98, no. 8 (2008): 1398–1406. https://doi.org/10.2105/AJPH.2007.125757.

Cooke, Bill, and Uma Kothari, eds. *Participation: The New Tyranny?* New York: Zed Books, 2001.

Gaventa, John, et al. "Participatory Research in North America; A Perspective on Participatory Research in Latin America; Participatory Research in Southern Europe." *Convergence: An International Journal of Adult Education* 21, no. 2–3 (1998): 19–48.

Golob, Matias I., and Audrey R. Giles. "Transforming Power Relations within Community-based Participatory Research: The Promise of a Foucauldian Analysis." *Qualitative Research in Sport, Exercise and Health* 5, no. 3 (2013): 356–372. https://doi.org/10.1080/2159676X.2013.846273.

Greene, Saara, Amrita Ahluwalia, James Watson, Ruthann Tucker, Sean B. Rourke, Jay Koornstra, Michael Sobota, LaVerne Monette, and Steve Byers. "Between Skepticism and Empowerment: The Experiences of Peer Research Assistants in HIV/AIDS, Housing and Homelessness Community-based Research." *International Journal of Social Research Methodology* 12, no. 4 (2009): 361–373. https://doi.org/10.1080/13645570802553780.

Greenwood, Davydd J., and Morten Levin. *Introduction to Action Research: Social Research for Social Change*, 2nd edition. Thousand Oaks: Sage, 2007.

Greer, Alissa, and Jane Buxton. *A Guide for Paying Peer Research Assistants: Challenges and Opportunities*. Vancouver: BC Centre for Disease Control, 2017. https://towardtheheart.com/assets/uploads/1502392095pS7Cr8pMMC3xed4576edy2mHGOyNxJnLFCmcbzU.pdf.

Hall, Budd L. "From Margins to Center? The Development and Purpose of Participatory Research." *American Sociologist* 23, no. 4 (1992): 15–28. https://doi.org/10.1007/BF02691928.

Happel, Brenda, Sarah Gordon, Julia Bocking, Pete Ellis, Cath Roper, Jackie Liggins, Brett Scholz, and Chris Platania-Phung. "'Chipping Away': Non-consumer Researcher Perspectives on Barriers to Collaborating with Consumers in Mental Health Research." *Journal of Mental Health* 28, no. 1 (2018): 49–55. https://doi.org/10.1080/09638237.2018.1466051.

Higginbottom, Gina, and Pranee Liamputtong, eds. *Participatory Qualitative Research Methodologies in Health*. London: Sage, 2015.

Israel, Barbara A., Amy J. Schulz, Edith A. Parker, and Adam B. Becker. "Review of Community-based Research: Assessing Partnership Approaches to Improve Public Health." *Annual Review of Public Health* 19, no. 1 (1998): 173–202. https://doi.org/10.1146/annurev.publhealth.19.1.173.

Jagosh, Justin, Paula L. Bush, Jon Salsberg, Ann C. Macaulay, Trish Greenhalgh, Geoff Wong, Margaret Cargo, Lawrence W. Green, Carol P. Herbert, and Pierre Pluye. "A Realist Evaluation of Community-based Participatory Research: Partnership

Synergy, Trust Building and Related Ripple Effects." *BMC Public Health* 15 (2015): 725. https://doi.org/10.1186/s12889-015-1949-1.

Lazarus, Sandy, Abdulsamed Bulbulia, Naiema Taliep, and Tony Naidoo. "Community-Based Participatory Research as a Critical Enactment of Community Psychology." *Journal of Community Psychology* 43, no. 1 (2015): 87-98. https://doi.org/10.1002/jcop.21689.

MacKinnon, Kinnon R., Adrian Guta, Jijian Voronka, Merrick Pilling, Charmaine C. Williams, Carol Strike, and Lori E. Ross. "The Political Economy of Peer Research: Mapping the Possibilities and Precarities of Paying People for Lived Experience." *British Journal of Social Work* 51 (2021): 888-906.

Ochocka, Joanna, Rich Janzen, and Geoffrey Nelson. "Sharing Power and Knowledge: Professional and Mental Health Consumer/Survivor Researchers Working Together in a Participatory Action Project." *Psychiatric Rehabilitation Journal* 25, no. 4 (2002): 379-387. https://doi.org/10.1037/h0094999.

Roche, Brenda, Sarah Flicker, and Adrian Guta. *Peer Research in Action: Models of Practice*. Toronto: The Wellesley Institute, 2010. http://www.wellesleyinstitute.com/wp-content/uploads/2011/02/Models_of_Practice_WEB.pdf.

Salmon, Amy, Annette J. Browne, and Ann Pederson. "'Now We Call It Research': Participatory Health Research Involving Marginalized Women Who Use Drugs." *Nursing Inquiry* 17, no. 4 (2010): 336-345. https://doi.org/10.1111/j.1440-1800.2010.00507.x.

Stoecker, Randy. "Are We Talking the Walk of Community-Based Research?" *Action Research* 7, no. 4 (2009): 385-404. https://doi.org/10.1177/1476750309340944.

Travers, Robb, Jake Pyne, Greta Bauer, Lauren Munro, Brody Giambrone, Rebecca Hammond, and Kyle Scanlon. "'Community Control' in CBPR: Challenges Experienced and Questions Raised from the Trans PULSE Project." *Action Research* 11, no. 4 (2013): 403-422. https://doi.org/10.1177/1476750313507093.

Voronka, Jijian, and Carole King. "Reflections on Peer Research: Powers, Pleasures, Pains." *British Journal of Social Work* 53, no. 3 (2023): 1692-1699.

Wallerstein, Nina, Bonnie Duran, John G. Oetzel, and Meredith Minkler, eds. *Community-based Participatory Research for Health: Advancing Social and Health Equity*. Hoboken: John Wiley & Sons, 2017.

Whitman, Geoff P., Rachel Pain, and David G. Milledge. "Going with the Flow? Using Participatory Action Research in Physical Geography." *Progress in Physical Geography* 39, no. 5 (2015): 622-639. https://doi.org/10.1177/0309133315589707.

IV

Reflections on Creative Research Collaborations and Relationships

11

Building Collaboration through (Embodied) Conversation
An Indigenist and a Feminist Reflect on Writing and Learning Together

Melissa Schnarr and Eva Cupchik

Introduction

In the spring of 2020, two things happened: COVID-19 shut down the world and we (Eva and Melissa) began our writing partnership. While new to the realm of academic publishing, we were confident in our expertise and in the strength of our relationship—as colleagues, friends, and occasionally co-conspirators. As a feminist and an Indigenist, we felt the gravitational pull of academic recognition (publishing) while also being guided by internal motivations for what we envisioned as purposeful and inclusive knowledge translation. As scholars whose knowledge systems exist on the margins,[1] the opportunity to engage in knowledge co-production that would reach an international audience was both exciting and empowering. We, the subaltern, would speak, and we chose to do so in a way that purposefully confronted and played with conventional academic writing.[2]

Our co-writing work has evolved from conversations in which we have naturally engaged with one another as scholars and lifelong learners. We take inspiration from writers like Absolon and Willett[3] by translating informal conversation into textual presentation. Our methodology is realized through unfolding dialogue (often over the phone) as we navigate the development of our collaborations. Our conversations are both data gathering and analysis. There is an inherent, a priori vulnerability in learning about concepts that extend across cultures. To resist a polarization of epistemologies and ontological subject positions, we made space for mistakes, failure, and uncertainty, holding each other's subject positions in the writing. (There is a vulnerability in admitting that "I do not know.") With each intellectual meeting and every story, metaphor, and citation shared, our understandings of each person's unique perspective continued to build and deepen.

In this chapter, we reflect on our experiences of collaboration and view this as a continued evolution from the conversations that first informed our work. We invite you to join us as we share thoughts and experiences from our writing process, while interrogating the tensions encountered along the way. Such tensions include the politics of navigating divergent writing styles, academic subject positions, relationships with editors, citational practices, and the complexities of co-writing through a pandemic. Through this journey, we have come to understand vulnerability as an essential practice of collaborative writing.

It is important that we introduce ourselves. Introductions serve as the first means of relationship building; in Indigenous ways of knowing and being, introductions are an integral component of relationality, which, as a practice, connects Indigenous epistemologies, ontologies, and axiologies. This has become a common practice within Indigenous scholarship; we elucidate our self-location first so that you might know us.

> **Eva:** I am a queer Jewish (Ashkenazi) independent researcher, athlete scholar, teacher, and outsider. Despite communicative barriers, Mel and I continue an open-ended dialogue across positionalities, lived experiences in publishing, and ethnic/cultural backgrounds.
>
> **Melissa:** Boozhoo. She:kon. I am an Anishinaabe and Haudenosaunee writer, scholar, and educator currently living in Deshkan Ziibii (London, Ontario, Canada). My mother's family comes from Bkejwanong Territory (Walpole Island First Nation) and my father's family is Mohawk of the Six Nations of the

Grand River Territory. I'm currently a PhD candidate at Western University studying Indigenous education and an instructor at Western's Faculty of Ed. As an author and poet, I approach the co-writing process as a wilful practice of my culture's ways of knowing and being, embodying collectivity and valuing multiple truths as we attempt to understand the world.

Tension 1: Navigating Writing Styles

Eva: I encounter difficulties responding to Indigenous knowledge translation within a feminist lens, often defaulting to Eurocentric paradigms. Working across oral traditions (traditional and contemporary Jewish and Indigenous cultures) offers a creative, fruitful platform for discussion. However, research through storytelling must translate into grounded idea sharing and respectful knowledge dissemination. Theoretical constraints from Eurocentric traditions (feminist phenomenology) can impart a technicality of style and content within the writing. They are not inherently colonial schools of thought but need to expand from deductive reasoning into a non-linear method for collecting and sharing information. I am humbled by Indigenous methodologies but feel disconnected from their central tenets. I struggle to balance the creativity of abstraction (esoteric language of feminist phenomenology) with grounded wisdom through dialogues with Elders, scholars, and Knowledge Keepers. In our research collaboration, I engage an iterative form of dialogue, while Melissa fosters a playful form of writing akin to her poetic style. An embodied hermeneutic (a holistic means for contextual interpretation) that makes space for both Indigenous and feminist discourses is important for contingent knowledge sharing/translation. What is the purpose of publishing across Indigenous and Settler paradigms? Whom does this work affect and what is at stake? I will not help the cause of reconciliation by the mere publication of words in an article.

Melissa: As a (creative) writer, the prospect of developing academic writing with a trusted colleague and friend was both exciting and also subversive to me. Here I was, a lowly PhD candidate who now had the opportunity and vehicle to share knowledge that had rarely been seen throughout my graduate studies curriculum. (The idea of *giving voice* is a frequent topic during our phone calls.) When we began writing together, I expected tension. I expected tension in finding ways to bring our respective knowledge systems together without one superseding the other. I also expected tension in translating embodied knowledge (Indigenous knowledge systems) via the static medium of text. What I did not anticipate was the confrontations that arose as Eva and I attempted to reconcile an academic way of writing with an Indigenous way of knowing. Eva's training as a phenomenologist did not always mesh with my sensibilities as a poet. Our writing styles, while divergent, were a strength, though, allowing for dissonance and space to question and better apprehend. We practised Two-Eyed Seeing by enacting Two-Eyed writing. For us, when we write together, we become a community rather than two individuals striving for voice.

Dialogic interaction opens the hermeneutic enclosure to allow us a centred learning experience. Eva often felt constrained by Eurocentric critical theory, relegated by the conventions of form and limitations of academic prose, while Melissa experienced anxiety in the perceived rigidity of the academic form. Through dialogue, however, these constraints and perceptions became less stark and humbler in their engagements. In conversation (and through dissensus), we were able to examine the elemental components of our given medium and discard the trappings that did not serve the heart of our message. We eschew a traditional format in favour of a structure that embodies the knowledges we are translating. We embody our dialogue in the texts that we co-write. Being vulnerable is about permission to fail in style, intent, audience, and literary purpose. Vetting internal dialogue through a cross-cultural perspective can permit asynchronicity, as power for resistance. This power is built on relationships first, allowing for those spaces to open up for disagreement, iteration, and occasionally failure. When writing together there is no "wrong"; there is only what does or does not breathe life into your words.

At first, we allowed these vulnerabilities out of necessity—what seemed like an ontological condition of the pandemic. We were two disembodied voices attempting to connect and complement two unique systems of knowledge on one (virtual) page. With nothing except the enunciations of our English language holding us together, we negotiated murky understandings of each other's lens. We told stories and invoked imagery beyond the scope of our intellectual debates, and when our meaning (or clarity) waffled, this became an opportunity for internal reflection. We disagreed; we misunderstood; we explained poorly at times. We entered into and shared this space willingly, experiencing it not so much as a collision of jagged worldviews[4] but as a graceless dance, punctuated by the clacking of keys. Accepting our (frequent) gracelessness became the foundation for our collaboration. We wrote into our subject positions, and into our misunderstandings, finding that falling and dancing can sometimes be the same thing.

This graceless space is a mutual responsibility. Our research was/is a pact. As co-authors, scholars, and libraries of our own respective expertise, when we engage in co-writing, we engage in treaty making. Here, we gather as sovereign scholars, codifying our relationship as co-authors through the sharing of intellectual territory and through "patience and persistence."[5] Ultimately, the co-writing and the dialogue across cultures/ways of knowing and being invigorated a deeper understanding of our own knowledge systems as we engaged the protocols of treaty: respect, reciprocity, and balance. Working with editors also engenders a treaty relationship. We come together, each with gifts to share: subject-matter expertise (the authors) and audience expertise (the editors). Our book chapter promotes a wampum mindset:[6] cementing an oral agreement into material form.

Tension 2: Negotiating Indigenous and Embodied Knowledges into English (Forms)

Eva: There is inherent difficulty in locating knowledge production between Settler editors and feminist/Indigenous authors. Melissa and I had reservations about footnoting (sacred teachings, e.g., the Seven Grandfather Teachings and blood memory). There are tenets of Anishinaabek knowledge that are not citable for Settler consumption in publications. Moreover, using language that gestures to Grandfather Teachings (e.g., Speaking Bravely) may be more appropriate than an explanatory footnote. Indigenous Knowledge can be written in metaphor through specific words, their meanings are not inherently explicit or translatable in literary terms; a difficult reality to contend with between Settler editors and researchers. It is important to balance the readerly elements of Eurocentric scholarship with embedded Indigenous Knowledge.

Melissa: We talk extensively about theory and theorizing. Indigenous Knowledge is inherently embodied—how do you theorize something that exists as a verb rather than a noun? In writing together, we attempt to impart the motion and vibrancy of Anishinaabemowin through metaphor and imagery. There is a responsibility to not only express the knowledge in a good (accurate) way in terms of meaning, but also in terms of spirit.

English is problematic as one of the colonizer's first tools. Settler education systems strip Indigenous populations of their languages; the Discovery Doctrine and naming rights strip the land of its first identity, replacing it with European signifiers. The imposition of English on Indigenous Peoples has eroded the "symbolic code" we have for understanding our world and how we commune with Creation.[7] To put Indigenous Knowledges into English words, then, is a precarious endeavour.

The literal use of English does not always afford justice to Indigenous Knowledges. (It is not possible to explicate all signified content to a Settler audience.) Creating a dichotomy between Settler and Indigenous Knowledge is a tautology with little room for creative nuances; we find it more constructive to accept the fragility of this linguistic bridge rather than shore it up with abstraction and theory. Settler and Indigenous perspectives can work in concert if we tread carefully and respectfully. It is important to foster intertextual understandings of Eurocentric and Indigenous ways of knowing rather than impose criticisms or comparatives that assert binaries across texts.

Enacting our wampum mindset and our Two-Eyed Seeing methodology poised our writership for appreciating what both English and Anishinaabemowin had to offer us. Noun-based English holds at its core a relationship between subject and object; Anishinaabemowin (verb-based) carries a story in every action.[8] We engendered linguistic bridging on metaphoric levels when the literal held too many obstacles. We encountered adversity in balancing the complexity of Anishinaabek concepts with reader accessibility, footnoting to provide more context as necessary without colonizing the ideas themselves. Some things we chose to simply cut rather than explain; the knowledge was too inherent to expose to the ink of the page. Reconciling the vulnerability of English (to hold certain knowledges) becomes a pre- and post-writing exercise in courting decolonial practices.

Tension 3: Navigating the Academic Subject Position

Eva: It is not easy to relate through rigid methods that sustain academic formats. Institutional bureaucracy engenders a kinship with hypocrisy, increasing enrolment by restricting faculty. I am gutted by limits associated rigid academic methodologies that do not engage lived-world phenomena. Words are empty unless they connect with actual processes—the sentient beings who experience culture, life, family, and self. Where is the line between academic conventions, form, and integrity of self in writing? I feel pressured to write for publishers, not Indigenous communities, Jewish, or queer realms.

Melissa: Indigenous ways of knowing and being are predicated on relationality. We are accountable to our communities and yet, as an Indigenous scholar, I am also beholden to an institution—one that has the authority to grant me status within the academic community or not. Being an Indigenous academic is fraught with ethical conundrums like this, not to mention having to carry the colonial legacy of research that has often seen Indigenous Knowledges transacted at the expense of the community and for the benefit of the researcher. I always come back to language and form. Who will read my/our work? How will it be received? What will my community think? Will my/our work create meaningful change (in the heart/mind of someone) somewhere in the world? If the answer is "no," then my path forward ceases to exist. There is no such thing as an Indigenous scholar who isn't relatable.

As co-authors, we aim to balance a complementarity of knowledge, eradicate dichotomies, and foster peaceful co-existence that engenders the axioms of treaty making, echoing Indigenous epistemologies.[9] The dialectic of Two-Eyed Seeing is creative and outward reaching, not self-centring its premises on positivist results.[10] A question arises: Who are we in the *doing of research* (enacting Indigenous and feminist epistemologies across cultures and lived experiences)? Theorizing in the abstract necessarily evades the purposes of embodying a scholarly community through actions.

Relatability is a nuanced experience. Feminist phenomenologist Radhika Mohanram clarifies that "place" and "body" intersect, where "meaning" emerges, across layers of epistemologies.[11] The concepts of place and body "do not have meaning, prior to their discursive practice," as emerging cross-cultural expressions.[12] We focus on relatability in dialogues to perform a phenomenological framework of experience that engenders Two-Eyed Seeing, which expresses theoretical and practical stakes for culturally safe learning and exploratory writing.[13]

Phenomenological but not wholly Eurocentric, our framework has been carefully constructed. By weaving together considerations for the marginalized experiences (communities) we aim to elevate, tenets of transnational feminism and the principles of Indigenous Research: respect, relevance, reciprocity, responsibility, relationships, and (right of) refusal.[14] Embodying relatability is a key measure of relating Indigenous-Settler experiences through written text in the absence of face-to-face engagements, where relationship building occurs in real time, in real space. Our bodies (our selves, our bodies of knowledge) can only constitute meaning for our communities when they intersect with places of relevance (local grounded spaces and conceptual spaces that hold our communities' subject positions as pre-eminent); our reciprocity comes to life in how we share and activate the knowledges we transpose. None of this is possible without walking with respect in our hearts. Our relationships are sustained through these practices only with the ongoing accountability and maintenance of all these responsibilities. It is a lifelong commitment to engage in this good way.[15]

But there is vulnerability in practising such relatability as an academic. While our framework is stalwart—firmly grounded and built with the connective tissue of ethical accountability—it invites interrogations (on objectivity, bias, editorializing) and exposes us to the vicissitudes of the academic realm. Our framework is a ladder reaching up into the possibilities of our field(s), but we must cling to it against the strong winds of convention and the vortices of continuing academic debates and paradigm shifts.

Tension 4: Negotiating the Intimate Distance of the Pandemic

Eva: What does it mean to be vulnerable during a pandemic (are the words parallel or divergent)? Is the university during COVID a mere aesthetic?

Are scholars thinking critically during pandemics amid a turn to economic advancement/research production? Is the virtual aspect of phone or Zoom dialogue aiding or restricting communication? Are folks passively observing the world as void, rather than engaging the lived experiences of marginalized communities during COVID? E-learning through academic communication enters the private sphere, while sexuality, race, protest, and politics return as public means of engagement.

Walking through downtown London/Toronto, I note the present absences, silenced voices, and unmarked territories soliciting narrative validation. Human sidewalk evasion in fear of viral infection reveals classist divisions and intersections of difference. I do not theorize a departure from the phenomenology of COVID; beyond actual illness resides internalized anxieties, justifications for avoidance, scientific arrogance, government resistance, and confession. It is possible to theorize amid global pandemic intervention; is abstraction feasible during times of suffering? Is it possible to distill contemporary and Indigenous Knowledges to a Settler audience or publisher in COVID times? The impetus to produce (positivist data) is curtailed by human suffering in its most raw iteration. Indigenous epistemologies require the teacher to embody the subject position of the learner. I learn from Melissa's poetry, a discursive contribution that fills the gaps of nothingness.

Melissa: I think we inadvertently conducted a methodology of visiting out of instinctual self-care. I looked forward to our phone calls, not only because it was connection with the outside world but because we always took the time to visit with one another first. While our days were similar and uneventful (we were each in our own quarantine silo), we still took the time to share unimportant details about our daily lives before diving into the work. Collaborating through a pandemic was a challenge and an intellectual lifeline. In my darkest moments of the shutdown, I couldn't help but reflect on the state that we, as human beings, had found ourselves in. In the shutdown, Eva and I traded physical proximity for the intimate distance of a shared headspace via our conversations.

Embodying writing can be visceral, translating and reproducing salient knowledge.[16] Embodied writing devises the self in plurality, exploring self-understandings as they inspire cultural experiences and social worlds. Travelling across Indigenous and Eurocentric worlds, our chapter "becomes-with" theory and embodies intersectional learning that permits dynamic relationships and practices.[17] Distance does not immediately bear on liminal spaces: as co-authors, we negotiate personal, cultural, and professional boundaries in travelling across worlds into discursive communities.[18]

Negotiating meaning across liminal spaces can bridge epistemological gaps and their power dynamics. In co-writing, we negotiate personal and professional boundaries that intersect and superimpose, instantiating an "interstitial space" wherein "different knowledge systems can be equitably compared rather than absorbed into an imperialist archive";[19] our interstitial space, unlike Gough's, however, is not neutral but shared, invoking our wampum mindset.

Our liminality comes to the fore as we collaborate across physical distances (two different cities) within worlds largely cut off from human connectivity. This can be a space of vulnerability in its rawest form; we invite outsiders into our headspace, our homes. In this space, wholism becomes a precondition. There is no quarantining one's mental, physical, emotional, or spiritual aspects when we share our understandings of that which we hold dear (our worldviews, in this case). Rhythm and inflection fluctuate as we discuss topics of passion, stimulating more thought (apprehension) and even memory. Yet we tread within each other's headspace and heartspace, noting the traumas of our internal landscapes. We hold each other's subject positions as we write, out of methodology as much as treaty, understanding that this shared space permits creation, but always with the danger of destruction (harm) if we do not hold each other with care in the work.

A Manifesto of Extant Conditions (a Pandemic Poetic)

This is a time of getting lost.

Forgotten, jettisoned, left in between the cracks. Languid anxiety and frantic hesitation quell search and rescue attempts.

Missed connections, marginalia, and slow internet are the means for misplacements, stagnating lack thereof conditions as the world executes a nimble pivot.

People disappear every day and our neuroses mask the absence, compelling platitudes in the place of questions, cavorting empathy as a type of witchcraft.

These frenetic dispositions tinge the world in garish shades of migraine yellow and visceral puce—afflicting the sight, averting eyes to more aesthetic scenes and narratives easier to parse.

Balcony concerts and neighbourhood yoga might soothe the soul of the social body, but they do not fill empty bellies or assuage the dread of coming tomorrows.

Meanwhile, we're building terrariums on a hope that changed states will revert, even though entropy only moves in one direction.

This is a time of bitter medicine we leave on the shelf.

Better to remember the sweet syrup of yore. Better to forget that societal panacea has never been an easy pill to swallow.

Is poetry a living medicine to heal broken spaces? We navigate held spaces that foster anachronistic experiences of space/time.[20] As co-authors, we are reframing discourses about Eurocentric methods by modelling paradigms from multiple lenses, demonstrating creative knowledge. We do not juxtapose formal, professionally acquired knowledge (Eurocentric learning practices) against Indigenous traditional knowledge systems, but "come to know" in a liminal space that welcomes change.[21] We write poetry into our research as means to stimulate all aspects of the reader. Poetry, Richardson notes, is a "*a practical* and *powerful* method for analysing social worlds."[22]

Final Thoughts

Eva: My writing is self-serving without outreach to Indigenous, Settler, Jewish, and queer communities; the world outside of critical theory narrows into nothingness. Academic rhetoric can obscure relationships between Indigenous and Settler people, by asserting a leitmotif of academic production, or abstraction in lieu of fostering community. I wonder if the words that we are speaking as scholars on Eurocentric and Indigenous understandings connect with actual communities (are we telling people who they are without listening)?

Melissa: Richardson[23] reminds us that all texts are constructed. Likewise, all knowledge is constructed, though these facts are often obscured by dominant narratives of "truth" and validity. I think in choosing to produce our work as dialogues, we enact a truth-telling of our learning journeys while also gesturing to the artifice of the written word. Is that enough? Did we push enough?

As scholars invested in social justice work (research, activism, education), part of our responsibility to our work and ourselves (collaborations, larger communities) is to recognize and interrogate the power and oppression embedded in the structures and grammars in which we are trained to communicate. If we take for granted the academic writing style or even conventional scholarly forms, we risk perpetuating oppression even as we work to dismantle it. We are emboldened by scholars like Smith, Tuck, and Yang, who promote marginalized experiences while eschewing the expected structure of an academic volume.[24] Research, including writing, can be activism if we are intentional in how we choose to give it life.

Moreover, English, as a tool of colonization, remains as an open-ended question on how to navigate marginalized knowledges; if writing is to be our method, then we must implement each word, punctuation mark, and syntax with deep care (even if such attentions render us unwilling to share, actively withholding certain information). We must also engender an ethic of accountable meaning making, practising relatability rather than objectivity. Lastly, we recognize that the pandemic ensconced individuals from the interpersonal, tangible world into virtuality, abstracting relationships and the realities of suffering as individuals endured under a blanket of global anxiety. Connecting as sentient beings fell privy to an interfering mechanism of technology, not in keeping with Indigenous epistemologies or transnational feminist methodologies. In building collaboration, we must affirm the adversity experienced by our partners-in-writing and walk in kindness as we navigate worldviews, expertise, and learning. We are vulnerable when we walk together like this, and in this cosmology of vulnerabilities, we become community; we *become* co-authors.

In this collaboration, we do not strive for absolutes, but rather a spectrum of questions and experiences, honouring the plurality of truths embodied in our respective knowledge systems. This text is our most genuine attempt to represent who we are; we share ourselves so that you might know us.

Notes

1. Margaret Kovach, "Emerging from the Margins: Indigenous Methodologies," in *Research as Resistance: Critical, Indigenous and Anti-Oppressive Approaches*, eds. Leslie Brown and Susan Strega (Toronto: Canadian Scholars' Press, 2004), 19–36.
2. Gayatri Spivak, "Can the Subaltern Speak?" in *Colonial Discourse and Post-Colonial Theory*, eds. Patrick Williams and Laura Chrisman (New York: Columbia University Press, 1993), 66–107.
3. Kathy Absolon and Cam Willett, "Putting Ourselves Forward: Location in Aboriginal Research," in *Research as Resistance: Critical, Indigenous and Anti-Oppressive Approaches*, eds. Leslie Brown and Susan Strega (Toronto: Canadian Scholars' Press, 2004), 97–126.
4. Leroy Little Bear, "Jagged Worldviews Colliding," in *Reclaiming Indigenous Voice and Vision*, ed. Marie Battiste (Vancouver: UBC Press, 2000), 77–85.
5. Leanne Betasamosake Simpson, *Dancing on Our Turtle's Back: Stories of Nishnaabeg Re-Creation, Resurgence, and a New Emergence* (Winnipeg: ARP Books, 2011).
6. Wampum covenants are traditional nation-to-nation agreements (treaties) that take form as wampum belts, which depict the terms of the agreement through symbolic encoding via white and purple shells. The Haudenosaunee Two-Row Wampum Belt is a well-known example that holds in it a treaty between the Haudenosaunee and Dutch peoples.
7. Gregory Cajete, "Philosophy of Native Science," in *American Indian Thought: Philosophical Essays*, ed. Anne Waters (Oxford: Blackwell Publishing, 2004), 50.
8. Darnell clarifies how time and space are coded into Ojibway "polysynthetic" verbal structures wherein word parts have independent meanings, sharing "entailments of personhood" that describe the language's ontological functions. Expert speakers do not directly address themselves "as individual or community," without grounding land-based relations in terms of developing their collective being. Regna Darnell, "Walking Alongside Wisahketchak: Fieldwork, a Retrospective Exercise that Takes a Long Time," *Journal of Anthropological Research* 71, no. 1 (2020), 55.
9. Andrea Reid, Lauren Eckert, John-Francis Lane, Nathan Young, Scott Hinch, Chris Darimont, Steven Cooke, Natalie Ban, and Albert Marshall, "'Two-Eye Seeing': An Indigenous Framework to Transform Fisheries Research and Management," *Fish and Fisheries* 17, no. 14 (2021): 243–261.

10. Audre Lorde, "The Master's Tools Will Never Dismantle the Master's House," in *This Bridge Called My Back: Writings by Radical Women of Color*, eds. Cherríe Moraga and Gloria Anzaldúa (New York: Kitchen Table Press, 1984), 94–101.
11. Radhika Mohanram, *Black Body: Women, Colonialism and Space* (Minneapolis: University of Minnesota Press, 1999), 200.
12. Mohanram, *Black Body*, 200.
13. Andrea McKivett, Judith Hudson, Dennis McDermott, and David Paul, "Two-eyed Seeing: A Useful Gaze in Indigenous Medical Education Research," *Medical Education* 54 no. 3 (2020): 217–224.
14. As updated by Deborah McGregor, Jean-Paul Restoule, and Rochelle Johnston, *Indigenous Research: Theories, Practices and Relationships* (Toronto: Canadian Scholars' Press, 2018).
15. Cora Weber-Pillwax, "Indigenous Researchers and Indigenous Research Methods: Cultural Influences or Cultural Determinants of Research Methods," *Pimatisiwin* 2 no. 1 (2004): 78–90.
16. Joan W. Scott, "The Evidence of Experience," *Critical Inquiry* 17 no. 4 (1991): 773–797.
17. Marian Ortega, *In-Between: Latina Feminist Phenomenology, Multiplicity, and the Self* (New York: SUNY Press, 2016).
18. Kurt Danziger, *Naming the Mind: How Psychology Found Its Language* (London: Sage, 1997).
19. Noel Gough, "Globalization and Curriculum Inquiry: Performing Transnational Imaginaries," in *Globalization Education*, eds. Nelly Stromquist and Karen Monkman (Lanham: Rowman & Littlefield, 2014), 132.
20. Anne McClintock, *Imperial Leather: Race, Gender and Sexuality in the Colonial Context* (New York: Routledge, 1995).
21. Kathleen E. Absolon (Minogiizhigokwe), *Kaandossiwin: How We Come to Know* (Halifax: Fernwood Publishing, 2011).
22. Laurel Richardson, "Writing: A Method of Inquiry," in *Handbook of Qualitative Research*, eds. N.K. Denzin and Y.S. Lincoln (Thousand Oaks: Sage, 1994), 522.
23. Richardson, "Writing: A Method of Inquiry."
24. Linda Tuhiwai Smith, Eve Tuck, and K.W. Yang, eds., *Indigenous and Decolonizing Studies in Education: Mapping the Long View* (New York: Routledge, 2019).

Bibliography

Absolon, Kathleen E. (Minogiizhigokwe). *Kaandossiwin: How We Come to Know*. Halifax: Fernwood Publishing, 2011.

Absolon, Kathy, and Cam Willett. "Putting Ourselves Forward: Location in Aboriginal Research." In *Research as Resistance: Critical, Indigenous, and Anti-Oppressive Approaches*, edited by Leslie Brown and Susan Strega, 97–126. Toronto: Canadian Scholars' Press, 2004.

Cajete, Gregory. "Philosophy of Native Science." In *American Indian Thought: Philosophical Essays*, edited by Anne Waters, 45–57. Oxford: Blackwell Publishing, 2004.

Danzinger, Kurt. *Naming the Mind: How Psychology Found Its Language.* London: Sage, 2017.

Darnell, Regna. "Walking Alongside Wisahketchak: Fieldwork, a Retrospective Exercise That Takes a Long Time." *Journal of Anthropological Research* 76, no. 1 (2020): 44-58.

Gough, Noel. "Globalization and Curriculum Inquiry: Performing Transnational Imaginaries." In *Globalization and Education: Integration and Contestation across Cultures*, edited by Nelly Stromquist and Karen Monkman, 125-43. Lanham: Rowman & Littlefield, 2014.

Kovach, Margaret. "Emerging from the Margins: Indigenous Methodologies." In *Research as Resistance: Critical, Indigenous, and Anti-Oppressive Approaches*, edited by Leslie Brown and Susan Strega, 19-36. Toronto: Canadian Scholars' Press, 2004.

Little Bear, Leroy. "Jagged Worldviews Colliding." In *Reclaiming Indigenous Voice and Vision*, edited by Marie Battiste, 77-85. Vancouver: UBC Press, 2000.

Lorde, Audre. "The Masters Tools Will Never Dismantle the Master's House." In *This Bridge Called My Back: Writings by Radical Women of Color*, edited by Cherrie Moraga and Gloria Anzaldúa, 94-101. New York: Kitchen Table Press, 1984.

McClintock, Anne. *Imperial Leather: Race, Gender and Sexuality in the Colonial Context.* New York: Routledge, 1995.

McGregor, Deborah, Jean-Paul Restoule and Rochelle Johnston. *Indigenous Research: Theories, Practices and Relationships.* Toronto: Canadian Scholars' Press, 2018.

McKivett, Andrea, Judith N. Hudson, Dennis McDermott, and David Paul. "Two-eyed Seeing: A Useful Gaze in Indigenous Medical Education Research." *Medical Education* 54, no. 3 (2020): 217-224.

Mohanram, Radhika. *Black Body: Women, Colonialism, and Space.* Minneapolis: University of Minnesota Press, 1999.

Ortega, Marian. *In-Between: Latina Feminist Phenomenology, Multiplicity, and the Self.* Albany: SUNY Press, 2016.

Reid, Andrea, Lauren Eckert, John-Francis Lane, Nathan Young, Scott Hinch, Chris Darimont, Steven Cooke, Natalie Ban, and Albert Marshall. "'Two-Eyed Seeing': An Indigenous Framework to Transform Fisheries Research and Management." *Fish and Fisheries* 22 no. 2 (2021): 243-261.

Scott, J.W. "The Evidence of Experience." *Critical Inquiry* 17 no. 4 (1991): 773-797.

Simpson, Leanne Betasamosake. *Dancing on Our Turtle's Back: Stories of Nishnaabeg Re-Creation, Resurgence, and a New Emergence.* Winnipeg: ARP Books, 2011.

Spivak, Gayatri. "Can the Subaltern Speak?" In *Colonial Discourse and Post-Colonial Theory*, edited by Patrick Williams and Laura Chrisman, 66-107. New York: Columbia University Press, 1993.

Smith, Linda Tuhiwai, Eve Tuck, and K.W. Yang, eds., *Indigenous and Decolonizing Studies in Education: Mapping the Long View.* New York: Routledge, 2019.

Weber-Pillwax, Cora. "Indigenous Researchers and Indigenous Research Methods: Cultural Influences or Cultural Determinants of Research Methods." *Pimatisiwin* 2, no. 1 (2004): 78-90.

12

Working Collectively across Our Minoritized Differences
Vulnerabilities and Possibilities of ReVisioning Fitness

Aly Bailey, Meredith Bessey, Carla Rice, Evadne Kelly, Tara-Leigh McHugh, Bongi Dube, Paul Tshuma, Skylar Sookpaiboon, Kayla Besse, Salima Punjani, and seeley quest

Across the Anglo-Western world, architects of the eugenics movement (race improvement through heredity) mobilized the word *fitness* to measure and discriminate against the physical and mental capacities of individuals.[1] Those coded as "unfit" included racialized, Indigenous, disabled, and impoverished peoples, whose bodies and minds were thought to deviate in problem-saturated ways from the dominant white, non-disabled, cisgendered, middle-to-upper-class standard.[2] Thus, their differences were targeted for containment and elimination through forced sterilization, institutionalization, restrictive immigration policies and marriage laws, and removal from public space.[3]

In present times, "fitness" continues to be tethered with morality. For instance, in neoliberal and healthist contexts, those with bodies categorized as "fit" (typically non-disabled, thin, white, and affluent) are presumed to make "healthy" life choices and become "good citizens" while those coded as "unfit" (often also fat, disabled, and racialized) are presumed to engage in "unhealthy" behaviours and as such, become "failed citizens" whose bio-psycho-moral "failures" justify their discrimination.[4] There is no doubt the word *fitness* continues to carry distressing connotations and implications for anyone labelled with difference,[5] and although blatant eugenics has waned, many scholars assert that eugenics takes a new form today, known as "new eugenics,"[6] "soft eugenics,"[7] "implicit eugenics,"[8] and "neo-eugenics."[9]

The new eugenics operates in more insidious ways than its earlier, overt form. Stern[10] argues that we can determine whether a practice is eugenic by examining its effects rather than its intentions. For example, seemingly "inclusive" campaigns (e.g., #InclusiveYoga) have been found to reinscribe ableist, racist, heteronormative, and fatphobic ideas about which bodies are worthy in today's society.[11] Furthermore, fitness contexts are known to be exclusive in their structural design, lack of diversity in employee representation, and narrow messaging about who is "fit."[12] Patriarchal, colonial, eugenic, and white supremist ideas permeate contemporary physical activity spaces, resulting in exclusion of people across minoritized differences.[13]

ReVisioning Fitness is an arts- and community-based participatory research project that directly counters these problematic discourses and structures by queering, cripping, and thickening fitness, and centring the lived experiences of people who are trans, non-binary, queer, Black, people of colour, disabled, and/or fat/thick/curvy/plus-sized. We have three main objectives: (1) to generate knowledge and explore new understandings about movement and fitness through centring the experiential insights of people with bodies of difference; (2) to explore potential contributions of digital storytelling and a minidocumentary to ongoing conversations about inclusion, accessibility, and difference within fitness and movement; and (3) to mobilize knowledge from queer, crip, and fat studies about experiences of non-normative embodiment within fitness, developing creative scholarly and professional resources to shift perspectives and practices, enhance policy, and advance academic knowledge about inclusion and fitness.

The research team comprises five (mostly) white cis women interdisciplinary academic scholars across kinesiology, feminism, critical dietetics, and dance studies. We all have varying relationships to non-normative embodiments, including queer, fat, thick/thicc, Mad, neurodivergent, and eating/dieting/exercise and other body-related struggles. In January 2021, we recruited six participant co-researchers to embark on an arts-based journey with us in re-conceptualizing fitness. Drawing from our community-university networks, we invited people with whom we had a sense of relationality and the topic of revisioning fitness would resonate deeply. In line with our participatory methodology, we use the term *participant co-researchers* to illustrate the blurred boundary between the academy and community and to challenge who is considered a "researcher." Participant co-researchers on the team hold varying relationships to difference (Black or person of colour, trans, non-binary, disabled, neurodivergent, fat, thick/thicc, and/or plus-sized) and are engaged in academia, community activism, art cultivation and creation, accessibility consulting and communications, relaxed performance, and disability coalitions.

We met biweekly on Zoom from January to May 2021, discussing ways to reimagine fitness in difference-affirming ways, with a common theme centred on connection, relationality, and joy/pleasure. We also completed an online digital storytelling workshop in June 2021, hosted by Re•Vision Centre's mobile media lab, where we created first-person multimedia films about our experiences with, inventiveness of, and complicated entanglement within, fitness. In this workshop, we created multimedia stories, which are short videos that pair audio recordings of first-person narratives with image and soundscapes (photos, videos, artwork, music, utterances, gestures, etc.). This story-making process included an in-depth framing of the themes/issues that brought us, the storytellers, together (e.g., interrogating notions of fitness). Further, part of this process was a story circle to share initial story ideas; participation in writing exercises to develop scripts; tutorials on editing software; and access to full technical, writing, and conceptual support from script development to finished video. To conclude the workshop, we shared our stories in a screening and everyone left the workshop as the creator and owner of their video.

Through our film-making and dissemination process, we have come together as a community of care working to reconceptualize "fitness" and have co-created a minidocumentary that highlights aspects of our digital stories and Zoom meetings. Our collective goal is to screen our films for non-profit and for-profit recreation, leisure, fitness, and wellness organizations as a pedagogical opportunity to disrupt normative, neoliberal, colonial, and capitalist-related dogmas that tend to permeate those spaces and preclude bodies of difference. We also intend to create access guides, difference-affirming teaching modules, and training programs designed to improve but also interrogate notions of access and inclusion in relation to fitness.

Since ReVisioning Fitness is a collective project, we took a collaborative writing approach to this chapter. Everyone, including the six participant co-researchers who joined the project, wrote a reflection about moments of vulnerability, disclosure, and witnessing, and/or their role on the project, which we integrate throughout the chapter. As part of this process, we surface our positionalities and relationalities to—and including for some, implicatedness in—fitness as a eugenic practice. As we each disclose and deconstruct our vulnerable relations to contemporary operations of "betterment" tethered to movement practices, we reflect on the challenges this type of social justice work involves, including what it means to engage vulnerably across our differences. We reflect, too, on the limits of vulnerability, particularly in the context of an extractive political economy that ranks/rewards bodies according to their money-making power, assigns little socioeconomic value to relational-care work, and relegates cared-for bodies to institutions and systems that ration basic necessities. The COVID-19 pandemic has laid bare how systems render unwanted bodies vulnerable through chronic under-resourcing and then weaponize that vulnerability as reason for people's untimely sickness and death. Against and through pandemic conditions, we created a tender online container to engage across difference, carving out space for radical alterity, and enacting what Jennifer Nash and other Black feminists theorize as a love politic.[14] As each co-researcher describes it, setting the terms of our engagement at the onset, which involved the intention to speak from our embodied experiences, individual and collective knowledges, and to witness these effects on each other, helped facilitate the sharing of vulnerabilities and accountabilities.

Participant Co-researcher Skylar Sookpaiboon's Reflections

When I was completing my BSc degree in Health Sciences, I came across the word *fitness* on a regular basis. Personally, I found the word itself often presented as a whole package full of rules, regulations, and expectations. Altogether, they formed a particular set of standards or goals that were predominantly ascribed onto white, thin, abled bodies. So for me as a queer, non-binary person of colour,

I have accepted the fact that I was not and could never be "fit" in the world of fitness.

Prior to our first meeting, I had no idea what to expect or how I would play a role in a research project about "fitness." In hindsight, I probably would not even consider participating if I did not know Aly on a personal level—her identities, her intentions behind this project, her integrity and values, and her reflexivity. Which is why it was almost instantaneous for me to feel comfortable and open to vulnerability on this project once we all had a chance to meet and introduce ourselves. In some ways, I was relieved to see that we were all coming from different places, different bodies, different identities, different abilities, and different walks of life. Since our first Zoom meeting, I realized that we were all there for a reason. More importantly, we were all holding space for each other to explore different parts of ourselves, to reflect, to learn, and to share our stories. Despite meeting virtually, I still felt a lot of love and care throughout the times that we had together. It was such an honour for me to get to know, learn from, and experience this whole journey with everyone on this project.

This collective journey of sharing our stories, knowledge, and practices of fitness involved a willingness to speak and hear uncertainty and vulnerability, as well as to question our individual project roles and, along with these, our relationships to and understandings of researching fitness.

Co-investigator Tara-Leigh McHugh's Reflections

As a researcher who has committed their career to working alongside participants in research that is driven by participatory and community-based approaches, I have always been very comfortable with the blurred lines between researcher and participant (i.e., co-researcher). I respect, and am motivated as a researcher by, the co-learning that can (and should) occur for all of those involved in participatory research. Within such research I have been fortunate to be involved in the co-creation of knowledge and the drive for social change. With two decades of experience working collaboratively with co-researchers, I am always amazed at how much co-learning occurs in each new research project. However, my involvement with ReVisioning Fitness was different. It was different in the most rewarding and humbling of ways.

For the first time in my career, I found myself *really* questioning what I, as a researcher, could offer to this group. After each meeting with co-researchers I went away feeling awakened and inspired by the shared experiences and stories. At the same time, I worried about what I was able to offer the group. Was it enough? I was learning so much, but what could this group learn from me? I left more than one meeting feeling overwhelmed with emotion. Feeling like I was taking so much and not giving enough. Feeling like I knew the harmful history of fitness, but then realizing, through the shared stories, that I don't *really* know. But these emotions have grounded me. Through ReVisioning Fitness I have developed a deeper discomfort with fitness. And I know that such discomfort, particularly discomfort experienced by people like me (professor in kinesiology) who play central roles in teaching and researching fitness, is necessary if we are to create change and reimagine fitness.

Principal Investigator Aly Bailey's Reflections
My role as a researcher has transformed since my involvement with ReVisioning Fitness—from being researcher-as-expert to researcher-as-facilitator—a humbling but important shift. This included a sudden pivot to my approach to writing this chapter from a solo author to collective writing project. This is because I do not know everything, and much of what I do know I am trying to unpack or undo. This disruption in authoritative knowledge is critical in order to resist and refuse legacies of eugenics in fitness and beyond.

Within this role, I feel like I am fumbling. Do I know what I am doing? I know that revisioning fitness is an endeavour that needs moments of pause, reflection, and creativity. Part of my role is to question what "fitness" is and means. My relationship to fitness is an imperfect one; a complicated entanglement of bodywork and body politics that contradict and rub up against each other. And although I may be the "project lead," my role is more about supporting everyone in this process of reimagining fitness and being gentle and thoughtful while confronting difficult topics about eugenics, white supremacy, ableism, fatphobia, and colonialism in its relation to fitness. I am a facilitator and space holder with hopes and dreams of dismantling violent fitness practices and creating something new in fitness.

Research Assistant Meredith Bessey's Reflections
I feel immensely grateful to have been invited to be a part of this project, which has enabled me to rethink fitness but also to fundamentally rethink the process of "doing" research. At the beginning of ReVisioning Fitness, I wasn't quite sure of my "place" in the project, especially given that my research training has often emphasized "objectivity." How much should I disclose? How vulnerable did I want to be? How much of my own subjectivity should I bring with me? As time has passed and I've witnessed others' vulnerability, I have felt more comfortable revealing parts of myself. However, I continue to grapple with how much space my own story should take up, how much of me, as a human being with my own personal history with fitness, should show up, versus me as a researcher. Can I even separate those parts of myself? Will I want those tender, vulnerable parts of myself to be tied to my "professional" self? Tension also arises from the dual role I hold in broader fitness spaces—I am a fitness participant, someone who has been damaged by one-size-fits-all fitness messages and by "no pain, no gain" mentality in fitness spaces. But I am also a yoga instructor, someone who has likely (consciously and unconsciously) perpetuated harmful messages. How can I navigate those dual roles within ReVisioning Fitness? Does this mean that I am the "wrong" person to be asking fundamental questions about normative fitness culture? I am left with uncertainty, but also hope and optimism for what the future holds.

In addition to questioning our positionalities, we witnessed each other's stories of pain and trauma with fitness.[15]

Co-investigator Evadne Kelly's Reflections
I felt vulnerable when I shared with the group an experience of precarity as a fitness instructor. For years, I taught Pilates to clients

who paid large sums for private instruction. While a small portion of this money actually made its way to my pocket, Pilates offered me something else that I needed: access to equipment and knowledge I could otherwise not afford.

Pilates helped to balance out the wacky things I did with my body as a modern dancer. I could start teaching Pilates at 7:30 a.m., dance and rehearse during the day, and teach again at night. These long days only gave me just enough to get by.

The flexibility of the hours as a fitness instructor allowed me to go on occasional performance tours. Once, on our way home from a national tour, we got into a bad car accident. I needed the extra money so I drove the van home from our final performance location. I hit slush, the van spun and rammed into a wall of rock. Pain, shock, disorientation. They tied my body down to a stretcher—tight—and they took me to the hospital in an ambulance.

Over the next few months, my body tried to heal. At first, I could barely move. Since my income was contingent on my body demonstrating fitness, agility, and strength, I lost all employment. With no income, I had no choice but to sublet my subsidized apartment. I couch surfed for three months.

The experience came with painful lessons: that my body and its movements were not highly valued (and led to low pay) yet part of a system that valued elite fitness spaces and those who could afford to pay to be fit.

The experience taught me about how our fitness culture upholds the privilege of elite fitness spaces and simultaneously disvalues those who labour in the fitness industry, especially when they don't uphold ableist ideals of physical fitness.

This was a period of difficult precarity caused by an extremely ableist and capitalistic world of elite fitness that I had to scramble my way out of. I'm still scrambling.

Exploring ways to undo ableist, heteronormative, fatphobic, racist, colonial, and sexist fitness practices was vulnerable work and involved attending closely to our relationships to privilege and experiences of being Othered.

Participant Co-researcher seeley quest's Reflections
It has been striking to me that this project has been led by people positioned as privileged, and yet participants have accessed enough safety to disclose some of our more vulnerable experiences related to concepts of fitness. I am privileged by whiteness and some other characteristics yet have experienced much ableism related to mainstream ignorance of compromised body or cognitive functions and adaptations of fitness practices that could be appropriate for those conditions. I've also experienced real barriers to equitably accessing fitness education or practices as a trans person marginalized by gender-conforming frameworks for health, athletic attire, and more. I've been Othered and left unwelcome by abled and gender-normative takes on fitness so many times that I slightly questioned the prospect of vulnerable sharing from a place of difference from the lead researchers.

However, witnessing other participants' emerging willingness to disclose vulnerabilities has reinforced a sense of more liberated possibilities for our relationships. I learned how bluntly a comrade participant was refused exercising assistance by a personal trainer. This person uses a motorized wheelchair and has some range-of-motion limits; he's faced barriers since youth and I haven't known him yet to bring up much about his own needs or comments on oppression he's survived. Somehow it still surprised me, when he disclosed one incidence of how unfairly he's treated: to learn a gym trainer would just say "no, I'm not going to try" working out exercises with a potential client who asked for them. Massage therapists are trained to work with bodies in many conditions; I'm struck by how much training a "personal trainer" needs and by the extent of rejection my friend got. Learning that even the lead researchers have had stigmatizing compromised health experiences, too, has fostered a sense of more connection than division.

But Who Is Listening?
After one of our difficult group conversations about eugenics, Bongi, a participant co-researcher on the team who identifies as plus-sized, texted, "but Aly, who is listening to us?!" Bongi asks this question after almost

a year of Black Lives Matter protests following the murder of George Floyd and decades of outcries that Black people are being murdered by police. She also asks this question during a global surge in anti-Asian hate crimes, elicited by racist fearmongering about the source of COVID-19, and only a couple of months before Tk'emlúps te Secwépemc Chief Rosanne Casimir announced that the remains of 215 children had been found at the Kamloops Indian Residential School (along with other unmarked graves, confirming what Indigenous Elders and residential school survivors have been lamenting for years).

Bongi asks this question within days of the Bill C-7 Senate amendment being passed in Canada allowing people with disabilities to access medical assistance in dying (MAiD) despite an online filibuster from disability activists around the world. Bongi also asked this question amid the COVID-19 global pandemic where, in several Canadian provinces, medical triage protocol continued to discriminate against COVID-19 patients with disabilities. The protocol allowed hospitals to violate basic human rights of COVID-19 patients with disabilities if a surge in COVID-19 cases meant there would not be enough ventilators for everyone.[16] This protocol remained despite months of efforts by disability advocates to reconsider disabled lives as lives worth living.

In many ways, these events shaped and also clarified many of the difficulties with and necessities of vulnerability and weaponization of "fitness" (e.g., in COVID-related protocols) in spaces of alterity, as the state of the world impacted how people showed up in the meeting space, what topics we raised and stories we told, and how we moved together slowly toward vulnerability, according to our openness to witness and willingness to unpack power/privilege.

Co-investigator Carla Rice's Reflections
I've been thinking about movement during this pandemic, when many privileged professionals enjoy the type of work that has allowed and required them to shelter in place, while many others, disproportionately racialized and working-class essential workers, have had to put their lives on the line for economic survival. The stay-at-home injunctions issued to professionals has

returned to those who are child-free, like me, the time stolen by neoliberalism—the productive time required to serve paid work, and the social reproduction time needed to maintain homes and care for kin. As a formerly fat and all-kinds-of-different-sizes woman, I have a fractious relationship with fitness: I have long avoided gyms due to traumatic gym class experiences, and I still refuse disciplinary practices, when not self-imposed, as relief from self-inflicted eating distress. Imagine my surprise when I experienced how recouping capitalism's stolen time opened new worlds of movement. In the midst of the lockdown with screens as my connection to life, I began walking. I walked all over Toronto, exploring many hidden and wild spaces, and connecting to the diverse lifeforms that call the city home.

This story can be read as a vulnerable disclosure for how it exposes my privilege and my pain and trauma. While practising vulnerability might open possibilities for connection and coalition, my story also alludes to ways that vulnerability can cause harm. I used to argue for vulnerability's political importance as a route to forging more equitable relations across differences. This is what Martha Fineman argues in making the case for the vulnerable rather than the autonomous subject as the basis for law; if we took vulnerability as a shared human experience, this would lead to more responsive state policies and a more equitable society. While I still believe in vulnerability's necessity—that all life is vulnerable and that we must acknowledge and respond to its frailty in life-affirming ways—I no longer think that recognizing shared vulnerability is a sufficient condition for achieving justice. Pandemic conditions wrought by turbo-capitalism have cleaved vulnerability onto disabled, old, fat, and racialized bodies and have used that vulnerability to explain away the disproportionate numbers of racialized people becoming infected with COVID, and the old, disabled, and fat people dying from it. Naturalizing disabled, racialized, and aged people's susceptibility to COVID has become a way of masking the structural inequities (e.g., COVID triaging policies, long-term care warehousing practices) that actually produce and exacerbate people's vulnerabilities. This has made me acutely aware that vulnerability can operate to nourish or harm and that vulnerability's mobilization must serve *all* life's flourishing, regardless of the form that life takes.

We feel despair with the oppressive meanings of "fitness," the state of the world more broadly, and the rising tides of hate, but we also feel hope, based on our collective work in ReVisioning Fitness. In many ways, our hope is rooted in our collective willingness to assert our vulnerabilities against the weaponization of vulnerability and, in this, express love, compassion, and crip joy.

Participant Co-researcher Salima Punjani's
When I think about Revisioning Fitness as a project, the words that come up for me are *crip joy*. These words came together as the central focus in a collective word cloud the group worked on.

This sentiment is why I found it difficult at times to be honest and vulnerable about how I was actually feeling. There was an underlying sense of solidarity and care that served as a core feature of this group. I didn't want to taint that.

When pondering an uncomfortable moment of disclosure, my mind immediately jumps to when I shared my thoughts on the word *inclusion*. We worked on a word cloud about the term *inclusion* and I was seeing all these light, joyful words pop up. The thing is, for me, the word *inclusion* is often linked with violence. Violence at the way people use this term—scripts that say all the "right" things, without doing the deep structural work it takes to actually create welcoming environments.

I felt the heat building up in my body, and I felt propelled to share. When I did, it resonated with others, and I felt supported and validated.

It helped me understand that I wasn't tainting the group by being transparent and honest about my observations and perspectives. I was trusting in our collective ability to hold space for each other in whatever way we show up.

That, to me, is crip joy.

Returning to Bongi's important social justice question, "who is listening to us?," we can think further about how our work will be consumed, and by whom.

Participant Co-researcher Kayla Besse's Reflections

I think the greatest moments of vulnerability in ReVisioning Fitness were not necessarily present during the co-researcher meetings themselves, but rather in the knowledge that we were trying to come up with stories and strategies that would eventually be consumed by a broader, presumably non-disabled audience. It's one thing to share struggles and questions with other marginalized people, but another entirely to know that our lived experiences run the risk of being decontextualized to suit a dominant narrative in the fitness industry.

A particular moment of vulnerability, for me, was when I shared that the goals of mainstream (and often toxic) fitness don't feel like they align with my reasons for exercising much at all—rather than prioritizing aesthetics, or strength for the sake of strength, or "earning" food, my truth is that I have to move carefully every day just to manage my disability, just to function at a baseline level. If I don't walk and stretch my hamstrings, it becomes painful to even sit in a chair for any length of time. I shared this with some resentment for the amount of time it eats up in my life, the constant vigilance I feel I must carry in all my movements (and even in the postures in which I sit and lie down), for the invisibility of this physical labour done in private, without most people in my life being aware of the toll it takes.

My experience was met with understanding and validation by the group, and hopefully contributed to expansive definitions of what fitness looks like and the different efforts it requires.

After months of coming together bi/weekly and creating digital stories and a mini documentary, our hope is that fitness-related organizations (e.g., the YMCA/YWCA, yoga studios, gyms) will learn what it means to reimagine fitness to promote accessibility and inclusion in holistic, difference-affirming, comprehensive, and fluid ways, but we also feel trepidation about the structural inequities that underpin and use our vulnerabilities against us.

Participant Co-researcher Paul Tshuma's Reflections
Life has its way of teaching us new things, but in order to get to the place that you will be reading about, it requires openness, humility, and willingness to be vulnerable. However, vulnerability has its pros and cons. The pros are overcoming insecurity, building trust, and teaching others about what you have faced or continue to encounter each day. The cons are being looked down at and being taken advantage of.

One of my biggest fears about creating a digital story for this project was that someone was going to take it and make a profit. Too often in the past I have been on research projects that suddenly end and use my ideas for their gain without my consent.

When I joined ReVisioning Fitness, my mind was set to allow myself to help others feel welcomed in this space and to know that everyone matters. I had to embrace vulnerability at the age 15, due to realizing that I will forever have people in my space because of the physical limitations that have forced me to be dependent on people. Today I use it to help others reach for their star.

Being part of ReVisioning Fitness for me, was coming first and foremost as a disabled individual without a job title but someone coming to learn and share my experiences as a Canadian citizen with a disability that has to constantly fight to prove to our community and fellow citizens that I am fit to be doing or participating in the activities most people are in. The one thing required is the willingness to learn from us as we do from some of you. I am an accessibility consultant representing people with disabilities because oftentimes, we almost seem to be thought of as expensive and complicated individuals because of our infinite needs.

My position has not changed, but what has is my focus attached to one question that I have taken away from this experience: Now, who am I going to represent moving forward? It may be your question too.

In this imperfect journey, we lean into Nash's[17] offering of *love politics* as a way of understanding our work as an affective politic that can produce social change. For some of us, joining ReVisioning Fitness brought up fears of judgment or not fitting in, but the community of care we created together supported people in opening up and sharing.

Participant Co-researcher Bongi Dube's Reflections

When I joined ReVisioning Fitness I thought, "how will I be accepted into this group being a big woman talking about fitness?" I thought, "is she asking me to join because she thinks I need to lose weight? Will I be judged?" I might be the only one who is big. Will they think because I'm big I'm not healthy or I don't exercise or I'm not "fit"...? I wasn't too sure about this group.

But the people made me feel so comfortable, so I started opening up. I'm a big woman but that doesn't mean I'm not happy or healthy. This group helped me understand that fitness is not about how others perceive you. I've learned a lot as a big woman and I've learned to accept myself and be comfortable around people who are lean. Weight doesn't define beauty or who I am.

I met the people and understood them better and even met someone else from my background and we talked in our own language! I realized we are all different in our own ways. Not everyone in this group can run or walk, and not everyone is big, but we have some common ground because we all have different relationships to fitness. That made me understand the group's agenda: to include everyone.

Final Remarks

In this chapter, we tenderly reveal our vulnerabilities in fitness, as politics of eugenics continue to weaponize problematic notions of "fitness" against certain bodies. Within fitness contexts today, eugenics materializes in ways packaged as "good for your health" or "improved well-being." For example, fitness tests involve measuring, comparing, assessing, and scoring bodies against "normative" tables based on population average scores. Those who do not "measure up" are instructed how to change their behaviours to be a healthier (and thus "better") citizen, while ignoring the structural inequities that preclude health and wellness opportunities for bodies of difference. We argue that this individualized approach to fitness is demoralizing and dehumanizing and, at best, demotivating. We also know that a livelihood within the fitness industry is typically precarious, with many employees (fitness instructors) holding posts at several locations simultaneously as independent contractors, without benefits, pension, or any prospect of permanency. In response to the current precarious "fitness" climate, global pandemic, the brink of world war, waves of new eugenics, and weaponization of vulnerabilities, we advocate for new, difference-affirming conceptualizations of fitness in hopes of truth and healing.

ReVisioning Fitness orients us toward a sense of temporality similar to Muñoz's[18] conceptualization of queerness as an embrace of "futurity," as "the map to a new world is in the imagination."[19] We dream of a not-yet-written future and reimagine fitness as a radical embrace and celebration of difference.[20] We envision fitness as a place that embraces joy, pleasure, and connection to ourselves, each other, and the land, and we reclaim the notion of self- and community care as a political act.[21] We orient to vulnerability as life giving and contest its weaponization. We move forward as a collective to push for change, challenge normative uptake of our work/ideas, and question the harmful traditional practices that permeate our research and praxis.

Notes

1. Jim Holt, "Measure for Measure: The Strange Science of Francis Galton," *New Yorker*, January 24, 2005, https://www.newyorker.com/magazine/2005/01/24/measure-for-measure-5.
2. Douglas Baynton, "Disability and the Justification of Inequality in American History," in *The New Disability History: American Perspectives*, eds. Paul K. Longmore and Lauri Umansky (New York: New York University Press, 2001).
3. Marsha Saxton, "Hard Bodies: Exploring Historical and Cultural Factors in Disabled People's Participation in Exercise; Applying Critical Disability Theory," *Sport in Society* 21, no. 1 (2018).
4. Carla Rice and Eliza Chandler, "Representing Difference: Disability, Digital Storytelling and Public Pedagogy," in *The Routledge Companion to Disability Media*, eds. Katie Ellis, Gerard Goggin, Beth Haller, and Rosemary Curtis (Oxfordshire: Routledge, 2019); Irving K. Zola, "Healthism and Disabling Medicalization," in *Disabling Professions*, eds. Ivan Illich, Irving K. Zola, John McKnight, Jonathan Caplan, and Harley Shaiken (London: Marion Boyars, 1977).
5. Saxton, "Hard Bodies."

6. Deborah McPhail, Andrea Bombak, Pamela Ward, and Jill Allison, "Wombs at Risk, Wombs as Risk: Fat Women's Experiences of Reproductive Care," *Fat Studies* 5, no. 2 (2016): 98-115.
7. Diane B. Paul and James Moore, "The Darwinian Context: Evolution and Inheritance," in *The Oxford Handbook of the History of Eugenics*, eds. Alison Bashford and Philippa Levine (Oxford: Oxford University Press, 2010).
8. Eugenics Archive, "Interviews+," accessed July 21, 2021, http://eugenicsarchive.ca/discover/interviews.
9. Rebecca M. Kluchin, "Fit to Be Tied? Sterilization and Reproductive Rights in America, 1960-1984" (PhD diss., Carnegie Mellon University, 2004).
10. Alexandra Minna Stern, "Eugenics and Historical Memory in America," *History Compass* 3, no. 1 (2005).
11. K. Alysse Bailey, Carla Rice, Melissa Gualtieri, and James Gillett, "Is #YogaForEveryone? The Idealised Flexible Bodymind in Instagram Yoga Posts," *Qualitative Research in Sport, Exercise and Health* 14, no. 5 (2021): 827-842.
12. Geraint Harvey, Sheena J. Vachhani, and Karen Williams, "Working Out: Aesthetic Labour, Affect and the Fitness Industry Personal Trainer," *Leisure Studies* 33, no. 5 (2014): 454-470.
13. Emma V. Richardson and Robert W. Motl, "Promoting Inclusion in a Fitness Center through Non-Impaired Staff: Creating a Multi-Narrative Environment," *Qualitative Research in Sport, Exercise and Health* 12, no. 4 (2019): 1-19.
14. Jennifer C. Nash, "Practicing Love: Black Feminism, Love-Politics, and Post-Intersectionality," *Meridians* 11, no. 2 (2013): 1-24; Nash, *Black Feminism Reimagined: After Intersectionality* (Durham: Duke University Press, 2019).
15. Carla Rice, Katie Cook, and K. Alysse Bailey, "Difference-Attuned Witnessing: Risks and Potentialities of Arts-Based Research," *Feminism & Psychology* 31, no. 3 (2021): 345-365.
16. Ruth Enns, "The Deadly Danger of Ableism in Health Care During a Pandemic," *CBC*, February 6, 2021, https://www.cbc.ca/news/canada/manitoba/opinion-ruth-ens-ableism-health-care-pandemic-1.5901494.
17. Nash, "Practicing Love"; Nash, *Black Feminism Reimagined*.
18. José Esteban Muñoz, *Cruising Utopia: The Then and There of Queer Futurity* (New York: New York University Press, 2009).
19. Robin D.G. Kelley, *Freedom Dreams: The Black Radical Imagination* (Boston: Beacon Press, 2003), 2.
20. Nash, *Black Feminism Reimagined*.
21. Audre Lorde, *A Burst of Light: Essays* (Ithaca: Firebrand Books, 1988).

Bibliography

Bailey, K. Alysse, Carla Rice, Melissa Gualtieri, and James Gillett. "Is #YogaForEveryone? The Idealised Flexible Bodymind in Instagram Yoga Posts." *Qualitative Research in Sport, Exercise and Health* 14, no. 5 (2021): 827-842.

Baynton, Douglas. "Disability and the Justification of Inequality in American History." In *The New Disability History: American Perspectives*, edited by Paul K. Longmore and Lauri Umansky, 33-57. New York: New York University Press, 2001.

Enns, Ruth. "The Deadly Danger of Ableism in Health Care During a Pandemic." *CBC*, February 6, 2021. https://www.cbc.ca/news/canada/manitoba/opinion-ruth-ens-ableism-health-care-pandemic-1.5901494.

Eugenics Archive. "Interviews+." Accessed July 21, 2021. http://eugenicsarchive.ca/discover/interviews.

Harvey, Geraint, Sheena J. Vachhani, and Karen Williams. "Working Out: Aesthetic Labour, Affect and the Fitness Industry Personal Trainer." *Leisure Studies* 33, no. 5 (2014): 454-70. https://doi.org/10.1080/02614367.2013.770548.

Holt, Jim. "Measure for Measure: The Strange Science of Francis Galton," *New Yorker*, January 24, 2005. https://www.newyorker.com/magazine/2005/01/24/measure-for-measure-5.

Kelley, Robin D.G. *Freedom Dreams: The Black Radical Imagination*. Boston: Beacon Press, 2003.

Kluchin, Rebecca M. "Fit to Be Tied? Sterilization and Reproductive Rights in America, 1960-1984." PhD dissertation, Carnegie Mellon University, 2004.

Lorde, Audre. *A Burst of Light: Essays*. Ithaca: Firebrand Books, 1988.

McPhail, Deborah, Andrea Bombak, Pamela Ward, and Jill Allison. "Wombs at Risk, Wombs as Risk: Fat Women's Experiences of Reproductive Care." *Fat Studies* 5, no. 2 (2016): 98-115. https://doi.org/10.1080/21604851.2016.1143754.

Muñoz, José Esteban. *Cruising Utopia: The Then and There of Queer Futurity*. New York: New York University Press, 2009.

Nash, Jennifer C. *Black Feminism Reimagined: After Intersectionality*. Durham: Duke University Press, 2019.

Nash, Jennifer C. "Practicing Love: Black Feminism, Love-Politics, and Post-Intersectionality." *Meridians* 11, no. 2 (2013): 1-24. https://doi.org/10.2979/meridians.11.2.1.

Paul, Diane B., and James Moore. "The Darwinian Context: Evolution and Inheritance." In *The Oxford Handbook of the History of Eugenics*, edited by Alison Bashford and Philippa Levine, 27-42. Oxford: Oxford University Press, 2010.

Rice, Carla, and Eliza Chandler. "Representing Difference: Disability, Digital Storytelling and Public Pedagogy." In *The Routledge Companion to Disability Media*, edited by Katie Ellis, Gerard Goggin, Beth Haller, and Rosemary Curtis, 367-376. Oxfordshire: Routledge, 2019.

Rice, Carla, Katie Cook, and K. Alysse Bailey. "Difference-Attuned Witnessing: Risks and Potentialities of Arts-Based Research." *Feminism & Psychology* 31, no. 3 (2021): 345-365. https://doi.org/10.1177/0959353520955142.

Richardson, Emma V., and Robert W. Motl. "Promoting Inclusion in a Fitness Center through Non-Impaired Staff: Creating a Multi-Narrative Environment." *Qualitative Research in Sport, Exercise and Health* 12, no. 4 (2019): 1-19. https://doi.org/10.1080/2159676X.2019.1637926.

Saxton, Marsha. "Hard Bodies: Exploring Historical and Cultural Factors in Disabled People's Participation in Exercise; Applying Critical Disability Theory." *Sport in Society* 21, no. 1 (2018): 22-39. https://doi.org/10.1080/17430437.2016.1225914.

Stern, Alexandra Minna. "Eugenics and Historical Memory in America." *History Compass* 3, no. 1 (2005). https://doi.org/10.1111/j.1478-0542.2005.00145.x.

Zola, Irving K. "Healthism and Disabling Medicalization." In *Disabling Professions*, edited by Ivan Illich, Irving K. Zola, John McKnight, Jonathan Caplan, and Harley Shaiken, 41-67. London: Marion Boyars, 1977.

13

"Sorry, My Child Is Kicking Me under the Desk"
Intersectional Challenges to Research during the COVID-19 Pandemic

Irene Shankar and Corinne Mason

In March 2020, with infection cases surging nationwide, stay-at-home public health policies were introduced across Canada to curb the spread of COVID-19. As we write this chapter, we are entering the fourth wave of pandemic with a return to "lockdown" measures in most of Canada. These necessary health measures have had far-reaching social and economic consequences. Studies show an increased disparity in employment, economic, safety, and well-being outcomes for women, especially those with young children.[1] While the pandemic has been devastating for our entire society, those marginalized because of race, class, Indigeneity, gender identity and expression, disability, and neurodiversity have been disproportionately affected.[2] These effects are heightened due to some provincial governments' resistance to implementing the public health safety measures needed to curb the spread of the infectious and mutating coronavirus. As feminist philosopher Rosi Braidotti writes, "Yes, we are connected...But we differ tremendously in terms of our respective locations and access to social and legal entitlements, technologies, safety, prosperity, and good health services."[3]

Within the post-secondary education sector, the COVID-19 pandemic has further entrenched existing inequities.[4] As tenured faculty members who identify, respectively, as racialized and as a queer non-binary femme, and who are both located in the Canadian Prairies, we have benefited from certain privileges—namely class—and have also been negatively affected by other aspects of this pandemic, including Conservative provincial governments whose cuts to the social safety net have worsened the outcomes for those affected by COVID-19. This autoethnographic chapter explores the impacts of moving to online data collection during the pandemic. Using an intersectional framework, we deconstruct the privileges that allowed us to continue with our research. We also outline the personal and methodological challenges that stemmed from our own subject locations and that of our intended research participants. We focus our attention on three major challenges to our research: (1) institutional constraints; (2) participant strain; and (3) researcher fatigue and guilt. In each section, we theorize and reflect upon our positionalities within the broader context of the pandemic as we sought to keep our research projects moving while paying attention to the pandemic's disproportionate impact on marginalized communities. We examine the mental health and well-being implications of trying to adhere to the neoliberal standard of productivity and achievement within corporatized institutions of higher learning while surviving a global pandemic.

Disability scholar Michael Orsini asks scholars to think through the emotional landscape of COVID-19, positing that emotions are sense-making mechanisms and can provide "thicker accounts" of the pandemic.[5] For Orsini, taking an emotional lens to COVID-19 allows us to pay attention to intersections of inequity, especially as discourses of individual and collective resilience surround us.[6] He writes:

> It is not a coincidence, for instance, that discourses of resilience have permeated the COVID-19 policy landscape in countries such as Canada: communities affected by COVID-19 are hailed by anxious governments as brimming with grit and determination. Resilience cuts across a number of different emotional registers. *Is its ubiquity evidence of a public desire to find an emotional reset switch—something*

that will allow weary citizens to feel better about the world, and about their place in it? (Our emphasis)[7]

In this chapter, we feel through our own attachments to resiliency in the face of mounting negative feelings during the pandemic. While we both wanted to pause our data collection in 2020, we kept going. Perhaps we were motivated by the promise of resiliency? If we kept going, would we find an emotional reset switch? If we spoke to people about our research—rather than about case numbers, transmission links, and death rates—might we feel better about the world and about our place in it? Beyond overcoming obstacles to our work, were we aiming to build (our research) back better? In writing this, we reflected on the emotions of the pandemic to "thicken" our account of conducting qualitative research interviews despite the challenges of continuing our work. Descriptions of our emotions easily bubbled to the surface as we spoke, often taking us by surprise as we articulated the affect of our resilience. We begin each section of this chapter by offering a transcription of our conversational reflections on intersectional challenges to research during the COVID-19 pandemic.

Privilege and Pivots: Institutional Constraints

Irene: I didn't have time to strategize about online research. There was this pressure to continue but the ability to proceed was contingent upon certain privileges. While I didn't come from privilege, my position as an associate professor has made my life comfortable. I found out that my university had Zoom licences, and when those expired, we had SSHRC funding to purchase a licence for each of us. There were a few hiccups with the university placing additional requirements for our ethics application to move data collection online. However, these were minor inconveniences.

Corinne: I feel similarly about my ability to "pivot." I don't think I ever used the language of "pivot" prior to the COVID-19 pandemic, and now the word is as ubiquitous as "unprecedented." There was an institutional expectation for faculty to pivot teaching, research, and conferencing online and because of class privilege, it was somewhat simple for me. And in so many ways I could follow public health mitigation efforts, like working from home, and continue to meet the expectations of my university because of my well-paying and secure job. I could make my life as narrow as it needed to be to avoid public spaces and people beyond my household.

Although academic faculty in Canada have not dealt with the same COVID-19–induced employment disparities as the rest of the population, their research and publications plans have been affected, which could potentially have a long-term impact on their tenure and promotion plans. This is especially the case for women.[8] Researcher Jennifer Davis illustrates that despite narratives of the pandemic as a "leveler," COVID-19 has disproportionately impacted the health, well-being, and research activities of marginalized faculty.[9] In Davis and her team's study of 696 faculty, women and racialized faculty reported the highest levels of stress, social isolation, and lowered well-being. Overall, 53 per cent of faculty reported less research productivity during the pandemic. A greater portion of racialized faculty reported reduced research productivity (64%) than their non-racialized counterparts. On the other hand, 73 per cent of those who reported increased productivity were men.[10] Such studies reflect what we know about the pandemic more broadly: marginalized communities within and outside of academia have been most acutely affected by COVID-19 and subsequent public health mitigation efforts.[11]

Considering these findings, our almost seamless transition to online interviews speaks to our privileges. As we both have supportive partners, safe homes, food security, and other forms of social capital, we were able to complete 48 qualitative interviews (each approximately an hour to an hour and a half long) over eight months during a pandemic. As tenured faculty members,[12] we had secured internal and external research funding that we used to purchase Zoom licences and laptops and to employ transcribers and multiple research assistants to provide administrative labour. As tenured faculty members, our teaching is not as closely scrutinized and, similarly, a negative teaching evaluation does not carry the same ramifications as it does for our tenure-track and contract faculty colleagues.[13] Thus, we have room to experiment with teaching styles that provide a bit more time for research. We also shifted some of our service expectations to make space for research. To reiterate, these privileges are not equally accessible to all faculty members. Due to institutional pressure and need, racialized, women, and gender-diverse faculty members engage in a disproportionate amount of service to the institution and often provide much-needed services and resources to the larger community as well.[14] Still, scholarship is understood to be the result of individualized work ethic and resolve, a discourse that hides the social capital and myriad resources that are required for successful research and publishing.

Climbing the academic ladder to tenure and promotion has meant that we are no longer closely situated within our home communities, meaning that even before the pandemic, we often felt alone and alienated. For instance, in part due to necessary relocation to secure her current position, Irene is no longer involved in the larger Indo-Fijian community in which she grew up, and being three hours away from her elderly parents, she is not involved in the daily care of her extended family.

In absence of these extended family caregiving obligations, we had more time to complete our research during COVID-19. This absence of care obligations for our elderly relatives marks our privilege, but at the same time, we bonded over feelings of isolation and loneliness during the pandemic as we experienced further disconnection from family and community due to geographical distance and public health physical distancing mandates (an issue that we will return to later in this chapter). These feelings of isolation and loneliness during the pandemic are not unique; however, research on the experiences of communities of colour and 2SLGBTQIA+ individuals show more severe and systemic experiences of ill mental health and lack of well-being.[15]

The Depths of Resilience: Participant Strain

> **Corinne:** My motivation to keep going was based on feelings of obligation to the participants we invited to interview and to the research itself. My feelings of obligation were about not letting participants down after scheduling interviews and because I felt that the stories held by faculty about the harms associated with transforming universities needed to be told. At the time, I was on my first sabbatical, and I think I was also in denial about my protected research time being interrupted by a global pandemic after

working for seven years to be eligible for research leave. As a junior academic, I had let go of much of my research ambitions to teach and serve. As one of the only out queer faculty at my small rural university, I had spent too much time on equity and inclusion committees and had become burnt out. Now, as a mid-career academic, I desired nothing more than to settle into research life and come back to the institution with new lines on my CV.

At the same time, I was watching the "she-session" unfold and felt a defiant refusal to be the one in my relationship to leave work to take care of our child. My partner is non-binary transmasculine, and while we are both gender nonconforming, we are often misrecognized and treated as cisgender man and woman by those outside of our community. For example, on the daycare run, teachers assume I am responsible for childrearing while my partner is treated as merely a chauffeur. We refuse these normative gender expectations in our home, but we are not immune to the functioning of cissexism and heterosexism outside of it. Looking back, I don't know whether I was more invested in some kind of feminist activism by refusing to let go of my research sabbatical and planned projects or if I was more concerned about what it would mean for my identity and well-being to parent full time when schools and daycares were closed. As someone who experienced postpartum depression and anxiety, I held a deep fear about how shifting my focus from work to childcare might affect my mental health. I saw no other option than to keep going.

Irene: Looking back, I am upset that I kept going. Like you, I wanted to be respectful to the participants and do justice to our research. It did get harder as we went on and one of the main things was the combination of full-time parenting, homeschooling, teaching, and doing interviews. Honestly, it was a nightmare. Often my daughter would come in as I was getting ready to go online with various requests and needs—ranging from not being able to log on to Google meets or the computer's battery was dying and she couldn't find the cord, or she was just told to print something out and the printer is in my office. As the title of this paper indicates, sometimes she would lie in frustration underneath the desk (along with my dog) and kick me to get my attention. She was tired, frustrated, and lonely and I was busy with my work. In hindsight, it seems a bit absurd.

Part of the drive to continue was due to my own positionality. As a racialized and gendered scholar, I get treated as unknowledgeable and I am rendered invisible in professional settings. Thus, I have had to work hard at being seen as "professional"—which in my world means not cancelling meetings, not asking for extensions, always being super prepared. This is exhausting and unrealistic. I am not endorsing this but articulating what many scholars like me must do to survive in a society that is often dismissive of our knowledge and expertise. So, it is not surprising that I didn't see cancelling our interviews or rearranging them as an option. I also continued because there was this hope for meeting other feminist scholars like us. I wanted to learn about how they have survived resistance and dismissal of their expertise on campus. I was hoping to alleviate this sense of isolation of working and being invisible.

As stated above, we continued with the project because of the research topic itself. Like many other scholars, our research on sexualized violence at Canadian post-secondary institutions (PSIs) is motivated by our commitment to and experiences of working towards social justice and resistance. At Corinne's home institution, Brandon University, a student sought media assistance to expose the university's use of "behavioural contracts"—which include threat of expulsion— on victims of sexualized violence.[16] Corinne had advocated alongside this student within the institution for almost a year prior to the student leveraging the media. As a new professor of gender and women's studies at the university, Corinne experienced other student disclosures of sexualized violence, and when they sought campus resources, they quickly realized there were none. All attempts to encourage their institution to establish a sexualized violence policy and an officer failed until the student survivor went public.[17] Corinne's role on campus became that of a whistleblower by calling the behavioural contract a "gag order" in the media and speaking out against the institution's betrayal of sexualized violence survivors.[18] While there is now an officer for sexualized violence complaints, the position was cut by 75 per cent in the midst of the pandemic and more mishandlings of complaints have come to light.[19]

Irene's experience at Mount Royal University[20] also centred on students' experiences of unmet services. Students kept asking for referrals to services on campus, but these services were hard to locate, and some students would return from referred services without being helped.[21] The available services and policies were geared toward privileged cisgender white women and did not reflect the needs of anyone else.[22] Irene's request for policies and services based on an intersectional understanding of sexualized violence or the pressing need to address the underlying heteronormativity of available services was often met with uncomfortable silence. Another alienating feature was the overwhelming lack of racialized faculty and staff working in this area.

Driven by this context, we developed our research project to centre and make visible the expertise and experiences of racialized, gendered, and queer scholars working to address violence and other inequities on campus, and in doing so, we hoped to create a network of critical scholars working in the area who were missing from this conversation.

The continued exclusion of BIPOC, 2SLGBTQ+, disabled, and neurodivergent scholars and scholarship within the field of sexualized violence is facilitated by the ways in which higher education has been constructed and shaped. PSIs have a long history of being spaces devoted to the "enlightenment" of privileged groups, which have historically been heterosexual white able-bodied men. Academic spaces have been conceptualized and constructed (as both physical and theoretical spaces) around the needs and desires of these privileged bodies.[23] Like the construction of physical space that fails to consider the needs of disabled students and staff, the theoretical space of academia is also defined by its original inhabitants. We see this in our definitions of "knowledge" and which bodies are deemed to be the proper knowledge holders. The very positivist understanding of knowledge and exclusionary understandings of knowledge holders continue to define pedagogy and expertise. As explained by Avery Gordon, we are haunted by our history: "haunting is part of our social world, and understanding it is essential to grasping the nature of our society and for changing it."[24]

It is precisely because of this haunting of our history that Sara Ahmed[25] talks about universities as institutional spaces where some are more at home than others, specifying that those who adhere to the somatic norm get to be more at home in PSIs. Theorist Nirmal Puwar has fleshed this out in her own work on institutional spaces—she states that academia's construction around the somatic norm of privileged and abled-bodied white males renders all others that enter academia as "space invaders,"[26] meaning that they are perceived as not belonging in this space, nor do they have the right to be knowledge holders and experts. As space invaders, Other theorists and researchers are intruders whose expertise and knowledge are always suspect and carry the ever-present marker/resonance of Otherness. Those who are located within the category of Other, or "space invaders," encounter overt discrimination through lack of hiring and promotion, pay inequity, tokenization, microaggressions, overt racism, and other forms of violence and exclusion.[27]

For data collection, we sent participant recruitment letters to all faculty with research expertise in sexualized violence or who were known advocates on campus. We outlined our specific interest in speaking with those most underrepresented in campus governance at the highest levels[28] and those whose voices and experiences are rarely heard on this topic. Who interprets themselves as an expert is a functioning of power, and we found that primarily white women responded to our call for participants. Of course, white people make up the majority of faculty (including faculty who are women or other marginalized genders) and they occupy the most powerful and highest-paid positions.[29] In Canada, white women are the established and recognized experts in feminist academic circles because they are most likely to be hired into those programs. Once hired, white women have made contributions to the field of sexualized violence either because they have either lived experience or because they occupy faculty positions in fields such as gender and women's studies. These participants were incredibly generous with their time and graciously shared the gender-based barriers they have encountered in academia. They also discussed their accumulated privileges, such as being at a later stage of their career, having grown children, financial stability, secure households that facilitated their tenured positions and made participating in our research feasible.

The feasibility of participation for some faculty contrasted with lack of participation by others. Perhaps our research title "#MeTooAcademia" dissuaded potential participants. As Phipps maintains, although #MeToo was originally used by Black activist Tarana Burke to help women of colour heal by connecting and supporting survivors, the Hollywoodization of #MeToo has whitewashed the movement. The testimonial nature of the current iteration of #MeToo offers space to "the cultural power of white tears" that relies on the illegibility of women of colour as victims of violence and, in this case, experts on the issue.[30] For Tambe, the racial and class politics of #MeToo has led women of colour to ask: "Is #MeToo a white women's movement?"[31] As she reminds readers, the current #MeToo movement relies on the power of public shaming and calls for the criminalization of perpetrators. For racialized communities, these public calls add to the historical and entrenched stigmatization of Black men as predators. Protecting communities from further punishment during mass incarceration falls beyond the purview of social media callouts of abusers by victims—leaving #MeToo activism to white women. Research on #MeToo in academic settings carries this baggage of white women's centrality in the current formulation of this movement,[32] even as racialized women experience insidious sexualized violence across campuses and carry the burden of advocating for survivors who have been betrayed by institutional misogynoir.

The overextension and overburdening of those faculty who are often hailed as "space invaders" was another barrier in accessing participants. We did manage to connect with some racialized and queer people who spoke about their fatigue and the invisibility of their labour and knowledge. In many interviews, 2SLGBTQ+ and BIPOC scholars who participated in our interviews spoke about how they have expertise in sexualized violence—academic and/or lived experience—but the mushrooming of "EDI Inc" at their institutions meant that they were asked to sit on equity-focused committees or were tokenized as "diverse representatives" at tables where administrations needed to illustrate their inclusivity. 2SLGBTQ+ and BIPOC scholars told us about how they were tapped for service work based on how the university could deploy their embodiment, which left sexualized violence committees to primarily white women.

Many of the 2SLGBTQ+ and BIPOC faculty we wanted to talk to responded that they were already fully committed to supporting their respective communities at a time when multiple crises were happening. In one case, a Black scholar expressed her interest in the research and its results but stated she could not participate because she was deeply involved in local anti-racist organizing in the summer of 2020 while also surviving ongoing white supremacy. The increasing recognition of continued state-sanctioned violence against Black and Indigenous people—heightened by the murders of George Floyd and Breonna Taylor in the US and Regis Korchinski-Paquet and Eishia Hudson in Canada—has promoted reluctant post-secondary institutions to finally begin to address institutional racism. This call to address racism on campus has resulted in increased demands on the labour, time, and expertise of Black, Indigenous, and other racialized faculty members. Increasing racist attacks against Southeast Asians in Canada and ongoing colonial violence against Indigenous people left some faculty depleted and without the time or resources to participate in interviews.

As seen above, our decisions to continue despite the outstanding issues of societal racialized violence and ill health meant that some faculty that we desperately wanted to talk to were unable to take part in our research. This was disappointing for both of us. As discussed earlier, we are quite isolated in our institutions and were eager to form connections with other scholars like us. Moreover, our resulting data largely reflects the experiences of privileged white scholars, while the realities of space invaders continue to be largely invisible. We inevitably reinforced the same narrative and voices by our desire to proceed in doing qualitative research during the pandemic, which had concrete and frustrating implications. In hindsight, it was unrealistic to expect 2SLGBTQIA+ and BIPOC participants to participate in an hour-long interview while they were caring for their larger community and fighting for survival during global health and social crises.

Angry, Tired, and So Sad: Lingering Researcher Fatigue and Guilt

> **Irene:** Continuing at all costs was detrimental to my health. I was tired of working while parenting full time—which became very gendered, because my partner was working outside of the home, so it fell on me to arrange for day-to-day managing of life under the pandemic. While I know that child was well taken care of, I was not the parent I wanted to be while conducting the online interviews. Along with the emotional labour of caregiving, homeschooling and managing life under the pandemic, I felt

overwhelmed listening to people's trauma over the screen but then robotically moving to the next task on the list. There was no time to sit with the participant or process what they had experienced. I would turn off the camera and then proceed with the work that awaited me: my child's homework, preparing breakfast/lunch/snacks or feeding and walking the dog. The move was so quick from one task to the other that the feelings of discomfort and despair from the interviews didn't leave but lingered and accumulated with each new interview. It's akin to haunting, whereby I couldn't sleep because interview excerpts would continuously play in my head. However, there was no room or space to be distraught. I also feel guilty for making the participants relieve their trauma online and not being able to sit with them afterwards. I would stay up late wondering how they are doing and whether it would be appropriate for us to check on them, or would following up create even more labour for the participants, whereby they would be forced to reassure us of their well-being?

Alongside all these struggles, the reality of being a racialized scholar in white academia intensified during the pandemic. The racialized and gendered microaggressions and sometimes outright racist acts continued over Zoom and Google meets. I was unprepared for dealing with the harshness of discrimination in online meetings and classrooms.

Corinne: For me, juggling childcare while continuing to work was the hardest part of the early days of the pandemic. It was incredibly stressful in our household and led my partner and me to work late nights and early mornings to get our to-do lists done.

I couldn't keep up with any responsibility in my life, and I was often rushed when preparing for interviews or could not prepare at all. My guilt about being a bad parent was matched with guilt for being a bad researcher when a participant scolded me for being unprepared for an interview. She told me I had not done my research about her specific expertise on the issue of sexualized violence and cut off our conversation before it could even start. I remember calling you, Irene, shaking, crying, and apologizing for ruining our research reputations, worried that no one would speak to us again, and thinking that you wouldn't want to keep working with me. I've never felt more like an imposter as an academic.

At the beginning of our project, we had planned on travelling together for research interviews. I knew that the conversations we would have with faculty would be difficult to process, but I also knew that we would have each other in the interview and for debriefs. I had every expectation that we would be away from our homes and families to do this work and would be able to use nights at hotels and flights back to our respective cities as boundary markers. Instead, I would walk out of my office and into a chaotic family scene after listening to faculty describe institutional betrayals, experiences of harassment and assaults, death threats, career stagnation, and burnout. My life was spilling over into my research, and the research spilled over into my life.

Researching sensitive issues is taxing and emotionally depleting for the participants and for researchers.[33] In qualitative research, there is careful attention to potential trauma participants may encounter within data collection. As such, the ethics board has procedures for mediating some of this risk and requires a detailed plan on researchers' proposals to mediate any emerging trauma. While we followed and often exceeded the procedures we outlined in our ethics application, there was still an outstanding discomfort that our efforts were insignificant. Despite the participants' assurances and consent to discuss their experiences, the online communication felt cold and distant, and we felt limited in our ability to properly emphasize our shock and/or offer to stand with them in their struggles against their institution. Also, we often worried that the distractions caused by simultaneously providing for children and conducting interviews made us appear uninterested in the interviews. This was an ongoing source of tension and anxiety for both of us.

As scholars, we are aware of societal discrimination and structural barriers. However, this pandemic brought these inequities to the forefront in intensified ways that made it overwhelming and painful to encounter. For instance, due to unsafe working and living conditions, Indigenous and racialized people are disproportionately impacted by COVID.[34] Not only are marginalized communities more at risk for COVID-19, but there were also increased incidences of racialized violence[35] and scapegoating of communities by government officials. For instance, in Alberta, Premier Kenney's conservative government blamed Northeast Calgary, which has a higher rate of poor and racialized residents, for the spread of COVID-19.[36] Similarly, in other parts of Canada, violence against Asian communities escalated, with Vancouver police citing an increase of 717 per cent in anti-Asian hate crimes reports.[37] In Manitoba, former premier Brian Pallister blamed Indigenous people for the province's slow rollout of vaccines. He claimed that "Manitobans" would wait longer due to the prioritization of North and remote communities, saying, "This puts Manitobans at the back of the line. This hurts Manitobans, to put it mildly."[38]

Considering the increased hate attacks and rising infection rates in BIPOC communities, Irene found herself working on EDI policies, public editorials, webinars, and other equity measures while being subjected to harassment, microaggressions, and continual skepticism of her expertise and position within university committees. Being asked to do the work of informing campus EDI initiatives, while simultaneously distrusting the administration to enact the recommendations, was an infuriating experience. Within PSIs, space invaders are often asked to spearhead EDI initiatives that, in turn, place us at increased risk for harassment and bullying. Sadly, the very institutions that ask for such labour fail to provide any protection. For Irene, working online during the pandemic made these harrowing experiences more frequent and harder to avoid.

The discriminatory COVID-19 vaccination rollout prompted Corinne to focus on vaccination advocacy in Manitoba. In Manitoba, vaccine consent forms proved to be a barrier for trans and non-binary people. Without consultation with the community, the first rollout of consent forms included the language for gender markers as "female," "male," "intersex," and "unknown." After a public apology, the Manitoba government changed the form to "male," "female," and "other," which neither fixed the issue nor removed barriers. Due to misgendering on forms and in-person at vaccine supersites, individuals from the advocacy group TransManitoba set up vaccine buddy systems at supersites and organized affirming vaccination clinics with local non-profits. Through their networks, Corinne provided media interviews on the subject to educate the public and to contribute to vaccine uptake among trans and non-binary people.[39] Research by the Tegan and Sara Foundation found that while a majority of 2SLGBTQ+

people in the US and Canada were in favour of vaccinations to protect their community, one in four transgender and one in three genderqueer respondents cited previous medical trauma as a reason they would delay getting the vaccine. Of those who stated they would "wait a while" to get the vaccine when available, 12 per cent were BIPOC.[40] These health disparities related to COVID-19 are perhaps unsurprising given the well-documented array of health inequities in racialized and 2SLGBTQ+ communities throughout Canada arising from discrimination in the healthcare system.

Given the contexts in which we were operating, our research interviews were particularly strenuous. In our brief conversations about how interviews were going while we were research active, Irene would speak about feeling dread as she looked through her calendar of scheduled interviews and then having palpable nausea as she waited for participants to join Zoom meetings. Corinne reflected on sweating and shaking from anxiety prior to interviews and then dissociating during them, where they felt as if they floated above their physical being while trying to maintain embodied professionalism. We both feared that the outside world (our family life, the pandemic) and our emotional states (anxiety, dread) would be made visible through our computer screens. Despite our stress levels, we continued in part due to this constant pressure to perform and adhere to the white supremacist and patriarchal standards of academia that expect productivity and output—even during a pandemic. With the looming threat of PSI budget cuts and restructuring, the pressure to perform and be productive will continue to escalate, leaving us without room to slow down or take care of ourselves during societal crises like a pandemic.

Conclusion

In this chapter, we offered a "thickened" account of our experiences as researchers during COVID-19. By reflecting on our feelings about qualitative research during the pandemic, we illustrated how expectations of resiliency during the pandemic—our own and institutionally based—left us exhausted and disappointed. Pivoting and carrying on despite the multiple crises occurring in our communities and beyond meant that the data we collected did not reflect our intentions for the research. While we aimed to interview Othered faculty members—Black, Indigenous, racially minoritized, 2SLGBTQ+, disabled, and neurodiverse—our resilience and institutional pressure to perform meant that we left these people behind.

Michael Orsini's call to scholars to thicken our accounts of the pandemic by paying attention to feelings is a call to refuse public commentary that "we are in this together," "we are in the same boat," and "we are on the same team."[41] As Rosi Braidotti reminds us, we may be in this together, but we are "not one and the same."[42] Our connectedness as individuals who are navigating a global pandemic need not obscure our stratification. During COVID-19, governments have offered discourses of resiliency as means to survive this pandemic and future crises. Under the pressures of flailing neoliberal capitalism, resiliency is offered to those who are otherwise left to bear the consequences of a nonexistent social safety net. Those most impacted by the pandemic are asked to find an emotional reset switch and continue "as normal." As disability scholarship makes clear, resiliency narratives have long marked individuals as responsible for systemic barriers.[43] In our pivot to online data collection, we bought into this resilience narrative. As we show in this chapter, those most acutely affected by the pandemic are not "in the same boat" as those most privileged. Because of both pressure and desire to be resilient, our data set excluded the intended participants for our research and it does not reflect the diversity of faculty on Canadian campuses. As we prepare for the inevitability of future pandemics, we as researchers need to pay closer attention to the impact of structural inequities on our research practices and demand that our faculty unions and scholarly associations provide us with strategies and protection so that we can refuse pressures from our institutions—and our own institutionalization—to just carry on.

Notes

1. Yue Qian and Sylvia Fuller, "COVID-19 and the Gender Employment Gap among Parents of Young Children," *Canadian Public Policy* 46, no. S2 (2020), S89; Melissa Moyser, "The Mental Health of Population Groups Designated as Visible Minorities in Canada during the COVID-19 Pandemic," *StatCan COVID-19: Data to Insights for a Better Canada*, September 2, 2020.
2. Neeta Kantamneni, "The Impact of the COVID-19 Pandemic on Marginalized Populations in the United States: A Research Agenda," *Journal of Vocational Behavior* 119, 103439 (2020); Jackie Marchildon, "Canada's Economy Will Only Recover if Marginalized Communities Get Support: Report," *Global Citizen*, July 31, 2020, https://www.globalcitizen.org/en/content/canada-economy-marginalized-communities-covid/; Elizabeth Pellicano and Mark Stears, "The Hidden Inequalities

of COVID-19," *Autism* 24, no. 6 (2020): 1309–1310; Jackie Leach Scully, "Disability, Disablism, and COVID-19 Pandemic Triage," *Bioethical Inquiry* 17 (2020): 601–605; Adia Harvey Wingfield, "The Disproportionate Impact of Covid-19 on Black Health Care Workers in the US," *Harvard Business Review*, May 14, 2020, https://hbr.org/2020/05/the-disproportionate-impact-of-covid-19-on-black-health-care-workers-in-the-u-s.

3. Rosi Braidotti, "'We' Are In This Together, But We Are Not One and the Same," *Bioethical Inquiry* 17 (2020): 465–469.

4. Jennifer Davis, "University Survey Shows How COVID-19 Pandemic is Hampering Career Progress for Women and Racialized Faculty," *The Conversation*, March 2, 2021, https://theconversation.com/university-survey-shows-how-covid-19-pandemic-is-hampering-career-progress-for-women-and-racialized-faculty-153169; Anna Maria Górska et al., "Deepening Inequalities: What did COVID-19 Reveal about the Gendered Nature of Academic Work?" *Gender, Work, and Organization* 28, no. 4 (2021): 1546–1561; Merin Oleschuk, "Gender Equity Considerations for Tenure and Promotion during COVID-19," *Canadian Review of Sociology* 57, no. 3 (2020): 502–515.

5. Michael Orsini, "Feeling Critical: Navigating the Emotional Worlds of COVID-19," *Critical Policy Studies* 15, no. 3 (2021): 387–397.

6. "Thick description" was developed as an ethnographic tool in 1973 by Clifford Geertz to ensure context was analyzed in addition to behaviour. In 2019, fat scholars May Friedman, Carla Rice, and Jen Rinaldi used the term *thicken* as a descriptor of intersectional and "liminal analyses" of fat subjectivities. Following Orsini, we use *thicken* to signal that our analysis of research practices includes a focus on the emotional register of this pandemic resilience paradigm. See Clifford Geertz, *The Interpretation of Cultures* (New York: Basic Books, 1973); May Friedman, Carla Rice, and Jen Rinaldi, *Thickening Fat: Fat Bodies, Intersectionality, and Social Justice* (New York: Routledge, 2019).

7. Orsini, "Feeling Critical," 391.

8. Mariah Bohanon, "Pandemic Expected to Cause Additional Barriers to Tenure for Marginalized Academics," *Insight into Diversity*, September 15, 2020, https://www.insightintodiversity.com/pandemic-expected-to-cause-additional-barriers-to-tenure-for-marginalized-academics/; Colleen Flaherty, "Covid-19: A Moment for Women in STEM?" *Inside Higher Education*, March 10, 2021, https://www.insidehighered.com/news/2021/03/10/covid-19-moment-women-stem; Juliet Isselbacher, "Women Researchers are Publishing Less Since the Pandemic Hit. What Can Their Employers Do to Help?" *STAT*, July 9, 2020, https://www.statnews.com/2020/07/09/women-research-covid19-pandemic/; Oleschuk, "Gender Equity Considerations."

9. Davis, "University Survey Shows," n.p.

10. Davis, "University Survey Shows," n.p.

11. Gillian R. Bentley, "Don't Blame the BAME: Ethnic and Structural Inequalities in Susceptibilities to COVID-19," *American Journal of Human Biology* 32, no. 5 (2020):

e23478; Caitlyn Collins et al., "COVID-19 and the Gender Gap in Work Hours," *Gender, Work, and Organization* 28, no. 1 (2020): 101–112; James K. Gibb et al., "Sexual and Gender Minority Health Vulnerabilities during the COVID-19 Health Crisis," *American Journal of Human Biology* 32, no. 5 (2020): e23499; Górska et al., "What Did COVID-19 Reveal"; Megan Kinch, "Filipinos across Canada Respond to Pandemic Inequalities: From Live-in Caregivers to Meat Packers, Filipino Workers Have Been at the Front Lines of COVID—But Have Received Little Protection or Recognition," *Briarpatch Magazine*, July 5, 2021, https://briarpatchmagazine.com/articles/view/filipinos-across-canada-respond-to-pandemic-inequalities; Oleschuk, "Gender Equity Considerations."

12. In most post-secondary institutions, research funding is restricted to tenure-track/tenured faculty members, making contract faculty members ineligible for such funding. Moreover, the precarious employment conditions of contract work necessitate a heavy teaching load, which presents a significant barrier for research.

13. For most contract faculty, rehiring decisions are contingent upon teaching evaluation results. Moreover, as numerous studies have demonstrated, racialized, gendered, queer, and disabled faculty are more likely to be negatively evaluated by students due to their subject position and/or their critical pedagogical focus on societal inequalities and power structure.

14. Cassandra M. Guarino and Victor M.H. Borden, "Faculty Service Loads and Gender: Are Women Taking Care of the Academic Family?" *Research in Higher Education* 58 (2017): 672–694; Frances Henry, Enakshi Dua, Carl E. James, Audrey Kobayashi, Peter Li, Howard Ramos, and Malinda S. Smith, eds., *The Equity Myth: Racialization and Indigeneity at Canadian Universities* (Vancouver: UBC Press, 2017); University of Oregon Social Sciences Feminist Network Research Interest Group, "The Burden of Invisible Work in Academia," *Humboldt Journal of Social Relations* 39 (2017): 228–245.

15. Moyser, "The Mental Health of Population Groups"; Megan Ruprecht, Wang Xinzi, Amy K. Johnson, Jiayi Xu, Dylan Felt, Siobhan Ihenacho, Patrick Stonehouse, Caleb W. Curry, Catherine DeBroux, Diogo Costa, and Gregory Phillips II. "Evidence of Social and Structural COVID-19 Disparities by Sexual Orientation, Gender Identity, and Race/Ethnicity in an Urban Environment," *Journal of Urban Health* 98, no. 1 (2021): 27–40; Lela R. McKnight-Eily, Catherine A. Okoro, Tara W. Strine, Jorge Verlenden, NaTasha D. Hollis, Rashid Njai, Elizabeth W. Mitchell, Amy Board, Richard Puddy, and Craig Thomas, "Racial and Ethnic Disparities in the Prevalence of Stress and Worry, Mental Health Conditions, and Increased Substance Use Among Adults During the COVID-19 Pandemic," *Centers for Disease Control and Prevention*, February 5, 2021, https://www.cdc.gov/mmwr/volumes/70/wr/mm7005a3.htm.

16. Riley Laychuk, "Brandon University Sexual Assault Victims Forced to Sign Contract that Keeps Them Silent," *CBC News*, April 5, 2016, https://www.cbc.ca/news/canada/manitoba/brandon-university-behavioural-contract-1.35205680568.

17. Emma Jones, "How These Students Fought Their School's Sexual-Assault 'Gag Order'—and Won," *The Discourse*, May 29, 2018, https://thediscourse.ca/gender/students-fought-schools-sexual-assault-gag-order-won.
18. Laychuk, "Brandon University."
19. Maggie Macintosh, "Embattled BU Cut Sexual Violence Education Coordinator Hours," *Winnipeg Free Press*, September 16, 2021. https://www.winnipegfreepress.com/local/embattled-bu-cut-sexual-violence-education-coordinator-hours-575331172.html.
20. Currently, MRU has a dedicated full-time staff to address sexual and dating violence, a one-day-per-week visit by a counsellor for specialized counselling, and a coordinator who is responsible for year-round programming and prevention campaigns.
21. There are many reasons for the lack of adequate services, ranging from the neoliberal funding structure of post-secondary institutions, the constant budget cuts, lack of attention to and funding of gendered and often racialized labour (such as counselling) and needs (sexual violence)—all of which leads to services being provided by generic health professionals who are not trained on the intersections of sexual violence.
22. Sara Carrigan Wooten, "Revealing a Hidden Curriculum of Black Women's Erasure in Sexual Violence Prevention Policy," *Gender and Education* 29, no. 3 (2016): 405–417.
23. Nirmal Puwar, *Space Invaders: Race, Gender and Bodies out of Place* (Oxford: Berg, 2004). We can see this in the lack of universal design in our classrooms, the lack of consideration of mobility and learning needs of disabled students—there are countless examples.
24. Avery Gordon, *Ghostly Matters: Haunting and the Sociological Imagination* (Minneapolis: University of Minnesota, 1997), 27.
25. Sara Ahmed, *On Being Included: Racism and Diversity in Institutional Life* (Durham: Duke University Press, 2012).
26. Puwar, *Space Invaders*.
27. Kelly Ervin, "The Experiences of an Academic Misfit,'" in *Presumed Incompetent: The Intersections of Race and Class for Women in Academia*, eds. Gabriella y Muhs Gutiérrez, Yolanda Flores Niemann, Carmen. G.Gonzalez, and Angela P. Harris (Boulder: University Press of Colorado, 2012), 439–445; Michelle A. Holling, May C. Fu, and Roe Bubar, "Dis/jointed Appointments: Solidarity Amidst Inequity, Tokenism, and Marginalization," in *Presumed Incompetent: The Intersections of Race and Class for Women in Academia*, eds. Gabriella y Muhs Gutiérrez, Yolanda Flores Niemann, Carmen. G. Gonzalez, and Angela P. Harris (Boulder: University Press of Colorado, 2012): 250–265; Carl E. James, "You Know Why You Were Hired, Don't You?" Expectations and Challenges in University Appointments," in *The Equity Myth: Racialization and Indigeneity at Canadian Universities*, eds. Frances Henry, Enakshi Dua, Carl E. James, Audrey Kobayashi, Peter Li, Howard Ramos, and

Malinda S. Smith (Vancouver: UBC Press, 2017), 155-170; Yolanda Flores Niemann, "Lessons from the Experiences of Women of Colour Working in Academia," in *Presumed Incompetent: The Intersections of Race and Class for Women in Academia*, eds. Gabriella y Muhs Gutiérrez, Yolanda Flores Niemann, Carmen. G. Gonzalez, and Angela P. Harris (Boulder: University Press of Colorado, 2012), 446-500; Howard Ramos, and Peter Li, "Differences in Representation and Employment Income of Racialized University Professors in Canada," in *The Equity Myth: Racialization and Indigeneity at Canadian Universities*, eds. Frances Henry, Enakshi Dua, Carl E. James, Audrey Kobayashi, Peter Li, Howard Ramos, and Malinda S. Smith (Vancouver: UBC Press, 2017), 46-64; Howard Ramos and Rochelle Wijesingha, "Academic Production, Reward and Perceptions of Racialized Faculty Members," in *The Equity Myth: Racialization and Indigeneity at Canadian Universities*, eds. Frances Henry, Enakshi Dua, Carl E. James, Audrey Kobayashi, Peter Li, Howard Ramos, and Malinda S. Smith (Vancouver: UBC Press, 2017), 65-83; Malinda S. Smith, Kimberly Gamarro, and Mansharn Toor, "A Dirty Dozen: Unconscious Race and Gender Biases in the Academy," in *The Equity Myth: Racialization and Indigeneity at Canadian Universities*, eds. Frances Henry, Enakshi Dua, Carl E. James, Audrey Kobayashi, Peter Li, Howard Ramos, and Malinda S. Smith (Vancouver: UBC Press, 2017), 263-287.

28. Robyn Dolittle and Chen Wang, "The Power Gap," *Globe and Mail*, January 21, 2021, https://www.theglobeandmail.com/canada/article-power-gap-main/.
29. Canadian Association of University Teachers (CAUT). "Underrepresented and Underpaid: Diversity and Equity Among Canada's Post-Secondary Education Teachers," April 2018, https://www.caut.ca/sites/default/files/caut_equity_report_2018-04final.pdf; Henry et al., *The Equity Myth*.
30. Alison Phipps, "White Tears, White Rage: Victimhood and (as) Violence in Mainstream Feminism," *European Journal of Cultural Studies* 24, no. 1 (2021): 81-93.
31. Ashwini Tambe, "Reckoning with the Silences of #MeToo," *Feminist Studies* 44, no. 1 (2018): 198.
32. Wooten, "Revealing a Hidden Curriculum," 405-417.
33. Roni Berger, "Studying Trauma: Indirect Effects on Researchers and Self—and Strategies for Addressing Them." *European Journal of Trauma & Dissociation* 5, no. 1 (2021): 100149; Jan Coles et al., "A Qualitative Exploration of Researcher Trauma and Researchers' Responses to Investigating Sexual Violence," *Violence Against Women* 20, no. 1 (2014): 95-117; Amelia van der Merwe and Xanthe Hunt, "Secondary Trauma Among Trauma Researchers: Lessons from the Field," *Psychological Trauma* 11, no. 1 (2019): 10-18.
34. Megan Kinch, "Covid-19 Makes a Bad Situation Worse for Agricultural Workers in Canada," *Equal Times*, April 23, 2021, https://www.equaltimes.org/covid-19-makes-a-bad-situation?lang=en#.YUi8O2ZKiw5; Tamara Power et al., "COVID-19 and Indigenous Peoples: An Imperative for Action," *Journal of Clinical Nursing* 29, no. 15-16 (2020): 2737-2741; Rajendra Subedi, Lawson Greenberg, and Martin

Turcotte, "COVID-19 Mortality Rates in Canada's Ethno-cultural Neighbourhoods," *StatCan Covid-19: Data to Insights for a Better Canada*, October 28, 2020, https://www150.statcan.gc.ca/n1/en/pub/45-28-0001/2020001/article/00079-eng.pdf?st=H8p8jEeP; Roberta K. Timothy, "Coronavirus Is Not the Great Equalizer—Race Matters," *The Conversation*, April 6, 2020, https://theconversation.com/coronavirus-is-not-the-great-equalizer-race-matters-133867.

35. Statistics Canada, "Experiences of Discrimination during the COVID-19 Pandemic," *The Daily*, September 17, 2020, https://www150.statcan.gc.ca/n1/daily-quotidien/200917/dq200917a-eng.htm; Statistics Canada, "Perceptions of Personal Safety Among Population Groups Designated as Visible Minorities in Canada during the COVID-19 Pandemic," *Statcan Covid: Data to Insights for a Better Canada*, July 8, 2020, https://www150.statcan.gc.ca/n1/pub/45-28-0001/2020001/article/00046-eng.htm.

36. Sammy Hudes, "Kenny's 'Wake-up Call' to Northeast Calgary Condemned as Scapegoating," *Calgary Herald*, November 30, 2020, https://calgaryherald.com/news/politics/kenneys-wake-up-call-to-northeast-calgary-condemned-as-scapegoating.

37. Stephanie Liu, "Reports of Anti-Asian Hate Crimes are Surging in Canada during the COVID-19 Pandemic," *CTV News*, March 17, 2021, https://www.ctvnews.ca/canada/reports-of-anti-asian-hate-crimes-are-surging-in-canada-during-the-covid-19-pandemic-1.5351481; Statistics Canada, "Experiences of Discrimination."

38. Cameron MacLean, "Manitoba Premier Wants Extra Dose of Vaccine if Ottawa Reserves a Portion for First Nations," *CBC News*, December 3, 2020, https://www.cbc.ca/news/canada/manitoba/manitoba-first-nations-covid-19-vaccines-1.5826960.

39. Rachel Bergen, "Vaccine Consent Form Invalidating for Non-binary and Trans People, Manitoban Says," *CBC News*, May 13, 2020, https://www.cbc.ca/news/canada/manitoba/covid-19-vaccines-manitoba-transgender-1.6023988.

40. Tegan and Sara Foundation. "It's For Us: COVID-19 Vaccination and the LGBTQ+ community," June 2021, https://static1.squarespace.com/static/582601b4440243fc471a91d0/t/60c76c654a25e73bb1fc850d/1623682153103/It%27s+For+US-+COVID-19+Vaccination+and+the+LGBTQ%2B+Community.pdf.

41. Orsini, "Feeling Critical."

42. Braidotti, "'We' Are In This Together."

43. Eli Clare, *Exile and Pride: Disability, Queerness, and Liberation* (Durham: Duke University Press, 2015); Michael Oliver, "The Social Model in Context," in *Rethinking Normalcy: A Disability Studies Reader*, eds. Tanya Titchkosky and Rod Michalko (Toronto: Canadian Scholars' Press, 2009), 19–30.

Bibliography

Ahmed, Sara. *On Being Included: Racism and Diversity in Institutional Life*. Durham: Duke University Press, 2012.

Bentley, Gillian. R. "Don't blame the BAME: Ethnic and Structural Inequalities in Susceptibilities to COVID-19." *American Journal of Human Biology* 32, no. 5 (July 2020): e23478. https://doi.org/10.1002/ajhb.23478.

Bergen, Rachel. "Vaccine Consent Form Invalidating for Non-binary and Trans People, Manitoban Says." *CBC News*, May 13, 2020. https://www.cbc.ca/news/canada/manitoba/covid-19-vaccines-manitoba-transgender-1.6023988.

Berger, Roni. "Studying Trauma: Indirect Effects on Researchers and Self—and Strategies for Addressing Them." *European Journal of Trauma & Dissociation* 5, no. 1 (February 2021): 100149. https://doi.org/10.1016/j.ejtd.2020.100149.

Bohanon, Mariah. "Pandemic Expected to Cause Additional Barriers to Tenure for Marginalized Academics." *Insight into Diversity*, September 15, 2020. https://www.insightintodiversity.com/pandemic-expected-to-cause-additional-barriers-to-tenure-for-marginalized-academics/.

Braidotti, Rosi. "'We' Are In This Together, But We Are Not One and the Same." *Bioethical Inquiry* 17 (2020): 465-469. https://doi.org/10.1007/s11673-020-10017-8.

Canadian Association of University Teachers (CAUT). "Underrepresented & Underpaid: Diversity & Equity Among Canada's Post-Secondary Education Teachers." April 2018. https://www.caut.ca/sites/default/files/caut_equity_report_2018-04final.pdf.

Clare, Eli. *Exile and Pride: Disability, Queerness, and Liberation.* Durham: Duke University Press, 2015.

Coles, Jan, Jill Astbury, Elizabeth Dartnall, and Shazeen Limjerwala. "A Qualitative Exploration of Researcher Trauma and Researchers' Responses to Investigating Sexual Violence." *Violence Against Women* 20, no. 1 (2014): 95-117. https://doi.org/10.1177/1077801213520578.

Collins, Caitlyn, Liana Christin Landivar, Leah Ruppanner, and William. J. Scarborough. "COVID-19 and the Gender Gap in Work Hours." *Gender, Work, and Organization* 28, no. 1 (2020): 101-112. https://doi.org/10.1111/gwao.12506.

Davis, Jennifer. "University Survey Shows How COVID-19 Pandemic is Hampering Career Progress for Women and Racialized Faculty." *The Conversation*, March 2, 2021. https://theconversation.com/university-survey-shows-how-covid-19-pandemic-is-hampering-career-progress-for-women-and-racialized-faculty-153169.

Dolittle, Robyn, and Chen Wang. "The Power Gap." *Globe and Mail*, January 21, 2021. https://www.theglobeandmail.com/canada/article-power-gap-main/.

Ervin, Kelly. "The Experiences of an Academic 'Misfit.'" In *Presumed Incompetent: The Intersections of Race and Class for Women in Academia*, edited by Gabriella y Muhs Gutiérrez, Yolanda Flores Niemann, Carmen. G. Gonzalez, and Angela P. Harris, 439-445 (Boulder: University Press of Colorado, 2012).

Flaherty, Colleen. "Covid-19: A Moment for Women in STEM?" *Inside Higher Education*. March 10, 2021. https://www.insidehighered.com/news/2021/03/10/covid-19-moment-women-stem.

Friedman, May, Carla Rice, and Jen Rinaldi. *Thickening Fat: Fat Bodies, Intersectionality, and Social Justice*. New York: Routledge, 2019.

Geertz, Clifford. *The Interpretation of Cultures*. New York: Basic Books, 1973.

Gibb, James K., L. Zackary DuBois, Sarah Williams, Luserad McKerracher, Robert-Paul Juster, and Jessica Fields. "Sexual and Gender Minority Health Vulnerabilities during the COVID-19 Health Crisis." *American Journal of Human Biology* 32, no. 5 (2020): e23499. https://doi.org/10.1002/ajhb.23499.

Gordon, Avery. *Ghostly Matters: Haunting and the Sociological Imagination*. Minneapolis: University of Minnesota, 1997.

Górska, Anna Maria, Karolina Kulicka, Zuzanna Staniszewska, and Dorata Dobija. "Deepening Inequalities: What did COVID-19 Reveal about the Gendered Nature of Academic Work?" *Gender, Work, and Organization* 28, no. 4 (2021): 1546–1561. https://doi.org/10.1111/gwao.12696.

Guarino, Cassandra M., and Victor M.H. Borden. "Faculty Service Loads and Gender: Are Women Taking Care of the Academic Family?" *Research in Higher Education* 58 (2017): 672–694. https://doi.org/10.1007/s11162-017-9454-2.

Henry, Frances, Enakshi Dua, Carl E. James, Audrey Kobayashi, Peter Li, Howard Ramos, and Malinda S. Smith, eds. *The Equity Myth: Racialization and Indigeneity at Canadian Universities*. Vancouver: UBC Press, 2017.

Holling, Michelle A., May C. Fu, and Roe Bubar. "Dis/jointed Appointments: Solidarity Amidst Inequity, Tokenism, and Marginalization." In *Presumed Incompetent: The Intersections of Race and Class for Women in Academia*, edited by Gabriella y Muhs Gutiérrez, Yolanda Flores Niemann, Carmen. G. Gonzalez, and Angela P. Harris, 250–265. Boulder: University Press of Colorado, 2012.

Hudes, Sammy. "Kenny's 'Wake-up Call' to Northeast Calgary Condemned as Scapegoating." *Calgary Herald*, November 30, 2020. https://calgaryherald.com/news/politics/kenneys-wake-up-call-to-northeast-calgary-condemned-as-scapegoating.

Isselbacher, Juliet. "Women Researchers are Publishing Less Since the Pandemic Hit. What Can Their Employers Do to Help?" *STAT*, July 9, 2020. https://www.statnews.com/2020/07/09/women-research-covid19-pandemic/.

James, Carl E. "You Know Why You Were Hired, Don't You?" Expectations and Challenges in University Appointments." In *The Equity Myth: Racialization and Indigeneity at Canadian Universities*, edited by Frances Henry, Enakshi Dua, Carl E. James, Audrey Kobayashi, Peter Li, Howard Ramos, and Malinda S. Smith, 155–170. Vancouver: UBC Press, 2017.

Jones, Emma. "How These Students Fought Their School's Sexual-Assault 'Gag Order'—and Won." *The Discourse*, May 29, 2018. https://thediscourse.ca/gender/students-fought-schools-sexual-assault-gag-order-won.

Kantamneni, Neeta. "The Impact of the COVID-19 Pandemic on Marginalized Populations in the United States: A Research Agenda." *Journal of Vocational Behavior* 119 (2020): 103439. https://doi.org/10.1016/j.jvb.2020.103439.

Kinch, Megan. "Covid-19 Makes a Bad Situation Worse for Agricultural Workers in Canada." *Equal Times*, April 23, 2021. https://www.equaltimes.org/covid-19-makes-a-bad-situation?lang=en#.YUi8O2ZKiw5.

Kinch, Megan. "Filipinos across Canada Respond to Pandemic Inequalities: From Live-in Caregivers to Meat Packers, Filipino Workers Have Been at the Front Lines of COVID—But Have Received Little Protection or Recognition." *Briarpatch Magazine*, July 5, 2021. https://briarpatchmagazine.com/articles/view/filipinos-across-canada-respond-to-pandemic-inequalities.

Laychuk, Riley. "Brandon University Sexual Assault Victims Forced to Sign Contract that Keeps Them Silent." *CBC News*, April 5, 2016. https://www.cbc.ca/news/canada/manitoba/brandon-university-behavioural-contract-1.3520568.

Liu, Stephanie. "Reports of Anti-Asian Hate Crimes are Surging in Canada during the COVID-19 Pandemic." *CTV News*, March 17, 2021. https://www.ctvnews.ca/canada/reports-of-anti-asian-hate-crimes-are-surging-in-canada-during-the-covid-19-pandemic-1.5351481.

Macintosh, Maggie. "Embattled BU Cut Sexual Violence Education Co-ordinator Hours." *Winnipeg Free Press*, September 16, 2021. https://www.winnipegfreepress.com/local/embattled-bu-cut-sexual-violence-education-co-ordinator-hours-575331172.html.

MacLean, Cameron. "Manitoba Premier Wants Extra Dose of Vaccine if Ottawa Reserves a Portion for First Nations." *CBC News*, December 3, 2020. https://www.cbc.ca/news/canada/manitoba/manitoba-first-nations-covid-19-vaccines-1.5826960.

Marchildon, Jackie. "Canada's Economy Will Only Recover if Marginalized Communities Get Support: Report." *Global Citizen*, July 31, 2020. https://www.globalcitizen.org/en/content/canada-economy-marginalized-communities-covid/.

McKnight-Eily, Lela R, Catherine A. Okoro, Tara W. Strine, Jorge Verlenden, NaTasha D. Hollis, Rashid Njai, Elizabeth W. Mitchell, Amy Board, Richard Puddy, and Craig Thomas. "Racial and Ethnic Disparities in the Prevalence of Stress and Worry, Mental Health Conditions, and Increased Substance Use Among Adults During the COVID-19 Pandemic." *Centers for Disease Control and Prevention*, February 5, 2021. https://www.cdc.gov/mmwr/volumes/70/wr/mm7005a3.htm.

Moyser, Melissa. "The Mental Health of Population Groups Designated as Visible Minorities in Canada during the COVID-19 Pandemic." *StatCan COVID-19: Data to Insights for a Better Canada*, September 2, 2020. https://www150.statcan.gc.ca/n1/pub/45-28-0001/2020001/article/00077-eng.htm.

Niemann, Yolanda Flores. "Lessons from the Experiences of Women of Colour Working in Academia" In *Presumed Incompetent: The Intersections of Race and Class for Women in Academia*, edited by Gabriella y Muhs Gutiérrez, Yolanda Flores Niemann, Carmen. G. Gonzalez, and Angela P. Harris, 446–500. Boulder: University Press of Colorado, 2012.

Oleschuk, Merin. "Gender Equity Considerations for Tenure and Promotion during COVID-19." *Canadian Review of Sociology* 57, no. 3 (2020): 502–515. https://doi.org/10.1111/cars.12295.

Oliver, Michael. "The Social Model in Context." In *Rethinking Normalcy: A Disability Studies Reader*, edited by Tanya Titchkosky and Rod Michalko, 19-30. Toronto: Canadian Scholars Press, 2009.

Orsini, Michael. "Feeling Critical: Navigating the Emotional Worlds of COVID-19." *Critical Policy Studies* 15, no. 3 (2021): 387-397. https://doi.org/10.1080/19460171.2021.1963793.

Pellicano, Elizabeth, and Mark Stears. "The Hidden Inequalities of COVID-19." *Autism* 24, no. 6 (2020): 1309-1310. https://doi.org/10.1177/1362361320927590.

Phipps, Alison. "White Tears, White Rage: Victimhood and (as) Violence in Mainstream Feminism." *European Journal of Cultural Studies* 24, no. 1 (2021): 81-93. https://doi.org/10.1177/1367549420985852.

Power, Tamara, Denise Wilson, Odette Best, Teresa Brockie, Lisa Bourque Bearskin, Eugenia Millender, and John Lowe. "COVID-19 and Indigenous Peoples: An Imperative for Action." *Journal of Clinical Nursing* 29, no. 15-16 (2020): 2737-2741. https://doi.org/10.1111/jocn.15320.

Puwar, Nirmal. *Space Invaders: Race, Gender and Bodies Out of Place*. Oxford: Berg, 2004.

Qian, Yue, and Syliva Fuller. "COVID-19 and the Gender Employment Gap among Parents of Young Children." *Canadian Public Policy* 46, no. S2 (2020): S89-S101. https://doi.org/10.3138/cpp.2020-077.

Ramos, Howard, and Peter Li. "Differences in Representation and Employment Income of Racialized University Professors in Canada." In *The Equity Myth: Racialization and Indigeneity at Canadian Universities*, edited by Frances Henry, Enakshi Dua, Carl E. James, Audrey Kobayashi, Peter Li, Howard Ramos, and Malinda S. Smith, 46-64. Vancouver: UBC Press, 2017.

Ramos, Howard, and Rochelle Wijesingha. "Academic Production, Reward and Perceptions of Racialized Faculty Members." In *The Equity Myth: Racialization and Indigeneity at Canadian Universities*, edited by Frances Henry, Enakshi Dua, Carl E. James, Audrey Kobayashi, Peter Li, Howard Ramos, and Malinda S. Smith, 65-83. Vancouver: UBC Press, 2017.

Ruprecht, Megan, Xinzi Wang, Amy K. Johnson, Jiayi Xu, Dylan Felt, Siobhan Ihenacho, Patrick Stonehouse, Caleb W. Curry, Catherine DeBroux, Diogo Costa, and Gregory Phillips II. (2021). "Evidence of Social and Structural COVID-19 Disparities by Sexual Orientation, Gender Identity, and Race/Ethnicity in an Urban Environment." *Journal of Urban Health* 98, no. 1 (2021): 27-40. DOI: 10.1007/s11524-020-00497-9.

Scully, Jackie Leach. "Disability, Disablism, and COVID-19 Pandemic Triage." *Bioethical Inquiry* 17 (2020): 601-605. https://doi.org/10.1007/s11673-020-10005-y.

Smith, Malinda S., Gamarro, Kimberly, and Mansharn Toor. "A Dirty Dozen: Unconscious Race and Gender Biases in the Academy." In *The Equity Myth: Racialization and Indigeneity at Canadian Universities*, edited by Frances Henry, Enakshi Dua, Carl E. James, Audrey Kobayashi, Peter Li, Howard Ramos, and Malinda S. Smith. Vancouver, 263-87. UBC Press, 2017.

Statistics Canada. "Experiences of Discrimination during the COVID-19 Pandemic." *The Daily*, September 17, 2020. https://www150.statcan.gc.ca/n1/daily-quotidien/200917/dq200917a-eng.htm.

Statistics Canada. "Perceptions of Personal Safety Among Population Groups Designated as Visible Minorities in Canada during the COVID-19 Pandemic." *Statcan Covid: Data to Insights for a Better Canada*, July 8, 2020. https://www150.statcan.gc.ca/n1/pub/45-28-0001/2020001/article/00046-eng.htm.

Subedi, Rajendra, Greenberg, Lawson, and Martin Turcotte. "COVID-19 Mortality Rates in Canada's Ethno-cultural Neighbourhoods." *StatCan Covid-19: Data to Insights for a Better Canada*, October 28, 2020. https://www150.statcan.gc.ca/n1/en/pub/45-28-0001/2020001/article/00079-eng.pdf?st=H8p8jEeP.

Tambe, Ashwini. "Reckoning with the Silences of #MeToo." *Feminist Studies* 44, no. 1 (2018): 197-203. https://doi.org/10.15767/feministstudies.44.1.0197.

Tegan and Sara Foundation. "It's For Us: COVID-19 Vaccination and the LGBTQ+ community." June 2021. https://static1.squarespace.com/static/582601b4440243f-c471a91d0/t/60c76c654a25e73bb1fc850d/1623682153103/It%27s+For+US-+COVID-19+Vaccination+and+the+LGBTQ%2B+Community.pdf.

Timothy, Roberta K. "Coronavirus Is Not the Great Equalizer—Race Matters." *The Conversation*, April 6, 2020. https://theconversation.com/coronavirus-is-not-the-great-equalizer-race-matters-133867.

University of Oregon Social Sciences Feminist Network Research Interest Group. "The Burden of Invisible Work in Academia." *Humboldt Journal of Social Relations* 39 (2017): 228-245.

van der Merwe, Amelia, and Xanthe Hunt. Secondary Trauma Among Trauma Researchers: Lessons from the Field. *Psychological Trauma* 11, no. 1 (2019): 10-18. https://doi.org/10.1037/tra0000414.

Wingfield, Adia Harvey. "The Disproportionate Impact of Covid-19 on Black Health Care Workers in the US." *Harvard Business Review*, May 14, 2020. https://hbr.org/2020/05/the-disproportionate-impact-of-covid-19-on-black-health-care-workers-in-the-u-s

Wooten, Sara Carrigan. "Revealing a Hidden Curriculum of Black Women's Erasure in Sexual Violence Prevention Policy." *Gender and Education* 29, no. 3 (2016): 405-417. https://doi.org/10.1080/09540253.2016.1225012.

14

"It Was the Worst Place I Ever Lived"..."It Was the Best Place I Ever Worked"
Exploring the Productive Potential of Narrative Discrepancies and Bias in Qualitative Research

Madeline Burghardt

Introduction

Troubling differences between narratives from different groups of participants in a research project present methodological and interpretive challenges for the qualitative researcher. Postmodern interpretation, which acknowledges "uncertainty about what constitutes an adequate depiction of social 'reality'"[1] and which suggests that there may be more than one truth to a story,[2] offers a methodology that runs counter to the often-seductive investigative path through which the researcher might be tempted to determine the real story. Attending to troublingly different narratives which purportedly describe the same phenomenon, however, suggest that the task for the researcher is not simply to determine which truth is more truthful, but to determine what the gap between the two social realities reveals. The charge becomes to not only expose different sides to the story, but to determine the nature and extent of the entity uncovered between them. What can the variance between these two versions tell us about the larger phenomenon in question, and why should we be concerned about it? To what is this space inviting us to understand?

I encountered this methodological conundrum while doing my doctoral research, an exploration of the effects of institutionalization on family relationships and understandings of disability.[3] Among other participants, I interviewed institutional survivors[4]—those who had lived in an institution for people labelled/with intellectual disabilities—as well as people who had worked in one. Most of my interviews with former staff took place after I had spoken with survivors. Throughout the interviews with former staff, I found it challenging to remain non-judgmental and open (in other words, to be a good listener) to their descriptions of the institution as "the best place I ever worked," in some cases only days after I had heard survivors tell me that it was "the worst place I ever lived."

When reflecting on the interviews afterward, it would have been easy to take a descriptive approach and conclude that the two groups simply conveyed vastly different experiences and interpretations of the same phenomenon. Yet the differences invited me into an interrogative space, the gap between them a rich if irresolvable source of insight. Important questions emerged: To what degree could these different accounts be reconciled? And if reconciliation was not possible, what and how could I learn from that irresolvability? What is the meaning behind these narrative differences? Importantly, what is at stake when such an exposure is undertaken?

What became clear was that the goal was not about trying to determine the extent to which each account was accurate, but to determine what the discrepancy between them revealed. When held against the particularities of the phenomenon being studied—a system of incarceration specifically designed to remove people designated as feebleminded from the population, against their will, and sometimes for their entire lives—then the space between the two versions of the same story was not only a discrepancy but was an indication of the extent of the injustice embedded in the system from which the discrepant narratives had emerged. That the two versions were given by two groups of people in possession of vastly different amounts of power—one marginalized and rejected by society, their lives governed by the dictates of the running of the institution; the other, that which oversaw and performed the governing—was the impetus to excavate the space between them.

Moreover, my exposure to these very different accounts, and the analysis that followed, generated reflection on the productive potential of bias in qualitative research. I knew, through my own allegiances with the institutional survivor community, and a desire to facilitate the articulation of experiences from those whose voices have historically been suppressed or deliberately neglected, that I entered the project with a bias of foregrounding survivors' experiences over those who had held power over them during their time in the institution. While bias has traditionally been considered an unfortunate consequence of preformed alliances between researchers and research participants, a contrivance that can allow research to arrive at predetermined and desired outcomes, I contend, rather, that bias can galvanize the illumination of previously excluded narratives[5] and can expose normalized research practices that maintain the status quo of hegemonic knowledges.

In this chapter, I use the aforementioned example, in which two groups of participants presented vastly different accounts of their experiences within the same social and geographic location (that is, the staff and inmates at an institution for people labelled/with intellectual disabilities) in order to explore the productive potential of narrative discrepancy. I examine the accounts shared during the research process and demonstrate how the irresolvability between the two groups is not indicative of methodological failure per se, nor of the need to reconcile them under one, all-embracing analytical umbrella, but signal, rather, the injustice embedded between these two groups' distinct and inequitable social positions, and thus point the way towards future academic and advocacy work that can address the injustice revealed. Second, I discuss the productive potential of bias in qualitative research. I posit that bias is not something to be avoided—for, by doing so, we risk obfuscating the emergence of uncomfortable truths with emancipatory potential—rather, it is a tool to formulate new, previously repressed knowledges and to expose social inequities within our research populations and within society more generally.

Further, in alignment with this volume's focus on vulnerabilities revealed through research committed to social change, the stories contained herein reveal the paradoxical nature of the vulnerability experienced by the oppressed group in this dichotomy—that is, those who were institutionalized: on the one hand, a vulnerability that is heightened and real, while simultaneously necessarily constructed[6] in order to justify institutions' ongoing use—a contradiction that generally goes assumed and unnoticed in public discourse. Moreover, while I would not define my position as researcher in this situation as vulnerable, owing the multiple privileged positions I occupy, this project also reveals the ways in which engaging with research with an aim towards justice can land one in irresolvable and uncomfortable spaces. My stance of intentionally aligning with one group—one that has historically been deemed unreliable—positions me on shaky methodological ground within the framework of traditional research methodologies. And while this work exposes my allegiances, it also allows the survivors in this project to hold me to account.

The chapter consists of three parts. First, I briefly describe the research project that was the source of the findings introduced above. Second, I discuss the investigative possibilities and the insights that can emerge when the spaces between narratives in qualitative research projects are interrogated and when the systems that allow such discrepancies to exist are exposed. In the third section, I discuss the productive potential of bias in qualitative research, not as something to be avoided in order to maintain the strict standards of traditional, case-based research, but as a tool that can reveal previously obscured experiences.

Project: Institutionalization and Its Effects

For the project upon which this chapter is based, I interviewed nine institutional survivors, eleven siblings and six parents of survivors (as well as two parents who chose not to institutionalize their child, contributions that provided important insights), four key informants on the issue, and four former institutional staff. The research was qualitative in nature, and thus my aim was to allow participants to share their experiences of institutionalization and its effects as freely as they wished. I followed a rough interview guide, yet space was made in the interviews such that participants could reflect on issues and memories that were important to them. While the research uncovered several important findings—such as the extent to which parents' interpretations of disability and difference affected their degree of allegiance to institutionalization as a viable and reasonable form of care, as well as siblings' interpretations of how the institutionalization of a brother or sister had affected their own childhood[7]—in this chapter, I focus on the interviews with survivors and former staff and the discrepancies between them, with some reference to statements made by key informants. I begin with a brief summary of general themes that emerged and then move to a discussion of three main areas of comparison: institutions as paradoxical sites of abundance/injustice; degrees of freedom; and relationships between staff and residents.

"The Worst Place I Ever Lived"..."The Best Place I Ever Worked"
All of the survivors indicated that the time they had spent in the institution was the darkest and unhappiest period of their lives. Some of the survivors provided horrific examples of the oppression, regimentation, dehumanization, and physical and sexual abuse that they had suffered while institutionalized. They had lived the failures of the institutional system and continue to advocate fiercely that anyone can live in the community, so long as adequate supports are imagined and implemented. They all indicated that they are much happier now, even in community living situations in which there exist some ongoing difficulties such as loneliness and poverty, or struggles regarding the inadequacy of social supports and their accompanying bureaucratic obstacles.

In contrast, the former institutional staff with whom I spoke considered the time they had spent working in the institution as one of the happiest of their lives: a solid government job with good pay, excellent benefits, and (seeming) job security. They also described the significant sense of loss they had experienced when the provincial government followed through on promises made years earlier and closed the last, large, government-run institution in Ontario for good in 2009, forcing an end to their relationships with residents, people for whom they had provided care for years and sometimes decades. In some cases, this meant the end of a longstanding family tradition in which several generations of the same family had been employed at the same institution. For many staff, it also meant the end of a close and tightly knit community of friends, other staff with whom they had become close through their work at the facility. Further, in contrast to what survivors unequivocally stated regarding the possibility that everyone can live in the community with adequate support, former staff indicated that they believe that there will always be a need for some institutions. Not abolitionists, they confirmed their adherence to some system of control and shared their belief that sometimes it is not possible to support people in the community. Thus, for the staff I interviewed, the principal characterization of institutional closure was one of loss.

Institutions: Abundance/Injustice

Accounts from survivors and former staff reveal a discrepancy between interpretations of what institutions provided to the people who lived there. Throughout institutions' history, the amenities and activities provided shifted in emphasis and scope, depending on the philosophical underpinnings of programming considered necessary for residents' long-term rehabilitation and development. For example, in the mid-1930s, the names of the major institutions for people labelled/with intellectual disabilities in Ontario were changed from Asylum to Ontario Hospital School,[8] suggesting that these were not merely residents for people with intellectual disabilities but were educational facilities that provided a basic curriculum and skills training with qualified instructors. Further, as professional rehabilitative roles in institutions became increasingly prolific and specialized throughout the second half of the twentieth century, amenities were added to institutions' list of offerings. For example, each of the three largest Schedule One[9] facilities had a pool, an exercise program, walkways, and various activities, all of which purportedly met the physical, social, and cultural needs of its residents. The former staff saw these as positive features of institutional life. As one of them stated, "the residents lacked for nothing...there were so many options for them."

Survivors offered different interpretations. One survivor said she attended school in the institution as "an escape from the abuse." Several others described their labour within the institution, historically included in institutions' mandates as a form of moral therapy that had therapeutic benefits. These included descriptions of labour in the laundry room[10] and the supply room, not as rewarding work but as imposed labour for which they were not compensated. In addition, survivors' internal labour paradoxically helped to keep the institution running and thus contributed to their own incarceration. Yet no survivors mentioned the pool, or exercise, or other programs that the staff held in such high regard. This omission is not necessarily evidence that these services were not available to this particular group of survivors, nor that their use was not enjoyable, but it is indicative of the lack of centrality that these amenities held in the survivors' depictions of their institutional experience. Further, it was clear that for survivors, one of the central characterizations of institutional life was not the services offered, but rather, the fact that they had no choice regarding how and on whose terms they made use of them.

It is tempting to consider these divergences simply as different interpretations of what was offered at the institution based on peoples' variant opinions and preferences. More troublingly, the reluctance of survivors to frame their recollections of the better features of institutional life in a positive light can also be interpreted by non-disabled observers as examples of an undeveloped lack of appreciation towards their possible benefits. To better understand the discrepancies presented from these two groups, I turned to explanations that key informants offered regarding the institutions and what they purportedly offered. Key informants were participants in the project who had extensive experience and expertise in the support of people labelled/with intellectual disabilities and their families, and many of them had also been active in the deinstitutionalization movement, yet they did not have familial or personal connections. The key informants offered a more nuanced interpretation of what amenities in the institutions represented and why it is important to not simply embrace them as beneficial programming that supported residents' development. They pointed out that it is essential to be skeptical of the progressive appearance of amenities and to invert our initial understandings of them as positive features in order to see the injustice of the system within which they were embedded. Key informants pointed out that it was not in spite of those services that institutionalization was a fundamentally unjust way of life, but because of them. That is, if residents could learn to read and write in a classroom setting, then why did they have to come to an institution, spending years away from their families, in order to have access to one? Why was it that the one place where people labelled/with intellectual disabilities could learn to swim was not in their home communities, but in a segregated, isolated facility? This interpretive inversion—from amenities as evidence of the positive aspects of institutions to evidence of their injustice—is counterintuitive yet fundamental to understanding institutions for what they actually performed and accomplished and also to foregrounding the voices, preferences, and experiences of people labelled/with intellectual disabilities.

Further, what became clear through the research and the reflection that followed was the extent to which former staff, entrenched as they were in institutional life,[11] did not recognize these contradictions. Staff observations that residents "lacked for nothing" reflect their embeddedness in a lens of abundance that masks the injustice of people labelled/with intellectual disabilities having to become incarcerated in order to access the basic supports and amenities—education, healthcare, exercise—that the rest of the population takes for granted. Intentional or not, staff demonstrated an inability or an unwillingness to extricate themselves from the framing of institutions as rich locations of support, not acknowledging that most people can choose to engage, or not to engage, with these kinds of supports and amenities on their own terms rather than having those choices always made on their behalf.

For these reasons and as indicated previously, all of the staff interviewed described the deinstitutionalization process in Ontario as a loss. Framing the community as a place where supports and amenities for people with more complex needs could not be guaranteed, where more vulnerable people would be exposed to increased risk, and, paradoxically, as a location in which people labelled/with intellectual disabilities would have less freedom as opposed to more (discussed below), staff were adamant that for many of the residents, government-run institutions were the better option.

Degrees of Freedom

Drawing from the preceding discussion, the second point of divergence between survivor and staff narratives concerns interpretations regarding the amount of freedom available to institutional residents. Survivors' principal characterization of the institution was that these were places over which they had no control. They had had no authority regarding their arrival at the facility (most had been admitted as children or adolescents as a result of decisions made by either their parents, medical doctors, or social service agencies), and this was a place from which they could not leave. Indeed, some of the survivors provided harrowing accounts of the sudden loss of autonomy that they encountered upon their admission. Peter[12] described being stripped of his "new blue suit," purchased especially for his move to the institution, which his family had understood as a place where he might be healed of his epilepsy, and Joe also described being stripped upon entry at the age of 12 for a full-body examination in front of strangers. Peter and Joe's accounts provide evidence of Goffman's observation that upon admission, inmates are "stripped of almost everything,"[13] not only of personal possessions such as clothing, but of their identity and individuality.

The loss of freedom initiated at admission to the facility became a persistent feature of institutional life that survivors had to endure for the duration of their time there. Institutional life reminded survivors daily of their exclusion from decision making concerning their own lives, from the smallest, seemingly insignificant decisions such as choosing what clothes to wear each day and what time to get up in the morning, to life-altering ones such as where to live and what dreams to follow. Survivors' experiences of exclusion and constraint contrast sharply with one staff observation that "[residents] had free run; they could go wherever they wanted," a comment made in reference to his estimation that people experienced fewer obstacles on the grounds of the institution than they would in an unregulated community setting. Residents could indeed go "wherever they wanted," both physically and metaphorically, so long as their journey did not take them beyond the gates or mandate of the institution, limits to which institutional residents had not agreed.

The regimented "machinery of the establishment,"[14] in which the running of the institution consistently superseded residents' individual needs and desires, dictated all aspects of residents' lives. Survivors' choices and volition were subservient to the bigger goal of maintaining the operation of a massive administrative arrangement specifically designed to keep a troublesome population out of public view and effectively dealt with. The goal of efficiency, or the "handling of many human needs by the bureaucratic organization of whole blocks of people,"[15] was paramount. This perspective was echoed by one of the staff, who noted that "a big place works. That's where you do economies of scale." In other words, it makes more sense to prioritize large-scale efficiencies over residents' preferences—indeed, in large-scale institutions, it is almost impossible to do otherwise.

In addition to highlighting discrepancies between staff and survivor experiences, these scenarios also raise troubling questions regarding the notion of freedom in general and the degree to which people in positions of power have the authority to make decisions regarding who is allowed to exercise it and to what extent. Survivor accounts point to the unchallenged lines of authority that removed their freedom and forced them into a life of incarceration. In their case, freedom was contingent on decision makers' assessment of intellectual capacity, defined by a narrow field of normative functioning.

In addition, survivors' observations carry ontological implications regarding the valuation of some lives over others, for it is only the largely unexplained reasoning of intellectual difference that prevented them from living a life in which they could exercise the freedoms that most people take for granted. Their accounts reveal the arbitrary nature of the boundaries that separated them from non-institutionalized people, thus warning of the potential for it to reach in directions not previously considered: What protective wall of able-bodiedness and intellectual capacity do the majority of people rest behind, unaware of the historical flexibility that characterizes its borders? Questions that survivors ask concerning the reasons for their institutionalization should not be limited to those who have lived through it. They must also be asked of those who assume immunity—indeed, the majority of people—forcing an acknowledgment of the universality and unknowable extent of human variation, as well as the universal vulnerability to the power of government preferences and the policy used to enact them.

Relationships between Staff and Residents

The third point of divergence concerns participants' interpretations of relationships between staff and residents. It is here that the power discrepancies between the two groups are most blatantly revealed. Staff were inclined to speak fondly of the relations between themselves and residents, to the point of referring to them as family. While naming relationships as family might have been a well-meaning gesture in light of the absence of residents' birth families, the metaphor is troubling as it suggests an inauthentic taking over of some of our most intimate relationships in a situation in which only one party (the staff) has consented to be there. Moreover, while staff could create what they perceived as family relationships, they had the authority to define those relationships as they wished, an option not available to residents. Dependent on staff for their survival, residents were vulnerable in relationships they could neither define nor escape. While staff could intensify or walk away from relationships or, in the worst cases, abuse residents in their interactions with them, institutional residents were only and always subjected to the relationships being imposed upon them. The staff, with more social capital,[16] had greater flexibility and control in the categorization of relationships, a semantic authority that must have been disorienting and troubling for those not doing the naming. Indeed, the characterization of relations between staff and residents as family is one that survivors never used.

It is important to note the intensity of emotion that was expressed by both survivors and staff in their depictions of the nature of their relationships. Tears were shed from both sides of the narrative gap; they were, however, for completely different reasons. While one former staff became visibly distraught over the losses she had suffered due to institutional closure—the loss of relationships with her family of institutional residents, the loss of relationships with colleagues, the loss of her place of employment—survivors cried when recounting the extent of their suffering at the expense of a carceral system. While some survivors did mention staff who had shown kindness or were helpful in the gradual process of preparing to leave the institution, their descriptions overwhelmingly suggested that relationships in the institution were characterized by fear, impermanence, and lack of control.

Moreover, the use of "family" is a particularly poignant and emotionally fraught point of reference due to survivors' experiences of loss and abandonment from their birth families. For survivors, this abandonment, whether due to a decision made within the family or by surveillant authorities such as Children's Aid Societies, was the central defining feature of their institutionalization. In spite of all the horrors of institutional life—the regimentation, social exclusion, oppression, and abuse—it was the abandonment from their families to those horrors that left the deepest wounds. Staff's naming of institutional residents as their family, therefore, while potentially well-intentioned, demonstrated an obliviousness to its potential to cause pain and confusion.

Narrative Discrepancies: Insights Revealed

Reflections on the narratives described in the foregoing section point to the need to interrogate the implications of their discrepancies. To repeat the questions posed in the introduction: What can be learned from the gaps between these accounts? What is this space inviting us to understand? What does the variance tell us about the larger phenomenon in question?

First, from a methodological standpoint, the irresolvability between the narratives shared by survivors and former staff invited me to listen differently, beyond the boundaries of each story and into the very structures that allowed and indeed facilitated their coexistence. That is, in addition to listening to the story each person told, I needed to consider the institutional and political frameworks that allowed these stories to exist—and allowed them to exist differently. How could it be that great jobs and miserable existences could exist simultaneously and in the same cultural location? Moreover, the narratives needed to be examined with regard to their emergence from a system that not only facilitated their coexistence but allowed the distinction between them to appear reasonable. What were the social, economic, and political factors that facilitated this evolution and how did these factors contribute to their perceived acceptability? Useful in this analysis is Foucault's notion of the "archeology of knowledge,"[17] which explores the conditions of possibility that delimit the boundaries of language and thought, to the point of allowing hegemonic power structures to remain intact and unchallenged.

Thusly considered, the divergences appear less as simply different experiences and are more accurately described as the culmination of significant power differences, reproduced over time within the confines of the institutional model. Thus, survivor and staff narratives are not only distinct, verbatim accounts, but are evidence of injustice embedded in the larger system from which they emerged. They also implicate institutionalization more generally as one facet of a broader system that supports great jobs and horrible existences simultaneously. Specifically, this simultaneous existence of polarized experiences—one an expression of power, the other of exploitation—is the bedrock upon which capitalism relies. As Ignatieff observes, the reproduction and success of capitalist society is not in spite of, but rather depends upon the "constant interposition of state... controls and repression...penal sanction is essential to the reproduction of the unequal and exploitative social relations of the capitalist system."[18] The narrative imbalance that appears in this project, therefore, is a reflection of the larger mechanisms of exploitation and control that are essential for the smooth functioning of the capitalist state, of which institutions are one piece. Bluntly put, the success of institutions depends on injustice.

I realize that I make these claims on challengeable terrain: two divergent accounts of the same phenomenon do not necessarily provide evidence of injustice. People can have different interpretations of the same situation even while possessing similar amounts of social and political power. However, although survivors and former staff described identical phenomena (the existence of a school within the institution, for example), each participant's unique position and relationship to power significantly shaped how those phenomena were perceived and experienced. To staff, the institution's school was evidence of a high degree of support from government and staff, one that ensured that residents were provided with the opportunity to achieve at least a minimal level of literacy and numeracy; to survivors, it was evidence of the fact that they were not allowed to attend school with their siblings and neighbours in a school close to home. This differential interpretation reveals the degree to which this amenity— and indeed, the underlying distribution of power within the institutional structure more generally—was differentially experienced and understood. Thus, when trying to understand gaps between narratives, the degree to which different participants hold or do not hold power in relation to the phenomenon in question must be taken into account.

The foregoing discussion leads to further questions regarding what is at stake in undertaking, or not undertaking, this kind of excavation. What is the extent of my responsibility, as a researcher, to do this work? For assistance with these questions, I draw from Karen Barad's work, which, although ostensibly a study of the relationship between scientific practice and ethics, reflects on the "ethics of mattering."[19] Barad posits that responsible analysis involves the "processing of small but consequential differences"[20] and that these "difference[s] [are] tied up with responsibility."[21] Barad's inquiry suggests that indeed much is at stake in understanding the divergent presentations of institutional life that are revealed here, not only in terms of hearing stories from multiple subject positions, but in the possibility that attending to such narrative gaps can open a way to redress historic imbalances in the presentation of facts and can begin to forge a more just way forward in the treatment of historically marginalized people.

Moreover, to what extent can such findings be used to dismantle the unjust structures that engendered them? I posit that such deconstructive work is possible, but only insofar as research communities are willing to enter the dangerous terrain of claiming bias as part of one's positionality in a research project. Rather than succumb to the investigative trap of allowing findings' arbitrariness to direct the analysis, or of compliantly embracing inconsistent interpretations with equanimity, I suggest that it is acceptable and indeed necessary to claim allegiance to some narratives over others in order that imbalances might be righted. This necessitates a discussion of bias, for in its traditional definition, bias signals an alignment with the accounts and experiences of one group over another. In the following and final section, I examine the notion of bias, traditionally relegated a no-go in the land of rigorous research, and explore its potential not as a restrictive limitation within research, but as an instrument that allows researchers to assert where oppression exists and to identify where our efforts for righting the imbalances of history are best directed.

Bias: Obstacle to Accuracy or "Epistemic Window"?

Since the latter part of the twentieth century, the postmodern turn in scholarly praxis has foregrounded the impossibility of a distanced, objective perspective on the part of the researcher when engaged in qualitative research and knowledge production.[22] As Breuer and Roth poetically summarize: "the bird's-eye perspective is an ideal that embodied subjects cannot ever take."[23] Recognition of the effect of the researcher's own context, history, and often-unexamined belief systems—one's positionality—on the ways in which data are collected, analyzed, and interpreted has been well documented,[24] and current practice in qualitative research suggests that in order for research to be truly liberatory, researchers must, at minimum, be aware of, and at best, reveal their positionality as part of the analytic process.[25] Moreover, the notion of landing securely at an objective truth through qualitative research has been deconstructed. Everything that we learn from qualitative research is done with an acknowledgement of the imbrication between the researcher's own history and the research findings. Moreover, Davison[26] and others[27] point out that this acknowledgement of uncertainty "trouble[s] the act of representation in research";[28] the interpretation and representation of the lives and experiences of others—primarily through the researcher's words and writing—will always, and not unproblematically, involve reproduction, replication, and transformation.

Taken further, an acknowledgement of one's positionality and the ways in which it interacts with the stories revealed in the research, and the spectre of irresolvability that results—both between research subjects and between oneself and one's subjects—can understandably dissuade the researcher from making definitive claims.[29] Yet scholars indicate that acknowledgement of the infinitely complex ways that researchers' histories interact with and indeed influence the ways in which information is gleaned and knowledge created[30] does not necessarily have to lead to a pit of "bottomless skepticism,"[31] nor to the conclusion that the researcher has failed due to their inability "to discipline a world that is [fundamentally] uncontainable."[32] Rather, such complexities and the discomfort they elicit can serve as a signpost, pointing in the direction to which the analysis must move.

First, to avoid plummeting into the "pit of skepticism" of which Mabry warns, researchers' acknowledgement of their positionality and the bias this unavoidably carries must be framed not as something to overcome, but as an inevitable encounter that can be worked with in order to arrive at new insights. As Breuer and Roth suggest in general terms, knowledge production that is elicited from situations that carry "traces of the epistemic subject"[33]—in other words, pieces of ourselves in the research findings as well as insights drawn from our research subjects—offer not only an "epistemological challenge...but a production opportunity, an *epistemic window* and a possibility for *methodological innovation.*"[34] Breuer and Roth's perspective reframes positionality and bias not as obstacles to meaningful analyses, but as a way to forge new and critical ways forward, free of the inaction that objectivity can elicit.

Second, bias must be considered a construction, not a natural or predetermined entity, impervious to critique or to fluctuations in discourse and hegemonic research standards. It is, rather, a manufactured notion imposed upon the process of qualitative research by the agreed-upon and historical governance of the broader purview of scholarly pursuit.[35] As feminist and Indigenous scholars have pointed out,[36] claims regarding the "essentials" of sound research, including the elimination of the deliberate foregrounding of the voices and experiences of marginalized people, emerge from a pre-existing academic community with preformed assumptions regarding race, gender, and ability.[37] By framing bias as a tool towards the unmasking of historically unheard voices, and by engaging the historical ontological work of Foucault[38] and Hacking,[39] the task, rather than obliterating bias, becomes uncovering the ways in which it has come to be understood as something to be feared and avoided.[40] That bias has historically been construed as a negative feature of research, the avoidance of which must be included in one's research plan in order to obtain ethical approval, indicates as much about the systems that govern research as it does about the practices (and the researchers) seemingly vulnerable to bias's preferential dangers. Treating bias as if it is a predetermined entity with inherent characteristics, without decoupling it from the social processes that have allowed its essentialness and importance to be brought, assumed and unchallenged, into being, prevents researchers from doing the necessary work of questioning why the fear of bias exists and what purposes this fear serves. Whose voices are being silenced as a result of this caution, and whose are allowed to flourish? In the words of feminist scholar Scott, in more general terms, interrogating bias in this way allows us to question how some "meanings have emerged as normative, and others have been eclipsed or disappeared."[41] More importantly, what can an interrogation of bias "reveal about how power is constituted and operates,"[42] even within the exploratory field of qualitative research?

The fear of bias and its potential to skew the results of research has historically affected the degree to which different voices are taken seriously and the degree to which they are silenced. Anxiety regarding bias's effects, and the concomitant desire to ensure that all voices in a research project are heard equally, paradoxically allows inequitable representations—and the inequitable power distribution upon which such representations rest—to remain intact. By aligning myself, openly, with the need to bring the stories of institutional survivors to the fore, I risked chastisement from other members of my research participant pool, and indeed from the larger research community, but this was necessary to ensure an equitable airing of all facets of an unjust historical practice and its debilitating effects. One of the goals of the project, besides revealing the effects of institutionalization, was to ensure that previously silenced voices could be heard within academic and lay communities; if assuming the role of "biased" was part of that process, that was a risk I was obliged to take.

An incident that took place several months after the completion of my research provides an example of the ways in which such a stance can be challenged and one's results questioned. During a medical rounds for healthcare professionals at which I was presenting my findings, an audience member questioned survivors' assessment that the institution "was the worst place they ever lived," in addition to my invoking their description as a comparator to staff's perceptions that it had been "the best job they ever had." She challenged survivors' position—surely, she asked, there had been moments of joy during their time in the institution? In her own experience of working at a long-stay institution for disabled children, she had witnessed moments of contentment and even happiness. It did not seem right, she stated, that I was taking survivors' conclusions at face value when they were being asked to describe their experience in retrospect, sometimes many years after they had lived there, thus having had the opportunity to contextualize their experience, and that they were presenting a summary that seemed to exclude moments of pleasure that might have made the experience "not all bad." One of the implications of her question was that my invocation of "the worst place I ever lived" revealed my bias and was being used to justify my conclusions. Perhaps she was right. Perhaps my inclusion of this statement did reveal my stance, and that on the surface, this made my findings "unfair." Rather than that being a problem, however, I contend that that is precisely the point. Revealing the perspective of people who have historically been unable to voice their opinions, even if that requires a disproportionate amount of advocacy and allyship, seems like a worthwhile endeavour, in research and beyond. In the attempt to right the scales of extreme historical oppression, perhaps "unfairness" is needed. If bias is required in order for those discomfiting observations to make their way into the public imaginary, then it is time for bias to be reconsidered—not as something to be avoided, but as a possible instrument of change.

The audience member's question, in spite of the moment of discomfort it produced, was ultimately purposeful, as it returned me to the bigger questions that underscore much of the thinking behind this chapter. First, it confirmed the importance of revealing the historical practice of challenging the accuracy of accounts from people labelled/with intellectual disabilities. What is the origin of the discomfort that emerges when a historically marginalized group says something challenging, disruptive, or destabilizing? Why is it acceptable to challenge these accounts in the first place; that is, for some group's accounts to be considered reasonable, and others not?

Second, her question uncovered the ubiquitous yet mostly masked assumption that the veracity of survivors' stories is challengeable due to the fact that they required my representation, support, and bias to bring them forward. What are the conditions that allow a particular group's stories to be challenged due to the "advantage" of allyship, despite that group's historic oppression, and for allyship to be interpreted as evidence of an increased risk of unaccountability? Moreover, the reverse of these assumptions was not questioned. Bias also supports non-disabled people; it is simply masked by social norms and expectations. The person in the audience did not question the veracity of the staff's accounts: embedded in accepted norms of language and demeanour, the accuracy of the non-disabled people's accounts was assumed.

The encounter confirmed that, in terms of my own assessment regarding where I stood in relation to my research subjects, and the degree to which I was doing justice to their stories, my alignment with survivors had been the right move. I fear that if I had not assumed a position of foregrounding the voices and experiences of institutional survivors and had worked instead to extinguish traces of my own "epistemic subject," then the discrepancy with staff, and the injustice this reveals, would not have appeared.

Conclusion

In the uncertain world of qualitative research, insofar as it concerns the stories of people's lives, one thing is certain: irresolvabilities will emerge. Stories conflict; experiences do not align. The world's "vibrancy...[and] its vitality and resistance to expectations, exceeds our attempts to understand it."[43] Sometimes, in order to ensure that some stories are heard, bias is needed. Alignment with the under-heard is needed to ensure some voices gain a place in the larger account of the human experience.

Yet the emergence of bias and irresolvability does not mean inaction. Rather, its presence might indicate the cusp of some new and bigger knowledge, one that exists in the gap between divergent discourses, one that has not been yet imagined due to the historical foregrounding of more powerful voices over those that have not yet had the chance to surface. Instead of allowing ourselves to remain tethered due to the presence of competing narratives, this irresolvability should instead push us to dig deeper, to listen into the spaces that emerge between different accounts, and to understand what it is that allows those differences to exist in the first place.

Notes

1. Patty Lather, *Getting Smart: Feminist and Research within the Postmodern* (New York: Routledge, 1991), 21.
2. Linda Mabry, "Postmodern Evaluation—or Not?" *American Journal of Evaluation* 23, no. 2 (2002): 141–157.
3. Madeline Burghardt, *Broken: Institutions, Families, and the Construction of Intellectual Disability* (Montreal: McGill-Queen's University Press, 2018).
4. The use of the term *survivor* in this chapter denotes people labelled/with intellectual disabilities who lived in large, government-run institutions. At the outset of this research, I was specifically asked to use the term by the first institutional survivor with whom I spoke. When I asked him how long he had lived in the institution, he corrected me by saying: "I did not live in the institution; I survived there." I acknowledge that the term is also widely used in other communities whose members have experienced and survived traumatic events and histories (for example, sexual assault survivors, survivors of Indian Residential Schools).
5. Franz Breuer and Wolff-Michael Roth, "Subjectivity and Reflexivity in the Social Sciences: Epistemic Windows and Methodical Consequences," *Forum: Qualitative Social Research* 4, no. 2 (2003): Art. 25.
6. Bill Hughes, "The Abject and the Vulnerable: The Twain Shall Meet: Reflections on Disability in the Moral Economy," *Sociological Review Monographs* 67, no. 4 (2019): 829–846.
7. Burghardt, *Broken*.
8. A complete history of the name changes undergone by Ontario institutions can be found on the Government of Ontario website: http://www.mcss.gov.on.ca/en/mcss/programs/developmental/HRC_history.aspx.
9. Schedule One facilities were large, residential, long-term facilities for people designated as having intellectual disabilities. At their peak in the 1960s, there were 16 such institutions in Ontario. The three largest were the Huronia Regional Centre in Orillia, the Rideau Regional Centre in Smiths Falls, and Southwest (or Cedar Springs) Regional Centre, near Chatham, Ontario.
10. It is interesting that a number of survivors mentioned that they had been forced to work in the laundry room of the institution. Some of the survivors described this work in explicit terms: the removal of residents' excrement from issued linens and clothing. My own personal reflection includes metaphorical inferences: the laundry room was located in the basement, the "bowels," so to speak, of the institution, where workers dealt with its waste.
11. Erving Goffman, *Asylums: Essays on the Social Situation of Mental Patients and Other Inmates* (Chicago: Aldine, 1961).
12. Actual names are used in this chapter, with written consent from participants.
13. Goffman, *Asylums*, 140.
14. Goffman, *Asylums*, 16.

15. Goffman, *Asylums*, 6.
16. Pierre Bourdieu, *The Logic of Practice*, trans. R. Rice (Stanford: Stanford University Press, 1990).
17. Michel Foucault, "What is Enlightenment?" in *Ethics, Subjectivity and Truth: Michel Foucault*, ed. Paul Rabinow (New York: The New Press, 1969).
18. Michael Ignatieff, "State, Civil Society and Total Institutions: A Critique of Recent Social Histories in Punishment," in *Social Control and the State: Historical and Comparative Essays*, eds. Stanley Cohen and Andrew Scull (Oxford: Basil Blackwell, 1983), 75-105, 96.
19. Karen Barad, *Meeting the Universe Halfway: Quantum Physics and the Entanglement of Matter and Meaning* (Durham: Duke University Press, 2007), 36.
20. Grossberg and Nelson, as cited in Barad, 29.
21. Barad, *Meeting the Universe Halfway*, 36.
22. Yvonna Lincoln, Susan Lynham, and Egon Guba, "Paradigmatic Controversies, Contradictions, and Emerging Confluences, Revisited," in *The Sage Handbook of Qualitative Research*, 4th ed., eds. Norman Denzin and Yvonna Lincoln (Thousand Oaks: Sage, 2011), 97-128.
23. Breuer and Roth, "Subjectivity and Reflexivity," 1.1.
24. Jessica Ringrose and Emma Renold, "'F**k Rape!': Exploring Affective Intensities in a Feminist Research Assemblage," *Qualitative Inquiry* 20, no. 6 (2014): 772-780.
25. Brian Bourke, "Positionality: Reflecting on the Research Process," *Qualitative Report* 19, no. 33 (2014): 1-9.
26. Kevin Davison, "Dialectical Imagery and Postmodern Research," *International Journal of Qualitative Studies in Education* 19, no. 2 (2006): 133-146.
27. See, for example, Martin Jay, *Downcast Eyes: The Degeneration of Vision in Twentieth-Century French Thought* (Berkeley: University of California Press, 1994) and John Van Maanen, *Tales of the Field: On Writing Ethnography* (Chicago: University of Chicago Press, 1988).
28. Davison, "Dialectical Imagery," 134.
29. Mabry, "Postmodern Evaluation—or Not?," 142.
30. Sara Childers, "Promiscuous Analysis in Qualitative Research," *Qualitative Inquiry* 20, no. 6 (2014): 819-826.
31. Mabry, "Postmodern Evaluation—or Not?," 152.
32. Childers, "Promiscuous Analysis," 819.
33. Breuer and Roth, "Subjectivity and Reflexivity," 1.1.
34. Breuer and Roth, "Subjectivity and Reflexivity," 2.1, original emphasis.
35. Linda Tuhiwai Smith, *Decolonizing Methodologies: Research and Indigenous Peoples* (New York: Zed Books, 2012).
36. See, for example, Abigail Brooks and Sharlene Nagy Hesse-Biber, "An Invitation to Feminist Research." In *Feminist Research Practice: A Primer*, eds. Patricia Leavy and Sharlene Nagy Hesse-Biber (Thousand Oaks: Sage, 2006), 1-24, and Smith, *Decolonizing Methodologies*, respectively.

37. Colleen Reid, Lorraine Grieves and Sandra Kirby, *Experience, Research, Social Change: Critical Methods*, 3rd ed. (Toronto: University of Toronto Press, 2016).
38. Foucault, "What is Enlightenment?"
39. Ian Hacking, *Historical Ontology* (Cambridge: Harvard University Press, 2002).
40. Linda Gilbert, "Going the Distance: 'Closeness' in Qualitative Data Analysis Software," *International Journal of Social Research Methodology* 5, no. 3 (2002): 215–228.
41. Joan Scott, "Deconstructing Equality-versus-Difference: Or, the Uses of Poststructuralist Theory for Feminism," *Feminist Studies* 14, no. 1 (1988): 32–50, 35.
42. Scott, "Deconstructing," 35.
43. Childers, "Promiscuous Analysis," 819.

Bibliography

Barad, Karen. *Meeting the Universe Halfway: Quantum Physics and the Entanglement of Matter and Meaning*. Durham: Duke University Press, 2007.

Bourdieu, Pierre. *The Logic of Practice*. Trans. R. Rice. Stanford: Stanford University Press, 1990.

Bourke, Brian. "Positionality: Reflecting on the Research Process." *The Qualitative Report* 19, no. 33 (2014): 1–9.

Breuer, Franz and Wolff-Michael Roth. "Subjectivity and Reflexivity in the Social Sciences: Epistemic Windows and Methodical Consequences." *Forum: Qualitative Social Research* 4, no. 2 (2003): Art. 25. https://doi.org/10.17169/fqs-4.2.698.

Brooks, Abigail and Sharlene Nagy Hesse-Biber. "An Invitation to Feminist Research." In *Feminist Research Practice: A Primer*, edited by Patricia Leavy and Sharlene Nagy Hesse-Biber, 1–24. Thousand Oaks: Sage, 2006.

Burghardt, Madeline C. *Broken: Institutions, Families, and the Construction of Intellectual Disability*. Montreal-Kingston: McGill-Queen's University Press, 2018.

Childers, Sara. "Promiscuous Analysis in Qualitative Research." *Qualitative Inquiry* 20, no. 6 (2014): 819–826.

Davison, Kevin. "Dialectical Imagery and Postmodern Research." *International Journal of Qualitative Studies in Education* 19, no. 2 (2006): 133–146.

Foucault, Michel. "What is Enlightenment?" In *Ethics, Subjectivity and Truth: Michel Foucault*, edited by Paul Rabinow. New York: The New Press, 1999.

Gilbert, Linda. "Going the Distance: 'Closeness' in Qualitative Data Analysis Software." *International Journal of Social Research Methodology* 5, no. 3 (2002): 215–228.

Goffman, Erving. *Asylums: Essays on the Social Situation of Mental Patients and Other Inmates*. Chicago: Aldine, 1961.

Hacking, Ian. *Historical Ontology*. Cambridge: Harvard University Press, 2002.

Hughes, Bill. "The Abject and the Vulnerable: The Twain Shall Meet: Reflections on Disability in the Moral Economy." *Sociological Review Monographs* 67, no. 4 (2019): 829–846.

Ignatieff, Michael. "State, Civil Society and Total Institutions: A Critique of Recent Social Histories in Punishment." In *Social Control and the State: Historical and*

Comparative Essays, edited by Stanley Cohen and Andrew Scull, 75-105. Oxford: Basil Blackwell, 1983.

Jay, Martin. *Downcast Eyes: The Degeneration of Vision in Twentieth-Century French Thought*. Berkeley: University of California Press, 1994.

Lather, Patty. *Getting Smart: Feminist Research and Pedagogy within the Postmodern*. New York: Routledge, 1991.

Lincoln, Yvonna, Susan Lynham, and Egon Guba. "Paradigmatic Controversies, Contradictions, and Emerging Confluences, Revisited." In *The Sage Handbook of Qualitative Research*, 4th edition, edited by Norman Denzin and Yvonna Lincoln, 97-128. Thousand Oaks: Sage, 2011.

Mabry, Linda. "Postmodern Evaluation—or Not?" *American Journal of Evaluation* 23, no. 2 (2002): 141-157.

Reid, Colleen, Lorraine Grieves and Sandra Kirby. *Experience, Research, Social Change: Critical Methods*, 3rd edition. Toronto: University of Toronto Press, 2017.

Ringrose, Jessica, and Emma Renold, "'F**k Rape!': Exploring Affective Intensities in a Feminist Research Assemblage." *Qualitative Inquiry* 20, no. 6 (2014): 772-780.

Scott, Joan. "Deconstructing Equality-versus-Difference: Or, the Uses of Poststructuralist Theory for Feminism," *Feminist Studies* 14, no.1 (1988): 32-50.

Smith, Linda Tuhiwai. *Decolonizing Methodologies: Research and Indigenous Peoples*. New York: Zed Books, 2012.

Van Maanen, John. *Tales of the Field: On Writing Ethnography*. Chicago: University of Chicago Press, 1988.

V

Reflections on the Methodologically Unresolved

Decolonial Co-Resistance as Indigenous Methodology
Deepening Resistance and Decolonizing the "Co-"

Jess Notwell

Freedom is an ongoing process, a collective practice that allows our sense of the very meaning of freedom to become ever richer, ever more complex.
—Angela Davis, "Freedom is a Constant Struggle," February 26, 2018

Across Palestine, women are practising and deepening freedom. Living under Israeli settler colonialism,[1] Palestinian women have become simultaneously victims of settler colonial violence and everyday warriors for freedom; "frontliners" in the ongoing struggle for liberation.[2] Each woman's life frames the contours of her struggle. Living in a city, village, or refugee camp, her family, religion, class, education, and myriad additional factors impact her choices and opportunities. From 2016 to 2018, using the Indigenous Methodology Decolonial Co-Resistance,[3] I deepened my understanding of 40 Palestinian women's intersectional[4] liberation struggles grounded in decolonial love:[5] a love of Palestinian identity and culture, commitment to liberating Palestine from the river to the sea, and reclaiming the belonging of all Palestinians in Gaza, the land colonized as the Israeli state, the West Bank including Jerusalem, and the diaspora. A praxis of decoloniality, the liberation struggle is both resistance *against* Israeli settler colonialism and action *for* a decolonial *otherwise*.[6] Through embodied struggle, these Palestinian women are co-creating the knowledges and modelling the actions necessary to liberate all Palestinians and all of Palestine.

Decolonial Co-Resistance developed iteratively through the research, conducted in response to a request by Palestinian colleagues to carry the stories of Palestinian women frontliners home to Turtle Island in order to influence more people to support the liberation of Palestine. Learning about their praxis of decolonial love, hope, beloved community, and co-liberation through embodied co-resistance[7] awakened my Ancestral knowledge about ᓵᑭᑐᐃᐧᐣ sâhkitowin [love] and fostered Indigenous knowledge "wholistically derived from Spirit, heart, mind and body."[8] While my methodology is grounded in Ancestral knowledge, and ᓀᐦᐃᔭᐤ nehiyaw [Cree] and ᐊᓂᔑᓇᐯ Anishinaabe traditional teachings from my Elders, my research is with women Indigenous to Palestine. This chapter explores Decolonial Co-Resistance through critical questions that have pushed me to reflect on the "co-": (1) What are the implications of developing and applying Indigenous Methodologies outside of our communities and cultures? (2) How has being a white-passing Indigenous person with a Canadian passport impacted and limited the "co-"? and (3) What are the tensions between Decolonial Co-Resistance as a research methodology and as ᒥᔪ ᐱᒫᑎᓯᐃᐧᐣ miyo pimâtisiwin [ᓀᐦᐃᔭᐤ nehiyaw for living in a good way] for liberation?

Decolonial Co-Resistance: An Indigenous Methodology

Decolonial Co-Resistance—the documentation and sharing of "lived experience stories"[9] gathered during co-resistance actions and life history interviews—centres decolonial love of our individual and collective identities despite the colonizer's hate, love as connectedness with the land, and love as enacting our collective freedom. Decolonial Co-Resistance developed organically through place-based *co-resistance* during visits to families of prisoners and martyrs, the prisoners' Freedom and Dignity Hunger Strike, defending al-Aqsa Mosque in July 2017 as co-liberation. It draws on Indigenous Storywork,[10] Leanne Betasamosake Simpson's work on co-resistance "creating doorways out of settler colonialism,"[11] and ᒋᔦ ᐱᒧᕐᐊᒋ miyo pimâtisiwin.

> Storywork illuminates pathways to liberation, harmonizing story research agendas with Indigenous resurgence movements globally.[12]

Indigenous Storywork is a research methodology based on relationships with and through the stories of Indigenous peoples. It honours these stories as both Indigenous ways of knowing and being and counter-narratives to the dominant stories of coloniality/modernity. Indigenous Storywork is a praxis of connection with community, decolonial love of Indigenous identity, and mobilizing stories for Indigenous resurgence. Four interconnected and indivisible principles guide Indigenous Storywork: respect, relationships, reverence, and reciprocity.

Indigenous Storywork is a way of speaking and writing back[13] to the objectification and exploitation of and attempts to eliminate Indigenous Peoples. It is meaning making in community, for community, to sustain community. First, listening with respect requires an understanding of the worldview, reality, and language of the storyteller to really hear what is being shared and understand the meaning of silences and omissions. The second principle, developing story relationships in a responsible manner, requires time to build trust and understanding between the listener and the storyteller. Developing these relationships may include co-resistance, which builds competency in the listener through experiencing the storyteller's context. Story relationships are also relations with the stories themselves.

In Palestine, I created space to listen with respect and develop story relationships by spending two years learning enough Palestinian Arabic to participate in everyday conversations, building trust with multiple networks of liberation strugglers, and working with different Palestinian organizations and groups as a researcher, advocacy assistant, and special events volunteer. Part of developing responsible story relationships was connecting with community members as requested, responding promptly when potential participants reached out, and stepping away when people chose not to engage. Over coffee and tea, over الإفطار *Al-Iftar* [breakfast eaten to break the fast], during رمضان *Ramadan*, at memorial services and عزاء *Azza* [condolences], through tear gas and sound grenades, I listened and learned. In the process, I developed the deep decolonial love in which my co-resistance is rooted.

The third principle of Indigenous Storywork is treating story knowledge with reverence. The listener's job is not to question the accuracy or veracity of the stories but to respect the lessons the storyteller is conveying and to honour the meanings made through the storytelling process. As knowledges created in embodied struggles for survival and liberation, the stories are key to decoloniality.[14] In Palestine, I built the capacity to treat stories with reverence by learning about the communities, families, and lives of research participants; deepening my understanding of Israeli settler colonialism; and participating in as many trainings, community meetings, and awareness-raising sessions as possible. These efforts grounded my understanding of women's experiences and analysis in their everyday realities rather than academic literature. I listened carefully to women's stories and silences, learning both what research participants wanted me to share and what I was being trusted *not* to share.

Strengthening storied impact through reciprocity is the fourth principle of Indigenous Storywork. It builds on respect, relationships, and reverence through action to share, amplify, and mobilize the story. Reciprocity connects Indigenous Peoples across generations, bringing together the past, present, and future in order to enact decolonial futurities informed by knowledges we have created, expanded, transformed, and reclaimed. In Palestine, I practised reciprocity through co-resistance in land defence actions, sit-ins to prevent houses from being demolished, and demonstrations to protect Palestinian communities. Six research participants regularly invited me to participate as a way to build my capacity to understand and share their stories, so that I could contribute my labour toward particular liberation efforts, in order to have a white-passing foreigner visibly in solidarity with them in front of media and as a form of mitigation against direct physical colonial violence. I have also shared women's stories with the Canada-Palestine Parliamentary Friendship Group, at dinner tables, in conferences, and in elementary school classrooms. Sharing the stories is an act of reciprocity in our struggles for co-liberation.

Decolonial Co-Resistance is an embodiment of the seven Sacred Teachings that comprise ᒥᔪ ᐱᒫᑎᓯᐃᐧᐣ miyo pimâtisiwin. As a Two Spirit ᓄᐦᐃᔪ nehiyaw Métis mom, land defender, activist and scholar, I strive to live ᒥᔪ ᐱᒫᑎᓯᐃᐧᐣ grounded in decolonial love of ᑲᐦᑮᔭᐤ ᓂᐊᐧᐦᑰᒪᑲᓇᐠ kahkîyâw niwâhkômakanak [All My Relations]. Critical reflection on the "co-" is itself resistance *informed by* ᒥᔪ ᐱᒫᑎᓯᐃᐧᐣ and the vulnerability[15] of: (1) being an Indigenous graduate student displaced by settler colonialism (Is my Indigenous Methodology truly Indigenous if my place-based learning has taken place outside of my traditional territory?), (2) still reclaiming my language (Am I "Indigenous enough" to be "living in a good way"?), and (3) standing with Palestine (Together with colleagues, can our collective vulnerability become a site of resistance and protection?).[16]

What Are the Implications of Developing and Applying Indigenous Methodologies outside of Our Communities and Cultures?

> We hope for the liberation of Palestine, but it may take us many years to get to that liberation that we are all trying to get to. Or it may be after a short period of time. But if everyone is convinced that one day Palestine is going to be free and independent, to work on this thing is enough. Instead of thinking negatively about us being under occupation, and we know that it is forced upon us, but at least we must have this beautiful image inside of us that we may one day be free. So now, when I feel like I'm acting freely, I think to myself, "if I feel free now imagine when Palestine is truly free." — دلال Dalal

دلال Dalal's words, and her commitment to teaching other Palestinian youth traditional Dabke dancing and Palestinian history, touched my ᓄᐦᐃᔪ and ᐋᓂᐢᑰ teachings about our responsibilities to seven generations of ᓂᑖᓂᐢᑯᐦᐱᒋᑲᓇᐠ nitâniskohpicikanak [a ᓄᐦᐃᔪ word that means both Ancestors and descendants]. دلال Dalal draws upon Palestinian history going back to the Canaanites to teach youth about Israeli appropriation of Palestinian culture, including Dabke dancing, as one of myriad settler colonial attempts to justify land theft.[17] دلال Dalal understands that her responsibility to past and future generations of Palestinians is to "take good care of this culture and tradition…[to] fight to keep hold of this culture and say, "no, this is Palestinian culture that our grandparents taught us" in the face of Israeli cultural appropriation. دلال Dalal explains that decolonial love for Palestinian culture and identity means that "you will feel like you are part of your culture and your country and that way you will keep holding on to the country itself."

دلال Dalal's truth helped me to understand that at the core of Decolonial Co-Resistance is decolonial love of my ᓴᐻᐅ Métis identity and culture. The Sacred Teaching of ᓵᑭᐦᐃᑐᐃᐣ sâkihitowin [love] teaches us to love all beings unconditionally, while ᑭᐦᒉᔨᐦᑖᑯᓱᐃᐣ kihceyihtâkosowin [respect] teaches us to respect all beings in a reciprocal way. Living these teachings through Decolonial Co-Resistance means loving and respecting the Palestinian women who were part of my research, their families, communities, and land in the same way I love and respect my own family, community, and territory. It means that when أم محمد Umm Mohammed took the time to mentor me, to help me to build competency to understand the lived realities of Palestinian women across the West Bank insofar as it is possible as an outsider, my co-resistance was an act of decolonial love. أم محمد Umm Mohammed helped me to unlearn settler-colonial narratives about Palestinians and deepen my praxis of ᓵᑭᐦᐃᑐᐃᐣ during solidarity visits with women who are mothers of martyrs and prisoners, during land defence actions for المسجد الأقصى al-Aqsa Mosque, and through distributing small plants at باب العامود Bab Al-Amoud to commemorate Palestinians' connection to the land on يوم الأرض Land Day. Through our shared embodied struggle, we cultivated decolonial love as a "practice of decolonization."[18]

As a ᓴᐻᐅ Métis person displaced from my family's Ancestral Territories, like so many Indigenous people on Turtle Island, I am not learning from the land that taught my Ancestors for millennia. In response to the question about the implications of developing and applying Indigenous Methodologies outside of my community and culture: I learn from the land on which my feet are planted, the people and More-than-Human relations around me, my Ancestral knowledge, and the teachings of my Elders. This is the settler-colonial reality in which I enact Indigenous radical resurgence and co-resistance.[19] The relational and embodied knowledge of Decolonial Co-Resistance has been co-created with the women I met in Palestine, and with the land, through ᒥᔪ ᐱᒫᑎᓯᐃᐣ miyo pimâtisiwin. The Sacred Teaching of ᑖᑉᐌᐃᐣ tâpwewin [truth] is to speak and act from my lived experience; from the knowledges, or truth, of my heart, body and mind. Watching دلال Dalal's troupe dance their stories through Dabke and standing with أم محمد Umm Mohammed when the Israeli soldiers attacked us for daring to invoke Palestinian belonging to the land, these experiences are part of the ĊV·Δ·ᗪ of Decolonial Co-Resistance.

ᑕᐸᐦᑌᔨᒥᓱᐏᐣ tapahtêyimisowin [humility] teaches us to lower ourselves in relation to ᑲᐦᑮᔮᐤ ᑳᐚᐦᑰᒪᑳᐤ kahkîyâw kâwâhkômakâw [All Our Relations]; to prioritize their well-being[20] and survivance.[21] Balanced with ᓵᑭᐦᐃᑐᐏᐣ sâkihitowin [love] and ᑭᐦᒉᔨᐦᑖᑯᓯᐏᐣ kihceyihtâkosowin [respect], ᑕᐸᐦᑌᔨᒥᓱᐏᐣ taught me to prioritize and learn from the Palestinian liberation struggle. In the process, I moved "beyond a politics of solidarity to a practice of decolonization" by "being humble and honouring frontline voices of resistance as well as offering tangible solidarity as needed and requested."[22] Key to this process was listening with respect to women's stories, silences and actions; showing up when asked, expected, and when it was useful; and mitigating the vulnerability of the women with whom I was in solidarity (and their children) by putting my (white-passing) body between them and the Israeli soldiers and police seeking to arrest, injure, or murder them in pursuit of ethnic cleansing and settler-colonial elimination.[23]

أم محمد Umm Mohammed, دلال Dalal, and many additional Palestinian women I met cultivate decolonial love of Palestinian-ness as an act of decolonization and liberation. Israeli settler-colonial narratives demonize Palestinians as "terrorists" and obstacles to the "imagined community"[24] of the Israeli state.[25] Countering the colonizer's hatred, including through love of individual and collective colonized identities, is necessary to liberation.[26] Chela Sandoval calls this love a "decolonizing activity," through which "love is reinvented as a political technology, as a body of knowledges, arts, practices, and procedures for re-forming the self and the world."[27] In Palestine I learned decolonial love of Palestinian-ness and of myself. Iterative development of Decolonial Co-Resistance with Palestinian women liberation strugglers did not detract from my Indigenous radical resurgence. In fact, it has deepened my embodied knowledge of ᓵᑭᐦᐃᑐᐏᐣ [love] as a co-creation of decolonial *otherwise*. At the same time, the development of Decolonial Co-Resistance has involved many tensions and challenges—not least because I hold a passport from settler-colonial Canada, well known for supporting the Israeli settler-colonial regime.

How Has Being a White-Passing Indigenous Person with a Canadian Passport Impacted and Limited the "Co-"?

Today, the Israeli soldiers attacked again. We were standing in باب الأسباط *Bab Al-Asbat* when the tear gas bombs and sound grenades came flying toward us. One burned the back of my leg. We ran to the nearby playground in باب حطة *Bab Hatta*, hoping they wouldn't follow us. The two Palestinian women beside me started whispering to one another. Looking over at me, one woman asked in a nervous voice, من هي؟ *Min he?* [Who is she?] The second woman shook her head and said, هي دائما معنا *He daiman m3ana* [She is always with us]. (Research notes, July 20, 2017)

أم محمد Umm Mohammed, اقرأ Iqra, دلال Dalal, فاطمة Fatima, and additional women who were part of the research invited me to stand with and learn from them for multiple reasons. The first was to build my understanding of their lived realities so I could return to Turtle Island with the competency to tell their stories. The second was to celebrate Palestinian identity and culture within relationships of mutual respect and trust. The third was maximize the value of my white-passing body and Canadian passport. When أم محمد Umm Mohammed and اقرأ Iqra invited me to the يوم الأرض Land Day action in باب العامود *Bab Al-Amoud*, they reasoned that Israeli soldiers and police would be less likely to shoot at a white-passing person who, from their perspective, might be a Jewish Israeli or a foreign journalist. فاطمة Fatima invited me to eat إفطار فوق الأنقاض ["Iftar in the Rubble," a collective breaking of the daily Ramadan fast] at the site of a local family's demolished home as an act of solidarity with the family and to deepen my understanding of collective punishment.[28] When اقرأ Iqra took me to visit a local women's centre, she wanted me to understand the community-building work being done through the centre and to share my knowledge of potential funding opportunities through settler-colonial Canada. While these were instances in which my identity was useful, there were also times when my identity and presence were extremely problematic.

While living in Jerusalem, I became close with a group of liberation strugglers through a long-time friend. I spent time with some of the families in this group, making and eating meals together, staying at their family homes, and participating in weddings, memorial services, and land defence activities. When a disagreement arose between one of the liberation strugglers and another good friend of mine, he circulated a rumour that I was actually collaborating with the Israeli secret police to gather information about the group. In part, the rumour was believable because settler-colonial Canada is a strong supporter of Israeli settler colonialism.[29] A man from one of the families was re-arrested (all Palestinians are vulnerable to arrest, torture, and incarceration), and this was attributed to my supposed status as a collaborator. It was heartbreaking. Most importantly, the man who was arrested is one of the most amazing human beings I will ever meet and I grieve the suffering he and his family endured. I am also devastated that I no longer have any relationship with that family of strong, beautiful people who have sacrificed so much for Palestine. The sister-like relationship I had with my friend made me vulnerable to a kind of lateral violence that is fostered through settler colonialism to fracture trust among people Indigenous to the land and allies; to fragment families and communities. This fragmentation is intended to weaken resistance against settler-colonial violence.[30] My friend shared her ᐃᔨᓂᐃᐧ iyinisowin [wisdom] about this experience, teaching me to see settler-colonial violence as the root cause of the rumour and to refuse to allow it to diminish my decolonial love.

My friend's ᐃᔨᓂᐃᐧ [wisdom] recalled Leanne Simpson's "generative refusal" as learning to "live as an individual and as part of a collective in a way that ensures I recognize my great-great-great-grandchildren as Indigenous peoples."[31] The limit of the "co-" in the experience I have just described is that in Palestine I will always be an outsider, someone who never be completely trusted except by people with whom I share decolonial love-based relationships. My responsibility to respond in a good way can be explained, in part, through the Sacred Teaching of ᓱᐦᑭᑌᐦᐁᐃᐧᐣ sôhkitêhêwin [courage]: facing fears and challenges with bravery. I decided to move to another city because my presence in the community was causing further fragmentation. I wrote a letter (which I did not send) to the family from which the man had been arrested, explaining how much I loved them and offering prayers for his safe return. I later burned the letter in the Sacred Fire. I continued my research for another year, keeping my commitment to learn women's stories and carry them home to Turtle Island. When I told this story months later, another young struggler, دانة Danah, shared her own ᐃᔨᓂᐃᐧ, saying, "every day, I ask myself what course of action will make my children proud when they are old enough to understand. And that's what I do. It doesn't matter that it's hard. What matters is their future."

My mobility as a white-passing Indigenous person with a Canadian passport has also impacted the "co-." In Palestine, the Israeli settler-colonial regime enforces separation and mobility restrictions against Palestinians through ethnic cleansing, collective punishment, mass incarceration, and legal and physical barriers that include military checkpoints, The Wall, refusal of family reunification, and the permit and identity regimes that regulate where Palestinians can live, drive, and visit.[32] Instead, when it became impossible to complete my research in Jerusalem, I was able to move across The Wall and start a new phase of the research. My Canadian passport allowed me to purchase a car with a yellow licence plate and travel to many different communities to conduct interviews. (According to Israeli law, a car with a green "West Bank" licence plate is unable to cross The Wall or to drive on settler-only roads.) When my research was finished, I left Palestine to return to Turtle Island. While I have close friends and family in Palestine, the "co-" will always be limited by my holding a passport from a government that supports the colonizer and the fact that I am not Palestinian and am not vulnerable to Israeli settler-colonial violence as the drive for my own elimination.

How do these limitations of the "co-," impact the possibilities for Decolonial Co-Resistance as ᒥ ᐱᒫᑎᓯᐃᐧᐣ miyo pimâtisiwin? What is the threshold for Decolonial Co-Resistance to be considered good and to become a way of living? How will I know when/if I am practising Decolonial Co-Resistance in the way I had intended? How will I recognize decolonial love as I enact the Indigenous Storywork principle of reciprocity? Kathleen Absolon concludes that as Indigenous re-searchers, "we come to know because of a deep and profound love for our land, ancestors and Spirit."[33] It is love that elevates Indigenous Methodologies beyond mere research tools. Decolonial Co-Resistance is no exception.

What Are the Tensions between Decolonial Co-Resistance as a Research Methodology and as ᒥ ᐱᒫᑎᓯᐃᐧᐣ miyo pimâtisiwin for Liberation?

As an Indigenous Methodology, Decolonial Co-Resistance is not simply a way of doing research. It is a way of knowing and being consistent with the seven Sacred Teachings, including the teaching of ᖃ·ᑉᕐᓐᑲ·ᑎᐟᐁ·ᐅ kwehyaskwatisiwin [honesty]: to live rightly, with virtue. Together, the Sacred Teachings combine as ᒥᔭ ᐱᒫᑎᐟᐁ·ᐅ miyo pimâtisiwin. Indigenous re-search is a process of "regaining our humanity and embracing that Anishinaabek/Indigenous way of life."[34] Through re-search, we learn about ourselves "in relation with" ᑲᑉᕓᕐᐤ ᑲᐷ·ᑉᑯᒪᕐᐤ [All Our Relations] and heal through "being reconnected and remembered from the dismemberment and disconnections created by colonial policy and actions."[35] However, academic research is indivisible from colonial policy and actions. For over a century it has been deployed as a tool to "justify," expand, and entrench (settler) colonialism.[36] In recognition of this violence, the Boycott, Divestment and Sanctions movement in Palestine began with an academic and cultural boycott in the late 1970s.[37] Is the contradiction of enacting Decolonial Co-Resistance as a research methodology resolvable?

Western science enacts "damage-centred research"[38] to dehumanize Indigenous Peoples and justify imperialist white saviourism[39] *within* the structure of (settler) colonialism rather than pursuing liberation from it. Seeking to protect themselves, their families, and communities from foreign researchers who wittingly or unwittingly uphold anti-liberation agendas, a number of women I met in Palestine asked me questions designed to elicit my level of complicity with settler-colonial violence. These questions included from whom I had rented my house (renting from an Israeli landlord was complicit while renting from a Palestinian was not), whether or not I spoke Hebrew (the language of the colonizer), and if I believed in the work of organizations like Seeds of Peace (an NGO that brings Palestinian and Israeli youth together for activities framed within colonial peace). One potential participant asked, "Are you interviewing any Israeli women? If you are, I can't be part of your research." If my research was anti-liberation, if it considered Palestinian and Israeli women as equal participants from "two sides" rather than understanding settler-colonial relations of domination,[40] she was not interested. رشيدة Rashida explained that in Palestine anti-liberation research is used to justify the funneling of "aid" into donor-driven projects based on Western imperialist agendas and enacted through depoliticized international and local non-profit organizations:[41]

> I hate NGOs. We do not make real change. We promote whatever the project is promoting. And what is the word? To support the Palestinian

"resilience," or whatever. I worked under this [EU-funded] project with different NGOs...Nothing is changing, just putting us in this position to say, "no, I cannot do anything. I cannot promote change. I will lose my own source of income. Maybe I will go to jail...if I critique the project." So, if you become an NGO, you will become another rat in the same lab with no real change. —رشيدة) Rashida

Western scientific research that sees people's survival of settler colonial violence as an opportunity to learn about "resilience" rather than a call to join their struggles for liberation is the antithesis of ᒥᔪ ᐱᒫᑎᓯᐎᐣ miyo pimâtisiwin. Its claims of objectivity and superiority serve to reinforce the idea that only Western scientific research is valid and reliable.[42] Indigenous re-search gives voice to ᑖᐺᐎᐣ tâpwewin [truth]. Linda Tuhiwai Smith explains that self-determination for Indigenous Peoples is at the core of an Indigenous research agenda with "a goal of social justice... which necessarily involves the processes of transformation, of decolonization, of healing and mobilization as peoples."[43] My ᑖᐺᐎᐣ tells me that ᒥᔪ ᐱᒫᑎᓯᐎᐣ necessitates decolonization and liberation, on Turtle Island and in Palestine. There is still a long way to go.

Decolonial Co-Resistance is more than a research methodology. My Decolonial Co-Resistance did not end when I returned to Turtle Island from Palestine. It is an everyday practice of decolonization that includes taking every opportunity to share the stories of the Palestinian women who participated in the research, their families, communities, and the land. This sharing of stories is an act of ᓴᑭᐦᐃᑐᐎᐣ sâkihitowin [love]. It is also an act of freedom,[44] of liberation. Decolonial Co-Resistance is a co-creation of decolonial futurities in the present[45] through enacting the world we want to create: a world in which decolonial love has liberated us from settler colonial relations of domination. We learn this love from the land, from land defenders, from the knowledges of our Ancestors that we carry deep inside. عائشة Aisha explains that with every act of decolonial love, we incrementally decolonize ourselves and our world as a collective practice of freedom:

> Every word we say may change something. If we didn't have this belief, that one word can change everything, then we wouldn't be here. There wouldn't be something called Palestine. Or martyrs.

Or rocks thrown every day. We know that the rock doesn't change anything. But because we believe in it, it does. —عائشة Aisha

I believe in it too. I have witnessed Palestinian mothers pulling their children away from large groups of soldiers who were carrying semi-automatic weapons, willing to die to save them from arrest and torture. كفاح Kifah explained this decolonial love when she said, "the life we lived together, the hardship we faced in prison, the torture, the everything, made us one." The limits of the "co-" are not a reason to abandon Decolonial Co-Resistance as both practice and pursuit of ᒥᔪ ᐱᒫᑎᓯᐎᐣ miyo pimâtisiwin. Decolonial Co-Resistance is my gift to seven generations of ᓂᑖᓂᐢᑯᐦᐱᒋᑲᓇᐠ nitâniskohpicikanak [a ᓀᐦᐃᔭᐤ nehiyaw word that means both Ancestors and descendants], my ᓵᑭᐦᐃᑐᐎᐣ sâkihitowin [love] for Palestinian-ness and my ᓀᐦᐃᔭᐤ Métis identity, and my own struggle for liberation:

> Struggle because we are occupied, erased, displaced, and disconnected. Struggle because our bodies are still targets for settler colonial violence. Struggle because this is the mechanism our Ancestors engaged in to continuously rebirth the world. And our struggle is a beautiful, righteous struggle that is our collective gift to Indigenous worlds, because this way of living necessarily continually gives birth to ancient *Indigenous* futures in the present.[46]

I offer ᓇᓈᐢᑯᒧᐎᐣ nanâskomowin [gratitude] to دلال Dalal, أم محمد Umm Mohammed, اقرأ Iqra, فاطمة Fatima, رشيدة Rashida, دانة Danah, عائشة Aisha, كفاح Kifah, and all of the women I met and learned from in Palestine. عائشة Aisha shared that "when we are convinced that we have a reason to live here, that we have the right because this is our country and our land and our life, when we get to that point, not one of us will ever give up." ᑭᓇᓈᐢᑯᒥᑎᐣ kinanâskomitin [thank you], عائشة Aisha, for this teaching about our collective practice of freedom.

Notes

1. To learn more about Israeli settler colonialism, see, for example: Fayez Sayegh, "Zionist Colonialism in Palestine (1965)," *Settler Colonial Studies* 2, no. 1 (2012):

206–225; Lorenzo Veracini, *Israel and Settler Society* (London: Pluto Press, 2006); Patrick Wolfe, "Settler Colonialism and the Elimination of the Native," *Journal of Genocide Research* 8, no. 4 (2006): 387–409.
2. Nadera Shalhoub-Kevorkian, *Militarization and Violence against Women in Conflict Zones in the Middle East: A Palestinian Case Study* (Cambridge: Cambridge University Press, 2009).
3. Jess Notwell, "Decolonization is an Everyday Struggle: The (In)visible Revolution of Palestinian Women" (PhD diss., University of Guelph, 2022).
4. Kimberlé Crenshaw, "Mapping the Margins: Intersectionality, Identity Politics, and Violence against Women of Color," *Stanford Law Review* 43, no. 6 (1991): 1241–1299; Kimberlé Crenshaw, "Demarginalizing the Intersection of Race and Sex: A Black Feminist Critique of Antidiscrimination Doctrine, Feminist Theory and Antiracist Politics," *University of Chicago Legal Forum* 1 (1989): 139–167.
5. Yomaira C. Figueroa, "Reparation as Transformation: Radical Literary (Re)imaginings of Futurities through Decolonial Love," *Decolonization: Indigeneity, Education & Society* 4, no. 1 (2015): 41–58; Leanne Betasamosake Simpson, *Islands of Decolonial Love* (Winnipeg: ARP Books, 2013); Chela Sandoval, *Methodology of the Oppressed* (Minneapolis: University of Minnesota Press: 2000).
6. Walter Mignolo and Catherine Walsh, *On Decoloniality: Concepts, Analytics, Praxis* (Durham: Duke University Press, 2018).
7. Leanne Betasamosake Simpson, "Indigenous Resurgence and Co-resistance," *Critical Ethnic Studies* 2, no. 2 (2016): 19–34.
8. Kathleen E. Absolon (Minogiizhigokwe), *Kaandossiwin: How We Come to Know* (Halifax: Fernwood Publishing: 2011), 31.
9. Jo-ann Archibald (Q'um Q'um Xiiem), Jenny Bol Jun Lee-Morgan and Jason De Santolo, "Introduction: Decolonizing Research: Indigenous Storywork as Methodology," in *Decolonizing Research: Indigenous Storywork as Methodology*, eds. Jo-ann Archibald (Q'um Q'um Xiiem), Jenny Bol Jun Lee-Morgan, and Jason De Santolo (London: Zed Books, 2019), 1–16.
10. Archibald, Lee-Morgan and De Santolo, "Introduction."
11. Simpson, "Indigenous Resurgence and Co-resistance," 27.
12. Archibald, Lee-Morgan and De Santolo, "Introduction," 12.
13. Trinh T. Minh-Ha, *Woman, Native, Other: Writing Postcoloniality and Feminism* (Indianapolis: Indiana University Press, 2009).
14. Mignolo and Walsh, *On Decoloniality*.
15. See Judith Butler, "Rethinking Resistance," in *Vulnerability in Resistance*, eds. Judith Butler, Zeynep Gambetti and Leticia Sabsay (Durham: Duke University Press, 2016), 12–27.
16. See Heather Shotton, Amanda Tachine, Christine Nelson, Robin Zape-tah-hol-ah Minthorn, and Stephanie Waterman, "Living our Research through Indigenous Scholar Sisterhood Practices," *Qualitative Inquiry* 24, no. 9 (2018): 636–645.
17. Luma Zayad, "Systematic Cultural Appropriation and the Israeli-Palestinian Conflict," *DePaul Journal of Art, Technology & Intellectual Property Law* 28, no. 2

(2018): 81–125; Steven Salaita, "American Indian Studies and Palestine Solidarity: The Importance of Impetuous Definitions," *Decolonization: Indigeneity, Education and Society* 6, no. 1 (2017): 1–28.

18. Harsha Walia, "Decolonizing Together: Moving beyond a Politics of Solidarity toward a Practice of Decolonization," in *The Winter We Danced: Voices from the Past, the Future, and the Idle No More Movement*, ed. Kino-nda-niini Collective (Winnipeg: ARP Books: 2014), 44–51.
19. Leanne Betasamosake Simpson, *As We Have Always Done: Indigenous Freedom through Radical Resistance* (Minneapolis: University of Minnesota Press, 2017); Simpson, "Indigenous Resurgence and Co-resistance."
20. See Alex Wilson, *Living Well: Aboriginal Women, Cultural Identity and Wellness* (Winnipeg: Prairie Women's Centre of Health Excellence, 2004), 20, http://www.pwhce.ca/pdf/livingWell.pdf.
21. Gerald Vizenor, *Survivance: Narratives of Native Presence* (Lincoln: University of Nebraska Press, 2008).
22. Walia, "Decolonizing Together," 46.
23. See Wolfe, "Settler Colonialism"; Ilan Pappé, *The Ethnic Cleansing of Palestine* (Oxford: Oneworld, 2006); Rema Hammami, "Precarious Politics: The Activism of 'Bodies that Count' (Aligning with Those That Don't) in Palestine's Colonial Frontier," in *Vulnerability in Resistance*, eds. Judith Butler, Zeynep Gambetti, and Leticia Sabsay (Durham: Duke University Press, 2016), 167–190.
24. Partha Chatterjee, *The Nation and its Fragments: Colonial and Post-colonial Histories* (Princeton: Princeton University Press, 1993), 5.
25. Omar Jabary Salamanca, Mezna Qato, Kareem Rabie and Sobhi Samour, "Past is Present: Settler Colonialism in Palestine," *Settler Colonial Studies* 2, no. 1 (2012): 1–8.
26. bell hooks, *Salvation: Black People and Love* (New York: HarperCollins: 2001); Frantz Fanon, *Black Skin, White Masks* (1952), trans. R. Philcox (New York: Grove Press, 2008).
27. Sandoval, *Methodology of the Oppressed*, 10, 4.
28. In his report to the 44th session of the Human Rights Council, Michael Lynk, Special Rapporteur on the Situation of Human Rights in the Palestinian Territories occupied since 1967, explains that "[i]nternational humanitarian law has expressly forbidden the use of collective punishment against civilian populations under occupation. The 1907 Hague Regulations prohibited the imposition of general penalties on the occupied population. Expanding on this protection, Article 33 of the 1949 Fourth Geneva Convention provides that: 'No protected person may be punished for an offense he or she has not personally committed. Collective penalties and likewise all measures of intimidation or of terrorism are prohibited. Pillage is prohibited. Reprisals against protected persons and their property are prohibited.'" Lynk further details that "[collective punishment] methods used have included civilian executions, sustained curfews and closures of towns, food confiscation and starvation, punitive property destruction, the capture of

hostages, economic closures on civilian populations, cutting off of power and water supplies, withholding of medical supplies, collective fines and mass detentions" (see Lynk, Report of the Special Rapporteur on the Situation of Human Rights in the Palestinian Territories Occupied since 1967: A/HRC/44/60 [Geneva: United Nations Human Rights Council, 2020], paras 28, 26).

29. Jeremy Wildeman, "Neoliberalism as Aid for the Settler Colonization of the Occupied Palestinian Territories after Oslo," in *Palestine and Rule of Power*, eds. Alaa Tartir and Timothy Seidel (London: Palgrave Macmillan, 2018): 153-74; Yves Engler, *Canada and Israel: Building Apartheid* (Winnipeg: Fernwood: 2010).
30. Madalena Santos, "Relations of Ruling in the Colonial Present: An Intersectional View of the Israeli Imaginary," *Canadian Journal of Sociology* 38, no. 4 (2013): 509-531.
31. Simpson, *As We Have Always Done*, 179.
32. Nadia Abu-Zahra and Adah Kay, *Unfree in Palestine: Registration, Documentation and Movement Restriction* (London: Pluto Press, 2013); Lisa Taraki and Rita Giacaman, "Living Together in a Nation of Fragments: Dynamics of Kin, Place and Nation," in *Living Palestine: Family Survival, Resistance, and Mobility under Occupation*, eds. Lisa Taraki and Rita Giacaman (Syracuse: Syracuse University Press, 2006): 1-50.
33. Absolon, *Kaandossiwin*, 168.
34. Absolon, *Kaandossiwin*, 65.
35. Absolon, *Kaandossiwin*, 69.
36. Audra Simpson, "On Ethnographic Refusal: Indigeneity, 'Voice' and Colonial Citizenship," *Junctures* 9 (2007): 67-80; Linda Tuhiwai Smith, *Decolonizing Methodologies: Research and Indigenous Peoples* (London: Zed Books, 1999); Edward Said, *Orientalism* (New York: Vintage Books, 1979).
37. Gabi Baramki, *Peaceful Resistance: Building a Palestinian University under Occupation* (New York: Pluto Press: 2009).
38. Eve Tuck, "Suspending Damage: A Letter to Communities," *Harvard Educational Review* 79, no. 3 (2009): 409-427.
39. Chandra Mohanty, *Feminism without Borders: Decolonizing Theory, Practicing Solidarity* (Durham: Duke University Press, 2003); Smith, *Decolonizing Methodologies*.
40. Greg Shupak, *The Wrong Story: Palestine, Israel and the Media* (London: OR Books, 2018).
41. See also: Andy Clarno, "Neoliberal Colonization in the West Bank," *Social Problems* 65 (2018): 323-341; Raja Khalidi and Sobhi Samour, "Neoliberalism as Liberation: The Statehood Program and the Remaking of the Palestinian National Movement," *Journal of Palestine Studies* 11, no. 2 (2011): 6-25; Islah Jad, *The Demobilization of Women's Movements: The Case of Palestine* (Toronto: AWID, 2008).
42. Smith, *Decolonizing Methodologies*.
43. Smith, *Decolonizing Methodologies*, L2516/5873.
44. Angela Davis, *Freedom is a Constant Struggle: Ferguson, Palestine, and the Foundations of a Movement* (Chicago: Haymarket Books, 2016).
45. Figueroa, "Reparation as Transformation."
46. Simpson, *As We Have Always Done*, 21.

Bibliography

Absolon, Kathleen E. (Minogiizhigokwe). *Kaandossiwin: How We Come to Know*. Halifax: Fernwood Publishing, 2011.

Abu-Zahra, Nadia, and Adah Kay. *Unfree in Palestine: Registration, Documentation and Movement Restriction*. London: Pluto Press, 2013.

Archibald, Jo-ann (Q'um Q'um Xiiem), Jenny Bol Jun Lee-Morgan, and Jason De Santolo. "Introduction: Decolonizing Research: Indigenous Storywork as Methodology." In *Decolonizing Research: Indigenous Storywork as Methodology*, edited by Jo-ann Archibald (Q'um Q'um Xiiem), Jenny Bol Jun Lee-Morgan and Jason De Santolo, 1-16. London: Zed Books, 2019.

Baramki, Gabi. *Peaceful Resistance: Building a Palestinian University under Occupation*. New York: Pluto Press, 2009.

Butler, Judith. "Rethinking Resistance." In *Vulnerability in Resistance*, edited by Judith Butler, Zeynep Gambetti, and Leticia Sabsay, 12-27. Durham: Duke University Press, 2016.

Chatterjee, Partha. *The Nation and its Fragments: Colonial and Post-colonial Histories*. Princeton: Princeton University Press, 1993.

Clarno, Andy. "Neoliberal Colonization in the West Bank." *Social Problems* 65 (2018): 323-341.

Crenshaw, Kimberlé. "Demarginalizing the Intersection of Race and Sex: A Black Feminist Critique of Antidiscrimination Doctrine, Feminist Theory and Antiracist Politics." *University of Chicago Legal Forum* 1 (1989): 139-167.

Crenshaw, Kimberlé. "Mapping the Margins: Intersectionality, Identity Politics, and Violence against Women of Color." *Stanford Law Review* 43, no. 6 (1991): 1241-1299.

Davis, Angela. "Freedom is a Constant Struggle." Public talk at the University of Guelph: Guelph, Ontario, February 26, 2018.

Davis, Angela. *Freedom is a Constant Struggle: Ferguson, Palestine, and the Foundations of a Movement*. Chicago: Haymarket Books, 2016.

Engler, Yves. *Canada and Israel: Building Apartheid*. Winnipeg: Fernwood, 2010.

Fanon, Frantz. *Black Skin, White Masks*. Trans. R. Philcox. New York: Grove Press, 2008.

Figueroa, Yomaira C. "Reparation as Transformation: Radical Literary (Re)imaginings of Futurities through Decolonial Love." *Decolonization: Indigeneity, Education & Society* 4, no. 1 (2015): 41-58.

Hammami, Rema. "Precarious Politics: The Activism of "Bodies that Count" (Aligning with Those That Don't) in Palestine's Colonial Frontier." In *Vulnerability in Resistance*, edited by Judith Butler, Zeynep Gambetti, and Leticia Sabsay, 167-190. Durham: Duke University Press, 2016.

hooks, bell. *Salvation: Black People and Love*. New York: HarperCollins, 2001.

Jad, Islah. *The Demobilization of Women's Movements: The Case of Palestine*. Toronto: AWID, 2008.

Khalidi, Raja, and Sobhi Samour. "Neoliberalism as Liberation: The Statehood Program and the Remaking of the Palestinian National Movement." *Journal of Palestine Studies* 11, no. 2 (2011): 6-25.

Lynk, Michael. *Report of the Special Rapporteur on the Situation of Human Rights in the Palestinian Territories Occupied since 1967: A/HRC/44/60*. Geneva: United Nations Human Rights Council, 2020. https://www.ohchr.org/EN/HRBodies/HRC/RegularSessions/Session44/Documents/A_HRC_44_60.pdf.

Mignolo, Walter, and Catherine Walsh. *On Decoloniality: Concepts, Analytics, Praxis*. Durham: Duke University Press, 2018.

Minh-Ha, Trinh T. *Woman, Native, Other: Writing Postcoloniality and Feminism*. Indianapolis: Indiana University Press, 2009.

Mohanty, Chandra. *Feminism without Borders: Decolonizing Theory, Practicing Solidarity*. Durham: Duke University Press, 2003.

Notwell, Jess. "Decolonization is an Everyday Struggle: The (In)visible Revolution of Palestinian Women." PhD dissertation, University of Guelph, 2022.

Pappé, Ilan. *The Ethnic Cleansing of Palestine*. Oxford: Oneworld, 2006.

Said, Edward. *Orientalism*. New York: Vintage Books, 1979.

Salaita, Steven. "American Indian Studies and Palestine Solidarity: The Importance of Impetuous Definitions." *Decolonization: Indigeneity, Education and Society* 6, no. 1 (2017): 1–28.

Salamanca, Omar Jabary, Mezna Qato, Kareem Rabie, and Sobhi Samour. "Past is Present: Settler Colonialism in Palestine." *Settler Colonial Studies* 2, no. 1 (2012): 1–8.

Sandoval, Chela. *Methodology of the Oppressed*. Minneapolis: University of Minnesota Press, 2000.

Santos, Madalena. "Relations of Ruling in the Colonial Present: An Intersectional View of the Israeli Imaginary." *Canadian Journal of Sociology* 38, no. 4 (2013): 509–531.

Sayegh, Fayez. "Zionist Colonialism in Palestine" (1965). *Settler Colonial Studies* 2, no. 1 (2012): 206–225.

Shalhoub-Kevorkian, Nadera. *Militarization and Violence against Women in Conflict Zones in the Middle East: A Palestinian Case Study*. Cambridge: Cambridge University Press, 2009.

Shotton, Heather, Amanda Tachine, Christine Nelson, Robin Zape-tah-hol-ah Minthorn, and Stephanie Waterman. "Living our Research through Indigenous Scholar Sisterhood Practices." *Qualitative Inquiry* 24, no. 9 (2018): 636–645.

Shupak, Greg. *The Wrong Story: Palestine, Israel and the Media*. London: OR Books, 2018.

Simpson, Audra. "On Ethnographic Refusal: Indigeneity, 'Voice' and Colonial Citizenship." *Junctures* 9 (2007): 67–80.

Simpson, Leanne Betasamosake. *As We Have Always Done: Indigenous Freedom through Radical Resistance*. Minneapolis: University of Minnesota Press, 2017.

Simpson, Leanne Betasamosake. "Indigenous Resurgence and Co-resistance." *Critical Ethnic Studies* 2, no. 2 (2016): 19–34.

Simpson, Leanne Betasamosake. *Islands of Decolonial Love*. Winnipeg: ARP Books, 2013.

Smith, Linda Tuhiwai. *Decolonizing Methodologies: Research and Indigenous Peoples*. London: Zed Books, 1999.

Taraki, Lisa, and Rita Giacaman. "Living Together in a Nation of Fragments: Dynamics of Kin, Place and Nation." In *Living Palestine: Family Survival, Resistance,* and *Mobility under Occupation*, edited by Lisa Taraki, 1-50. Syracuse: Syracuse University Press, 2006.

Tuck, Eve. "Suspending Damage: A Letter to Communities." *Harvard Educational Review* 79, no. 3 (2009): 409-427.

Veracini, Lorenzo. *Israel and Settler Society*. London: Pluto Press, 2006.

Vizenor, Gerald. *Survivance: Narratives of Native Presence*. Lincoln: University of Nebraska Press, 2008.

Walia, Harsha. "Decolonizing Together: Moving beyond a Politics of Solidarity toward a Practice of Decolonization." In *The Winter We Danced: Voices from the Past, the Future, and the Idle No More Movement*, edited by Kino-nda-niini Collective, 44-51. Winnipeg: ARP Books, 2014.

Wildeman, Jeremy. "Neoliberalism as Aid for the Settler Colonization of the Occupied Palestinian Territories after Oslo." In *Palestine and Rule of Power*, edited by Alaa Tartir and Timothy Seidel, 153-74. London: Palgrave Macmillan, 2018.

Wilson, Alex. *Living Well: Aboriginal Women, Cultural Identity and Wellness*. Winnipeg: Prairie Women's Centre of Health Excellence, 2004. http://www.pwhce.ca/pdf/livingWell.pdf.

Wolfe, Patrick. "Settler Colonialism and the Elimination of the Native." *Journal of Genocide Research* 8, no. 4 (2006): 387-409.

Zayad, Luma. "Systematic Cultural Appropriation and the Israeli-Palestinian Conflict." *DePaul Journal of Art, Technology & Intellectual Property Law* 28, no. 2 (2018): 81-125.

16

The Weight of It All
Methodological Implications to Community-Engaged Research on Violent Memory

Jen Rinaldi, Kate Rossiter, and Siobhán Saravanamuttu

A content warning: this chapter contains descriptions of physical and sexual abuse of disabled children. We are asking readers to carry some of the weight of these stories with us.

I have been doing this work for so many years now, I sometimes forget how shocking the stories are. I can recall a conference where I paused mid-presentation when I realized I hadn't properly elaborated on the phrase *digging for worms*. To clear up any confusion, I rattled off the explanation: digging for worms is what Huronia Regional Centre survivors refer to when describing a disciplinary tactic that forced them to lie prostrate, hands behind their backs, faces pressed into the ground. It was an act of humiliation that strained the bodies of these then-children, in order to punish them for transgressions of arbitrary rules. My account was clipped and clinical, then I promptly returned to my reading. I was well into my scripted sentence before I clocked expressions of horror among my audience. *Oh, right*, I thought to myself, *this institutional practice was awful*. I already knew that, of course. I had just been told about digging for worms so often, and have had to brace myself for the story so many times before, that its affective residue must have worn off for me. Something in me had to calcify so I could keep being a conduit for that story.[1]

This chapter unpacks the researcher's role in projects where the success of the research necessitates shouldering the burden of participants' violent memories. Pivotal to this work is the notion of emotional *carrying*, which for Nirmal Puwar is "woven into methodological encounters, often as tight knots between life and research, which are grasped in partial fragments."[2] We argue that the work of carrying can be methodologically necessary in projects involving violent memory, even as it produces ethical complications regarding boundaries and emotional labour. We present this argument through our own methodological encounters, the partial fragments that stayed with us from our community-engaged research on institutional history.

Our analysis stems from research that documented survivors' accounts of the Huronia Regional Centre (Huronia or HRC for short). Huronia was an Ontario-run institution in operation from 1876 until 2009 that housed children with intellectual disability diagnoses. HRC residents—including survivors on our projects who had been institutionalized sometime between 1950 and 1975—were routinely exposed to verbal, physical, and sexual abuse while living at Huronia.[3] Our research collective sought to provide redress for these injustices by amplifying survivor histories in public fora. Along the way, we—the authors of this chapter—bore witness to powerful testimonials of violence and survival. We found that the work of surfacing these stories is not neutral, given the ways researchers can be pushed beyond the role of witness into a relational exchange.

In this chapter, we describe our project and situate it in methodological literature on community-engaged research, then we identify three strands of vulnerability that emerge from our work. In each instance, we show how the researcher takes on the work of carrying fraught memories. First, carrying the weight of traumatic memory involves embracing a blurring of boundaries between life and research. This work leaves us permanently altered such that we come to understand ourselves as both researchers and people reflected through the violence of institutionalization. Second, abuse at the HRC could be cyclical in ways that implicated survivors. We thus had a responsibility to provide support for the most painful memories of institutional life where survivors themselves were perpetrators. Third, violence can be injurious even as memory. Our collective processes of remembering bound participant and researcher, and left us both vulnerable, but there were moments when carrying the impact made it possible for survivors' narratives to be rendered differently comprehensible through the lens of the research.

Our Project

Located on the Lake Simcoe shoreline in Orillia, Ontario, the Orillia Asylum for Idiots and Imbeciles opened in 1876. It went by many names, each reflecting a new paradigm of institutional care (e.g., asylum, hospital school) and took on its final name, the Huronia Regional Centre, in 1974.[4] The facility was the first of its kind in Canada, and the last Ontarian institution to close—in 2009. Huronia came to be the largest and longest standing institution in Canada to house persons with intellectual disability diagnoses.[5]

As cited in watchdog investigations and provincially commissioned reports born of an era known for its deinstitutionalization movement[6] and a class-action lawsuit that former residents brought against the Government of Ontario for its negligent management of the facility,[7] the HRC provided poor living conditions and subjected residents to physical and sexual abuse. Residents were isolated from their families, made to sleep in cottage dormitories. They bathed and took their meals at the institution. They went to school on the grounds, and many were assigned labour for no pay in order to keep the institution running—including landscaping, cooking, mending, and janitorial responsibilities. These conditions meant that hired staff, superintendents, social workers, and medical professionals had considerable power over residents. This power imbalance, compounded by stress related to overcrowding, understaffing, and underfunding, led to hired caregivers routinely mistreating residents in the name of care, discipline, and even cruelty.

This is a history that has not been treated to a comprehensive accounting. The *Recounting Huronia* research collective formed in 2013 to document the history of the HRC from the vantage points of its survivors. The collective comprised scholars (including ourselves), artists, and Huronia survivors. We committed to a number of grant-funded projects that had scholarly and community outcomes, including a cabaret performance for a public audience, a speakers' bureau that enabled survivors to present to stakeholders across Canada, and an open-access digital archive.[8] Throughout survivors were not just research participants but invaluable members of the team. They were credited as co-researchers in all our academic projects. They presented at conferences, co-authored publications, and were named on grant applications. They generated content, and we sought their informed consent and detailed feedback across projects before putting anything tangible into the world.

Depending on the project and the researchers involved, our collective sought multi-jurisdictional approval from research ethics boards at various universities. Our ethics application process contended with complications related to working with a vulnerable population on research with a risk of psychological harm. Among other strategies, researchers worked to secure informed consent by writing documents in plain language and developing protocols for reading documents aloud and member checking. While our efforts to uphold research ethics principles were careful, this chapter addresses the complications to our research that exceeded the inquiries of the research ethics boards.

Community-Engaged Research on Trauma

Our collective is an example of community-engaged research, or a constellation of research approaches built on the premise that members of the marginalized community being researched are best positioned to identify the injustices they experience and the correctives they need.[9] Engagement implies participants play active roles in the design of the study, interpretation of findings, and dissemination of recommendations. This extensive involvement of participants as partners is meant to ensure the research is not extractive. By extractive, we mean the research is not just taking knowledge from community for the sake of the researcher's publications and clout, or making a spectacle of that knowledge in order to satisfy some collective morbid curiosity. When the community studied has power to shape the process, they can direct research toward social action that benefits them. When researchers take on community-engaged research, then, they are making a commitment to participants. Such a commitment tends to entail "sustained acquaintance,"[10] even friendship between researchers and participants, in an effort to build trust; careful attention to process as itself a good; and "exquisite sensitivity and reflexivity"[11] that does not let researchers off the hook.

Research of this nature cannot help but run into human vulnerabilities. Scott Neufeld and colleagues caution that "marginalized communities with high concentrations of poverty…compromised health, and other expressions of the many brutal effects of historical trauma attract more than their share of research attention."[12] These authors are referring to situational and structural vulnerabilities, or increased risk of exposure to various harms as a result of historical and ongoing disadvantage.[13] These communities are vulnerable-*ized*, wounded in ways that could have been prevented. Disabled populations—and intellectually disabled populations in particular—experience a great deal of vulnerability where ableist conditions expose them to impoverishment and abuse.[14] These populations have important stories to tell from their vantage point, so they deserve research that centres them and is geared toward their benefit.[15]

These stories can be incredibly painful to revisit. Communities with heightened vulnerabilities tend to have histories involving various forms of abandonment and violence, which means research tapping into these community histories consistently turns up trauma. Sharing in those memories can itself serve a social good by contributing to cross-cultural solidarity and building communities anew.[16] Where traumatic experiences can isolate a person and damage their sense of safety, security, and support, the sharing of trauma with others can do work to repair those wounds. In Emma Hutchison's words: "Trauma can be remembered and memorialized in ways that preserve the…injury and loss, thereby constituting communities around shared pain."[17]

But this act of sharing is not easy, especially since vulnerability is not only brought on by unjust circumstance—for it is also a universal human condition. Vulnerability is a deeply embodied experience rooted in material and emotional needs. It is felt in hunger, in ache, in grief.[18] A researcher coming into a wounded community straddles this tension, where comparatively they were spared key situational vulnerabilities, yet the relationships they forge through their research mark them as inheritors of trauma. They are inheritors in the sense that they can hold mediated or indirect memories.[19] The commitment to engage, to form a relation, exposes the researcher to vulnerabilities.

Nirmal Puwar writes about how the fragments of community-engaged research—not always or immediately fully grasped, often circulating about the research space as affects or resonances—can lodge themselves in the researcher's body, becoming a weight the researcher carries. She characterizes *carrying* as a physical methodological process, imprinting on the researcher and participant, marking those bodies as a collective archive. These embodied archives hold "histories, obsessions, dreams and materials."[20] The weight of traumatic history haunts the research relation, complicating all efforts to compartmentalize or create distance. The greater the weight, the stronger the researcher and participant are bound together. Puwar understands carrying to be a relational—even an intergenerational—process, where elders pass down their experience as teachings. These teachings can be painful gifts, intended to spare future generations the repetition of trauma. Rooting her analysis in Ann Cvetkovich's[21] earlier work on archives of feelings, Puwar focuses on sites of trauma for their potential for radical possibility to "enable the affects of trauma to serve as the basis of public cultures of mobilization, intimacy and support, which in turn constitute affective archives."[22]

Carrying thus becomes this necessary linchpin, "woven into methodological encounters, often as tight knots between life and research."[23] The act of carrying is not easy given the way it activates researchers' own life histories, and it is not always executed gracefully as a result. The relation forged in community-engaged research is not entirely reciprocal and constantly runs the risk of becoming exploitative. The privilege we as researchers brought into our research exchanges came with a call to share some of the weight survivors have had to shoulder—even when that sharing changed us and exposed our own vulnerabilities. We were left with questions of interest to this chapter on the contours of our commitment to survivors, on how our own feelings impacted us and the research relation.

Tracing the Knots from Archival Records to Family Photographs

This project is marked by the periodic tying and unravelling of the "tight knots between life and research."[24] Carrying the weight of the traumatic memory of institutionalization demands disavowing boundary-making between the academic and the personal. Working with HRC survivors does not finish after a speaking engagement, workshop, or telephone call. I find myself indelibly altered by the histories I have been entrusted with. Stories of once unspoken violence brought to the surface demand space in me now too. Testimonies that were silenced and not believed by many for too long take up residence in my own memory, appearing at whim, demanding my attention in the most benign moments. The voices of survivors confront me with the precarity of disabled life, many years after the HRC's 2009 closure. Innocuous tasks like taking a walk or cooking invoke vivid descriptions of institutional violence shared by survivors. These knots are not only psychic, but visceral too. Carrying this violence shows up as physical pain in my fascia, muscles, and joints. My body holds the traumatic memory of harm I did not experience myself.

I spent weeks poring over survivors' institutional records for work on *Recounting Huronia*'s digital archive. This collection of donated case files contains copious medical and social records about survivors over the course of many years, shaped by institutional staff, medical professionals, social workers, and elected representatives. Prior to this point, my primary source for understanding institutional life had been the testimony of survivors themselves. But in these records, I confronted the justifications of those in positions of power who enacted and enabled immense harm upon those who were kept at Huronia.

I am particularly haunted by the focus on families I noticed across record sets. In addition to institutional life, many records tell how children ended up at the HRC. Some were brought there voluntarily by families or guardians, while others were removed from their family home. Here were doctors and social workers commenting on the suitability of survivors' family structures and home environments. The state's medical and social service apparatuses positioned Huronia as fulfilling the caretaking of disabled children when their families supposedly could not. And yet I know directly from survivors themselves that they did not at all feel cared for or loved within HRC walls. Often, these instances of prolonged separation resulted in irreparable damage to survivors' relationships with their families long after leaving Huronia.

Perhaps the largest knot caught me when I understood how the authors of these records conceived of disabled children as a fundamental impediment to the ideal family structure. Reading people in positions of immense power use the protection of supposedly normal children as justification for their disabled siblings' institutionalization, and all that that entails, has broken me. Of course, I knew this intellectually as a researcher at some level prior to immersing myself in the records. But as I read through the detailed descriptions of disabled child and family, I began to carry these histories in a much more intimate way. This was not theoretical, but concretized in our work with survivors themselves, people who are real to me.

For me, the knot is even tighter than the interpersonal relationships I have built with these elders and teachers of a shared community that has coalesced around this work. I was raised a sibling of a disabled child very similar to those described in the records I read. Desperate to concretize the weight of what I was reading, I turned to my family photos albums. My father is committed to documenting our life, and there is a vast collection of images of my childhood. My disabled brother was a nonverbal child but is full of smiles and dimples in the photographs. The love and care he was surrounded by is evident, even if he did not have the language then to tell us. I look at a picture of him as a toddler, beaming in his new "big kid" room, lovingly painted and decorated by our parents to celebrate his transition out of a crib. I am reminded of the stories of HRC cribs—metal cages that children much older than babies were left in for hours or even days at a time. Next, images of Huronia's dormitory-style sleeping arrangements for older children flash to mind. The lack of privacy and safe sleeping quarters made bedtime a violent time for many.

My family was new to Canada then, so our home did not have much in it, but we were surrounded by our small immigrant community at every celebration. As I go through each birthday and holiday, I painfully but methodically look at my brother alone through Huronia's lens. I can see how starkly different his life might have been, if not for the gift of time. I then look at the images of myself as a child and the faces of the rest of our family. Those of us who might have been used as justification for my sibling's institutionalization. I am undone by the grief I imagine on our smiling faces had he not been present at those family events. For me, this grief is not imaginary nor hypothetical. I am beside myself with anger that I might have been used to justify the unspeakable violence of institutionalization against one of the people I care for most. How I relate to my family has changed now, whether in photos or in the flesh. I imagine the impact of our brother's ghost, even when he is in the room.

This knot between my life and this research becomes a little tighter, and as the ties to my life strengthen, I am brought back around more firmly to the work. It is, I suppose, deeply antithetical to notions of work/life balance and setting healthy boundaries. But it is (at least for me) the intimacy of life and research that drives the commitment to work underpinned by such violence.

Hearing the Stories Haunted by Guilt

An interview with Walter[25] unearthed stories that caught me off guard. On so many occasions across his time institutionalized, he was tasked with overseeing other HRC residents, usually children who were younger and classified as lower functioning. This itself was not a revelation. Coerced, unpaid resident labour was a theme knitting together survivor narratives because this labour contributed to the necessary upkeep of an understaffed, under-resourced facility. What struck me was that when supervising other residents, Walter was responsible for discipline to deter them from bring disruptive or breaking rules. Staff provided Walter with a limited set of techniques he could use to enforce rules, and among those options he employed the techniques he found to be more reasonable and humane. One such strategy entailed having residents push heavy wooden blocks up and down long hallways for hours, sometimes every day for weeks. This was a common practice at Huronia I recognized from other interviews with survivors who had been forced to perform it. They remember the punishment as arduous and unending, wearing down their small bodies, as well as degrading and undeserved, thus diminishing their self-worth. It pained me to hear Walter talk about this punishment as the lesser of other evils. At the time he had to use it, he understood the practice to be a way of advocating for residents and sparing them worse forms of violence. But there were other occasions where the punishment he found most humane did not lead to compliance. On those occasions he hit residents with his open hand.

Walter's confession stood out across different projects where the survivors we worked with had been much more likely to tell stories that framed them as perfect victims. I am far more accustomed to hearing harrowing accounts of victimization where residents absolutely did not deserve what they endured, as well as affirmative examples of resistance where residents fought back against injustices they experienced or witnessed. These stories are themselves true, and important to make public given the longevity of the total institutional model. Institutions like the HRC could only exist for as long as they did, and could only function on such a mass scale, if allegations of abuse were systematically discredited. The HRC survivors on our collective had their parents call them liars, and had staff punish them, whenever they alleged abuse. I have read through the institutional records that staff kept, records that left out any caregiver wrongdoing and sanitized disciplinary tactics but were quick to describe *residents* as volatile and oppositional. These examples illustrate that Huronia's legacy of violence was paired with an undermining of residents' credibility. Now survivors finally have an audience and opportunity to contribute to a public reckoning, but the arrangement is fragile. Morally complex stories risk exposing survivors to a continuation of what they have long encountered: people not believing them, even holding them at fault.

That Walter was made complicit in other survivors' traumatic histories, that he brought residents to harm, disabused me of the notion that HRC survivors approached the mythic perfect victim paradigm. I might well have been guilty along the way of believing and perpetuating constructions of institutional survivors as the "good" victims. Their diagnoses of intellectual disability culturally infantilize them,[26] and childhood is readily associated with a stark and inalienable innocence. Their institutionalization has been framed even within our collective work at times as imprisonment without committing crimes, which implies, however subtly, that violent carceral strategies are an acceptable way of dealing with wrongdoers. I don't think it hurts that all the survivors we worked with are white, given that racial privilege might mean they are more likely to be considered victims, not threats. And, personally, I spent so much time with these gentle elders, have been such a beneficiary of their kindness, my imagination for their capacity for violence was blunted. Walter entrusted me with knowledge that risked our relation, knowledge that pushed me to root my respect for him in something other than myth and misconception.

As a researcher committed to building platforms for survivor stories, I have a responsibility to "hear well." *Hearing well* refers to an "openness where what is said might be heard even if it threatens to break the order of the known world for those who listen."[27] That is, I hear well by not bringing all my preconceptions into the relational exchange with survivors like Walter. I hear well by being mindful of my own embodied archive that informs those preconceptions. I would welcome a world where my personal experiences of violence were tidy, and the people who assaulted me were simply monsters with inscrutable motivations. I would welcome not having to process the toxic lessons I took with me into other relationships. Walter was asking me to leave aside a light, clean-cut version of violence and instead to hold onto a story that anchored me to my old earned and unearned feelings of guilt, an affect with considerable heft.

We were breaking the order of my known world so we could collectively build a new one. Our work together entailed cultivating a moral community that had a place for Walter. His stories, these painful gifts, enabled me to envision how violence implicates survivors. The HRC was a closed system where a culture of abuse thrived. Residents were exposed to routine forms of degradation and violation that people in positions of authority called care or justified as discipline. Radical isolation meant residents had no access to advocates or comparators. They were young, the education they received at Huronia was insufficient, and they were told in many ways, over and over again, that they deserved violence. These conditions have suffocating force. It would be unreasonable to assume such relentless violence would produce perfect victims. Survival strategies could include compliance and negotiation with abusers, and constrained options prompt impossible choices. Living through institutionalization could entail re-enacting a learned, engrained, everyday brutality to process emotion or interact with others. Knowing all this, knowing concrete examples that illustrate how institutional violence inflicts moral injury, will haunt me as I continue to grapple with my own injuries. But *that's the work*: taking on the weight of the accounts that come with guilt so Walter does not have to keep holding that weight entirely on his own.

Carrying as Fuel, Carrying as Fire

I began this work in 2013 without a clear sense of what it would entail. I understood, in very broad strokes, that I would be collecting stories about experiences of institutionalization, which would likely include stories of abuse and neglect. But I was unprepared for the depth and profundity of these stories. Nor was I prepared for how much these stories, and the people who offered them, would change me as a person—how tangled my own subjectivity would be in terms of the methodology itself.

In 2014 our research team, comprised of academics, survivors, artists, and allies, made a collective trip to the closed Huronia site; survivors were permitted a few last visits to the institution before it was closed to the public permanently. This site visit was attended not only by our team, but by other survivors, family members, and members of the public interested in Huronia's history. While I had visited Huronia once previously, this visit was the first time I went with survivors, who narrated their own harrowing experiences through space. Survivors detailed horrific acts of sexual violence in the rooms where the violence took place, retraced steps to spaces of solitary confinement, pointed out areas where deep neglect had occurred and, in one case, tried on a straitjacket left over from Huronia's operation.

Most intense was witnessing moments of repressed memory surface suddenly for survivors who had not been at the site for many years. A moment with one survivor—a woman who had detailed her own profound neglect and abuse at the hands of staff—stands out in particular. As we walked between buildings she stopped suddenly and began to sniff loudly. We asked her what was troubling her and her body shook as she recounted an incident where she had been forced to care for another, more vulnerable resident (a common practice) and had become overwhelmed and irate, and she had hurt her charge badly. Wracked with sobs, this memory bubbled to the surface, and she haltingly recounted details that had long been submerged under layers of trauma. It was agonizing for everyone. As much as allies reassured her that her response to forced caregiving was entirely sensible given her own relationship to care and violence, it was not enough to assuage her guilt and horror at having been implicated in harming another survivor.

I came away from the site visit feeling viscerally impacted by what had transpired. I recall many frenzied days following this visit where I was unable to stop talking about what I had seen, and what survivors had endured. I felt compelled to tell everyone I encountered—friends, family, colleagues—about Huronia's legacy. I had the sense of feeling *infected* by traumatic memory and, as such, was compelled to infect others with the narratives that had impacted me so. This feeling drove me through much of the early stages of our research, fuelling my energetic commitment to intensive work alongside survivor colleagues to capture traumatic memories of Huronia. This included intensive focus group sessions, using arts-based methods to collect stories, and pouring over archival data such as resident files and in-depth interviews with survivors about their histories.

However, this drive was coupled with periods of despair and a sense of intense bodily anguish. At the time I described it as feeling as though I had sustained numerous emotional burns from the research and that any further exposure to traumatic narratives would be too intense for me to manage. Gone from my life were books, movies, TV shows, podcasts, or any other forms of media that contained graphic depictions of violence. These were not conscious choices; rather, I simply noticed myself unable to engage with any forms of media that featured harm. The same boundary materialized in my research trajectory. I once wondered if I should add a second wing to the project: a comparative analysis that included survivors of the residential schools built to warehouse Indigenous children in Canada. Before concretizing this plan, I had one informal interview with a residential school survivor who detailed experiences that were nearly identical to the stories Huronia survivors tell. In the moment of his recounting I felt numb and unfazed, observing only that the overlaps were uncanny. Within a day of this interview the numbness wore off and I fell to pieces. On a long walk alone, I began to cry harder than I ever had throughout the project. My tears were unstoppable. Despite enormous overlaps between the traumatic narratives, the thought of adding a second survivor group to the project was too much for me to bear. Some set of internal emotional boundaries that I had not been consciously aware of guided my decision to limit the project to Huronia survivors only.

What to make of this dual response to traumatic memory—a response which is at once a catalyst for momentum and a barrier to further exploration? I believe that holding these stories, as traumatic as they are, is critical to the work of understanding institutional violence and making these oft-private stories public. We as researchers are the medium through which private troubles become public issues.[28] While this act of holding is critical to the work of understanding, there is no neutral way to do it. These stories necessarily implicate researchers as complex witnesses to suffering. Making sense of these stories necessarily means carrying them, and carrying them is necessarily a painful process. The pain of this act of carrying may be key to the process of making sense of the brutality of a place like Huronia, for it is these experiences of vicarious pain that fuel an empathic attachment to the project at hand. However, managing this act of carrying also necessarily requires psychic boundary work on the part of the vessel. Methodology qua traumatic memory, then, becomes a kind of dance between utilizing the force of carrying pain and defending oneself against it.

Conclusion

This chapter sutures together disparate methods—from archival analysis to one-on-one interviews to on-site ethnography—in order to find a methodological truth that animates our research on traumatic memory. In each narrative fragment we describe our responsibility to the community members we serve, found in our tending to the grief that remembering induces, drawing out difficult stories, even honouring the dead. A responsibility to this wounded community binds us to the research, and exacts from us its pound of flesh. We can't do this work without ourselves being changed by it. But we commit to the impacts because it's work worth doing.

Notes

1. This chapter weaves together accounts from three separate authors. When telling stories in this chapter, we use the personal pronouns *I/me/my*, without citing by name which of us contributed any particular story. This ambiguous writing is informed by Janet Price and Margrit Shildrick, or more appropriately Janet/Margrit, whose retheorizing of relationship led them to suspend unique authorship in their joint writing. They characterize their co-writing as a "fluid encounter that expresses...the nature of the ever-changing relationship between, not just us, but all those who want to get away from the straitjacket of unified identities." Janet Price and Margrit Shildrick, "Bodies Together: Touch, Ethics and Disability," in *Disability/Postmodernity*, eds. Mairian Corker and Tom Shakespeare (London, Continuum, 2006), 64. The metaphor of the straitjacket in this quote is a poor choice for disability scholarship, particularly given that the institutional survivors affiliated with *Recounting Huronia* have memories of wearing and mending literal straitjackets. Our own writing team nonetheless finds value in slipping between author identities especially given that this chapter calls on each of us to express our vulnerabilities.
2. Nirmal Puwar, "Carrying as Method: Listening to Bodies as Archives," *Body & Society* 27, no. 1 (2020), 18.
3. The *Recounting Huronia* collective members who used to live at the HRC and endured abuse there self-identify as *survivors*, as a way of stressing the injustice of their institutionalization. We follow suit, using this term when referring to participants in our research projects. Additionally, when presenting history, we use the term *resident*, which is a non-medical, neutral term found in institutional records to reference a person during their time at a total institution.
4. Ontario Ministry of Children, Community and Social Services, "History of the Huronia Regional Centre," https://www.mcss.gov.on.ca/en/mcss/programs/developmental/HRC_history.aspx.

5. Harvey G. Simmons, *From Asylums to Welfare* (Toronto: National Institute on Mental Retardation, 1982).
6. Pierre Berton, "What's Wrong at Orillia: Out of Sight—Out of Mind," *Toronto Daily Star*, January 6, 1960; Robert Welch, *Community Living for the Mentally Retarded in Ontario: A New Policy Focus* (Ontario: Provincial Secretary for Social Development, March 1973); Joseph W. Willard, *Inquiry into the Management and Operation of the Huronia Regional Centre* (Ontario: Ministry of Community and Social Services, 1976); Walter B. Williston, *Present Arrangements for the Care and Supervision of Mentally Retarded Persons in Ontario* (Ontario: Ontario Department of Health, 1971).
7. *Dolmage v. Ontario* [2010] ONSC 1726.
8. Our work was originally supported by a Social Sciences and Humanities Research Council Insight Development Grant. Two spin-off projects received support from the Strategic Program Investment Fund, a one-time set of grants created through the settlement of a class-action lawsuit that HRC survivors brought against the Government of Ontario.
9. Vivien Runnels, Elizabeth Hay, Elise Sevigny, and Paddi O'Hara, "The Ethics of Conducting Community-Engaged Homelessness Research," *Journal of Academic Ethics* 7 (2009): 57-68; Naomi M. Wright, Julie M. Olomi, and Anne P. DePrince, "Community-Engaged Research: Exploring a Tool for Action and Advocacy," *Journal of Trauma & Dissociation* 21, no. 4 (2020): 452-467.
10. Henry Greenspan, "From Testimony to Recounting: Reflections from Forty Years of Listening to Holocaust Survivors," in *Beyond Testimony and Trauma: Oral History in the Aftermath of Mass Violence*, ed. Steven High (Vancouver: UBC Press, 2015), 352.
11. Greenspan, "From Testimony to Recounting," 353.
12. Scott D. Neufeld et al., "Research 101: A Process for Developing Local Guidelines for Ethical Research in Heavily Researched Communities," *Harm Reduction Journal* 16, no. 41 (2019): 1.
13. Catriona Mackenzie, Wendy Rogers, and Susan Dodds, "Introduction: What is Vulnerability and Why Does it Matter for Moral Theory?" in *Vulnerability: New Essays in Ethics and Feminist Philosophy*, eds. Catriona Mackenzie, Wendy Rogers, and Susan Dodds (New York: Oxford University Press, 2014), 1-32.
14. Talia Meer and Helene Combrinck, "Invisible Intersections: Understanding the Complex Stigmatization of Women with Intellectual Disabilities in their Vulnerability to Gender-Based Violence," *Agenda* 29, no. 2 (2015): 14-23; Jackie Leach Scully, "Disability and Vulnerability: On Bodies, Dependence, and Power," in *Vulnerability: New Essays in Ethics and Feminist Philosophy*, eds. Catriona Mackenzie, Wendy Rogers, and Susan Dodds (New York: Oxford University Press, 2014), 204-221.
15. Janette Welsby and Debbie Horsfall, "Everyday Practices of Exclusion/Inclusion: Women who have an Intellectual Disability Speaking for Themselves?" *Disability & Society* 26, no.7 (2011): 795-807.

16. Stef Craps, "Wor(l)ds of Grief: Traumatic Memory and Literary Witnessing in Cross-Cultural Perspective," *Textual Practice* 24, no.1 (2010): 51–68; bell hooks, *Teaching Critical Thinking: Practical Wisdom* (London: Routledge, 2010).
17. Emma Hutchison, *Affective Communities in World Politics: Collective Emotions After Trauma* (New York: Cambridge University Press, 2016), 64.
18. Mackenzie, Rogers, and Dodds, "Introduction," 1–32.
19. Maria Alina Asavei, "The Art and Politics of Imagination: Remembering Mass Violence Against Women," *Critical Review of International Social and Political Philosophy* 22, no. 5 (2019): 618–636; Yochai Ataria, "Traumatic Memories as Black Holes: A Qualitative-Phenomenological Approach," *Qualitative Psychology* 1, no. 2 (2014), 123–140.
20. Puwar, "Carrying as Method," 3–26, 4.
21. Ann Cvetkovich, *An Archive of Feelings: Trauma, Sexuality, and Lesbian Public Culture* (Durham: Duke University Press, 2003).
22. Puwar, "Carrying as Method," 9.
23. Puwar, "Carrying as Method," 20.
24. Puwar, "Carrying as Method," 18.
25. We use a pseudonym for the survivor we reference in this chapter.
26. Licia Carlson, *The Faces of Intellectual Disability: Philosophical Reflections* (Bloomington: Indiana University Press, 2010).
27. Jill Stauffer, *Ethical Loneliness: The Injustice of Not Being Heard* (New York: Columbia University Press, 2015), 69, 80.
28. C. Wright Mills, *The Sociological Imagination* (London: Oxford University Press, 1999).

Bibliography

Asavei, Maria Alina. "The Art and Politics of Imagination: Remembering Mass Violence Against Women." *Critical Review of International Social and Political Philosophy* 22, no. 5 (2019): 618–636.

Ataria, Yochai. "Traumatic Memories as Black Holes: A Qualitative-Phenomenological Approach." *Qualitative Psychology* 1, no. 2 (2014): 123–140.

Berton, Pierre. "What's Wrong at Orillia: Out of Sight—Out of Mind." *Toronto Daily Star*, January 6, 1960.

Carlson, Licia. *The Faces of Intellectual Disability: Philosophical Reflections*. Bloomington: Indiana University Press, 2010.

Craps, Stef. "Wor(l)ds of Grief: Traumatic Memory and Literary Witnessing Cross-Cultural Perspective." *Textual Practice* 24, no. 1 (2010): 51–68.

Cvetkovich, Ann. *An Archive of Feelings: Trauma, Sexuality, and Lesbian Public Culture*. Durham: Duke University Press, 2003.

Dolmage v. Ontario [2010] ONSC 1726.

Greenspan, Henry. "From Testimony to Recounting: Reflections from Forty Years of Listening to Holocaust Survivors." In *Beyond Testimony and Trauma: Oral History in the Aftermath of Mass Violence*, edited by Steven High, 141-169. Vancouver: UBC Press, 2015.

hooks, bell. *Teaching Critical Thinking: Practical Wisdom*. London: Routledge, 2010.

Hutchison, Emma. *Affective Communities in World Politics: Collective Emotions After Trauma*. New York: Cambridge University Press, 2016.

Mackenzie, Catriona, Wendy Rogers, and Susan Dodds. "Introduction: What Is Vulnerability and Why Does It Matter for Moral Theory?" In *Vulnerability: New Essays in Ethics and Feminist Philosophy*, edited by Catriona Mackenzie, Wendy Rogers, and Susan Dodds, 1-32. New York: Oxford University Press, 2014.

Meer, Talia, and Helene Combrinck. "Invisible Intersections: Understanding the Complex Stigmatization of Women with Intellectual Disabilities in their Vulnerability to Gender-Based Violence." *Agenda* 29, no. 2 (2015): 14-23.

Mills, C. Wright. *The Sociological Imagination*. London: Oxford University Press, 1999.

Neufeld, Scott D., Julie Chapman, Nicolas Crier, Samona Marsh, Jim McLeod, and Lindsay A. Deane. "Research 101: A Process for Developing Local Guidelines for Ethical Research in Heavily Researched Communities." *Harm Reduction Journal* 16, no. 41 (2019): 1-11.

Ontario Ministry of Children, Community and Social Services. "History of the Huronia Regional Centre." March 8, 2018. https://www.mcss.gov.on.ca/en/mcss/programs/developmental/HRC_history.aspx.

Price, Janet, and Margrit Shildrick. "Bodies Together: Touch, Ethics and Disability." In *Disability/Postmodernity*, edited by Mairian Corker and Tom Shakespeare, 62-75. London: Continuum, 2006.

Puwar, Nirmal. "Carrying as Method: Listening to Bodies as Archives." *Body & Society* 27, no. 1 (2020): 3-26.

Runnels, Vivien, Elizabeth Hay, Elise Sevigny, and Paddi O'Hara. "The Ethics of Conducting Community-Engaged Homelessness Research." *Journal of Academic Ethics* 7 (2009): 57-68.

Scully, Jackie Leach. "Disability and Vulnerability: On Bodies, Dependence, and Power." In *Vulnerability: New Essays in Ethics and Feminist Philosophy*, edited by Catriona Mackenzie, Wendy Rogers, and Susan Dodds, 204-221. New York: Oxford University Press, 2014.

Simmons, Harvey G. *From Asylums to Welfare*. Toronto: National Institute on Mental Retardation, 1982.

Stauffer, Jill. *Ethical Loneliness: The Injustice of Not Being Heard*. New York: Columbia University Press, 2015.

Welch, Robert. *Community Living for the Mentally Retarded in Ontario: A New Policy Focus*. Ontario: Provincial Secretary for Social Development, March 1973.

Welsby, Janette, and Debbie Horsfall. "Everyday Practices of Exclusion/Inclusion: Women Who have an Intellectual Disability Speaking for Themselves?" *Disability & Society* 26, no. 7 (2011): 795-807.

Willard, Joseph W. *Inquiry into the Management and Operation of the Huronia Regional Centre*. Ontario: Ministry of Community and Social Services, 1976.

Williston, Walter B. *Present Arrangements for the Care and Supervision of Mentally Retarded Persons in Ontario*. Ontario: Ontario Department of Health, 1971.

Wright, Naomi M., Julie M. Olomi, and Anne P. DePrince. "Community-Engaged Research: Exploring a Tool for Action and Advocacy." *Journal of Trauma & Dissociation* 21, no. 4 (2020): 452–467.

Vulnerabilities, Affects, and Solidarities
A Rape Survivor's Tale

Athanasia Francis

Introduction

My prior involvement in feminist and disabled activist communities prior to my social justice research work added an additional layer of experience where the political, the personal, and the academic constituted a continuum. I undertook doctoral research as a social anthropologist in 2018 and started exploring the communities of which I was part, with emphasis on the phenomenology of lived experiences and affectivity within them, drawing on autobiographic, ethnographic, creative, and collaborative material. It is in this context that I discuss researching activisms of feminist resistance to gender violence and its intersections as a disabled survivor of this violence, and this consequently entails a high level of personal investment and entanglements within research. These multilayered entanglements are attached to both the disability and the survivor aspects of my lived experience. While I cannot claim an essentialist, monolithic identity formulation and identification as a result of these experiences, they have impacted my perceptions of setting as well as the way concepualize, articulate, and constantly negotiate the research context and its perceived volatility and precarity. They are also directly and decisively affected by the claims and experiences vocalized within the disabled and activist communities with which I collaborate and to which I belong. However, when it comes to translating these complex and intimate experiences epistemologically and methodologically into academic discourse, there exists a sense of insufficiency, where tool kits and frameworks systematizing and validating knowledge fall short. This chapter explores the importance of centralizing vulnerability and affectivity in articulating embodied lived experiences and knowledges.

Whose Paradigm?

Interacting with several Western codes of academic practice, ethics committee documents, and various handbooks and research protocols, the normative ontological assumption around the concept of *the researcher* and its epistemological/methodological implications are hard to miss. Contrary to my felt reality of the self as a rather messy crip assemblage, often fragile and volatile, upon entering research I came across the implied imperative to possess full mastery of the body-environment relationship, of processes, as well as of able-bodied functions. Similarly, there was the assumption of linearity and regularity in the life of the researcher (and those of others), as if disconnected from the realities of their communities in the midst of facing violence and in turbulent times. I recall the statements about causing no harm to my collaborating "communities of vulnerable individuals," a rather overconfident stance stemming from an institutional articulation of a canonized paradigm that in principle, as Deanna Dadusc points out, places "'research objects' within an observational cage," treating approaching lived realities as visiting a zoo.[1] I also recall trying to sound as convincing as possible on an ethics application when I had to painstakingly defend the validity of my memory (affected by PTSD), which would be supposedly crucial in keeping accurate fieldnotes at the end of each day during ethnographic fieldwork, as that would determine the quality of the data. Mind, senses, physical anatomy are implicitly expected to be "fully functional"—adhering to an ableist model—not obstruct the accuracy of observation, not get in the way of the unblemished research process. Similarly, the "rigorousness" of research is often implicitly understood as the accurate recording of a detached, objective reality—a task of macro-scale light shedding on some mystifying community practice into which institutions and policy makers seek direct access. Normative expectations around generating knowledge seem to not leave much room for fractured, discontinued, messy embodied assemblages, affective crescendos generated in proximity and deep involvement—indeed, in direct and unashamed bias.

However, the obsession with unbiased research subjects, coherence, clarity, and able-bodiedness—assumed to perfect the quality of the inquiry—are the heavy heritage of the positivist paradigm that seems to sit particularly awkwardly within the qualitative exploration of social justice struggles of maligned communities. Despite the bodies of theories, most notably feminist thought, opposing such paradigms since the 1990s, as Deanna Dadusc points out,[2] there is still persistent scholarly attachment to the notion of "rigorous detachment" and critical distance and objectivity in order for the research "to be 'verifiable' and 'duplicable.'" There is also the institutional, f(o)unding, and ethics committees' alignment to these principles and, according to Dadusc,[3] compatibility of research practices with these interests does not guarantee exposing the institutional/structural power exercised during the formation of the expected knowledge. In similar lines of thought, activist-scholar Jeffrey Juris[4] criticizes this framework for lack of relevance and efficiency in terms of accessing and creating meaningful knowledge for the community, given the objectivist paradigm's imperative for raising imaginary boundaries between (unaffected) subjectivities that do research and those (distant ones) that are being researched. Disability scholars Emma Stone and Mark Priestly similarly warn about the harmful superficiality involved in research imperatives that are not explicitly committed to the participants' priorities and their collective claims, but are instead centred on "objectivity" and "detachment."[5] Indigenous/Native American studies scholar April Petillo uses the term *normative academic affects* to refer to the "unbiased (if not removed) observer stance,"[6] whereby there is an obvious lack of attunement to embodiment. These alternative approaches, signalling the rise of the "activist turn,"[7] expressed through activist research across disciplines, has already been addressing such issues in practice. Moving beyond the ontological researcher-researched binary and highlighting the value of situated knowledges through community collaborating and emphasis on engaged research has been a developing initiative across humanities, social sciences, and elsewhere, often referred to as "militant ethnography."[8] Its collective call involves abandoning objectivism in favour of explicit commitment to community needs and emphasis on embodied research practices.

However, the call for embodied practice seems to pose equally complex questions, because incorporating the body as a valid measuring tool into an academic system of knowledge production inevitably collides with a long history of merely tolerating its "imperfections." As social-cultural geographer Hester Parr aptly puts it, "bodies are messy and unstable sites of substances, desires, and disgust which can never really be fully controlled as tools of investigation."[9] How does embodiedness work in practice, what are its limits and, perhaps most importantly, what do these limits tell us about the kind of knowledge that is left outside of them? According to Juris, whose focus is social justice movements, embodied research should entail "helping to organize actions and workshops, facilitating meetings, weighing in during strategic and tactical debates, staking out political positions, and putting one's body on the line during mass direct actions."[10] Moreover, aligning with the embodied reflective practice of fellow activist researcher Nancy Scheper-Hughes on violence in the context of Brazil, Juris conceptualizes embodiment as the involvement in "mass direct actions [that] generate extremely intense emotions involving alternating sensations of tension, anxiety, fear, terror, collective solidarity, expectation, celebration, and joy."[11] Dadusc clusters such practices as a "method of the body," where research "is not separated from embodied experience, and theory is not situated on a different level from the affects and desires involved in the process of research."[12]

However, there is a meaningful gap between embodiment as witnessing or even partaking in affect and embodiment as affective synapses intrinsically binding one's body to the researcher-community continuum. There is also little focus on the ways in which these binding affects are inhabited and the potential they can carry. Particularly as the daily discomforting, micro-level, vulnerable, and painful experiences of intersecting violences generating these binding affects (and consequently alternative ways of knowing) can be rendered invisible, there is also the risk of overlooking these "negative affects"[13] because they might not directly centralize mass action, visible achievement, and narrowly defined political shifts and impact—a common narrative even in self-conscious and reflective activist scholarly theorizing. Moreover, as Petillo pointed out, established academic affects set the norm against which other affects are prioritized and conceptualized. What if embodied tuning involves building these synapses on, through, and with the vulnerabilities and discomforts experienced in volatile contexts, prioritizing the affects that do not take central stage? In this case, what embodied conceptualizations are created by bodies working together that have been raped or medically mistreated and maligned, or experienced chronically sustained physical and mental pain, racism, xenophobia, transphobia, police violence, precarity—structural violences with their various intersections?

Mapping Vulnerability

As is often the case in activist research, the community members with whom I work are my fellow activists. They are women, trans and nonbinary people, and long-term friends with whom I have been sharing experiences of feminist resistance, intimacy, and affection. Mostly immigrants in the UK, like myself, and/or members of various transnational collectives in Latin America and South Europe, including Argentina, Chile, Greece, Spain, and the autonomous communities of Catalonia and the Basque Country. They have been experiencing various types of gender-based violence in obvious and less obvious ways, while also—as is the case for most of us, including myself—navigating around the challenges of disability barriers and the various intersections with other positionings, including immigration status and financial precarity, in our lived realities in a "non-war" context. These realities are undoubtedly different, reflecting the various levels of violence inflicted upon us at the intersection of our identities and identifications, marginalizations, and privileges. Yet we all came together in protests against femicides and vigils of yet another victim of gender violence, bonded in anger, pain, discomfort, tearfulness, a sense of loss and despair.

One such occasion was the vigil for Verónica, who committed suicide when personal moments of her intimate life were circulated in the form of revenge video in her workplace by a former partner. The vigil took place outside the Spanish embassy, and its side door was temporarily transformed into a makeshift place for mourning:

For Verónica. Twelve candles for Verónica. It's windy and the wind blows them out. We light them again. And again. For over an hour. It's pointless. We figured a sitting arrangement where we sit by the steps leading to the door, by the candles, with our backs as windshields to keep them burning. We feel this will somehow ease your pain. Or ours. The sign placed in the middle decorated with a purple scarf reads: "*Lo virtual es real*.[14] Stop the violence." Rolling, smoking, lighting cigarettes, lighting the candles. Tears. Feeling each other's presence. Talking about how no one cares. How everyone is easy to judge you. Neighbours are concerned about your two kids growing up without a mother. But what about Verónica? It's rush hour and people walk past us. Some spare a glance. We're a bubble travelling in space. We talk about the points system, how you answer the questionnaire on the computer to see if you qualify as "abused," as "in danger." Wrong answer, bad luck. How many before you, how many after? In the shitshow of patriarchy, taking your own life becomes a gradation of privilege. (Fieldnotes)

While revisiting my notes, it was clear how a strong memory is not required to preserve the embodied affect (indeed, contrary to concerns around objectivity and accuracy). The phenomenology of despair, bitterness, and anger is inscribed on bodies and writings through its own grammar of emotion.[15] Moreover, it is a code that facilitates the converging of intersectional experiences; it gathers us around the fire, from the Balkans to Latin America, as a catalyst for encounters where openness to vulnerability and discomfort allows embodied connection and synergy, where such affects are welcome, undenied. Witnessing and performing the affect is important but what happens to this feminist listening, how does this embodiment transcend the barrier of the "bubble" beyond its locality and temporality, and how does it negotiate itself against the established academic affect?

Perceptions of precariousness and susceptibility to violence, in its various levels of impact, have been nurtured in contexts that are deemed as "non-war,"[16] yet they have been experienced otherwise by those who have been harmed by them. Tuning into the emotional grammar of violated and maligned groups and of their bodies might suggest that a quiet street is in fact a battleground. One of the most common phrases used by my fellow activists in this context has been *es una guerra* ["this is a war"]. Our communication through messages is a testimony to the ongoing list I record of commemorations, vigils, protests against femicides/hate crimes organized throughout the years:

Lucia Pérez
Melina Romero
Natalia Melman
Daiana García
Micaela García
Carly VG
Fatima Catan
Antonia Barra
Maria Trinidad
Eleni Topaloudi
Sarah Everard
Verónica
(Fieldnotes)

A considerable amount of our communication/messages also involved safety checks, asking each other's whereabouts, whether everyone arrived "in one piece" at their destination, whether they could access emergency provisions, especially at night during COVID lockdowns, whether they knew the number "for that line" for support. Some of us carry "kitty-knuckles," a cat-shaped keyring with pointy edges that can be turned into a self-defence tool, personal safety alarms, lemon spray, and makeshift sharp items whose legality we discuss with each other. An extra sofa is also available for when the violence affecting us is not just in the streets. A resource exchange of some basic pay jobs and temp work, or the occasional scholarship and job training is also shared in those messages. Immigration information, too, as well as information on benefits. Doxxing by far-right members, too, is present in our realities, as is continuous online sexual harassment, abuse directed toward our positionalities, rape and death threats, so our communication also includes relevant support and exchange of experiences. Violences are entangled, building a frame of vulnerability whose strands begin with gender oppression but do not end with it; they involve race, ethnicity, sexuality, disability, our (non-)citizen status, and the level of our precarity, among other circumstances. This phenomenology, the sensing of the surroundings in our perception of daily living, is shaped largely within and around these "negative" affects—unease, fear, anxiety, anger, insecurity, mourning, a sense of injustice—complemented with the corporeal imprint of past and present violence on our bodies, our physicality and mental health, and its constant accumulation while structural issues are indefinitely pending resolution and accountability.

However, when faced with vulnerability as the embodied lived experience—that is, as more than a theoretical discourse—acknowledging these affects and their corporeality is challenging when the means of articulation are potentially incompatible. The term *vulnerability* itself is controversial and has been regarded with suspicion by some scholars,[17] perhaps rightly so as it can be drawn upon as an ideological device and political excuse to inflict harm rather than expose it. Yet, the ethnographically grounded, contextualized, and corporeally informed vulnerability of one's daily lived experience is potentially a qualitatively different concept, particularly when approached though the lens of affect. Erinn Gilson proposes holding on to the notion of vulnerability despite the ideological risks, and measuring against them the potential harms from rejection or ignorance around how vulnerability is experienced; as Gilson observers, "when we fail to think about vulnerability we tend to presume a simple picture of what it is."[18] Such disavowal also forecloses openness to someone's own vulnerability as well as that of others.[19] Extending Gilson's thought, without thinking through vulnerability it is not possible to trace the affects generated in relation to it, or the link between them loses its meaning once viewed in isolation. In the words of fellow feminist anthropologist and friend Andrea García González, "[r]ecognizing vulnerability is inevitably linked to thinking through the body and emotions."[20]

Affective Practices

Recognizing vulnerability as a frame is particularly important when attempting to trace emotions that generate affective practices and with the view to understand these practices and their potential. The feminist activism of this research context is very much an affective activism, where openness to vulnerability of self and others allows the articulation of often discomfiting and abject emotions as well as the sharing of experiences of violence in volatile contexts with the aim to be heard. Perhaps the question is twofold but still inherently linked; on the one hand, how are these affects accounted for within the sociopolitical contexts they are articulated and, on the other hand, how are they accounted for within research, if at all? Both questions entail the element of discomfort toward certain (unsettling) affects generated by certain (unsettled) bodies whose lived experience is pointing toward uncomfortable truths. How are these unsettling, in-search-of-accountability affects negotiated, and who is taking over the reparative burden of violence when the claims are not addressed?

Disappointment at a perceived injustice, pain, anger, and a sense of solidarity or bonding in vulnerability were audibly present when most of my feminist group initially got together, to protest the treatment of *la manada* ["the wolfpack"] gang rape case, which started in 2016. The case involved a group of five men who raped a semi-conscious young woman during the San Fermin festival in Pamplona, Spain. The men were originally set free and not charged with rape, as consent was implied—according to one of the defence lawyers, she could have otherwise "bitten their penises."[21] The men had also recorded the rape and circulated the video online; one of them was a police officer, another a soldier. The mobilizations following the event were unprecedented and crossed local borders as millions of feminist activists protested gender violence and the role of institutions in the ways they addressed and maintained it. Our London group met outside the embassy building, wore purple scarves to recognize each other, and brought cardboard and paint to create signs, which were written in our native languages and dialects as well as in English: "*Hermana, No Estás Sola*,"[22] "*Nik sinesten dizut*,"[23] "The state is the biggest rapist," "The manada are 8-5 rapists and 3 judges," "Don't worry sister, *your* manada is here."

Sara Ahmed[24] speaks of the moment of "the snap," the time when something breaks after it reaches the point when enough pressure has been forced upon it, often slowly and gradually enough as to render this force invisible. She further defines the "feminist snap" as the way in which "we collectively acquire tendencies that can allow us to break ties that are damaging as well as to invest in new possibilities."[25] Susceptibility to violences and the phenomenology of this susceptibility are shaped within contexts where violences are normalized, become daily numbers, cases, unaccounted for and dismissed by institutions—in some contexts more habitually than others. This also generates powerful affects that demand acknowledgement and change. Yet, the caricature of the angry feminist and the "feminazi" were labels that were attached to activists during these and other protests, alongside verbal abuse, police kettling, and restriction measures against "any woman with a purple scarf who tries to approach the gate of the building" or wants to pin a poster on a gate. Amid fuelled anger, the tension exploded, the collective "snap" took the form of audible, embodied condemnation with words and movement. Unattended affect does not demand administration but attunement to the violences that preceded it. As activist Soraya Chemaly[26] points out, the "anger management" approach has been historically used to construct and oppress the racialized, gendered subject, which in this case reinforces the impact of the original violence. As in the case of Verónica, the vigil in front of a gated door involved the demand—literally and metaphorically—to tune into vulnerability and affect. Recognition should address all violences entangled in the encounter: the original violences inscribed on the bodies of activists/survivors of gender violence, the violence of denying their manifested affect, and the violence of enforcing its management. Snapping, in its performative embodiment, provides an alternative collective attunement to these affects that generate solidarity and care about the unaccounted violences.

However, these collective affective practices suggest that the emotional labour of dealing with the consequences of the lack of accountability falls with those who have already been affected by it. Leaving such intensive events, where emotions explode and survivors are faced with the task of their own aftercare, is often followed by meetings in quieter places like parks or sheltered spaces. This offers the opportunity for some time to rest, talk about the events of the day, check with each other, share our frustrations and encouragement. These moments can also be intense, as some might be disproportionately affected by incidents of our daily lives and activism. It is also a time for deeper bonding, serving as a collective resource for support, each offering knowledge where they can, and sharing experiences. Whenever a house is available, these meetings take the form of indoors *tuppersex* sessions.[27] These resemble our usual meet-ups with additional conversations about intimacy, sexuality, issues around consent, medical information, and our own personal experiences, the exchange of which enriches our knowledge through mutual learning. Talking intimacy as a survivor often presupposes an openness to vulnerability and affective bonding, which recognizes the various ways in which violence is inscribed on bodies. There is trust in those synapses built on this recognition and there is room for affective listening, or what Ahmed calls a "feminist ear,"[28] which does not traumatize. It is mostly during these moments that I recall the cognitive dissonance entailed in institutional understandings of this kind of care and ethical responsibility. Complying with university protocols, each of my consent forms were necessarily accompanied by a rather standard aftercare document to be distributed, which reflects the institutional understanding of "responsibility of care" when working with "vulnerable individuals": a risk assessment, a training session on disclosure, helplines for abused women. Though a welcome resource, I cannot help but think how a tick-boxing exercise evidently structured around institutional/legal accountability is completely detached from the caring listenings that demand to be heard in my research context; how in some contexts, what constitutes a trigger for the community might not be the mention of violence but the forced management of its negotiation, its self-containment and concealment.

The bonding built through vulnerability also came in other embodied ways accommodating affectivity. These involved drawings gifted to each other, care boxes when struggling with "lows," long hours of sitting down together until we felt it was all right to be alone, and also in the form of songs. My undisclosed surviving story, which took me decades to speak about, became a moving *bertso*[29] in feminist solidarity to be shared with others. It was inspired during an exchange of experiences of violence with G., him as a person medically transitioning and I as someone struggling with aspects of my disability. Our bonding was generated in emotional intimacy, and it allowed attunements resulting in the creation of a song, expressing his emotions during our exchange:

...Bortxatzailea kalean dago
beste askoren antzerako
ta hori noski min doblea da
dudik gabe zuretzako
baina elkartu egingo gera
ta egingo dugu planto,
oraindik ere zure begiek
dauzkate hainbeste malko

...The rapist is still out in these streets,
like many of them
and this is a double pain for you,
without a doubt
but we will get together
and stop this,
there are still so many tears
in your eyes

nahiz ta borroka egingo dugun,	and we will all fight out in the streets,
kalean, etxetik kanpo.	my support will be with you at all times,
Etxe barruan ere ez zaizu	both in the streets and in the
nere babesik faltako.	solitude of home.[30]

As opposed to the institutional response at the encounter during the *la manada* protest, this song offers an embodied alternative of acknowledging violences that are denied. In the song, there is recognition of the original violence, a process of listening to the affects it causes, and an affirmation of the need for accountability in solidarity. There is also extensive invested labour that is drawn upon to create the song, the affective listening that preceded it, as well as the care of gently transforming trauma into an affirmative narrative of support. My personal experience of the song was therapeutic—it felt physically calming upon my body as well as emotionally nurturing. It also enhanced my connection with G. and established a code of communication that made room for embodied understandings. It confirmed an aspect of the transformative potential that tuning into the affect entails when allowed to flow undenied.

Is It a "We"?

One of the greatest challenges for me when attempting to inscribe affective writing of encounters in this context into academic writing[31] has been choices around the use of "we," when referring to the experiences that I am narrating involving others. "We" can be problematic in several ways. Anthropology, which is one of the disciplines I have been trained in, has a long history of being the spearhead of colonialism, before reflexivity, positionality, and the notion of situated knowledges became widely incorporated into anthropological vocabulary and conceptualization. In the constant interrogating of positionality in research, the investigating "I" cannot be conceived as "we" without blissful ignorance, lack of reflexivity, or deep guilt. Particularly in activist research, where researchers are often activists themselves or members of collaborating communities, the dilemma is even greater, as the negotiation of positionality involves direct proximity and identification. This dilemma is painstakingly inscribed upon many such activist-scholar writings. The use of first-person plural goes against everything I have been taught and I am aware of the bulldozing character of "we" in certain contexts. I have concerns about the number of assumptions it might entail and the harm it can cause, about those vulnerabilities that are not shared and those violences that are disproportionate, particularly considering my whiteness, along other privileges. However, "they" feels like a denial of the affective proximity that ignited our bonding in the first place. The difference in register between academic and activist affects that render "we" almost methodologically untranslatable becomes obvious.

In one of my conversations with group members, I share my concerns. E., a fellow activist and survivor who emigrated from Latin America and with whom I have had intimate conversations about our experiences, added: "We are sisters. It's not a race, it's a war."[32] E.'s hometown had one of the highest percentages of femicides and disappearances in the country, which would render the level of vulnerability she was exposed to significantly different to mine. E.'s emphasis on the presence of vulnerability to violence rather than the degree of that vulnerability suggests an activist approach whose conceptualization relies on violence impact rather than violence quantification. Her feelings of queer kinship to me, *hermana*, as we call each other, are founded upon the affective bonding weaved through surviving gender violence and standing collectively in solidarity against it and its intersections. Another fellow activist, M., added to the conversation by commentating on the attitude she experienced in both her native and diasporic "homes": "They ignore me here, they ignore me there. We need to tell them the story." The ignorance was in reference to her reporting and protesting multilayered violence in the different geographical contexts. Despite the different backgrounds, there is a common pattern emerging in the development of this discussion. There is the notion of urgency in relation to the unheard complaint. My original intention to resolve the "we" concern took an activist turn, where my issue of whether I should be violently unstitching the collectiveness of "we" in favour of the more detached "they" seemed, at least temporarily, irrelevant.

During this discussion, I sensed more relevancy in the urgency to "tell the story"—although I am less optimistic that this is all it takes, just telling one's tale. There have been many attempts to tell the story of embodied violences, particularly by those who have been affected by them at the intersection of race and gender.[33] However, voicing these affects has been challenging because they are either sidelined by normative academic affects[34] or because there is an institutional/structural barrier preventing the sufficient articulation of the language of trauma.[35] Bonding in vulnerability with space for affective flow and affirmation has been an alternative way of finding articulation, embracing the "negative" affects and emitting their transformative potential. However, these clusters of care and solidarity are implicitly expected to carry the burden of reparation where accountability for structural violence is institutionally unaddressed. Moreover, not everyone has access to such clusters of support. How can this collectivity be expanded and reparation processes be extended to where the responsibility for the violences originally lies? In the meantime, lives need to continue with support and solidarity in the here and now, while these processes are pending. Practising affective listening, alluding to Ahmed's call for a "feminist ear," with attunement to those affects that are not always easy listenings, might render tales more audible and lives more livable as we continue in search of more answers.

Notes

1. Deanna Dadusc, "Power, Knowledge and Resistances in the Study of Social Movements," *Contention: The Multidisciplinary Journal of Social Protest* 1, no. 2 (2014), 48.
2. Dadusc, "Power, Knowledge," 50.
3. Dadusc, "Power, Knowledge," 48.
4. Jeffrey S. Juris, "Practicing Militant Ethnography with the Movement for Global Resistance in Barcelona," in *Constituent Imagination, Militant Investigations, Collective Theorization*, ed. S. Shukaitis, D. Graeber, and E. Biddle (Oakland: AK Press, 2007), 174.
5. Emma Stone and Mark Priestley, "Parasites, Pawns and Partners: Disability Research and the Role of Non-Disabled Researchers," 1996, http://eprints.whiterose.ac.uk/archive/00000927/, 5.
6. April Petillo, "Unsettling Ourselves: Notes on Reflective Listening beyond Discomfort," *Feminist Anthropology* 1, no. 1 (2020), 15.
7. The term first appeared in Michaela Wolf, "The Sociology of Translation and its Activist Turn," *Translation and Interpreting Studies* 7, no. 2 (2012): 129-143. Wolf used it in relation to the sociopolitical struggles of the recent years and the impact of activism on translation studies. However, the notion of the activist turn is also used in artistic, anthropological, and sociological contexts pointing towards a wider, interdisciplinary conceptualization of activism as a driving force.
8. An extensive analysis of "militant ethnography" agendas and practices can be found in Juris, "Practicing Militant Ethnography."
9. Hester Parr, "Feeling, Reading, and Making Bodies in Space," *Geographical Review* 91, no. 1/2 (2001), 166.

10. Juris, "Practicing Militant Ethnography," 165.
11. Juris, "Practicing Militant Ethnography,"166, following the thought of Nancy Scheper-Hughes, "The Primacy of the Ethical," *Current Anthropology* 36, no. 3 (1995): 409-420.
12. Dadusc, "Power, Knowledge," 54.
13. The term *negative affects* was used by Sianne Ngai in her book *Ugly Feelings* (Cambridge: Harvard University Press, 2005). She used the original term in reference to abject emotions (such as disgust and irritation) in the context of literary and cultural theory analysis. I use this term in a broader sense here but still echoing the core of Ngai's central idea that there are affects that might be overlooked but also extremely meaningful.
14. Translated in Spanish as "The virtual is real."
15. I use the concepts of *emotion* and *affect* indistinguishably here.
16. There is an ongoing criticism against the binary definition of peace/war in relation to violence; in other words, what can be safely called a "peaceful" environment as opposed to a "war zone." Focusing on everyday violence and its normalization can point to a certain level of crossing between these boundaries in some contexts. Some examples of scholars following this line of thought are: Rachel Pain, "Intimate War," *Political Geography* 44 (2015): 64-73; and Robin Luckham, "Whose Violence, Whose Security? Can Violence Reduction and Security Work for Poor, Excluded and Vulnerable People?" *Peacebuilding* 5, no. 2 (2017): 99-117.
17. Judith Butler, *Precarious Life: The Powers of Mourning and Violence* (London: Verso, 2004); and Alyson Cole, "All of Us Are Vulnerable, But Some Are More Vulnerable than Others," *Critical Horizons* 17, no. 2 (2016): 260-277.
18. Erinn Gilson, "Vulnerability, Ignorance, and Oppression," *Hypatia* 26, no. 2 (2011), 311.
19. Erinn Gilson, "Vulnerability, Ignorance, and Oppression," 319.
20. Andrea García González. "Desde el Conflicto: Epistemología y Política en las Etnografías Feministas," *Antípoda. Revista de Antropología y Arqueología* 35 (2019), 17.
21. Manuel Jabois, "Pamplona Gang Raped Victim: 'Don't Leave Me Alone, Please,'" *El País* 28 (November 2017), https://english.elpais.com/elpais/2017/11/28/inenglish/1511867397_302207.html.
22. Translated in Spanish as "You are not alone, sister."
23. Translated in Basque as "I believe you."
24. Sara Ahmed, *Living A Feminist Life* (Durham: Duke University Press, 2017), 189.
25. Ahmed, *Living A Feminist Life*, 162.
26. Soraya Chemaly, *Rage Becomes Her: The Power of Women's Anger* (London: Simon & Schuster, 2018), xvii, xx.
27. The word *tuppersex* is a term playfully coined from "Tupperware" and "sex." With an original reference to the Tupperware parties most of us witnessed as children, they resemble those original home gatherings where a "Tupperware consultant" would invite a group of women at her home in order to host a display of Tupperware products. Those original gatherings were often used as an excuse to

escape the domestic and heavily gendered responsibilities of some of our contexts, meet friends, and find comfort. A further analysis of *tuppersex* meetings is included in Athanasia Francis, "Resisting and Healing: Embodied Feminist Research as a Sexual Violence Survivor," in *The Routledge Companion to Gender, Sexuality and Culture*, ed. Emma Rees (London: Routledge, 2023).
28. Ahmed, *Living a Feminist Life*, 203.
29. A *bertso* is a particular type of improvised song/oral poetry sung in the Basque language, a minority language historically suppressed in favour of Spanish. These songs follow specific type of rules in rhyme and melody and are composed for a variety of occasions. The *bertsolaris*, the performers of these songs, usually need only a few seconds once a topic is suggested. This tradition has only recently normalized the participation of women; however, it is currently being reclaimed by activist performers.
30. Translated to English by G. and author.
31. The particular issue of academic writing in relation to affect with a specific focus on discomfort has been the topic of a fruitful exchange with four fellow feminist scholars in a conversation sharing our experiences and trying to learn collaboratively. This conversation can be found in Andrea García-González, Elona Hoover, Nancy (Athanasia) Francis, Kayla Rush, Ana María Forero Angel, "When Discomfort Enters Our Skin: Five Feminists in Conversation," *Feminist Anthropology* 3, no. 1 (2021): 151–169.
32. The original phrase in Spanish: "*Somos hermanas. No es una carrera, es una guerra.*"
33. I feel the following constitute powerful testimonies to these violences: Cherríe Moraga and Gloria Anzaldúa, eds. *This Bridge Called My Back: Writings by Radical Women of Color*, 2nd ed. (New York: Kitchen Table: Women of Color Press, 1983) and Sara C. Motta, *Liminal Subjects: Weaving (Our) Liberation* (Lanham: Rowman & Littlefield International, 2018).
34. Petillo, "Unsettling Ourselves,"15.
35. Motta, *Liminal Subjects*.

Bibliography
Ahmed, Sara. *Living A Feminist Life*. Durham: Duke University Press, 2017.
Butler, Judith. *Precarious Life: The Powers of Mourning and Violence*. London: Verso, 2004.
Chemaly, Soraya. *Rage Becomes Her: The Power of Women's Anger*. London: Simon & Schuster, 2018.
Cole, Alyson. "All of Us Are Vulnerable, But Some Are More Vulnerable than Others." *Critical Horizons* 17, no. 2 (2016): 260–277.
Dadusc, Deanna. "Power, Knowledge and Resistances in the Study of Social Movements." *Contention: The Multidisciplinary Journal of Social Protest* 1, no. 2 (2014): 47–60.
Francis, Athanasia. "Resisting and Healing: Embodied Feminist Research as a Sexual Violence Survivor." In *The Routledge Companion to Gender, Sexuality and Culture*, edited by Emma Rees, 402–412. London: Routledge, 2022.

García, González Andrea. "Desde el Conflicto: Epistemología y Política en las Etnografías Feministas." *Antípoda. Revista de Antropología y Arqueología* 35 (2019): 3-21. https://doi.org/10.7440/antipoda35.2019.01.

García-González, Andrea, Elona Hoover, Nancy (Athanasia) Francis, Kayla Rush, Ana María Forero Angel. "When Discomfort Enters Our Skin: Five Feminists in Conversation." *Feminist Anthropology* 3, no. 1 (2021): 151-169.

Gilson, Erinn. "Vulnerability, Ignorance, and Oppression." *Hypatia* 26, no. 2 (2011): 308-332.

Jabois, Manuel. "Pamplona Gang Raped Victim: 'Don't Leave Me Alone, Please.'" *El País* 28 (November 2017). https://english.elpais.com/elpais/2017/11/28/inenglish/1511867397_302207.html.

Juris, Jeffrey S. "Practicing Militant Ethnography with the Movement for Global Resistance in Barcelona." In *Constituent Imagination. Militant Investigations, Collective Theorization*, ed. S. Shukaitis, D. Graeber, and E. Biddle, 164-176. Oakland: AK Press, 2007.

Luckham, Robin. "Whose Violence, Whose Security? Can Violence Reduction and Security Work for Poor, Excluded and Vulnerable People?" *Peacebuilding* 5, no. 2 (2017): 99-117.

Moraga, Cherríe, and Gloria Anzaldúa, eds. *This Bridge Called My Back: Writings by Radical Women of Color*, 2nd edition. New York: Kitchen Table/Women of Color Press, 1983.

Motta, Sara C. *Liminal Subjects: Weaving (Our) Liberation*. Lanham: Rowman & Littlefield International, 2018.

Ngai, Sianne. *Ugly Feelings*. Cambridge: Harvard University Press, 2005.

Pain, Rachel. "Intimate War." *Political Geography* 44 (2015): 64-73.

Parr, Hester. "Feeling, Reading, and Making Bodies in Space." *Geographical Review* 91, no. 1/2 (2001): 158-167.

Petillo, April. "Unsettling Ourselves: Notes on Reflective Listening beyond Discomfort," *Feminist Anthropology* 1, no. 1 (2020): 14-23.

Scheper-Hughes, Nancy. "The Primacy of the Ethical." *Current Anthropology* 36, no. 3 (1995): 409-420.

Stone, Emma and Mark Priestley. "Parasites, Pawns and Partners: Disability Research and the Role of Non-Disabled Researchers." *British Journal of Sociology* 47, no. 4 (1996): 699-715. http://eprints.whiterose.ac.uk/archive/00000927/.

Wolf, Michaela. "The Sociology of Translation and its Activist Turn." *Translation and Interpreting Studies* 7, no. 2 (2012): 129-143.

Conclusion
Finding (a) Dwelling in Vulnerabilities

Caitlin Janzen, Chelsea Temple Jones, and Claire Carter

As with nearly everything that began around 2020, this book became delayed. Though it was conceived of earlier, the editing of the collection began in earnest around the summer of 2021. At the time, we—the editors—were sending and receiving emails with signature lines that included things like, "I am aware that my work hours may not be your work hours" or "please prioritize your health and well-being." We were wrapping up teaching terms that implemented greater access with little to no pushback, but also with mixed support amid a stressful context. Faculty members were themselves receiving automatic extensions on federal funding grants to compensate for halted data collection, the closure of labs, the cancellation of conferences and travel plans, and of course, the pressing demands of caring for family, friends, and community members in the midst of a global pandemic. The summer of 2021 was a moment sandwiched between the acute panic of uncertainty, and the later adaptation—and critical resistance to—a "new normal."

In no way do we wish to romanticize the weeks and months of lockdown. They were times of hardship and suffering for many reasons, isolation, poverty, violence, and illness common among them. Further, as Shankar and Mason detail in their chapter, the costs of COVID-19 in loss of life, loss of income, and loss of productivity have not been evenly distributed across Canadian society or around the globe. We must recognize that although COVID-19 is no longer classified as an active pandemic, it is far from "over." There are profound losses that can never be recovered, paramount among them the loss of those we knew and loved, and those we never met. What is more, an unknown number of people are suffering from what is now called "long COVID." And, of course, we continue to get sick and feel anxiety amid pressure to resume to a new normal informed by concerns for financial health within the neoliberal model of university education.

There is, however, a distinction to be made between romanticizing the time of the pandemic and taking an account of our social responses to it, as varied as they were between people and over time. In this period of so-called recovery, a reckoning must occur, and part of this reckoning involves looking at the import of those email signatures that told us to take care of ourselves, the impact of being told that you can take more time if you need it, and the benefit of realizing that as creatures, we share a fundamental vulnerability, even if it is not shared at the same level and for the same duration. Perhaps it is more accurate to say that COVID-19 made it painfully and frightening apparent that we all have the capacity to be—and in fact are—vulnerable and that there are very few of us that can afford to be fully independent, socially, economically, or physically. It is a hard lesson, and this knowledge has proven to be too difficult to retain at a cultural level in the Global North. But what would it mean to hold on to that realization that to be human is to have the capacity for vulnerability? And further, what might it entail *to mobilize vulnerability as shared capacity*? The contributors to this volume have provided some insights in this regard.

One such insight is to do away with preconceived notions of vulnerability as attached to a particular embodiment, identity, social position, or role. Virtually every chapter in this book encourages us to dismantle our beliefs about research subjects as categorically vulnerable, in need of protection or in search of some emancipatory knowledge from without. Indeed, as Cowper-Smith and Nayak so articulately write in the context of their work with Rohingya people:

> They are the ones who are developing the tools for their liberation against seemingly impenetrable structural obstacles. They are

agentic; they are not vulnerable as people, but the socioeconomic-political power structures have rendered them exposed to vulnerabilities on a scale others can barely imagine. Yes, they are put into conditions and situations that allow for extreme vulnerabilities. However, within structural oppression, there is always agentic power.

Breaking the binary of powerful/powerless in social justice research led to a further questioning of the boundaries between "us" as researcher and "them" as participants in many of the authors' chapters. Many authors spoke of their uncertain relation to the research as insider/outsider or, in Chatterjee's case, as an ethnographic "returnee," whose diasporic trajectory threatens to overwrite their queer identifications with a participant with classed political codes, both material and imagined. Many of the authors entered the field on the basis of a shared element of identity, experience, or political struggle and grappled with how to situate themselves in relation to their research and research participants. Thorpe's autoethnographic chapter about organizing Pride speaks to the competing investments and obligations that can arise when one is both behind and beneath the lens of inquiry. Notwell brings Indigenous Storywork and decolonial love into sites active in the work of decolonization of Palestine and powerfully demonstrates what research utilizing methodology of embodied co-resistance looks like in practice, endeavouring to do research in a good way.

Subjective boundaries between researcher and participant, self and other are at their most vulnerable when exposed to the affective resonances that inhabit the space between self and other, especially in the shared time-space of witnessing traumatic experiences. Writing of their community-engaged research with survivors of the Huronia Regional Centre, an institution that housed children with intellectual disability diagnoses until its closure in 2009, Rinaldi, Rossiter, and Saravanamuttu evocatively write:

> The weight of traumatic history haunts the research relation, complicating all efforts to compartmentalize or create distance. The greater the weight, the stronger the researcher and participant are bound together.

Like Rinaldi, Rossiter, and Saravanamuttu, Athanasia Francis calls on us to understand affective responses as an embodied methodology. As Francis argues in the context of her shared membership in an intersectional community of disabled feminist activists and survivors of gender-based violence, nurturing a space for such "affective flow" in research as a community-building practice is a means of mobilizing shared vulnerability toward social transformation.

In each of the chapters, authors returned to their research, opening their practices, decisions, translations, and interpretations. As readers, we benefit from them making themselves vulnerable. The hard questions Ross, Pilling, Pitt, and Voronka ask of themselves in revisiting their participatory research with students as peer collaborators allow us to consider the possibilities and limitations of embarking on participatory action research within the neoliberal academy. Problems of funding, timelines, labour, and institutional ethics are laid bare as so-called failures in the research process and serve as important teachings for emerging change-oriented researchers. For Varadi, the return to research is a gesture of "hindsight reflexivity"—a look back at the researcher's own performance, behaviour, and reactions as they emerge in interview transcripts. Such reflexivity is a challenge to traditional "textbook knowledges" of feminist qualitative interview inquiry, and a bid for an affective turn toward interviews for social change.

When presented with a discrepancy in narrative accounts between those who were institutionalized in a facility for people labelled as intellectually disabled and those who worked there, Burghardt leans into the space of irreconcilability. Instead of searching for a singular and unifying truth that would tie the narrative together, Burghardt interrogates the narrative gap, tracing the operation of power that allows for one cultural site to be constituted by multiple truths. For Burghardt, privileging the experiences of survivors of institutionalization demonstrated "the productive potential of bias in qualitative research."

The expansiveness we find in leaning into vulnerability is vast. The embrace of vulnerability situates us productively in the unknown, as Ngo details in their experience working at the interchange of language translation. Moving between English and Vietnamese, Ngo's positioning represents the lived experience of translation as an exercise of power, and a reach toward what is unknown and undiscoverable when we reach the real—but also rich—limits of language.

We opened with an invitation to dwell with us—and all the authors in this collection—in vulnerability. This invitation comes from a feminist place of unknowing—sometimes we don't know exactly how to do research in ethical ways, how to teach difficult moments, or how to reconcile with research problematics past, present, or future. Even after putting together this collection, we still wonder what is lost to restrictive axes of vulnerability that impose paternalistic exclusions of people from knowledge production. Knowing that you, the reader, come to this collection with your own experiences of vulnerability, we offer the collaborative thought in these pages as a new orientation toward vulnerability as an inevitable and unresolvable part of research in all its forms. Our own orientations toward vulnerability are overlapping, critical, and informed by both theory and our lived experiences. However, the questions guiding this collection ask many other people to explore vulnerability beyond this launching point, in ways that continually complexify vulnerability and challenge our thinking. By moving through moments of vulnerability, spaces of research, temporal disjunctures and allowances, multiple forms of resistance, challenges of research, and the unresolvable, we offer this collection as an open-ended invitation to dwell in the inseparability of research and vulnerability as a means of engaging in the expansiveness of justice-driven scholarship.

Contributors

Aly Bailey is a Mitacs postdoctoral fellow at McMaster University and adjunct professor at the University of Guelph. Her research interrogates relationships between fitness, access, and inclusion with a focus on participatory, community-, and arts-based approaches and critical feminist theories. Her recent (co-authored) publications include "Is #YogaForEveryone? The Idealised Flexible Bodymind in Instagram Posts," in *Qualitative Research in Sport, Exercise and Health* (2021), and "#BodyPositive? A Critical Exploration of the Body Positive Movement within Physical Cultures Taking an Intersectionality Approach" in *Frontiers in Sports and Active Living* (2022).

Kayla Besse is the accessibility coordinator for the Stratford Festival in Stratford, Ontario. She holds a master of arts in English literature and theatre studies from the University of Guelph. Her current work focuses on the intersections of disability, representation, care, and creativity in accessible performance. Her recent (co-authored) publications include "Letting Bodies be Bodies: Exploring Relaxed Performance in the Canadian Performance Landscape" in *Studies in Social Justice* (2021), and "Relaxed Performance: An Ethnography of Pedagogy in Praxis" in *Critical Stages/Scènes Critiques* (2020).

Meredith Bessey is a PhD candidate in Family Relations and Applied Nutrition at the University of Guelph. She is a registered dietitian, and her research is broadly focused on critical perspectives of food, bodies, health, and fitness, using qualitative, arts-based approaches. Her recent (co-authored) publications include "Transgressing Professional Boundaries through Fat and Disabled Embodiments" in *Canadian Woman Studies* (2023) and "Covid-19 Risk and 'Obesity': A Discourse Analysis of Canadian Media Coverage" *Critical Studies: An International and Interdisciplinary Journal* (2021).

Madeline Burghardt has a PhD in critical disability studies from York University and is the author of *Broken: Institutions, Families, and the Construction of Intellectual Disability* (McGill-Queen's University Press, 2018). Currently a faculty member in the College of Rehabilitation Sciences at the University of Manitoba, she has worked extensively with people labelled/with intellectual disabilities in professional and artistic capacities and is an ally of the institutional survivor community. Her research interests include the geopolitics and histories of difference and disability.

Claire Carter is associate professor and head of the Department of Gender, Religion, and Critical Studies at the University of Regina, Treaty 4 territory. Their research focuses on gendered embodiment, movement, and community engagement. Claire's recent collaborations focused on creating community leisure spaces for all bodies to feel welcome and engaged, through movement workshops led by trans, genderqueer, non-binary dance artists and choreographers. Her work with queer sports leagues from across Canada led to their book *Who's Coming Out to Play? Disorientation and Disruption in Queer Community Sports*.

Shraddha Chatterjee (they/she) is a postdoctoral visiting scholar in Women's, Gender, and Sexuality Studies at the University of Houston. They have a PhD in Gender, Feminist and Women's Studies from York University, Canada. Their research, funded by a Vanier Canada Graduate Scholarship (2019-2022) examines how queer and trans* activisms in India are being shaped by, and responding to, Hindu nationalism. Their work is situated at the interstice of queer and trans* of colour critique, South Asian studies, Lacanian psychoanalysis, and scholarship on authoritarianism and nationalism in the age of digital media. Their single-authored monograph is titled *Queer Politics in India: Towards Sexual Subaltern Subjects* (Routledge, 2018).

Yuriko Cowper-Smith holds a PhD in political science and international development from the University of Guelph. She is currently the research and engagement officer at the Sentinel Project. Her research focuses on the intersection of migration, social movements, statelessness, and mass atrocities. Yuriko has recently published in the *Global Responsibility to Protect* and the *Statelessness & Citizenship Review*.

Eva Cupchik is a queer-identified settler ally of Eastern European (Ashkenazi) Jewish descent. She defended a doctorate (2020) at Western University's Theory Centre that explored, through interviews, how Indigenous students at Western university experience identity, ways of knowing, health, truth, and reconciliation. She is pursuing a second master's degree in Carleton University's Law and Legal Studies department. She publishes in the areas of feminist phenomenology, equity, diversity, and inclusive education, queer expression, research methods, poetics, and Jewish studies.

Cheyanne Desnomie is a Plains Cree woman from Peepeekisis Cree Nation in the Treaty 4 territory of southern Saskatchewan. She holds a bachelor of arts honours degree in anthropology, and a master of arts in history from the University of Regina (U of R). Cheyanne is a sessional instructor for the Department of Indigenous Studies at the First Nations University of Canada and an adjunct professor at the U of R for the Department of Anthropology. Her research background focuses on oral history, social memory, identity, and the lasting influence of colonial policies on Indigenous people.

Bongi Dube is a senior education program associate in the department of Family Medicine at McMaster University, based in Hamilton, Ontario.

Athanasia (Nancy) Francis is a queer disabled PhD researcher at the University of Liverpool whose interdisciplinary background includes social anthropology and gender, European LGBTQ+ literature and culture, as well as history and archaeology. As an activist-scholar and rape survivor, Athanasia aims in her work to capture local and transnational claims and resistances articulated by gender/sexual violence survivors and trans, disabled and aligned activist communities in (semi)peripheries, as well as diasporic/immigrant and indigenous communities facing multiple systemic violences. Athanasia's most recent publications include "Resisting and Healing: Embodied Feminist Research as a Sexual Violence Survivor" in *The Routledge Companion to Gender, Sexuality and Culture* (2022).

Rebecca Godderis is an associate professor in the Department of Community Health and the Social Justice and Community Engagement master's program at Wilfrid Laurier University. The majority of her published academic work has focused on gender, sexuality, and health, including in the area of gendered and sexual violence on university campuses. Rebecca's recent publications have appeared in journals such as *Atlantis: Critical Studies in Gender, Culture & Social Justice, Engaged Scholar Journal: Community-Engaged Research, Teaching and Learning*, and *Sociology of Health & Illness*.

Moses Gordon is from the George Gordon First Nation in southern Saskatchewan. He holds a masters of public policy, a bachelor of arts in history, and a certificate in economics from the University of Regina. Moses is currently a PhD candidate with the Johnson-Shoyama Graduate School of Public Policy and a project manager with the Indigenous Peoples' Health Research Centre (IPHRC). Before assuming this role, he served in various capacities within the IPHRC since initially joining the organization in 2018. Prior to working at the IPHRC, Moses spent three years working in research at the First Nations University of Canada.

Emily Grafton (Métis Nation) has a PhD in Native Studies from the University of Manitoba. Emily has worked in community, provincial, and Indigenous politics. She was the research-curator, Indigenous content at the Canadian Museum for Human Rights and the Indigenous research lead and executive lead, Indigenization at the University of Regina. She is an associate professor of politics and international studies, University of Regina. Her work concerns settler colonialism, reconciliation, feminist theories, decolonization and reconciliation in museums and the academy, racialized tokenism, and provincial politics.

Caitlin Janzen is a doctoral candidate in sociology at York University. Janzen has been involved in a number of community-based research projects and has taught courses on qualitative research for social change. She currently works in research administration at the University of Calgary. Janzen is the author of articles published in *Hypatia*, *Somatechnics*, *Continuum*, and *Psychoanalysis, Culture, and Society* and is co-editor, along with Donna Jeffery and Kristin Smith, of *Unravelling Encounters: Ethics, Knowledge, and Resistance under Neoliberalism* (Wilfrid Laurier Press, 2015).

Evadne Kelly is an independent artist-scholar with a PhD in dance studies from York University. Her research investigates danced expression as a source of social change and social response-ability (and indeed responsibility). Her recent (co-authored) publications include "Towards Decolonial Choreographies of Co-resistance" in *Social Sciences* (2023) and "Projecting Eugenics and Performing Knowledges" in *Narrative Art and the Politics of Health* (2021).

Debra Langan is a sociologist and associate professor in Wilfrid Laurier University's Department of Criminology, situated on the Haldimand Tract of the traditional territory of the Haudenosaunee, Anishinaabe, and Neutral peoples. Debra's engagement with critical analyses incorporates qualitative methodologies to focus on exposing the complexities of gendered violence, police cultures, women's experiences in law enforcement, eating dis/orders, and families and intimate relations. Her recent journal publications include *Feminist Criminology*, *Policing and Society*, *Women & Criminal Justice*, and *Gender & Society*.

Rebecca Lennox is an assistant professor in the department of Criminology and Criminal Justice at the University of Missouri-St. Louis.

Her research areas include fear of crime, feminist criminology, and sexual violence. Her work appears in outlets including the *British Journal of Criminology*, *Violence Against Women*, and *Women's Studies International Forum*.

Corinne L. Mason is a professor of women's and gender studies at Mount Royal University. They research in the areas of sexualized and gendered violence, 2SLGBTQIA+ in/exclusion, EDI, and reproductive justice. Mason is the author of *Manufacturing Urgency: Violence Against Women and the Development Industry* (University of Regina Press, 2017), the editor of *Routledge Handbook of Queer Development Studies* (Routledge, 2018), the co-editor of a proposed collection called *Unmasking Academia: Institutional Inequities Laid Bare During COVID-19*, and *Reproduction in Crisis: White Feminism and the Queer Politics of End Times*.

Tara-Leigh McHugh is a professor in the Faculty of Kinesiology, Sport, and Recreation at the University of Alberta. Dr. McHugh's research is broadly focused on addressing gender equity in sport and enhancing the experiences of women and youth in sport and physical activity. Her recent (co-authored) publications include "Self-compassion in Sport: A Scoping Review" in *International Review of Sport and Exercise Psychology* (2023) and "'We're Categorized in These Sizes—That's All We Are': Uncovering the Social Organization of Young Women's Weight Work through Media and Fashion" in *BMC Public Health* (2022).

Preeti Nayak is a PhD candidate in curriculum and pedagogy at the Ontario Institute for Studies in Education, University of Toronto. Broadly, she is interested in climate justice education and how educators of colour engage marginalized learners in climate learning across formal and informal educational contexts. Preeti most recently co-edited a special issue of *Curriculum Inquiry* titled *Education and Ecological Precarity: Pedagogical, Curricular, and Conceptual Provocations*.

Anh Ngo is an associate professor at the Faculty of Social Work, Wilfrid Laurier University. Her scholarship focuses on the well-being of immigrant and refugee peoples through the lens of critical refugee and migration studies and critical social work. Anh's research aims to drive social change through community action and engaged scholarship. Her recent publications have appeared in *Studies in Social Justice, Canadian Social Work Review,* and *Refuge.*

Jess Notwell is citizen of the Métis Nation of Ontario and a ᐅᐦᐃᓯ nehiyaw ᑲ ᓂᐯᐃᑭᒋᐠ Métis and ᒍᓯᓯ settler ᑭᓂᐦᑳᐢᐃᓂᑳᐧ Two Spirit mom, activist, and assistant professor in sociology at King's University College. From Turtle Island to Palestine, Jess teaches, researches, and enacts decolonization mobilized through decolonial love. The CARE Collective @c.a.r.e.collective, Decolonize Now consultancy, and the Decolonization Advisory Circle at King's are some of the pathways Jess walks to co-create beloved community, stand with anti-colonial struggles around the world, and ᒥᔪ ᐯᒫᑎᓯᐃᐧᐣ miyo pimâtisiwin (live in a good way).

Marcia Oliver (she/her) is an associate professor in law and society and social justice and community engagement at Wilfrid Laurier University, situated on the traditional homelands of the Haudenosaunee, Anishinaabeg, and Attawandaron peoples. Her recent research projects address gendered and sexual violence, international law and refugee governance, and the role of the voluntary sector in regulating sex work and supporting anti-trafficking movements in Canada and the United States. Her most recent publications appear in *Violence Interrupted: Confronting Sexual Violence on University Campuses, Oñati Socio-Legal Series,* and *Refugee Survey Quarterly.*

Cassandra J. Opikokew Wajuntah is a member of Canoe Lake Cree Nation. She holds a BA in journalism (2009), a certificate in Indigenous communication arts (2009), a masters of public administration (2012), and a PhD in public policy (2022). She is director of the Indigenous Peoples' Health Research Centre, which has contributed over $20 million to Indigenous health research in Saskatchewan. She is an assistant professor of Indigenous health studies at the First Nations University of Canada, co-chair of U of Regina's Research Ethics Board, and an appointed member of the Public Health Agency of Canada's Ethics Consultative Group.

Merrick Pilling is an assistant professor in the School of Disability Studies at Toronto Metropolitan University. His work employs an intersectional, anti-racist lens that emphasizes the importance of lived experience, relevance to the communities being researched, and making changes to the systems that create marginalization. He is the author of *Queer and Trans Madness: Struggles for Social Justice* and co-editor of *Interrogating Psychiatric Narratives of Madness: Documented Lives*.

Kendra-Ann Pitt is a lecturer in the Social Work Unit at the University of the West Indies, STA. She holds a PhD in education and women and gender studies. Her research and teaching mobilize critical social work, transnational feminist, critical disability, and decolonial frameworks. A former postdoctoral fellow at the Dalla Lana School of Public Health, she has worked as a domestic violence advocate and counsellor and been involved in anti-violence work in the Caribbean, Canada, and the UK. Her current research projects explore issues related to gender-based violence, disability, and equity in Canada as well as in the postcolonial Caribbean and its diaspora.

Salima Punjabi is a Montreal-based multisensory artist and social worker. Her work focuses on the intersections of the arts and care.

seeley quest is a trans disabled writer, performer, educator, and environmentalist. Working in literary and body-based composition, curation, and facilitation, sie presented in San Francisco's Bay Area, including with Sins Invalid. Hir play "Crooked" is in *At the Intersection of Disability and Drama* and sie created an ecological assessment for Buddies in Bad Times' Rhubarb Festival. Sie inaugurated a Queer Disabled Joy movement workshop for Montreal's Studio 303's 2021 Queer Performance Camp. Hir script in progress, "Modeling," has had readings that have included Montreal's Wildside Festival, Vancouver's rEvolver Festival, and Dartmouth's Early Stages Festival. https://questletters.substack.com

Carla Rice is a professor and the Canada Research Chair in the College of Social and Applied Human Sciences and founding director of the

Re•Vision Centre for Art and Social Justice at the University of Guelph. She specializes in disability and embodiment studies and in arts-based research methodologies with a focus on changing systems and fostering social well-being and justice. Her recent (co-authored) publications include "Episodic Disability in the Neoliberal University: Stories from the Canadian Context" in *Gender, Work & Organization* (2023), and "Performing Fat Liberation: Pretty Porky and Pissed Off's Affective Politics and Archive" in *Social Sciences* (2023).

Jen Rinaldi is an associate professor in legal studies at Ontario Tech University. She earned a PhD in critical disability studies at York University, and an MA in philosophy at the University of Guelph. Her research takes up how law and socio-legal discourse read, mark, and produce non-normative bodies. Her publication record includes the journal articles "Huronia's Double Bind: How Institutionalization Bears Out on the Body" (co-authored, in *Somatechnics*, 2021), and "What Survivors See: Creative Condemnations of Total Institutionalization" (*Emotion, Space & Society*, 2021).

Lori Ross is associate professor in the Division of Social & Behavioural Health Sciences, Dalla Lana School of Public Health, University of Toronto. She draws from Mad Studies and other critical approaches to study mental health among 2SLGBTQ+ and other communities impacted by intersecting structural oppressions. Recent publications include: "Mad Studies Genealogy and Praxis," *International Mad Studies Journal* (2023), and "'Slighted and Unheard': The Psychiatrization of Bisexuality," in *Interrogating Psychiatric Narratives of Madness* (eds. Daley and M. Pilling, 2021).

Kate Rossiter is an associate professor in the Health Studies program at Wilfrid Laurier University. She received her PhD from the Dalla Lana School of Public Health at the University of Toronto in 2009 and her MA in performance studies from New York University in 2002. Her interdisciplinary work fuses critical theoretical scholarship in health with arts-based practices, including theatre and fiction. She was the principal investigator for the Recounting Huronia Collective projects. Her publications include *Institutional Violence and Disability: Punishing Conditions* (co-authored with Jen Rinaldi, Routledge, 2019) and *Population Control: Theorizing Institutional Violence* (co-edited with Rinaldi, McGill-Queen's University Press, 2023).

Brenda Rossow-Kimball is an associate professor in the Faculty of Kinesiology and Health Studies at the University of Regina. She works in the field of adaptive physical activity and recognizes how dominant social narratives are created/imposed through policy, attitudes, infrastructure, and more. Her most recent chapter, "Engaging in Reflexive Writing in Adaptive Physical Activity" (in Goodwin and Connolly's *Reflexivity and Change in Adaptive Physical Activity: Overcoming Hubris*, 2023, Routledge) invites readers to ask "Who might we be in others' lives, and who might others become in ours?"

Siobhán Saravanamuttu is a doctoral candidate in politics at York University. Her dissertation traces the politics of historic and contemporary forms of eugenic institutionalization and vocational rehabilitation as mechanisms of regulating both disability and the family. Her work integrates feminist-of-colour disability theory, feminist political economy, critical social policy, and abolitionist anti-work perspectives. Her publications include the co-authored chapter "The Huronia Survivors Speakers Bureau: Enacting a Cripped Feminist Solidarity with Intellectually Disabled Institutional Survivors" (*Hand-book of Feminist Research Methodologies in Management and Organization Studies*, 2023).

Melissa Schnarr is Anishinaabe and Haudenosaunee from Bkejwanong Territory (Walpole Island First Nation), with family in Six Nations of the Grand River. She is a scholar, writer, and educator pursuing a PhD in Indigenous Education at Western University. Her research focuses on land education practices within local First Nation communities. She is an instructor at Brescia University College and an SSHRC scholar. Academically, she has been published in *AlterNative: An International Journal of Indigenous Peoples* and co-wrote "Embodied Learning and Two-eyed Seeing: Indigenous and Feminist Perspectives in Professional Education" in *Embodiment and Professional Education: Body, Practice, Pedagogy*, published by Springer.

Bettina Schneider is an associate professor in Indigenous business and public administration at the First Nations University of Canada (FNUniv). She has a PhD in Native American studies with emphases in critical and feminist theory from the University of California, Davis. At FNUniv since 2007, she is formerly its associate dean of Community, Research, and Graduate Programs and associate VP academic. Her work has focused on Indigenous community and economic development strategies, Indigenous-relevant business and financial literacy curriculum, and Indigenous research methodologies. Recent publications include *Financial Empowerment: Personal Finance for Indigenous and Non-Indigenous People*.

Irene Shankar is a professor of sociology at Mount Royal University and is dedicated to critically engaging with intersections of marginalization and inequality in her work, which focuses on feminist theories, sociology of gender, critical race theory, qualitative methodology, and the sociology of health and illness. She has received the Distinguished Faculty Award and the Faculty of Arts Outstanding Researcher Award. Her co-authored article "Increasing Pathways for Leadership for Black, Indigenous and Women of Colour" was published in *Atlantis* and a co-authored chapter, "Academia and the Propagation of Privilege" is included in *Reading Sociology: Decolonizing Canada* (4th edition).

Skylar Sookpaiboon is an education coordinator at ARCH (HIV/AIDS Resources and Community Health) in Guelph, Ontario. They hold a master's of science in family relations and human development from the University of Guelph.

Chelsea Temple Jones's research focuses on storymaking through a critical disability studies lens. She is a research affiliate at Re·Vision: Centre for Art and Social Justice at the University of Guelph and an associate professor in the department of Child and Youth Studies at Brock University. Her research and teaching areas include critical digital accessible pedagogy, critical animal studies, and disability justice. Chelsea completed a postdoctoral fellowship at the University of Regina in the faculties of Social Work and Media, Art and Performance.

Amelia Thorpe is a PhD candidate and Vanier scholar at the University of New Brunswick. She holds a master's degree in social justice education from the University of Toronto and has extensive experience working with queer, trans, and non-binary youth and seniors. Amelia runs ConneQT NB and ElderPride in colonially named Fredericton, NB, and has worked closely with a wide range of community organizations both locally and nationally. Her research is focused on grassroots organizing and intergenerational community-building within 2SLGBTQ+ communities and queering concepts of identity, space, and education.

Paul Tshuma is a Zimbabwean-born musician, poet, and an alumnus of McGill and Concordia universities. He is a disability activist and an independent accessibility consultant.

Amber-Lee Varadi is a PhD candidate in the Department of Sociology at York University in Toronto, Canada. She holds an MA in critical sociology from Brock University and a BSc from the University of Toronto. Her research interests include gender and sexuality, motherhood, youth and girlhood studies, discourse studies, qualitative methods, research ethics, and action-based research. Her dissertation draws on youth and critical internet studies to learn about the intersections of gender, sexuality, race, and class in young people's online and offline experiences. She also has academic and outreach experience with anti-oppressive practices and trauma-informed care to learn about and prevent houselessness and violence against women.

Jijian Voronka is associate professor in the Department of Interdisciplinary and Critical Studies at the University of Windsor. Her research uses interdisciplinary critical theory to explore how systems of power contend with street-involved, mad, and disabled communities, and vice versa. She has recent publications in the *British Journal of Social Work*, *Social Work Education*, and *Schizophrenia Bulletin*.

Kristyn White is a graduate student at the University of Regina and works full time as the literacy facilitator for a not-for-profit organization that supports disabled individuals. She has worked within the disability sector for over 10 years, and her time as a caregiver and sexual health educator for disabled people led her to pursue her MSc with a research focus on sexuality and disability. She is passionate about supporting the sexuality of people with disabilities and their support networks and dismantling societal myths about sexuality and disability.

Printed in the USA
CPSIA information can be obtained
at www.ICGtesting.com
CBHW031734191024
15970CB00011B/57